AMSCO®

ADVANCED PLACEMENT® EDITION

HUMAN GEOGRAPHY

DAVID PALMER
Senior Consultant

PERFECTION LEARNING®

Advanced Placement® and AP® are trademarks registered and/or owned by the College Board, which was not involved in the production of, and does not endorse, this product.

AMSCO Advanced Placement* Human Geography:* is one of a series of
Advanced Placement* social studies texts first launched with the book now titled
AMSCO Advanced Placement* United States History.*

© 2022 Perfection Learning*

Please visit our websites at:
www.perfectionlearning.com

When ordering this book, please specify:
Softcover: ISBN 978-1-6636-0966-3 or **T403801**
eBook: ISBN 978-1-6636-0967-0 or **T4038D**

3 4 5 6 7 DR 27 26 25 24 23

Printed in the United States of America

Contributors

Senior Consultant

David L. Palmer is a national consultant for AP® Human Geography, and has served as a question leader, lead table leader, and test item creator for the AP® Human Geography Exam. He is a frequent speaker and leader at national and international seminars and conferences, and he has taught social studies at Eaglecrest High School in Centennial, Colorado, for more than 20 years. In 2012, he received the Distinguished Geography Teacher Award from the National Council for Geographic Education.

Writers

Dan Berry
Former Member, AP® Human Geography Test
  Development Committee
Morgantown High School
Morgantown, West Virginia

Christopher Hall
Former Member, AP® Human Geography Test
  Development Committee
Davis School District
Farmington, Utah

Jane Purcell
AP® Human Geography Exam Table Leader
Norman Public School System
Norman, Oklahoma

Dan Snyder
AP® Human Geography Exam Question Leader
NSU University School
Fort Lauderdale, Florida

John Trites
Former Member, AP® Human Geography
  Test Development Committee
Acadia University
Wolfville, Nova Scotia

David Valdez
AP® Human Geography Exam Table Leader
Cherry Creek High School
Greenwood Village, Colorado

Tom Wurst
AP® Human Geography Exam Table Leader
Magnolia West High School
Magnolia, Texas

Reviewers

Rick Gindele
Former Member, AP® Human Geography Test
  Development Committee
Retired Teacher, Chery Creek High School
Denver, Colorado

Greg Hill
AP® Human Geography Exam Lead
  Table Leader
Horn High School
Mesquite, Texas

Kenneth H. Keller
Former Member, AP® Human Geography
  Test Development Committee
George Walton Comprehensive High School
Marietta, Georgia

David Lanegran
Former Chair, AP® Human Geography
  Test Development Committee
Macalester College
St. Paul, Minnesota

Celeste Reynolds
AP® Human Geography Exam Table Leader
Mashpee Middle High School
Mashpee, Massachusetts

Sharon Shelerud
AP® Human Geography Exam Table Leader
Retired Teacher, Metcalf Middle School
Burnsville, Minnesota

Pam Wolfe
AP® Human Geography Teacher
Yeshiva of Greater Washington
Silver Spring, Maryland

Contents

UNIT 3—Cultural Patterns and Processes

UNIT 4—Political Patterns and Processes

UNIT 6—Cities and Urban Land-Use Patterns and Processes

Chapter 15 Origin, Distribution, and Systems of Cities

Chapter 20 Changing Global Economy and Sustainability

Preface

This edition of *AMSCO® Advanced Placement® Human Geography* provides a concise narrative, skills instruction and practice, multiple-choice questions, free-response questions, and essential questions designed to help students understand the significant content and develop the vital skills needed to master the subject. It can be used in classes as either the core textbook or along with other resources.

For teachers, a teacher resource with answers to all questions in the student edition is available from the publisher.

As of its publication, *AMSCO® Advanced Placement® Human Geography* was up to date with all standards and guidelines published by the College Board. For the latest information on AP® Human Geography courses and the exam, check the human geography section of apcentral.collegeboard.com and advancesinap.collegeboard.org.

Introduction

Studying Advanced Placement® Human Geography

The AP® Human Geography course has grown dramatically since it was first introduced in 2001. These are some of the reasons students give for enrolling in AP® courses:

- Evidence that the student has the ability to succeed as an undergraduate
- Increased eligibility for scholarships
- Evidence that taking AP® courses strengthens a college application
- Opportunity to save on college expenses by earning college credit
- Opportunity to test out of introductory college courses
- Evidence that AP® students have better college graduation rates
- Enrichment of the AP® student's high school experience

Because geography is often taught as part of more general social studies courses rather than as a discrete subject, you might feel you have not had much specific instruction in it. And for many students, AP® Human Geography is their first course at the advanced placement level, so it can appear very challenging. This introduction will help you understand the structure of the exam and the content of the course.

Overview of the AP® Human Geography Exam

The AP® Human Geography exam assesses understanding of geographic skills, concepts, and principles. It also looks at knowledge of foundational geographic facts and domain-specific vocabulary. Questions on the exam check a student's ability to apply spatial concepts, spatial relationships, scale analysis, data analysis, and visual landscape analysis to a variety of geographic contexts and scenarios. Every question on the exam measures a specific geographic skill and specific content learning objective. Checking for knowledge of the tools and methods used by geographers is also part of the exam. Importantly, part of the exam will assess your ability to use your understanding of the world's geography to analyze or illustrate geographic concepts in the real world. The exam consists of two parts.

ORGANIZATION OF THE AP® HUMAN GEOGRAPHY EXAM				
Section	Question Type	Number of Questions	Percentage of Total Exam Score	Timing
I	Multiple-Choice	60	50%	60 minutes
II	Free-Response	3	50%	75 minutes

Each component will be described in this introduction. AP® examinations, including the Human Geography exam, score student performance on a five-point scale. The following descriptions are used regarding the College Board's recommendation of a student's performance on the exam:

5 = Extremely well qualified

4 = Well qualified

3 = Qualified

2 = Possibly qualified

1 = No recommendation

Another way to think about exam scores is to compare them to the performance of a college student:

- A score of 5 indicates the equivalent of earning a grade of A in a college human geography course.
- A score of 4 is equivalent to a grade of A-, B+, or B.
- A score of 3 is equivalent to a grade of B-, C+, or C.

An AP® score of 3 or higher is usually considered evidence that a student has demonstrated proficiency with the material covered in an introductory college course in human geography.

The AP® Exam Compared to Classroom Tests

AP® exams are prepared differently from typical classroom tests prepared by a teacher. Teachers select questions to assess whether you have learned the materials that they have taught you. A teacher knows what you read, heard, practiced, and experienced in your course of study and creates a test that addresses those things specifically. Although you may not always know the answer on a test in your classroom, you most likely realize that it was something that had been covered in the reading or classroom activities.

The AP® test is different. It is prepared by a team of college professors and high school teachers from across the country. Because one single exam cannot assess every aspect of human geography, the team makes decisions about what material will be addressed on the test and how it will be presented.

In addition, the AP® exam is designed to be more difficult than tests used in classrooms. A teacher is pleased to see all students demonstrate understanding by performing well on a test. In contrast, the AP® test is designed so that it can distinguish students who are better prepared from those who are still attempting to master the material. You should not be surprised if you find that many of the questions seem more difficult than you expected. But you should not necessarily be worried because of this. Many other well-prepared students will experience the same feeling. The test writers do not expect that students will do as well on this exam as they do in their own classrooms. Finally, the AP® exam is scored differently than a classroom test. The cutoffs for the different scores vary a little each year depending on how well a control group of college students enrolled in introductory human geography courses who also took the test did. You may feel like you performed poorly on the exam and still receive a score of 5. Much depends on how your performance on the exam compares to that of others who also take it.

Organization of This Book

This book contains the following elements:

- *Course Introduction:* This introduction surveys the type of information covered in an AP® Human Geography course and that is tested on the exam.

- *Unit Introduction:* Each of the seven units in the book begins with a list of the chapters in the unit, an overview of the content, and a list of the essential understandings that are covered in the unit. The introduction to Unit 1 has been expanded to highlight the skills needed in AP® Human Geography. These are the Course Skills taken from the College Board's CED and are critical to your success on the national exam.

- *Chapter Narrative:* The 20 chapters are organized by topics that correspond to the course and exam description developed by the College Board. Each will present you with key terms, concepts, and geographic models of the topic. Additionally, you will find examples and scenarios from the real world that illustrate key concepts and skills.

- *Reflect on the Essential Question:* Each topic opens with a broad question based on a course learning objective that is then addressed by the content within that topic. These questions are repeated at the end of each topic to provide you an opportunity to answer them and strengthen your understanding important content.

- *Key Terms:* At the end of each chapter is a summative list of the vocabulary terms identified in the chapter narrative. Familiarity with these terms will be an important part of your success in understanding AP® Human Geography.

- *Geographic Perspectives:* This feature at the end of each chapter focuses on how geographers approach a topic by highlighting the spatial perspective that is distinctive to the field.

- *Think as a Geographer:* This feature at the end of each chapter builds one of the skills used by geographers, such as interpreting maps, understanding networks, recognizing scales of analysis, and defining regions.

- *Multiple-Choice Questions:* Each chapter is followed by seven multiple-choice items that you can use to review the chapter and check your understanding.

- *Free-Response Question:* A sample free-response question is included with every chapter. These are written to mirror the questions on the AP® exam. You should be able to answer them based on the content of this book.

- *Connecting Course Skills and Content:* At the end of each unit is a two-part feature dedicated to helping students apply geographic skills and improve writing.

  - *Applying Geographic Skills:* This skill-focused feature at the end of each unit asks student to apply specific geographic skills to the content and stimuli of the book.

  - *Write as a Geographer:* This feature at the end of each unit focuses on one of the writing skills needed to answer a free-response question on the AP® exam.

- *Practice Exam:* A complete practice examination, modeled on the AP® exam, follows the final chapter.

- *Index:* The index is useful for locating coverage of key terms and topics for review.

A separate Teacher Resource with multiple-choice answers, free-response rubrics, and feature sample answers is available for teachers and other authorized users of the book and can be accessed through the publisher's website.

The Study of AP® Human Geography

Geographers, like historians, economists, sociologists, and others, study human behavior and relationships. What makes geographers distinctive from these other groups is that they use a set of skills that emphasize spatial thinking. Spatial thinking is a way of looking at things "in space," which means understanding the location and distribution of things in terms of their relationship to other things.

Location, then, is at the heart of all geographic understanding. The thinking skills used by geographers help them understand why things and people are where they are, and why the location of an item or of people with particular traits is important.

Through the study of human geography, you will develop a set of skills that will enable you to think spatially. The AP® Human Geography test contains questions in both the multiple-choice and free-response sections that will attempt to assess how well a student can use these skills to analyze geographic information and think spatially. The course material can be broken down into three "big ideas" and a variety of key skills.

Big Ideas

The following Big Ideas are the foundation of AP® Human Geography. You will use these throughout the course to understand key concepts. Each unit introduction in this book has a series of Big Ideas from the College Board that are specific to the content of that unit.

1. *Patterns and Spatial Organization (PSO):* Spatial patterns and organization of society are arranged according to cultural, economic, historical, and political factors.

2. *Impacts and Interactions (IMP):* Complex cause and effect relationships exist among people, their environments, and historical and contemporary actions.

3. *Spatial Process and Societal Change (SPS):* A spatial perspective that focuses on the ways phenomena are related to one another, which in turn allows for the examination of human organization and its environmental consequences.

Essential Skills of Geographers

The AP® Human Geography exam will require students to not only learn the content and discipline-specific language of the course, but to also apply a set of essential skills to demonstrate their understanding of human geography. Below is a list of the five skills the College Board has determined are essential to student success in this course. (See the introduction of Unit 1 for an in-depth analysis of each skill.)

AP® HUMAN GEOGRAPHY COURSE SKILLS	
Skill Category	**Description**
Concepts and Processes	Analyze geographic theories, approaches, concepts, processes, or models in theoretical and applied contexts.
Spatial Relationships	Analyze geographic patterns, relationships, and outcomes in applied contexts.
Data Analysis	Analyze and interpret quantitative geographic data represented in maps, tables, charts, graphs, satellite images, and infographics.
Source Analysis	Analyze and interpret qualitative geographic information represented in maps, images (e.g., satellite, photographs, cartoons), and landscapes.
Scale Analysis	Analyze geographic theories, approaches, concepts, processes and models across geographic scales to explain spatial relationships.

Source: *AP® Human Geography Course and Exam Description.* Effective Fall 2020. (College Board).

Course Content

The AP® Human Geography course is divided into seven broad topics:

- *Thinking Geographically:* Geographers seek to understand the world through spatial analysis. They use location, distance, scale, and pattern to examine the distributions, what causes them, and what results they have. Students of human geography learn to examine the changing interrelationships between places, human-environment interactions, and the evolution of landscapes. Geographers often use the information provided by historians, biologists, and other scholars, yet the perspective of a geographer is distinctive because it focuses on spatial organization.

- *Population and Migration Patterns and Processes:* Critical to human geography is the human population. Geographers seek to understand the distribution of people on earth, why people decide to live where they do, why they migrate from one place to another, and the effects of migration. The demographic characteristics of populations, such as their birth rates, death rates, and life expectancy, are key to understanding population change.

- *Cultural Patterns and Processes:* The languages, religions, and ethnicities of people vary tremendously. The regional patterns exhibited by these elements of culture are part of human geography. Geographers study conflict, cooperation, cultural exchange, and cultural evolution. In recent years, gender and the cultural role it plays in the spatial distribution of human activities has become a greater component of human geography.

- *Political Patterns and Processes:* People divide the world into political units, such as countries, cities, and neighborhoods. Geographers are interested in how units at each scale evolved and how they function both internally and with each other. Political geography examines the forces that create and strengthen countries as well as those that work to tear them apart.

- *Agriculture and Rural Land-Use Patterns and Processes:* Food is central to all human life. Hence, human geographers examine questions relating to how people grow, process, and consume food. Key issues include how and why the techniques and purposes of farmers vary by region and why farmers decide to grow certain crops in certain places. Geographers study the impact of modern food production on the population, the environment, rural landscapes, and society in general.

- *Cities and Urban Land-Use Patterns and Processes:* Geographers study why cities are where they are and how those reasons continue to evolve. They develop models to explain the spatial organization within cities that determine which regions are business districts, cultural zones, residential areas, and manufacturing zones. These models can help explain how urban areas vary from country to country.

- *Industrial and Economic Development Patterns and Processes:* The distribution of manufacturing facilities, the reasons why certain industries locate where they do, and how those reasons evolve are essential to understanding the geography of industry. Geographers analyze where resources are located, how people use them, and the impact of resource use on the environment, as well as how sectors of the economy change over time. Large questions include sustainability, economic and social development and how people respond to economic inequality and the growing economic interdependence in the world.

These topics can be learned in any sequence and subdivided in several ways. This book is organized into units, chapters, and specific topics based on the seven broad categories above.

The AP® Exam Questions

The Course and Exam Description describes both the content of AP® Human Geography and the basic skills you need to develop. Every question will assess a skill and a geographic concept.

Answering the Multiple-Choice Questions

The AP® Human Geography exam includes 60 multiple-choice questions, which students have 60 minutes to answer. This portion of the exam accounts for 50 percent of a student's score. Each question will consist of a stem that can be either a question or statement and will have five possible choices. One choice is correct, and the others are distractors, or incorrect choices, that are often plausible.

Analyzing the Stimulus A graphic stimulus, such as a map, chart, graph, or photograph will be referenced in 30 to 40 percent of the multiple-choice questions on the exam. Take a moment to read the question, refer to the graphic, and then reread the question. Be careful to look at elements of the graphic that may be important:

- *Maps:* Check the scale of the data being represented. Is it showing a local community? a state or province? a country? Look at all information given to you in the map legend. If the map includes a title, it will probably also give you information you can use in answering the question.

- *Graphs:* Check each axis of any graph. Notice where each begins and ends. For example, does the axis go from 0 to 2,000, or did it begin at 1,200 and then end at 2,000? If an axis denotes a time period using years, notice the time period it covers. How big are the intervals or increments between elements on the axes?

- *Photographs:* Clues to interpreting a photograph might not be obvious but look closely for them. One strategy is to examine the photograph systematically in quarters—top left, bottom left, bottom right, top right— so that you don't miss anything.

- *Tables and Charts:* As with other types of graphics, note carefully titles and any words on the chart. Details such as the geographic scale, units of measurement, and the regions that are included or excluded can give you clues or information that you can use.

Only some multiple-choice questions will have a graphic stimulus. Read them carefully. If, as you are reading the stem, your eyes glance at the choices and you see what you believe is the correct answer, finish reading the question before you select it. Information given at the end of the stem may reverse any initial interpretation of the question itself. Always note if specific time periods or geographic regions are part of the question.

Tips on Making a Choice You will often know the right answer to a question quickly and with confidence, but sometimes you will not. Here are a few suggestions to help when you are uncertain about an answer.

| HOW TO ANSWER CHALLENGING QUESTIONS ||
Advice	Rationale
Answer every question	Your score will be based on how many correct answers you give. Unlike some standardized tests, the AP® Human Geography exam does not penalize for a wrong answer, so you should make your best guess if you are not confident in the answer.
Apply what you know	If a question asks about a specific place or situation that you have not studied, focus on the general concept, such as sustainability or distance decay, that the question addresses. Use what you know to determine the most reasonable answer.
Move forward	Since you have 60 minutes to answer 60 questions, you can spend an average of 60 seconds on each question. If you find a question difficult, guess the answer, note the question's number, and return to it if you have time at the end. Note: If taking the AP® exam in a digital format you will not be able to return to a previous question.

Recommended Activities Answering multiple-choice questions is a powerful way to review content and practice skills. Each chapter in this book presents several multiple-choice items to help you check your understanding of important concepts in AP® Human Geography. Often the questions include a map, diagram, chart, photo, or other source that you need to analyze in order to determine the best answer to the question.

Answering the Free-Response Questions (FRQ)

There are three free-response questions on Section II of the AP® Human Geography exam. The first free-response question will not have a stimulus. The second question will have one stimulus and the third question will have two stimuli. Each FRQ will typically include seven parts, lettered A through G with each part worth one point, for a total of seven points.

You are expected to answer all three questions in 75 minutes. That means you have an average of 25 minutes per question. However, you can divide this block of time in any way you would like, spending more time on one particular question and less time on another. You will be scored based solely on the quality of the content of your response. Try to use correct grammar so that you make your ideas clear, but you will not be penalized for grammatical errors.

Note: If taking the exam online you will not be able to move back and forth between questions.

Composing Your Response The free-response questions used on the AP® Human Geography exam are sometimes called *constructed response items*. Remember each FRQ is equally weighted on the exam. This type of question consists of a statement or short, topical introduction followed by a series of seven related questions or response prompts each worth one point. Each chapter in this book ends with a free-response question.

Your response should be written in prose rather than as an outline or a bulleted list. The format, or construction, of your response should reflect the verb used in the question and the required geographic content and skills.

An effective method for answering the questions is to label each part of your answer. That is, when you are answering part A of the question, label it "A" in your test book. Then label "B," etc. Within each labeled portion of your response, you may still want to use paragraphing to provide clarity to your writing. If you take the exam digitally follow the same structure in your response.

Analyzing the Question The stem of the free-response question sets up parameters for your response. You can often think of it as a sort of introduction to your answer. You do not need to restate, rephrase, or incorporate the stem in your answer. Pay attention to any limitations it places on you. Make note of any dates or time periods indicated in the question. Some questions may require you to consider a specific period, such as "in recent decades" or "after 1950." Evidence in your response that falls out of these historical periods will not be counted, even if it otherwise supports your point. Notice if you are required to provide evidence or examples from specific world regions. As with time periods, information provided from other regions cannot be counted toward your score. The use of world regions on the AP® Human Geography exam is discussed in Chapter 2, Topic 1.7 of this book.

Many previous questions have asked for information from one or more specific categories. Generally, these are economic, social/cultural, political, environmental, and demographic. Your response should clearly relate to the category or categories indicated in the question. The chart below gives you more specific examples to think about in each category.

ORGANIZING CONTENT TO ANSWER QUESTIONS	
Category	**Examples**
Economic	• Levels of development • Wealth and poverty • Employment and types of jobs • Structure and sectors of the economy
Social/Cultural	• Language, religion, and ethnicity • Gender and age roles • Cultural perspectives and views • Health, education, and welfare

ORGANIZING CONTENT TO ANSWER QUESTIONS	
Political	• Government structure • International relationships • Laws, policies, and legal systems
Environmental	• The physical environment, such as landforms • The natural environment, such as plants and animals • Climate • Pollution and resources
Demographic	• Total population, age structure and density • Births, deaths, natural increase, fertility rate, infant mortality, and life expectancy • Migration, immigration, and emigration

Task Verbs The key words in a question's prompts that indicate what you are to do are known as *task verbs*. The ones that will be used most often on the exam are shown in the chart below.

RESPONDING TO VERBS USED IN PROMPTS		
Task Verb	Definition	Expectation
Identify	To state a clear, concise, specific answer	Often a single and well-written sentence is sufficient, but you can add clarifying details. However, do not contradict or add confusion to your original answer.
Define	To give the precise meaning or the basic qualities of something	Provide a concrete, real-world example to strengthen a definition.
Describe	To provide a representation in words	Provide the attributes or characteristics of a concept, process, model, or theory.
Explain	To give an account or add details as to why or how processes, outcomes, relationships, or patterns occurred	Offer reasons, evidence, or examples to make an idea plainly understood or state how a process occurs.
Compare	To describe or explain similarities and/or differences	Provide a description or explanation of similarities and/or differences between two things, stimuli, or concepts.

If a prompt asks you to describe, explain, or compare, you will probably need to write approximately one paragraph for each part of the question. Your first sentence should be a clear claim about what you think is the correct answer. Then support this claim with evidence, examples, and clear reasoning. This paragraph should be three to five sentences.

For compare answers, you need to look for similarities and differences within the items being compared. Since the focus is on comparison, write about both concepts, not one just one. Failure to discuss both concepts specifically results in no points awarded. Support your comparisons with evidence and examples.

The structure of a compare difference claim is: "Concept A is different than concept B because concept A . . . while concept B . . . ." Then continue with evidence and examples to support your claim using both concepts. Follow this format for a compare a similarity claim also.

Questions with Qualitative or Quantitative Sources Free-response questions might contain a stimulus such as a graph, table, photograph, or map. If there is more than one graphic, you will be asked to compare the graphics. *Quantitative sources* include data (numbers), while *qualitative sources* do not use numbers.

As with the graphics in multiple-choice questions, take time to examine and analyze the prompt carefully. Understand how the graphic relates to the question prompt itself. Some parts of the free-response question might relate directly to the graphic, while others might be linked more generally by the concept. You don't need to refer to the graphic in those parts of your response. On the other hand, when you answer the parts of the question that relate to the graphic, you should clearly link your response to evidence in the graphic. See the Unit 1 Introduction and Topics 1.2 and 6.9 for more details.

Questions About Geographic Models Free-response questions often ask about one or more geographic models and will be discussed in more detail in Chapter 1. You should be able to comment on the models in several ways:

- *Analyze the model.* You should identify the various elements of the model, understand the role each plays in the model, and know how the model is applied in real-world contexts or scenarios.

- *Evaluate the model.* Geographic models rarely describe or predict reality perfectly for several reasons. Be aware of the times and places in which models were developed so that you can explain why a model might or might not be useful in specific situations. Be aware of the strengths, weaknesses, and limitations of models and theories.

Questions Requiring Examples Many of the free-response questions on the AP® Human Geography exam ask you to supply examples or reasons to illustrate or explain a concept. To answer these questions, begin by brainstorming a list of several ideas and selecting the best ones to include in your answer. Provide exactly the number of examples called for in the prompt. You will not get full credit if you provide too few examples. You will waste time if you provide extra examples. Always put your best example first in your response.

Some questions require you to examine two sides of an issue. You might be asked to give both a positive and negative impact of a certain process or trend. Many of the topics studied in geography are complex and can be understood from multiple perspectives. What one person considers a positive, another might view as a negative. Practice seeing topics from opposing viewpoints.

A question may ask that you provide evidence for a concept from a specific category of information, such as economic, social, cultural, political, demographic, or environmental. For example, you could be asked to describe one social impact and one environmental impact of the rise of industrialization in China and Southeast Asia. A social impact could be changing roles for women. An environmental impact could be increasing air pollution. Follow up your claims with specific details, explanations, and/or evidence.

General Writing Advice The principles of good writing that you have learned in school will help you write a good answer to a free-response question:

- *Plan your time.* Take time to plan your answer before you begin writing. A few minutes taken for brainstorming your ideas, selecting good examples, and organizing your response is time well spent.

- *Consider whether to include introductions and conclusions.* You do not need to restate the prompt or write an introduction to your answer. Conclusions are also not necessary. If you choose to write them, information contained in them that responds correctly to the prompt will be considered as part of your answer.

- *Make changes.* If you think of something you would like to add to part A (or B, or another part) of your response but you have already moved on to another part, simply add it and indicate which part of your response it belongs in with a label or arrow. If you write something that you decide you do not want included in your response, draw a line through it and it will not be scored.

- *Do not let grammar, spelling, and handwriting limit you.* Your answer to a free-response question will not be graded on grammar, spelling, or handwriting. So, think of it as a rough draft. Try to use correct grammar, spell words as best you can, and write legibly so that readers understand what you are saying. But focus on the geographic content and skills, not on these other concerns.

Evaluation of Your Answer Your answer to a free-response question will be graded using scoring guidelines that are sometimes called a single-point rubric. Each is designed to relate to one specific free-response question on the exam.

This type of rubric identifies what correct responses to the writing prompt include and how many points they are worth. When your response is scored, the scorer will look for particular information that has been predetermined to be correct.

At least one map will appear in the set of FRQs. None of the questions are intended to be easier or harder than the others, and none matter more than any other to the overall score.

Recommended Activities As with the multiple-choice questions, you should practice writing answers to free-response items. Each chapter in this book contains one that is clearly related to the material contained within the chapter. Each unit concludes with a writing activity that draws upon content from that entire unit and will help you sharpen your writing skills.

Free-response questions from previous AP® exams are available online. If you choose to practice with these, be aware that many of them are meant to cut across the various major topics in the course. Therefore, you may see parts of questions that you have not studied yet. Using the accompanying online scoring guides as a study and review tool is also very helpful.

Effective Review Strategies

Use every possible way to make the material your own—read it, take notes on it, talk about it, create visualizations of it, and relate the ideas in this book to your prior experience and learning. In other words, think about how it connects to ideas in your other courses and to your personal life experiences. The following approaches will help you accomplish this goal:

- *Form a weekly study group.* Use the Essential Question from each Topic as the starting point for your discussion, focusing on how the material you learned during the week helps to answer that question. Ask questions about anything you do not understand. The weekly meetings ensure that you will prepare on a regular basis, and they also give you a chance to speak about and listen to the concepts you are learning in addition to reading and writing about them.
- *Work collaboratively.* Work with a study group in other ways, such as doing the free-response questions in the Chapter Reviews.
- *Use the techniques of cognitive scientists.* The table on this page and the next, offers a summary six strategies which have been proven in research to help people learn. (For more details on learning strategies, visit *http://www.learningscientists.org/.*)

RESEARCH-BASED LEARNING STRATEGIES	
Strategy	**Details**
Distributed Practice	**Spread out** your studying over the entire course in manageable amounts.
Retrieval	After every class, or on another regular schedule, close your book and try to recall the important points, using a practice called **retrieval**. You can use the Reflect on the Essential Question feature at the end of each topic as a framework.

Write whatever you can't retrieve from memory alone by going back into the book for the missing pieces.

Whether you use sample multiple-choice questions, flash cards, or an online program such as Quizlet, take the time to test yourself with a friend or on your own. |

RESEARCH-BASED LEARNING STRATEGIES	
Strategy	**Details**
Elaboration	When studying, **ask yourself questions** about what you are reading. How does this material connect to other material in the unit or in other units? As you learn material, elaborate on it by connecting it to how you make economic decisions in your daily life.
Interleaving	When you study, occasionally **interleave** the material by switching up the order of your review. Instead or reviewing units and topics in the order presented in the book, review them in another order.
Concrete Examples	Write down all **concrete examples** your teacher uses in class. Note the examples given in this book. Use these examples to understand the application of the abstract concepts and ideas you are studying.
Dual Coding	Use **dual coding**, different ways of representing the information. Take notes or write reflections on a segment of text. Then create a visual representation of the same knowledge using graphic organizers, concept maps, or other graphics.

Review Schedule

Set up a review schedule as you prepare for the exam in the weeks prior to the test date. Studying with a group of fellow students can be helpful. Below is a sample of a eight-week review schedule, including information on the chapters in this book that cover the content to review. Because AP® tests are given during the first two full weeks of May, this review schedule assumes you begin your review in mid-March.

PROPOSED REVIEW SCHEDULE		
Week	**Content**	**Chapters in This Book**
1	Thinking Geographically	1, 2
2	Population and Migration Patterns and Processes	3, 4, 5
3	Cultural Patterns and Processes	6, 7
4	Political Patterns and Processes	8, 9, 10
5	Agriculture and Rural Land-Use Patterns and Processes	11, 12
6	Agriculture and Rural Land-Use Patterns and Processes	13, 14
7	Cities and Urban Land-Use Cities	15, 16, 17
8	Industrial and Economic Development Patterns and Processes	18, 19, 20

You should also plan to review the information in this introduction and the introduction to Unit 1 that details the geographic skills students need for this course. This skill information and the suggestions about answering multiple-choice questions and free-response items will be helpful to you.

UNIT 1

Thinking Geographically

Chapter 1 *Maps and Geographic Data*

Chapter 2 *Spatial Concepts and Geographic Analysis*

Unit Overview

What distinguishes geography from all other fields is its focus on a particular perspective, or way of looking at things. That distinctive perspective is spatial and a concern for the interactions between humans and the physical environment. Geographers are certainly interested in *where* questions, but more importantly, they focus on the *why there* question, often expressed as "the why of where."

A spatial approach considers the arrangement of the phenomena being studied across the surface of the earth. The course's Big Ideas (see pages xxiv–xxv), Four-Level Analysis (described below through page 3), and the five skill categories (see pages 3–7) will serve as reliable frameworks for understanding topics from a geographic perspective.

Branches of Geography

Geography is commonly divided into two major branches that bridge the gap between the physical and social sciences:

- **Physical geography** is the study of the spatial characteristics of various elements of the physical environment. Physical geographers study topics such as landforms, bodies of water, climate, ecosystems, and erosion.
- **Human geography** is the study of the spatial characteristics of humans and human activities. Human geographers study topics such as population, culture, politics, urban areas, and economics.

Four-Level Analysis Spatial Framework

Location is at the heart of all geographic understanding. The thinking skills used by geographers help them understand why things and people are where they are, and why the location of an item or of people with particular traits are important. The **Four-Level Analysis** spatial framework will guide your thinking, provide an approach to spatial thinking, and help you think like a geographer. You will use this process when looking at a map, chart, graph, data table, landscape, or an image such as Earth at night (shown on the following page).

Source: nasa.gov

2016 global scale Earth at night

FOUR-LEVEL ANALYSIS SPATIAL FRAMEWORK		
Level	**Key Questions**	**Possible Answers for Earth at Night Image Above**
Comprehension L1	*What?* *Where?* *When?* *Scale?* *Source?*	• What? Earth at night • Where? Earth • When? 2016 • Scale? Global scale • Source? nasa.gov
Identification L2	*Are there patterns in the source?* The source could be a map, chart, graph, etc. There could be multiple patterns.	Numerous patterns • Coasts are brighter than interior • Northern Hemisphere is brighter than Southern Hemisphere • Eastern China is brighter than Western China
Explanation L3	Pick a pattern from the source and explain: *Why did this pattern occur there?* or *How did this pattern occur?* You will use the content of the course to help answer these questions.	Why do so many people live near the coasts? Access to global trade networks or natural resources from oceans (fish), which results in more job opportunities, income, and food. The interior often has harsher climates (deserts or cold) and often less access to natural resources.
Prediction L4	*What will be the impact on the economy, society, politics, or the environment?* or *What if the pattern continues into the future?* Describe the impact or effects and make predictions.	Impacts: • *Economic*—Cost of living (rent) is higher on the coasts because of the high demand for housing. • *Environmental*—Human and factory waste can pollute the ocean, killing fish and wildlife.

The chart on the previous page is designed to be just an introduction to the process with relatively simple responses and is not meant to include all possible answers. The depth and quality of responses should improve as you develop a deeper understanding of human geography. Throughout the text, references will be made to the different levels by using L1, L2, L3, or L4.

Essential Geography Skill Categories 1–5

The AP® Human Geography exam will require students to not only learn the content and discipline-specific language of the course, but utilize and apply a set of essential skills to demonstrate their understanding of human geography. This section introduces these skills and prepares students to apply these skills using real world scenarios across all units of the course and both parts of the exam.

Skill Category 1: Concepts and Processes

Analyze geographic theories, approaches, concepts, processes, or models in theoretical and applied contexts.

This skill contains a large amount of the content of the course and is the most tested skill on the exam:

- **Analyze** means to break down into parts and study each part carefully.
- A **theory** is a system of ideas and concepts that attempt to explain and prove why or how interactions have occurred in the past or will occur in the future.
- **Concepts** are key vocabulary, ideas, and building blocks that geographers use to describe our world.
- **Processes** involve a series of steps or actions that explain why or how geographic patterns occur.

Models in Geography The most important element of this skill involves understanding and applying geographic models. Geographers, similar to biologists, meteorologists, and others who deal with complex reality, create geographic models. **Models** are representations of reality or theories about reality, to help geographers see general spatial patterns, focus on the influence of specific factors, and understand variations from place to place. Models help explain, describe, and sometimes even predict spatial activity and phenomena. There are two basic types of geographic models—spatial and nonspatial:

- **Spatial models** look like stylized maps, and they illustrate theories about spatial distributions. Spatial models have been developed for agricultural and urban land use, distributions of cities, and store or factory location.
- **Nonspatial models** illustrate theories and concepts using words, graphs, or tables. They often depict changes over time rather than across space with more accuracy than spatial models.

Data Driven Models (Formulas and Graphs) Geographers use mathematic formulas to help them understand how the world works. These formulas function much like models. Some formulas, such as those that determine crude birth and death rates, doubling times for populations, and population densities, are mathematical calculations that are used to produce a statistic.

One model that helps explain some patterns evident on the Earth at night image is what geographers call **time-distance decay**. Basically, the idea is that things, such as cities, near each other are more closely connected or related than things that are far apart, as shown in the graph below. The bright lights on the border between the United States and Mexico on the Earth at night map are partly explained because the lights show cities on both sides of the border. This illustrates the countries have lots of connections economically and culturally because they are close to each other.

TIME/DISTANCE DECAY MODEL

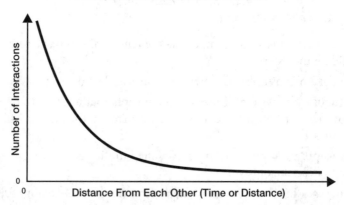

The Time-Distance Decay Model illustrates decreasing interactions and connections as distance increases.

Applying Concepts and Processes In order to be successful in all elements of this skill, you will need to describe, explain, and compare concepts, processes, models, and theories. Students will have to apply the models in various contexts from around the world. The most challenging part of this skill will be to explain the strengths, weaknesses, and limitations of the model. Another way of saying this is, where a model works and where it doesn't work and explain why.

Skill Category 2: Spatial Relationships

Analyze geographic patterns, relationships, and outcomes in applied contexts.

Maps are the signature element of geography. Geographers examine maps to look for clues and patterns in the location and distribution of phenomena (L1 and L2). **Spatial patterns** refer to the general arrangement of things being studied. Describing these spatial patterns, networks, and relationships with precise language is critical to understanding spatial relationships. Geographers use specific terms—density, dispersion, clustered, scattered, linked, etc.—to communicate about locations and distributions.

Applying Spatial Relationships In order to be successful in this skill, students will view a source such as the North America at night image and then use the concepts, models, and theories to explain why and how the patterns on the image occurred (L3 and L4) and some likely outcomes (L4).

Geographers look at the networks, patterns, and relationships that exist between locations, how they evolve, and what their effects are. **Networks** are a set of interconnected entities, sometimes called nodes. The image below shows a network of cities that are connected by numerous strings of lights. These lights follow highways, rail lines, or river routes of transportation and illustrate a connectiveness to U.S. urban and transportation systems.

The last element of this skill requires explaining the degree to which a geographic concept or model effectively describes or explains expected outcomes. This skill requires a deep understanding of different regions of the world and an ability to understand the strengths and weaknesses of various models and theories.

Source: nasa.gov
2016 North America at night

Skill Category 3: Data Analysis

Analyze and interpret quantitative geographic data represented in maps, tables, charts, graphs, satellite images, and infographics.

Quantitative data is any information that can be measured and recorded using numbers such as total number of immigrants to a city. More specifically, **geospatial data** is quantitative and spatial. It has a geographic location component to it such as a country, city, zip code, latitude, longitude, or address and is often used with geographic information systems (see Topics 1.2 and 1.3) because it lends itself to analysis using formulas and is mappable. An example would be average annual income by country.

Applying Data Analysis This skill is similar to Skill 2 except it involves interpreting quantitative statistical data expressed in numbers. This numerical data can be shown in a variety of ways, and examples include life expectancy, income, birth rate, etc. If the data is shown in a map, describing the spatial pattern (L2) accurately and with precision is critical for analysis. If the data is in a graph or chart, describing the variables and trend on the graph or chart (L2) is very important to an accurate interpretation.

The data analysis skill requires the use of concepts, models, and theories to explain why and how these patterns occurred (L3) and some likely outcomes and/or impacts (L4). Using the global scale Earth at night, you can use quantitative data, such as income, to explain why some places are brighter than others. Places that have higher income are more likely to afford electricity in their homes. But be careful, because a difference in income isn't the only reason why some places are bright or dark. Some of the dark areas may be difficult to live in due to extreme climates, such as the regions within the Sahara in northern Africa.

The most difficult part of this skill will be to recognize the limitations of the data. This will require an understanding of trustworthy sources of information, incomplete or inaccurate data, and possible mistakes in gathering the data.

Skill Category 4: Source Analysis

Analyze and interpret qualitative geographic information represented in maps, images (e.g., satellite, photographic, cartoon), and landscapes.

Qualitative sources are not usually represented by numbers. This data is collected as interviews, photographs, remote satellite images, descriptions, or cartoons. For example, asking people if they feel an intersection is dangerous is qualitative as is reviewing a photograph of a city's landscape.

Applying Source Analysis When viewing qualitative sources, you can use Four-Level Analysis to help guide your approach. Geographers look for the following elements: types of information within the source, patterns within a source, and similarities and differences between sources (L1 and L2).

Once this has been accomplished, geographers turn their attention to explaining the reasons why or how geographic concepts and ideas explain the patterns (L3) within the source and the possible impacts of the patterns (L4).

Like all data, there are limitations of visual and other qualitative resources such as only showing a part of the overall landscape, the time of day that the information was gathered, interviews that may include opinions not based on accurate information, or the author's lack of understanding of a culture's beliefs or values. In the case of the Earth at night image, one of the major limitations is that the image does not show lights where all people in the world live, just the places that can afford to have electricity. The image really only shows wealthier populations and larger cities where electricity is available.

Skill Category 5: Scale Analysis

Analyze geographic theories, approaches, concepts, processes, and models across geographic scales to explain spatial relationships.

One of the most powerful skills of geographers is changing **scales of analysis**, or looking at topics at the local, regional, country, or global scale. This process will be described in greater detail in Chapter 2 (see Topic 1.6), but essentially, changing scale of analysis involves studying phenomena by zooming in and zooming out in order to develop a more complete understanding of the topics being studied.

Applying Scale Analysis The Earth at night image can be used again to solidify your understanding. The map shows an image at the global or worldwide scale, and the pattern of more people living on the coast than the interior is a strong global scale pattern. However, the pattern that more people live in eastern China than western China is a country level scale of analysis. To take this one step further, a geographer could zoom into the local or city scale to see the border between the United States and Mexico, near San Diego. What is important is that at each scale, we may observe different patterns and reasons of why or how (L3) or the impacts (L4) that may be different or the same at each scale of analysis.

Source: nasa.gov
A zoomed in view of the U.S.-Mexico border showing San Diego, California, and Tijuana, Mexico.

Mastering the strategy of Four-Level Analysis spatial framework and the five essential skills of this course will take your ability to understand human geography to the next level.

ENDURING UNDERSTANDINGS

IMP-1: Geographers use maps and data to depict relationships of time, space, and scale.

PSO-1: Geographers analyze relationships among and between places to reveal important spatial patterns.

SPS-1: Geographers analyze complex issues and relationships with a distinctively spatial perspective.

Source: *AP® Human Geography Course and Exam Description*. Effective Fall 2020. (College Board).

CHAPTER 1

Maps and Geographic Data

Topics 1.1–1.3

Topic 1.1 Introduction to Maps

Learning Objective: Identify types of maps, the types of information presented in maps, and different kinds of spatial patterns and relationships portrayed in maps. (IMP-1.A)

Topic 1.2 Geographic Data

Learning Objective: Identify different methods of geographic data collection. (IMP-1.B)

Topic 1.3 The Power of Geographic Data

Learning Objective: Explain the geographical effects of decisions made using geographical information. (IMP-1.C)

The map—what a great idea!—is also one of the oldest and perhaps the most powerful and constant of geographic ideas. . . . Although they may be as beautiful as any work of art, we distinguish maps from art in the way we look at them. . . . The map's message does not lie in its overall effect but in the locational information it carries.

—Anne Godlewska, *Ten Geographic Ideas That Changed the World*

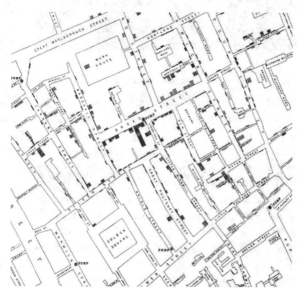

Source: Wikimedia Commons

John Snow used geographic reasoning to locate the source of a cholera outbreak to a water pump on Broad Street in London in 1854. The black dashes are cases of cholera. (See Topic 1.3 for how geographic data is used.)

Introduction to Maps

Essential Question: What information is presented in different types of maps, and how do those maps show spatial patterns, the power of geographic data, and relationships among places?

Geographers emphasize spatial patterns, which are the general arrangements of things being studied and the repeated sequences of events, or processes, that create them. Learning to recognize and use geographical patterns is a fundamental skill in understanding the discipline. One of the most important tools of geographers are maps. Improvements in geospatial and computer technologies have dramatically increased the quality of maps, the accuracy of data, and the variety of maps available to study and use. Maps and geospatial data now influence everyday life with the use of smartphones and apps that allow us to not only view maps but interact, modify, and show our own location within the map.

Maps

Maps are the most important tool of a geographer and help to organize complex information. No tool communicates spatial information more effectively than a map. Maps are essential in highlighting and analyzing patterns. There are two broad categories of maps: reference maps and thematic maps:

Reference Maps

Reference maps are aptly named because they are designed for people to refer to for general information about places.

- **Political maps** show and label human-created boundaries and designations, such as countries, states, cities, and capitals.
- **Physical maps** show and label natural features, such as mountains, rivers, and deserts.
- **Road maps** show and label highways, streets, and alleys.
- **Plat maps** show and label property lines and details of land ownership.

REFERENCE MAP OF MEXICO

Reference map of Mexico from 2020. What type of reference material is included in the map? For what purpose might this map be useful?

Thematic Maps

Thematic maps show spatial aspects of information or of a phenomenon. Following are descriptions of four common types of thematic maps.

Choropleth maps use various colors, shades of one color, or patterns to show the location and distribution of spatial data. They often show rates or other quantitative data in defined areas, such as the percentage of people who speak English.

Dot distribution maps are used to show the specific location and distribution of something across a map. Each dot represents a specified quantity. One dot might stand for one school building or for millions of people who own dogs. While these maps are known as dot distribution maps, any kind of symbol—a triangle, the outline of a house, a cow—can be used instead of dots.

MAP PATTERNS

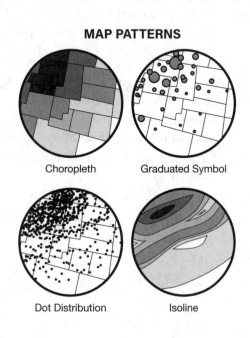

Choropleth   Graduated Symbol

Dot Distribution   Isoline

Graduated symbol maps use symbols of different sizes to indicate different amounts of something. Larger sizes indicate more of something, and smaller sizes indicate less. These maps make it easy to see where the largest and smallest of some phenomena are by simply comparing the symbols to each other. The map key is used to determine the exact amount. The symbols themselves are arranged on the map centered over the location represented by the data, so they may overlap. Graduated symbol maps are also called proportional symbol maps.

Isoline maps, also called isometric maps, use lines that connect points of equal value to depict variations in the data across space. Where lines are close together, the map depicts rapid change, and where the lines are farther apart, the phenomenon is relatively the same. The most common type of isoline maps are **topographic maps**, which are popular among hikers. Points of equal elevation are connected on these maps, creating contours that depict surface features. Other examples of isoline maps are weather maps showing changes in barometric pressure, temperature, or precipitation across space.

In a **cartogram**, the sizes of countries (or states, counties, or other areal units) are shown according to some specific statistic. In the example below, the cartogram of world population shows Canada and Morocco as roughly the same size because they have similar populations (about 35 million people), even though Canada is more than 20 times larger in area. Any variable for which there are statistics can be substituted for the size of the country and mapped in the same way. Cartograms are useful because they allow for data to be compared, much like a graph, and distance and distribution are also visible, like on a traditional map.

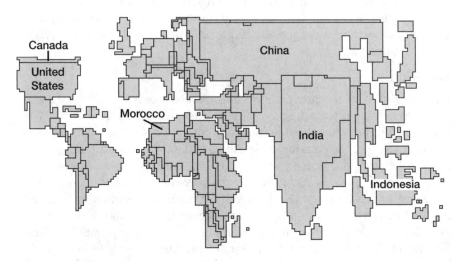

The size of each country reflects the total population. Based on the graphic, which countries have the largest populations?

Scale

Nearly every map is a smaller version of a larger portion of the earth's surface. In other words, a map is a reduction of the actual land area it represents. **Scale** is the ratio between the size of things in the real world and the size of those same things on the map. A map has three types of scale: cartographic scale, geographic scale and the scale of the data represented on the map. (See Topic 1.6 for more about scale.)

Cartographic scale refers to the way the map communicates the ratio of its size to the size of what it represents:

- Words: for example, "1 inch equals 10 miles." In this case, 2 inches on the map would be 20 miles on the surface of the Earth.

- A ratio: for example, 1/200,000 or 1:200,000. This means that 1 unit of measurement on the map is equal to 200,000 of the same unit in reality. For example, 1 inch on the map represents 200,000 inches (or 3.15 miles) on the ground.

- A line: for example, the map may show a line and indicate that its distance on the map represents ten miles in reality. This is sometimes called a linear, or graphic, scale.

- Scale: **Small-scale maps** show a larger amount of area with less detail—global scale Earth at night is an example. **Large-scale maps** show a smaller amount of area with a greater amount of detail—North America at night is an example.

Types of Spatial Patterns Represented on a Map

Spatial patterns refer to the general arrangement of phenomena on a map. Spatial patterns can be described in a variety of way utilizing important geographic tools and concepts including location, direction, distance, elevation, or distribution pattern.

Location

Locations may be absolute or relative. **Absolute location** is the precise spot where something is according to a system. The most widely used system is the global grid of lines known as latitude and longitude. **Latitude** is the distance north or south of the **equator**, an imaginary line that circles the globe exactly halfway between the North and South Poles. The equator is designated as 0 degrees and the poles as 90 degrees north and 90 degrees south.

Longitude is the distance east or west of the **prime meridian**, an imaginary line that runs from pole to pole through Greenwich, England. It is designated as 0 degrees. On the opposite side of the globe from the prime meridian is 180 degrees longitude. The **International Date Line** roughly follows this line but makes deviations to accommodate international boundaries. Thus, on this system, the absolute location of Mexico City is 19 degrees north latitude and 99 degrees west longitude.

THE GLOBAL GRID

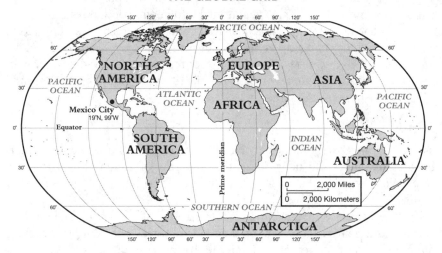

Relative location is a description of where something is in relation to other things. To describe Salt Lake City, Utah, as being "just south of the Great Salt Lake and just west of the Rocky Mountains, on Interstate 15 about halfway between Las Vegas, Nevada, and Butte, Montana," is one way (of many) to describe its relative location. Relative location is often described in terms of **connectivity**, how well two locations are tied together by roads or other links, and **accessibility**, how quickly and easily people in one location can interact with people in another location.

Direction is used in order to describe where things are in relation to each other. Cardinal directions such as north, east, south, or west or intermediate directions such as southeast or southwest are commonly used to describe direction. On most maps, north will be the top of the map, but be sure to look on the map for cardinal direction clues.

THE RELATIVE LOCATION OF SALT LAKE CITY

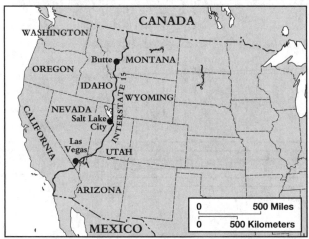

This map shows the relative location of Salt Lake City along Interstate 15. What are advantages for business or cities being located near an interstate?

Relative locations can change over time and as accessibility changes. For example, the many ghost towns (abandoned settlements) of the western United States once had relative locations near water sources (which dried up), along trade routes (which changed), or near mines (which closed). Their good relative locations lost the advantages of access to resources or trade that they once had. However, their absolute locations, as described by the global grid of latitude and longitude, remain the same.

Distance

Distance is a measurement of how far or how near things are to one another. **Absolute distance** is usually measured in terms of feet, miles, meters or kilometers. For example, the absolute distance from home to your school is 2.2 miles.

The term **relative distance** indicates the degree of nearness based on time or money and is often dependent on the mode of travel. For example, traveling from home to your school takes 10 minutes by car or 25 minutes walking.

Elevation

Elevation is the distance of features above sea level, usually measured in feet or meters. The elevation of the summit of Mount Everest is over 29,000 feet. Elevation can impact a variety of things including climate, weather, and agriculture. Usually, the higher the elevation, the cooler the temperature gets and at very high elevations, it becomes more difficult for certain crops to grow. Elevation is usually shown on maps with contours (isolines).

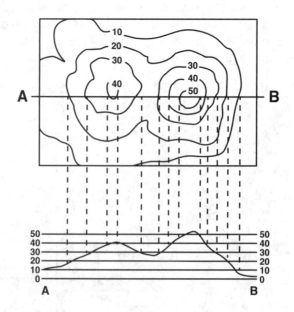

Source: usgs.gov

A contour map (isoline), like the one above, shows elevation of physical features.

Pattern Distribution

Geographers are also interested in **distribution**, the way a phenomenon is spread out over an area (L2). Essentially, distribution is a description of the pattern of where specific phenomenon are located. Geographers look for **patterns**, or the general arrangement of things, in the distribution of phenomena across space that give clues about causes or effects of the distribution. Common distribution patterns include the following:

- **Clustered or agglomerated** phenomena are arranged in a group or concentrated area such as restaurants in a food court at a mall or the clustering of cities along the border of the United States and Mexico.
- **Linear** phenomena are arranged in a straight line, such as the distribution of towns along a railroad line.
- **Dispersed** phenomena are spread out over a large area, such as the distribution of large malls in a city.
- **Circular** phenomena are equally spaced from a central point, forming a circle, such as the distribution of the homes of people who shop at a particular store.
- **Geometric** phenomena are in a regular arrangement, such as the squares or blocks formed by roads in the Midwest.
- **Random** phenomena appear to have no order to their position, such as the distribution of pet owners in a city.

Projections

Because the earth is a sphere and maps are flat, all maps distort some aspect of reality. The process of showing a curved surface on a flat surface is done using a map projection. Cartographers decide whether they want to preserve area, shape, distance, or direction on their map accurately, knowing that other elements will have to be less accurate as the earth is "flattened" on their map. Essentially all maps are distorted, but cartographers use different maps for different purposes.

The Mercator, one of the most famous projections, was designed for navigation because the lines of directions are straight and easy to follow. A weakness of the Mercator on a global scale is that it makes the land masses appear larger than reality as you move north or south from the equator. This results in the countries of North America and Europe appearing larger and possibly more powerful than the countries near the equator. Greenland's size on a Mercator looks to be the same size of Africa, however, in reality, Africa is 14 times the size of Greenland.

Geographers are concerned by the political and economic bias of power, wealth, and superiority that can be subconsciously reinforced by using an incorrect projection. All projections and maps have strengths and weaknesses. The key is to understand this and select the best projection for the map.

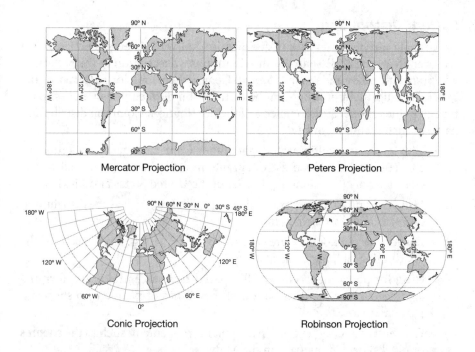

Mercator Projection

Peters Projection

Conic Projection

Robinson Projection

COMPARING MAP PROJECTIONS			
Projection	**Purpose**	**Strengths**	**Distortion (Weaknesses)**
Mercator	Navigation	• Directions are shown accurately • Lines of latitude and longitude meet at right angles	• Distance between lines of longitude appears constant • Land masses near the poles appear large
Peters	Spatial distributions related to area	• Sizes of land masses are accurate	• Shapes are inaccurate, especially near the poles
Conic	General use in midlatitude countries	• Lines of longitude converge • Lines of latitude are curved • Size and shape are both close to reality	• Direction is not constant • On a world map, longitude lines converge at only one pole
Robinson	General use	• No major distortion • Oval shape appears more like a globe than does a rectangle	• Area, shape, size, and direction are all slightly distorted

REFLECT ON THE ESSENTIAL QUESTION

Essential Question: *What information is presented in different types of maps, and how do those maps show spatial patterns, the power of geographic data, and relationships among places?*

Types of Maps	Types of Information in Maps	Ways to Describe Spatial Patterns

KEY TERMS

physical geography
human geography
Four-Level Analysis
analyze
theory
concepts
processes
models
spatial models
nonspatial models
time-distance decay
spatial patterns
networks
quantitative data
geospatial data
qualitative sources
scales of analysis
reference maps
political maps

physical maps
road maps
plat maps
thematic maps
choropleth maps
dot distribution maps
graduated symbol maps
isoline maps
topographic maps
cartogram
scale
cartographic scale
small-scale maps
large-scale maps
absolute location
latitude
equator
longitude
prime meridian

International Date Line
relative location
connectivity
accessibility
direction
patterns
absolute distance
relative distance
elevation
distribution
clustered (agglomerated)
   distribution
linear distribution
dispersed distribution
circular distribution
geometric distribution
random distribution

Geographic Data

Essential Question: What are different methods of geographical data collection?

Geographers often refer to the current era as being part of a geospatial revolution because they gather data through technical mapping and via satellites or aerial photos. Geographers also have the ability to gather data by visiting places, interviewing people, or observing events in the field. The quality of data gathered by individuals or institutions is important because patterns within the data will influence real-life individual choices and policy decisions.

Landscape Analysis

The word *landscape* comes from older Germanic words that refer to the condition of the land. The term can also imply a specific area, as in a "desert landscape" or the "landscape of Tuscany." The task of defining and describing landscapes is called **landscape analysis**.

Observation and Interpretation

The first part of landscape analysis is careful observation. Geographers are keen observers of phenomena and collect data about what they see. The term **field observation** is used to refer to the act of physically visiting a location, place, or region and recording, firsthand, information there. Geographers can often be found writing notes, taking photographs, sketching maps, counting and measuring things, and interviewing people as they walk through an area that they are interested in studying. For most of the history of geography, this was the only way to gather data about places. All of the information that can be tied to specific locations is called **spatial data**.

Developments in Gathering Data Modern technology has increased the ways in which geographers can obtain spatial data including remote sensing and aerial sources. **Remote sensing** gathers information from satellites that orbit the earth or other craft above the atmosphere. **Aerial photography**, professional images captured from planes within the atmosphere, is an important source of observed data available today. Ground-level photography has replaced sketching as a tool for capturing information about landscapes. Sound recordings and the ability to get chemical analyses of air, water, and soil have also changed the way geographers observe a landscape.

Interpreting Data Once data has been gathered, it must be interpreted. Geographers depend on their skills of synthesizing and integrating, or putting together, all of the collected information to better understand the place, area, or landscape being studied. A common example clearly observable today is the changes that occur in the landscapes of rural and urban areas over time. A geographer may be interested in understanding what changes are likely to occur as people move into or out of an area:

- Who are the people migrating into this area? Who is leaving?
- What are the cultures of these groups of people?
- What effects will the changes have on the local economy?
- What are the causes of people moving?
- What types of human-environment interaction are occurring?

Geospatial Data

Geospatial data can be quantitative or qualitative and may be gathered by organizations or individuals. Geospatial data includes all information that can be tied to a specific place. Besides locations of things, such as mountains or roads or boundaries, it includes human activities and traits. Where do speakers of Mandarin live? How common is poverty in each U.S. county? Where is the dividing line in a city between students who attend one high school and those who attend another school?

SOURCES OF QUANTITATIVE DATA

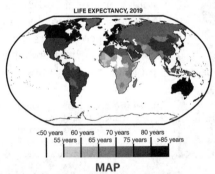

MAP

GRAPH

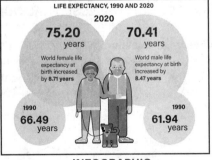

DATA TABLE

INFOGRAPHIC

Source: ourworldindata.org

The images illustrate different ways that quantitative geospatial data related to life expectancy can be presented. What are strengths and weaknesses of data presented in each image?

Obtaining Geospatial Data

Geographers collect geospatial data by doing **fieldwork**, or observing and recording information on location, or in the field. Important sources of this type of data can come from a census of the population, from interviews, or even from informal observations made by geographers. Land surveys, photographs, and sketches are also important ways in which this data is obtained. Technology is making the collection, storage, analysis, and display of geospatial data easier, as well as more accurate, than at any time in the past. The chart in Topic 1.3 illustrates three technologies that have revolutionized the importance of geospatial data.

Other Sources of Geospatial Data

Additional sources of data can come from government policy documents such as treaties or agreements, articles and videos from news media outlets, or photos of an area. Many tech companies who design apps for smartphones use locational data elements that make suggestions on food options or activities that are near to you. Most photos taken with smartphones have geospatial data embedded into the image that can be mapped in interactive online maps sites. In fact, many companies and some governments are interested in buying your smartphone geospatial data so they can make targeted advertisements or

policy decisions related to your locational activities. Students of geography can be local geographers who gather information for projects or field studies.

Qualitative data can include photos (as of Tokyo to the left), satellite photos (as seen on page 2), cartoons, or interviews. How can qualitative data better help geographers to understand a place?

REFLECT ON THE ESSENTIAL QUESTION

Essential Question: *What are different methods of geographical data collection?*

Individual Sources	Institutional Sources

KEY TERMS

landscape analysis	spatial data	aerial photography
field observations	remote sensing	fieldwork

The Power of Geographic Data

Essential Question: What are the effects of decisions made using geographical information?

Geographic data is powerful. When used properly and ethically, it can have many positive benefits for individuals, companies, governments, and society. However, misusing it can lead people to draw inaccurate conclusions or make poor decisions. So, understanding the limitations of the data and carefully monitoring improper uses of this information are essential to ensure that the data is beneficial, not harmful, to individuals or a society.

Using Geographic Data to Solve Problems

There are many technological sources of geospatial data and many ways the data obtained from those sources is used in our everyday life. As computers and technology has rapidly improved, large quantities of information can now be rapidly gathered and stored. This data can then be turned into amazing 2D or even 3D interactive maps, or **geovisualizations**, that allow people to zoom in or out to see the data in ways that were previously impossible. When skillfully used, tools such as Google Earth, ESRI 3D GIS, OpenStreetMap, or the COVID-19 map (produced by Johns Hopkins University) allow viewers to see the world and data in new and interesting ways. These geovisualizations can help people better understand the world they live.

More importantly, the data helps solve real world problems. For example, accurately tracking and mapping the COVID-19 pandemic that began in 2019 resulted in saving lives in hot spots. At same time, it allowed areas that were less affected by the virus to open businesses and to allow students back into classrooms.

Even with all of these techniques, all data has limitations and geographers must be careful to accurately gather and interpret the data. Maps are only as valuable as the data used to create the map. Interview data may be from only a small percentage of the population and not represent all of the views in a community. Sometimes data sets may exclude segments of the population, such as the homeless or undocumented workers. A constant concern for geographers and others who interpret data is that people may make simple errors by typing information incorrectly into a computer.

These limitations may not make the data completely useless, but they can create gaps and inaccuracies in the data. Potentially, bad data can cause people using the map to draw inaccurate conclusions.

GEOSPATIAL TECHNOLOGIES		
Type	**Description**	**Uses**
Global Positioning System (GPS)	GPS receivers on the earth's surface use the locations of multiple satellites to determine and record a receiver's exact location	• Locating borders precisely • Navigating ships, aircraft, and cars • Mapping lines (trails) or points (fire hydrants)
Remote Sensing	The use of cameras or other sensors mounted on aircraft or satellites to collect digital images or video of the earth's surface	• Determining land cover and use • Monitoring environmental changes • Assessing spread of spatial phenomena • Monitoring the weather
Geographic Information Systems (GIS)	Computer system that can store, analyze, and display information from multiple digital maps or geospatial data sets	• Analyzing of crime data • Monitoring the effects of pollution • Analyzing transportation/travel time • Planning urban area
Smartphone and Computer Applications	Location-aware apps that gather, store, and use locational data from computers or other personal devices	• Suggesting restaurants, stores, or best routes to users • Contact tracing related to tracking diseases or exposure to chemicals • Mapping of photos from geotags

GEOGRAPHIC INFORMATION SYSTEMS (GIS)

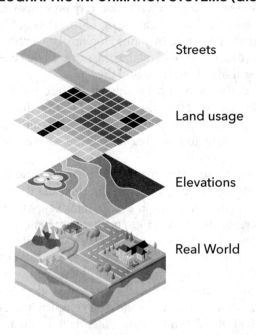

Streets

Land usage

Elevations

Real World

GIS are computer-based tools that are used gather, manage, and analyze data related to position on the Earth's surface

Solutions in Action

Geographers can use geospatial data tools to identify problems that exist in our world such as water shortages, potential famine, or rising conflicts. One case study involves the people of the Nuba Mountains in Sudan. Using maps and remote sensing technologies, such as satellite and aerial images, researchers observed possible humanitarian concerns. These concerns were related to conflicts in the area that resulted in a lack of access to clean drinking water or infrastructure such as hospitals or schools. A team of researchers decided to visit the community in order to assess the situation from the ground using landscape analysis techniques. The hope was to develop a **community-based solution** and the power of governmental and non-governmental organizations (NGO) to help the people improve their standard of

Source: cosv.org

Many people in Africa struggle with access to clean drinking water. This water pumps provides access to water for young girls their family in Darfur Sudan. Why is cooperation with the local community and researchers important?

living. Community-based solutions increase the likelihood of success because they create buy-in from local residents and are more likely to be culturally accepted. As a result, geographers and Sudanese family members living in the United States are working with organizations such as the Nuba Water Project to develop solutions to bring better access to water, medicine, and education to the people of the Nuba Mountains in Sudan. Geography in action!

REFLECT ON THE ESSENTIAL QUESTION

Essential Question: *What are the effects of decisions made using geographical information?*

Sources of Geospatial Data	Benefits of Using Geospatial Data

KEY TERMS

geovisualization

Global Positioning Systems (GPS)

remote sensing

Geographic Information System (GIS)

community-based solutions

One of the most useful maps in history is also one of the most inaccurate. And its inaccuracies are what make it so useful. The map of the London subway system, known as the Underground, demonstrates the value of the concept of relative location. A portion of this map is shown below.

Beck's Map

By 1931, the Underground had become so complex that an accurate but conveniently small map was hard to read. Harry Beck, an Underground employee, realized that a simpler map would be more useful. Passengers did not need to know every twist and turn in the routes, so he created a map with straight lines. Passengers were also not particularly concerned with distances, so he adjusted the space between stops on the map. He spread out the ones in the congested central city and reduced space between the outlying stops so they fit on the map easily.

The result was a map based on relative location that was easy to read and convenient to use. Passengers knew where to get on, where to get off, and at which stops they could transfer from one line to another.

Popular Demand

When the first version of the map was distributed to a few passengers in 1933, people demanded more. Since then, the map has been revised regularly to add new subway lines, more information about which lines have limited service, which stations are accessible to people using wheelchairs, and other improvements. Other transit systems have adopted a similar approach.

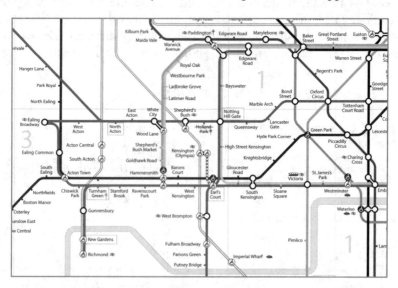

1. Even though the underground map has inaccuracies why is it still useful?

2. What other maps do you find useful that may have some inaccuracies? Explain.

THINK AS A GEOGRAPHER: *GROUPING DATA*

How people group information can emphasize certain patterns in the data. In turn, this can influence how readers interpret it. Imagine you are creating a map based on the data in the table.

POPULATION CHANGE FOR THE LARGEST CITIES, 1900 TO 2015				
City	Population in 1900	Population in 2015 (estimate)	Total Change	Percentage Change
New York	3,437,202	8,550,405	+5,113,203	+149%
Chicago	1,698,575	2,720,546	+1,021,971	+60%
Philadelphia	1,293,697	1,567,442	+273,745	+21%
St. Louis	575,238	315,685	–259,553	–45%
Boston	560,892	667,137	+106,245	+19%
Baltimore	508,957	621,849	+112,892	+22%
Cleveland	381,768	388,072	+6,304	+2%
Buffalo	352,387	258,071	–94,316	–27%
San Francisco	342,782	864,816	+522,034	+152%
Cincinnati	325,902	298,550	–27,352	–8%

1. If you use large dots to show cities of three million or more people in 1900 and small dots for the other cities, what impression would the map give readers about the relative size of cities?

2. If you use large dots to show cities of 600,000 or more people in 1900 and small dots for the other cities, what impression would the map give readers about the relative size of cities?

CHAPTER 1 REVIEW:
Maps and Geographic Data

Topics 1.1–1.3

MULTIPLE-CHOICE QUESTIONS

Questions 1 and 2 refer to the map below.

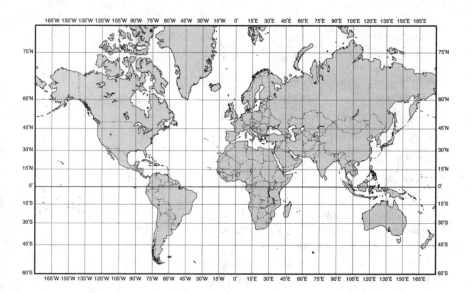

1. Why is the map projection shown here especially useful for navigation on the surface of the earth?

   (A) Distortion of shape is minimized.

   (B) Direction is constant across the map.

   (C) Distances are correctly portrayed.

   (D) Area of land masses is shown accurately.

   (E) It shows the sizes of bodies of water realistically.

2. Like the map above, all maps have some kind of distortion. Why?

   (A) The earth's surface is curved and a map is flat.

   (B) All maps are smaller than the areas they actually represent.

   (C) Human error is always present when a map is made.

   (D) Maps can depict only a small number of the many details of the earth's surface.

   (E) The world constantly changes, so maps are never current.

3. Which phrase refers to the collection of geospatial data through the use of satellite imagery?

(A) Creating a projection

(B) Gathering information through fieldwork

(C) Using a global positioning system

(D) Forming a mental map

(E) Using remote sensing

4. Which is the best example of qualitative data used by geographers?

(A) Personal descriptions of processes and events

(B) Surveys about how often people visit other places

(C) Census counts such as population statistics

(D) Measurements of distance made using GPS receivers

(E) Tables showing the age distribution of people in a community

Question 5 refers to the passage below.

Smartphones, each one with a tiny GPS pinging, have revolutionized cartography. Matthew Zook, a geographer at the University of Kentucky, has partnered with data scientists there to create what they call the DOLLY Project (Digital OnLine Life and You)—it's a searchable repository of every geotagged tweet since December 2011, meaning Zook and his team have compiled billions of interrelated sentiments, each with a latitude and longitude attached.

—Christian Rudder, "The United States of Reddit," *Slate*, 2014.

5. Why are geographers interested in the information in DOLLY?

(A) It provides information about spatial distribution of people's reactions to events.

(B) It provides an opportunity for geographers to work with data scientists.

(C) Geographers focus on the sentiments of people more than do other scientists.

(D) Geographers are more likely to use new technology than are other scientists.

(E) The data is searchable, and most geographic information is hard to organize.

Questions 6 to 7 refer to the map below.

6. Which statement best describes the absolute location of Paris, France?
   (A) 127 miles away from the English Channel
   (B) In the Northern Hemisphere and Eastern Hemisphere
   (C) 49 degrees north, 2 degrees east
   (D) The capital of France
   (E) In the heart of France

7. Which statement describes the relative location of Barcelona, Spain?
   (A) The capital of the Catalonia region
   (B) 41 degrees north, 2 degrees east
   (C) In the Northern Hemisphere and Eastern Hemisphere
   (D) 386 miles west of Madrid and 644 miles south of Paris
   (E) One of the largest cities in Spain

1. Use the image of Earth at night above, your knowledge of Four-Level Analysis, and the course skills to answer the prompts. Also refer to the introduction discussion on verbs (page xxx) to assist you on how much to write for each part of the question.

   (A) Identify the overall scale of the Earth at night image.

   (B) Describe TWO patterns on the map.

   (C) Explain why the Earth at night image is considered a qualitative source and not quantitative.

   (D) Explain ONE reason why eastern China is brighter than western China.

   (E) Explain ONE economic impact of so many people living on the coasts of the world's continents.

   (F) Explain ONE environmental impact of so many people living on the coasts.

   (G) Describe a major limitation of using the Earth at night image to illustrate the location of the world's population.

CHAPTER 2

Spatial Concepts and Geographic Analysis

Topics 1.4–1.7

Topic 1.4 Spatial Concepts

Learning Objective: Define the major geographic concepts that illustrate spatial relationships. (PSO-1.A)

Topic 1.5 Human-Environmental Interaction

Learning Objective: Explain how major geographic concepts illustrate spatial relationships. (PSO-1.B)

Topic 1.6 Scales of Analysis

Learning Objectives: Define scales of analysis used by geographers. (PSO-1.C)
Explain what scales of analysis reveal. (PSO-1.D)

Topic 1.7 Regional Analysis

Learning Objective: Define different ways that geographers define regions. (SPS-1.A)

A lot of these regional boundaries are porous and messy, allowing for a rich diversity of cultural flow. But knowing how we interact as part of a complex society, instead of only looking at political borders, can explain a lot more than we might have imagined.

—Samuel Arbesman, Bloomberg.com, 2012

Source: Getty Images

Much of the Netherlands has been reclaimed from the sea. Wind turbines were built on *polders* along highway A6 of the country's west coast, and are one of the most recognizable elements of the built environment. (See Topic 1.5 for more on how humans interact with the environment.)

Spatial Concepts

Essential Question: What are the major geographic concepts that illustrate spatial relationships and patterns?

A **spatial approach** considers the arrangement of the phenomena being studied across the surface of the earth. This approach focuses on things such as location, distance, direction, orientation, flow, pattern, and interconnection. A spatial approach also looks at elements such as the movements of people and things, changes in places over time, and even human perceptions of space and place. Using Four-Level Analysis from Unit 1 Overview, geographers ask and attempt to answer questions about spatial distributions such as these:

- Why are things where they are?
- How did things become distributed as they are?
- What is changing the pattern of distribution?
- What are the implications of the spatial distribution for people?

Major Geographic Spatial Concepts

Historians look through the lens of time to understand the past. Similarly, geographers look through the lens of **space** to understand place. Space is the area between two or more phenomena or things. Space is at the heart of geography and geographers are intensely interested in how space is arranged, used, and reflected in people's attitudes and beliefs.

Location

Location is an important spatial concept to geographers. (See Topic 1.1.) **Location** identifies where specific phenomena are located either on a grid system or relative to another location. The concepts of absolute and relative location are essential to define the amount of space and relative or absolute distance between locations. Additionally, geographers use the concepts of place, site, and situation to further develop an understanding of a specific location.

Place

Place refers to the specific human and physical characteristics of a location. A group of places in the same area that share a characteristic form a **region**. (See Topic 1.7 for more about regions.)

Two ways to refer to place are its site and situation. **Site** can be described as the characteristics at the immediate location—for example, the soil type, climate, labor force, and human structures. In contrast, **situation** refers to the location of a place relative to its surroundings and its connectivity to other places.

The site of Riyadh, the capital and most populated city in Saudi Arabia, is a desert climate, a large labor force, and a modern Islamic city. The city's situation includes being located roughly in the center of the Arabian Peninsula. The situation of the Arabian Peninsula is between the continents of Africa and Asia and Riyadh is connected to the world with a large modern airport. Another example of how situation can change relates to when the interstate highway system was created in the United States in the 1950s. The situation of many small towns changed dramatically. Towns along old railroad lines became less important as centers of trade, while towns along the new interstate suddenly became more important.

Sense of Place Related to the concept of place is a **sense of place**. Humans tend to perceive the characteristics of places in different ways based on their personal beliefs. For example, the characteristics of Rome, Italy, might be described differently by a local resident than by an outsider or by a Catholic than by a Hindu. If a place inspires no strong emotional ties in people or lacks uniqueness, it has placelessness.

Toponyms Finally, locations can also be designated using **toponyms**, or place names. Some toponyms provide insights into the physical geography, the history, or the culture of the location. The entire coast of Florida is dotted with communities with "beach" in the name—Fernandina Beach, Miami Beach, Pensacola Beach—all of which are on beaches. Iowa is named for a Native American tribe. Pikes Peak is named for an explorer, Zebulon Pike.

Sometimes toponyms get confusing. Greenland is icier than Iceland, while Iceland is greener than Greenland. And some toponyms are deceiving. Lake City, Iowa, is not on a lake, and few people consider Mount Prospect, Illinois, a mountain—at an elevation of only 665 feet above sea level. Toponyms are often created to inspire an ideal view of a location, memorialize an event or person, or even to express power and ownership and can be full of controversy and disagreement. One such controversy involved the debate over the name of the tallest mountain in the United States. Should the Alaskan mountain take the name Mt. McKinley after the former U.S. President, William McKinley? Or Denali, the name from the traditional Native American Koyukon language, meaning Great One? In 2015, President Obama restored the mountain's name back to Denali.

Distance and Time

Distance (see Topic 1.1) can be measured in terms of absolute or relative distance. **Time-space compression** is the shrinking "time-distance," or relative distance, between locations because of improved methods of transportation and communication. New York City and London are separated by an ocean, but the development of air travel greatly reduced travel time between them. As a result, they feel much closer today than they did in the 19th century even though the absolute distance of 3,500 miles has not changed.

One result of time-space compression is that global forces are influencing culture everywhere and reducing local diversity more than ever before. In the 19th century, the mountainous regions of southeastern Europe were famous for the local variations in their music. Today, because of radio, Internet, and other changes, people in southeastern Europe listen to the same music as everyone else in the world.

The Impact of Distance The increasing connection between places is reflected in the growth of **spatial interaction**. Spatial interaction refers to the contact, movement, and flow of things between locations. Connections might be physical, such as through roads. Or they can be through information, such as through radios or Internet service. Places with more connections will have increased spatial interaction. **Flow** refers to the patterns and movement of ideas, people, products, and other phenomena. You will learn about specific flows in every unit and apply Four-Level Analysis to better understand the flows of culture, migration, and trade in the world.

The **friction of distance** indicates that when things are farther apart, they tend to be less connected. This inverse relationship between distance and connection is a concept called **distance decay**. A clear illustration of this concept is the weakening of a radio signal as it travels across space away from a radio tower. Friction of distance causes the decay, or weakening, of the signal. Natural characteristics like waves, earthquakes, and storm systems exhibit the distance-decay function. Human characteristics also exhibit distance decay, although the key issue is more accurately described as connectedness than distance. When a new pet store opens, its influence is strongest in the area closest to the store but only among the pet owners who have a connection to the store. Improvements to infrastructure, such as transportation and communication, have reduced the friction of distance between places as they have increased the spatial interaction.

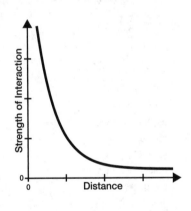

Declining Influence of Distance Concepts such as accessibility and remoteness are changing. The world is more spatially connected than ever before in history. The Internet can be used to illustrate several of these concepts. It allows a person living in El Paso, Texas, to shop at a store in New York City (via its website) and receive a product shipped from a warehouse in Atlanta, Georgia. Distance decay is less influential than it once was.

Patterns and Distribution

Patterns (see Topic 1.1) refer to the general arrangement of things being studied, and geographers must be able to describe patterns accurately and with precision. Geographers often use the concept of **distribution**, the way a phenomenon is spread out or arranged over an area to describe patterns.

Geographers look for patterns in the distribution of phenomena across space that give clues about causes or effects of the distribution. Common distribution patterns include but are not limited to the following: clustered, linear, dispersed, circular, geometric or random. (See Topic 1.1 for more on distribution patterns.)

Matching patterns of distribution is called **spatial association** and indicates that two (or more) phenomena may be related or associated with one another. For example, the distribution of malaria matches the distribution of the mosquito that carries it. However, just because two distributions have a similar pattern does not mean one is necessarily the cause of the other. The distribution of bicycle shops in a large city might be similar to the distribution of athletic wear stores—but one probably does not cause the other. They both might reflect the distribution of active people.

REFLECT ON THE ESSENTIAL QUESTION

Essential Question: *What are the major geographic concepts that illustrate spatial relationships and patterns?*

Geographic Spatial Concepts	Use of Concepts

KEY TERMS

spatial approach	time-space compression
space	spatial interaction
location	flow
place	friction of distance
region	distance decay
site	patterns
situation	distribution
sense of place	spatial association
toponyms	

Human-Environmental Interaction

Essential Question: How do human-environmental interaction and major geographic concepts explain spatial relationships and patterns?

The dual relationship between humans and the natural world is at the heart of human geography. The connection and exchange between them are referred to as **human-environmental interaction**. Geographers who focus on how humans influence the physical world often specialize in studying sustainability, natural resources, land use pollution, and environmental issues. But the environment can also have large influences on humans, so geographers also study the impacts of this interaction and how people respond. Topics of natural hazards, physical geography, water scarcity, poor soil, extreme climates, and a changing climate are often discussed and analyzed.

Geographic Concepts

Human-environmental interaction can be understood through the geographic concepts of natural resources, sustainability, and land use.

Natural Resources

The world is made up of mostly neutral matter that is of little value to people, but that matter is considered a resource is when it becomes useful or beneficial to people. The term **natural resource** includes items that occur in the natural environment that people can use. Examples usually include air, water, oil, fish, soil, and minerals.

Natural resources are usually classified as either renewable or non-renewable resources. **Renewable natural resources** theoretically are unlimited and will not be depleted based on use by people. **Non-renewable natural resources** are limited and can be exhausted by human uses. These resources are often discussed in terms of energy resources to power the world's societies but also include uses related to human consumption, agriculture, and building materials.

The world's natural resources are not distributed evenly—some countries have abundant natural resources, while others have few. In addition, the level of development of a country may influence whether a group of people can gain access to the resources within their borders because they lack the technological tools or finances to acquire and utilize the resources. This uneven access to resources can have an impact on cultures, political systems, and the rate of economic development from the local to global scale.

NATURAL RESOURCES	
Renewable Natural Resources	**Non-Renewable Natural Resources**
• Air: wind power • Water: surface water and hydro-electric • Solar: sun's energy • Biomass: organic material from plants and animals; examples include wood, crops, and sewage	• Fossil fuels: from a biological origin; examples include petroleum, natural gas, and coal • Earth minerals: natural inorganic substances; examples include gold, copper, and silver • Underground fresh water: from deep aquifers • Soil

Sustainability

Sustainability is an overarching theme of human geography and relates to trying to use resources now in ways that allow their use in the future while minimizing negative impacts on the environment. Sustainable development policies attempt to solve problems stemming from natural resource depletion, mass consumption, the effects of pollution, and the impact of climate change. Geographers are concerned with sustainability issues because of the influence that people have on the environment at the local, regional and global scale. An example of a sustainable policy would be to encourage companies to increase the use of renewable, less air-polluting energy sources and decrease the use of non-renewable fossil fuels.

Land Use

The study of how land is utilized, modified, and organized by people is the essence of **land use**. Geographers study the patterns of this land use and draw conclusions on the reasons for the specific use and the varying impacts on the environment, landscapes, and people. The word "environment" is usually a reference to nature and natural things. Plants, air, water, and animals are all part of the natural environment.

Human geographers consider the **built environment**, the physical artifacts that humans have created and that form part of the landscape, in their understanding of land use. Buildings, roads, signs, farms, and fences are examples of the built environment.

The architectural style of buildings varies from place to place. Think of typical homes and buildings in China, and then think of homes and buildings in Germany. These differences occur because people with different cultures who live in different physical landscapes will construct buildings, roads, and other elements to create a unique built environment. Anything built by humans is part of the **cultural landscape** and is in the realm of land use.

Theories of Human-Environmental Interaction

The study of how humans adapt to the environment is known as **cultural ecology.** The belief that landforms and climate are the most powerful forces shaping human behavior and societal development while ignoring the influence of culture is called **environmental determinism**. In the 19th and early 20th centuries, geographers developed a theory using environmental determinism to argue that people in some climates were superior to those of other climates. The theory is largely discredited because of its reliance on the use of Europe as a case study and it does not account for the rise of non-European powers such as China today and in the past. Additionally, the theory is usually criticized for overstating the role of the environment in the development of and the success or failure of a country or society.

In reaction to environmental determinism, contemporary geographers developed a theory known as **possibilism**, a view that acknowledges limits on the effects of the natural environment and focuses more on the role that human culture plays. Different cultures may respond to the same natural environment in diverse ways, depending on their beliefs, goals, and available technologies. Possibilism views humans as having more power and influence over their circumstances than the environment. Societies may face environmental challenges of fewer natural resources or harsh environments, but people can overcome these limitations with ingenuity and creativity.

The Netherlands, with nearly 35 percent of its land below sea level, is an example of possibilism in action. The threat of floods and rising sea levels is a legitimate challenge to the country. For centuries, the Dutch have developed a water management system of dykes (dams), walls, canals, and pumps. These developments allow low-lying land to be reclaimed from the sea (creating *polders*), keeping land suitable for settlement or agriculture.

REFLECT ON THE ESSENTIAL QUESTION

Essential Question: *How do human-environmental interaction and major geographic concepts explain spatial relationships and patterns?*

Human-Environmental Interaction	Major Geographic Concepts

KEY TERMS

human-environmental interaction	built environment
natural resources	cultural landscape
renewable natural resources	cultural ecology
non-renewable natural resources	environmental determinism
sustainability	possibilism
land use	

Scales of Analysis

Essential Question: What are scales of analysis, and what do they reveal to geographers?

Scale of analysis, or level of generalization, allows geographers to look at the local, regional, country, or global scale and is one of the most powerful concepts in geography. **Geographic scale**, sometimes called **relative scale,** refers to the area of the world being studied. For example, global scale means a map of the entire planet, showing data that covers the whole world. In contrast, local scale means using a map of a city or neighborhood to study local issues. Geographers often zoom in and out of maps that use different scales in order to see the patterns that exist at each scale. In addition, the reasons patterns exist can often be explained differently depending on the scale of analysis. A rise in unemployment might be shaped by global forces at a global scale or by local forces at a local scale.

Different Scales of Analysis

Changing scale of analysis involves studying phenomena by zooming in and zooming out in order to develop a more complete understanding of the topics being studied. Geographers will reference a continuum of different scales running from global, regional, national, and local. Each of these scales will show more or less area on the map.

SCALES OF ANALYSIS		
Scale	**Area Shown**	**Examples**
Global	The entire world	• Global Earth at night image • world population density map
World Regional	Multiple countries of the world	• North America • South Asia
National	One country	• the United States • Thailand
National Regional	A portion of a country or a region(s) within a country	• the Midwest • eastern China
Local	A province, state, city, county, or neighborhood	• Tennessee • Moscow

Data Aggregation

While the geographic scale of a map is important, it is only half of the story. Understanding the scale of the data is just as important. Data on maps can also be organized, or aggregated, at different scales. **Aggregation** is when geographers organize data into different scales such as by census tract, city, county, or country. This allows the data to be more easily mapped or organized in a chart or graph.

Importance of Scales of Analysis

Geographers seek to identify patterns, but patterns may differ depending on the scale of analysis. In order to fully understand a topic in depth, geographers must be able to analyze and understand the patterns and processes at multiple scales of analysis. A world map with data aggregated by country can be used to identify global patterns. The world is more interconnected than ever, and looking for trends and patterns on a global scale can help geographers study real world circumstances.

The "2019 Life Expectancy" map shows a variety of patterns of where life expectancy is high, medium, or low. The life expectancy in most African countries is less than 65 years, while in most of North America, the life expectancy is more than 75 years. This is an example of using a global scale map to describe world regional scale patterns. However, this map does not show a complete picture of life expectancy and doesn't allow for a local analysis of the data.

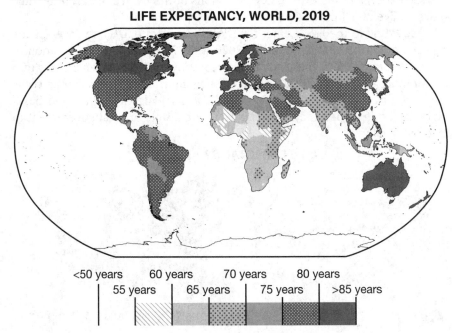

LIFE EXPECTANCY, WORLD, 2019

<50 years   60 years   70 years   80 years
55 years   65 years   75 years   >85 years

Source: ourworldindata.org

Use this map to practice Four-Level Analysis—specifically levels 1 and 2. What is the scale of the map? What is the scale of the data? Describe a global and regional pattern visible on the map.

LIFE EXPECTANCY, NORTH AMERICA, 2019

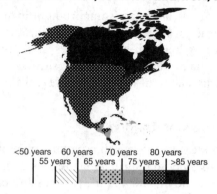

<50 years | 60 years | 70 years | 80 years
55 years | 65 years | 75 years | >85 years

Source: ourworldindata.org

This is a zoomed-in map of North America showing the world regional scale with data aggregated by country. What are the benefits of zooming into this scale of analysis?

Zooming in to a Map and Data

If geographers want to dig deep into the data and discover patterns about the different states, regions, or local communities of the United States, the maps above do not work because the scale of the data is too generalized. The solution is to find data or maps that zoom in to different scales of analysis to study the data. Both maps below are national scale maps of the United States, but the data is aggregated by U.S. state (left) and by county (right). Using these maps, we can see patterns of life expectancy by regions of the United States, individual states, or even the local scale.

According to the U.S. Center for Disease Control (CDC), the average life expectancy in the United States for 2020 was 77.8 years but the variation of life expectancy in the country varied greatly depending on where you live. By zooming in farther, all the way to the neighborhood or census tract scale, more localized patterns can be studied. If a particular neighborhood has a much lower life expectancy, this might require a state or local government to investigate why.

LIFE EXPECTANCY AT BIRTH

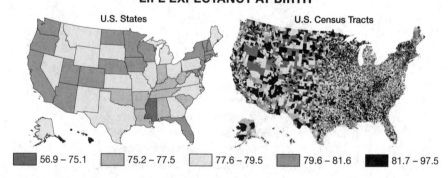

56.9 – 75.1 | 75.2 – 77.5 | 77.6 – 79.5 | 79.6 – 81.6 | 81.7 – 97.5

Source: Centers for Disease Control and Prevention

What regions of the United States tend to have life expectancies above the national average? Below? What are the benefits of using the map aggregated by counties?

Graphs and Other Visuals

The concept of scale of analysis can also be used on charts, graphs, or other visualizations. The process is essentially the same for charts and graphs as it is for maps—look at the data set and attempt to understand the data at different scales. Graphs often show change over time, but pay attention to the scale of the data for clues as to why the changes occurred.

The graph below shows trends in life expectancy for select countries and the world. Part of the data is aggregated by country, while part of the data is aggregated at the world scale. A reasonable global scale pattern description would be that the world's average life expectancy increased from 30 years in 1850 to over 70 years in 2015. A national scale pattern would be that U.S. life expectancy steadily increased from 40 years in the late 1800s to nearly 80 years in 2015. The graph below does not really support any regional or local analysis because the data lack the detail required for these scales of analysis.

LIFE EXPECTANCY, 1770 TO 2015

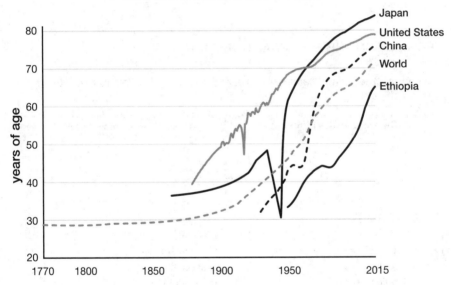

Source: ourworldindata.org

When viewing images, it is also appropriate to apply scale of analysis. Consider what is being shown in an image and the limits of what you can see in the image. Is it a picture of a local landscape of a neighborhood, or is it showing a larger aerial photo of an entire city or region of the world?

Different Interpretations of Data

Drawing conclusions and generalizations based on patterns in data sources is a critical skill, but be careful with your conclusions. It is easy to draw **false conclusions**, or inaccurate generalizations, that are not supported by the data or logical reasoning. Accurate conclusions need to be supported with accurate and scale-appropriate data. An example of a false conclusion would be to use national U.S. data to support that life expectancy in your local community is increasing. To avoid false conclusions, consider the following questions:

- Is the conclusion supported by the scale of the data?
- Is the scale of the conclusion appropriate for the scale of the data?
- Is the data accurate and trustworthy?
- Is there other data that could support or negate the conclusion?

It is possible that different interpretations of data can occur depending on the scale of the data. Recall the graph above related to life expectancy. The global trend of life expectancy between 1940–1950 was increasing; however, the life expectancy of Japan during the same time frame dropped dramatically. Which conclusion is true? Both are correct because the answers change based on the scale and time frame of analysis. Geographers must be precise and accurate for their conclusions to be accurate and use scale-appropriate data to support their reasoning.

REFLECT ON THE ESSENTIAL QUESTION

Essential Question: *What are scales of analysis, and what do they reveal to geographers?*

Different Scales of Analysis	Uses of Data from Each Scale

KEY TERMS

geographic scale (relative scale)
global scale
world regional scale
national scale

national regional scale
local scale
aggregation
false conclusion

Regional Analysis

Essential Question: What are the ways geographers define regions?

Geographers often find it necessary to divide and categorize space into smaller areal units. This regionalization process is much like how a writer divides a book into chapters and then names (or classifies) them. **Regions** have boundaries, unifying characteristics, cover space, and are created by people. What makes identifying regions challenging is that they are often dynamic, and the boundaries can change depending on who defines them and the scale of analysis used. Often the boundaries of regions overlap, which can result in tension or disagreements.

Types of Regions

Regions can exist at every scale of analysis from the local to the global. Geographers classify regions into one of three basic types—formal, functional, or perceptual.

Formal Regions These are sometimes called **uniform regions**, or **homogeneous regions**, and are united by one or more traits:

- political, such as Brazil in South America
- physical, such as the Sahara, a vast desert in northern Africa
- cultural, such as southwestern Nigeria, an area where most people speak Yoruba
- economic, such as the Gold Coast of Africa (Ghana), which exports gold

Functional Regions These regions are organized around a focal point and are defined by an activity, usually political, social, or economic, that occurs across the region. Functional regions or **nodal regions** are united by networks of communication, transportation, and other interactions:

- Pizza delivery areas are functional regions; the pizza shop is the node.
- A state or country is a political functional region because its government makes regulations that apply within its boundaries; the capital city is the political node.
- An airport is a node, and the locations that flights connect form a functional region.

A necessary part of any functional region is the flow of some phenomenon across the networks that unite the region, whether the flow is visible (cars delivering pizza using roads) or invisible (political and legal authority from the capital city).

Perceptual Regions Perceptual regions differ from formal and functional regions in that they are defined by the informal sense of place that people ascribe to them. The boundaries of perceptual regions vary widely because people have a different sense of what defines and unites these regions. The American South, the Middle East, and Upstate New York are examples. While all of these regions exist, their exact boundaries depend upon the person who is defining them. Perceptual regions are also known as **vernacular regions**.

World Regions

In the same way that historians divide history into eras and periods, geographers divide the world into regions and subregions. One type of large region is a continent. However, dividing the world into continents is not simple. Are Europe and Asia two continents or one? Where is the dividing line between North and South America? Is Greenland its own continent? Notice that all of the maps shown in this topic are global scale but the aggregation or classifications within the maps change.

Large World Regions

The following map shows the ten large regions used in AP® Human Geography. It includes the seven continents that are based on physical features. It also includes three cultural regions that are based on shared languages and histories:

- Central America is part of North America, but its culture is more influenced by Spain and Portugal than by Great Britain and France.
- Sub-Saharan Africa is distinguished from the rest of Africa.
- The Russian Federation spans Eastern Europe and northern Asia.

WORLD REGIONS: A BIG PICTURE VIEW

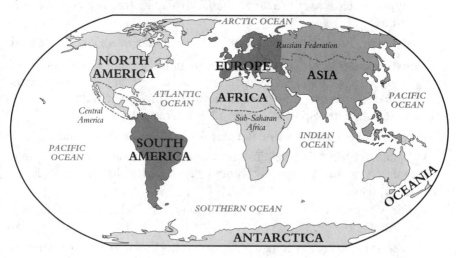

World Subregions

Geographers divide regions into smaller areas, or **subregions**. A subregion shares some characteristics with the rest of the larger region but is distinctive in some ways. For example, the region of Latin America covers parts of North and South America, from Mexico to Chile. Within it is the subregion of Brazil. As in other Latin American countries, most people in Brazil are Roman Catholics. However, Brazil's primary language is Portuguese, which makes it unlike any other country in the mostly Spanish-speaking Latin America. Because of its language, Brazil is a distinct subregion.

The map below shows the standard subregions used in AP® Human Geography. For example, Sub-Saharan Africa is subdivided into West, Central, East, and Southern Africa. Asia is divided into five subregions: Middle East, Central Asia, South Asia, East Asia, and Southeast Asia.

WORLD REGIONS: A CLOSER LOOK

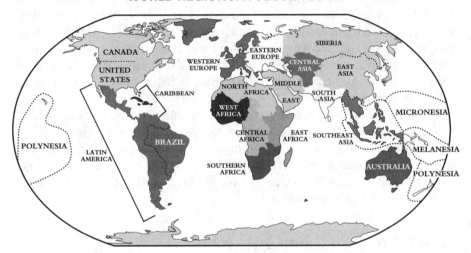

National, Subnational, and Local Regions

By changing the scale and zooming in, subregions can be even further divided. The further subdivisions can be based on elements of physical geography—such as climate and landform—or human geography—such as culture, politics, or economics. Western Europe can be divided into Northwestern Europe and Southern Europe, each unified by more specific traits. Additionally, regions can occur at the national, subnational (within a country), or at the local scale such as cities or counties within a state.

Since many kinds of regions exist, any one place is part of many regions or subregions at the same time. For example, Georgia is part of numerous regions:

- a climate region based on its warm weather
- a cultural subnational region known as the South
- an economic region known as the Sun Belt
- a political region known as the United States

Problems with Regions

Regions are generalizations. Just like generalizations in spoken language, they can lead people to overlook variations and differences. Think of the languges spoken in the United States. On a map showing languages, the United States is usually shown as an English-speaking country. This accurately reflects that more than 78 percent of people in the country speak English at home and more than 90 percent of the population speak English well.

However, showing the United States as an English-speaking country does not tell the entire story. Some people, mostly immigrants, primarily speak a non-English language. Far more are bilingual, speaking English and another language comfortably. Taken together, these two groups make up approximately 20 percent of the population. As a region, the United States might be described as English-speaking, but it is also a country where dozens of languages are widely spoken.

Additionally, people and characteristics within a region are transitional and often do not create a sharp boundary. Just because there is a formal political border between the United States and Mexico does not mean that people suddenly stop speaking Spanish or English when they cross the border. The reality is that people who live in the borderland region on either side of the border often speak both English and Spanish. Being aware of such realities helps a geographer understand how complex the world is.

When regions overlap, occasionally tension and disagreements can occur. These differences can be good-natured teasing such as when rival football teams' fan bases live close to each other. The differences can also be deadly serious disagreements over territory, political power, resources, or cultural views that have occurred in numerous hot spot locations of the world, such as between Sudan and South Sudan.

REFLECT ON THE ESSENTIAL QUESTION

Essential Question: *What are the ways geographers define regions?*

Types of Regions	Characteristics of Each Region

KEY TERMS

regions	functional regions (nodal regions)
formal regions (uniform regions or	perceptual regions (vernacular regions)
homogeneous regions)	subregions

GEOGRAPHIC PERSPECTIVES: *THINKING ABOUT DISTANCE*

Geographers use the concept of distance to study the spatial distribution of phenomena. The perception of distance reflects context. Neighboring families in a small town in Iowa might live 50 feet apart. To a family in a high-rise apartment in Manhattan, 50 feet might seem like a long distance. To a family living on a ranch in Wyoming, miles from their nearest neighbor, 50 feet might feel uncomfortably close.

Time and Distance

In addition, what people consider a long distance changes over time. In the mid-1800s, Irish families held funeral-like ceremonies for emigrants leaving for the United States, Australia, and elsewhere. Trips by ship to these other lands were so long, expensive, and dangerous that families expected they would never see the departing person again. And they often didn't. But what seemed far away in the 1800s seems much closer today. A flight by jet from Dublin to Boston takes about seven hours, costs only two days' pay for many people, and is remarkably safe.

Scale and Distance

A third factor shaping the perception of distance is scale. At a personal level, eight people crowded into an elevator, separated by inches, probably feel close together. At the community level, Tampa and Orlando seem close together, even though they are about 85 miles apart. At the global level, the countries of Mali and Chad seem close together, separated by only 1,500 miles.

Other Disciplines and Distance

Geographers are not alone in studying distance. Historians might research the change over time in how immigrants viewed distance. Sociologists might focus on how distance affects how neighbors interact. However, unlike others who study human actions, geographers emphasize the role of distance and other concepts that describe spatial distribution.

1. Why do people living in different locations and cultures experience and think about distance differently?

2. How can scale of analysis change people's view of closeness or relative distance?

THINK AS A GEOGRAPHER: *GROUPING DATA*

SOUTH CENTRAL STATES					
State	Adult Population Whose Primary Language is English	Corn Production (tons)	Largest Religious Denomination	Annual Precipitation (inches)	Athletic Conference of the Largest State University
New Mexico	64%	2,075,000	Catholic (34%)	14.6	Mountain West
Texas	65%	5,250,000	Catholic (23%)	28.9	Big 12 (Big 12 headquarters are in Irving, Texas)
Oklahoma	90%	255,000	Baptist (28%)	36.5	Big 12
Kansas	89%	3,145,000	Catholic (18%)	28.9	Big 12
Arkansas	93%	30,000	Baptist (27%)	50.6	Southeastern
Louisiana	91%	14,000	Catholic (26%)	60.1	Southeastern

1. What characteristics could you use to create a formal region from these six states? Explain your answer.

2. What characteristics could you use to create a functional/nodal region? Explain your answer.

3. What characteristics could be used to create a vernacular (perceptual) region? Explain your answer.

4. What problems are inherent in trying to classify places into regions?

CHAPTER 2 REVIEW:
Spatial Concepts and Geographic Analysis
Topics 1.4–1.7

MULTIPLE-CHOICE QUESTIONS

Question 1 refers to the following image.

1. Which best explains why the above image is considered part of the built environment?

   (A) It is found primarily in rural areas.

   (B) It is often used as part of boundaries.

   (C) It is designed to regulate the movement of animals.

   (D) It is part of the landscape made by humans.

   (E) It is a product that was invented to solve a problem.

2. Which technology had the greatest effect on the application of the distance-decay function?

   (A) Food preservatives because they reduce decay

   (B) Cars because they weakened family connections

   (C) Barbed wire because it stretches for long distances

   (D) New medicines because they keep people healthier

   (E) A jet because it strengthens the connections between distant places

3. The way a phenomenon is spread out or arranged over an area is

   (A) density

   (B) distribution

   (C) incidence

   (D) interconnection

   (E) distance

Questions 4 and 5 refer to the image below.

4. Which renewable resource is best illustrated in the image?

   (A) Soil

   (B) Natural gas

   (C) Petroleum

   (D) Wind

   (E) Solar

5. The use of canal, dykes (dams), pumps, and electricity to protect and reclaim land in the Netherlands best exemplifies which theory?

   (A) Environmental determinism

   (B) Possibilism

   (C) Scale analysis

   (D) Distance decay

   (E) Time-space compression

Questions 6 and 7 refer to the table below.

Location	Life Expectancy 1950	Life Expectancy 1980	Life Expectancy 2010
World	46	61	70
Africa	37	50	59
Asia	41	60	71
Europe	62	71	76

6. Using the chart on the previous page, which of the following conclusions is best supported by the data related to the period of 1950–2010?

(A) Life expectancy in most of the countries of the world has declined.

(B) Life expectancy of both France and China increased.

(C) Almost all of the countries of Africa had an increase in life expectancy.

(D) Of the regions listed, Asia had the largest increase of life expectancy.

(E) The United States and specifically New York City had the greatest increase in life expectancy.

7. Which response best illustrates the scale of analysis being shown in the table on the previous page?

(A) Local

(B) Regional

(C) Functional

(D) Perceptual

(E) National

FREE-RESPONSE QUESTION

1. Geographers use regions to make sense of the world in which we live and a variety of data sources to create regions.

(A) Explain the concept of region and how geographers use the term to make sense of locations.

(B) Describe ONE major difference between formal and nodal regions.

(C) Explain how changing the scale of analysis can help geographers develop a deeper understanding of a region.

(D) Identify TWO political regions shown on the map of Mexico on page 10.

(E) Identify TWO physical regions shown on the map of Mexico on page 10.

(F) Describe how quantitative spatial data is used on the map of Mexico on page 10.

(G) Explain the type of qualitative data researchers use to develop a better understanding of migration from Mexico to the United States.

UNIT 1 REVIEW:
Connecting Course Skills and Content

APPLYING GEOGRAPHIC SKILLS

Applying and utilizing geographic skills are critical for success on the AP® Exam. For each skill listed, write a one-paragraph response that illustrates your understanding of that course skill. Support your response with specific examples and evidence. Refer to the Unit 1 introduction (pages 3–7) for tips on how to apply geographic skills.

1A Describe three geographic concepts, processes, models or theories discussed in Unit 1.

2E Explain the degree to which environmental determinism fails to adequately explain the human-environmental interaction responses.

3A Using maps, data tables and images from Unit 1, identify three examples of quantitative data. List the page number, title, and explain why they are each quantitative.

4B Using images or aerial photos from Unit 1, describe three patterns presented in the visual sources.

5A Identify Unit 1 maps, data, and/or images that illustrate each of the following scales of analysis: global, regional, national, and local.

WRITE AS A GEOGRAPHER: *COMPREHEND THE PROMPT*

The first step in writing a good answer to a free-response question is to understand the question. First, note or circle the key content vocabulary used in the question. If the prompt asks about "squatter settlements," then your answer should as well. Second, note the type of task verbs that are being used in the prompt. The *verbs* will indicate the type of thinking and the depth and length of your response.(See page xxx of the introduction.) Only after understanding the prompt fully can you write an answer that includes relevant claims and sufficient evidence, examples and reasoning to support your claims.

In the following questions, identify the key content vocabulary, the task verb, and write how long your response should be. Do not answer the prompts.

1. Identify one consequences of rapid urbanization on the transportation system of a region.

2. Explain how distance-decay applies to the customer base for a retail store.

3. Explain the difference between absolute location and relative location with reference to a specific city.

4. Describe the distribution pattern of main highways in Florida.

5. Define the concept of formal region and provide a cultural example.

UNIT 2
Population and Migration Patterns and Processes

Unit Overview

The distribution of people influences all other elements of human geography. Where people live, whether spread out in small communities or concentrated in large cities, affects how they relate to one another, what demands they place on the environment, and what decisions they make as a community.

People decide where to live based on many factors. Some are physical: people want to be near sources of food and water and where the climate is not too extreme. Some factors are human: people might move to take a job or to be close to family.

Changes in Populations

For most of human history, women typically gave birth to many children, but so few children survived to adulthood that the total human population grew slowly. However, in the past two centuries, advances in public health, medical care, and the economy have enabled people to live longer. As a result of these new patterns, the global population has exploded. However, in recent decades, population growth has leveled off in many wealthy countries, such as Germany, South Korea, the United States.

Why People Move

People have always been on the move. Usually, they migrated by choice, wanting to leave a place of poverty or persecution or warfare in order to live in a place with economic opportunity, religious liberty, political freedom, and peace. In some cases, people had no choice. For example, for nearly four centuries, Africans were enslaved and brought to the Americas.

ENDURING UNDERSTANDINGS

PSO-2: Understanding where and how people live is essential to understanding global cultural, political, and economic patterns.

IMP-2: Changes in population are due to mortality, fertility, and migration, which are influenced by the interplay of environmental, economic, cultural, and political factors.

SPS-2: Changes in population have long- and short-term effects on a place's economy, culture, and politics.

Source: *AP® Human Geography Course and Exam Description.* Effective Fall 2020. (College Board).

CHAPTER 3

Population Distribution and Composition

Topics 2.1–2.3

Topic 2.1 Population Distribution

Learning Objectives: Identify the factors that influence the distribution of human populations at different scales. (PSO-2.A)

Define methods geographers use to calculate population density. (PSO-2.B)

Explain the differences between and the impact of methods used to calculate population density. (PSO-2.C)

Topic 2.2 Consequences of Population Distribution

Learning Objective: Explain how population distribution and density affect society and the environment. (PSO-2.D)

Topic 2.3 Population Composition

Learning Objectives: Describe elements of population composition used by geographers. (PSO-2.E)

Explain ways that geographers depict and analyze population composition. (PSO-2.F)

Half the world's population lives in just 1 percent of the land.

—Max Galka, *Metrocosm*, January 4, 2016

Source: Getty Images

The image shows city traffic in India. Rapid population growth and density impacts society and the environment. (See Topic 2.2 for the effects of population growth.)

Population Distribution

Essential Question: What are the factors that influence population distribution and what are the impacts of different methods used to calculate population density?

Humans live on a small percentage of the planet. The world contains seven times as many people today as it did two centuries ago. Population density has increased significantly. However, population distribution has not. The vast majority of growth has been in areas already settled. For example, eastern China was one of the most populated parts of the world in 1800—and it still is today. Why have people chosen to live in such crowded places?

Where People Live

People want to live in places where they can survive with relative ease and comfort—places where they can raise or obtain food and live in moderate climates. Around 1800, when the population was only one billion, people were dispersed throughout such desirable lands. As population increased, the amount of suitable land stayed about the same, so people chose to live in greater densities on that same land.

Human geography tries to explain why people live where they do. It includes the study of two distinct but related concepts:

- **Population distribution** is the pattern of human settlement—the spread of people across the earth. Representing it on a map highlights places that are crowded, sparsely settled, or even empty.

- **Population density** is a measure of the average population per square mile or kilometer of an area. It measures how crowded a place is.

Understanding both population distribution and density helps people make important decisions on issues such as where to set the boundaries of an electoral district or where to develop new housing. These are among the many issues influenced by the number, distribution, and density of current and projected populations.

Physical Factors Influencing Population Distribution

Survival for the earliest humans depended on food, water, and shelter. Thus, these hunter-gatherers settled where these features were most readily available. Similarly, people today have the same basic needs, which helps explain why the population distribution has remained so similar over time. The map of Earth's population distribution today below shows where the highest densities and largest numbers of people live today.

Midlatitudes Most people live in the **midlatitudes**, the regions between 30 degrees and 60 degrees, north and south of the equator. These areas have more moderate climates and better soils than do regions at higher or lower latitudes. This pattern is particularly noticeable in the northern hemisphere because it includes more land than the southern hemisphere.

Low-Lying Areas Most people live in low-lying areas rather than high-alititude areas, such as mountains. Low-lying areas typically have better soils for raising crops than do upland or high-altitude areas. In addition, these areas are often close to oceans, which facilitate transportation, provide a source of food, and have a moderating effect on temperature. Oceans keep the land warmer in the winter and cooler in the summer.

Other Factors Most people live near lakes or rivers. People need fresh water to drink, and they can use it for irrigation, transportation, and to provide food. Regions of the world where it is difficult for humans to live typically have low population numbers and densities. These include mountainous areas, deserts, and high latitude/cold climates where agriculture is challenging. Lower population densities are also found in the tropics where disease is more prevalent and poor soils make farming difficult. Polar regions have no permanent human populations.

WORLD POPULATION DISTRIBUTION

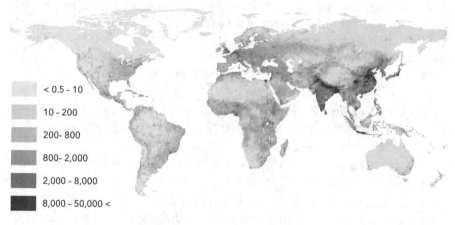

- < 0.5 - 10
- 10 - 200
- 200- 800
- 800- 2,000
- 2,000 - 8,000
- 8,000 - 50,000 <

Source: Wikimedia Commons

Human Factors Influencing Population Distribution

The places humans first settled included natural features that attracted them. However, then people themselves became an attraction. Newcomers moved in for safety, to find a job, or to be with friends or relatives. The populations and densities of cities have continued to grow, often to extreme levels.

Where people place transportation networks also has a significant impact on population distribution. People prefer to live close to trade routes. Roads, train lines, and rivers often produce a linear settlement pattern in which houses and communities stretch out in a line.

Political decisions sometimes bring clusters of populations to isolated locations where physical attributes would not normally attract settlement. For example, in 1950, Canada wanted a military base that could monitor possibly hostile actions by the country then known as the Soviet Union. So, it established a military base named Alert on the northern edge of its territory, in a land of ice, snow, and bitterly cold temperatures. Alert remains the most northerly community in the world.

Scale of Analysis and Physical Factors

The basic principle that people want to live on the most desirable land applies at any scale, or level of analysis by size. (See Topic 1.6 for more on scales of analysis.) As the scale of analysis changes, the relevance of certain factors such as climate, elevation, and industrialization changes as well.

At the global scale, regions with very high elevations—mountainous regions such as in the Himalayas, the Andes, and the Rocky Mountains—have cold climates, so such places usually have limited populations. However, elevation is sometimes important at the city level. People might prefer living at the highest elevations in a city because these spots offer cool breezes, safety from floods, and inspiring views of the landscape. At a regional scale, climate can also explain population distribution of a state such as California, where climate varies greatly within the state. For example, coastal California has a very large population compared to the desert and mountain regions of the interior. On a larger or local scale, such as a city, the spatial climate variation is usually too small to affect settlement.

Scale of Analysis and Human Factors

Polluted air is a health hazard, yet it may signal industrialization, economic development, and employment opportunities. On a global or national scale, millions of people are attracted to cities in search of economic opportunities and they might knowingly move to a polluted area. At a local scale, few people intentionally choose to settle near a pollution source unless they have to live there because lower property values make it more affordable.

Governments also have a significant influence on population distribution at different scales. A national government might increase the population of an area by building a new military base. A state might reduce population in an area by creating a new state park. A city government might affect population distribution by allowing high-rise apartment buildings in some areas and reserving other areas for single-family homes. (See Topic 6.6.)

Factors influencing a city's population distribution such as elevation, proximity to desirable land, and land use laws commonly result in a population distribution that reflects **social stratification**—the hierarchical division of people into groups based on factors such as economic status, power, and/or ethnicity. Cities are characterized by regions and neighborhoods where the local population shares a characteristic that distinguishes it from other neighborhoods. For example, a neighborhood with large homes and parks would be likely to have families with children and an industrial zone might have few residences. In most countries, stratification is largely based on wealth, but sometimes policies and cultural beliefs have limited the areas where certain groups of people can live.

Population Density

Population density is calculated by comparing the area's population to its size, and is expressed in the number of people per square mile or square kilometer. Demographers, people who study human populations, identify three types of population density: arithmetic, physiological, and agricultural.

Arithmetic Population Density

The most commonly used population density is the **arithmetic population density**, calculated by dividing a region's population by its total area. In 2019, the United States had a population of approximately 328,239,523 in a total area of 3,841,999 square miles. Therefore, its arithmetic population density was 85.4 people per square mile, or 35.9 people per square kilometer. These figures are given in various styles. Two common styles are 85.4/sq. mi. and $85.4/mi^2$.

But arithmetic density says little about population distribution. Population density is simply an average number of people overall in an area. It does not indicate where in the total area they live. The diagram below shows three areas with ten people per square mile, but with different distributions:

- In A, people are evenly dispersed throughout the area. This pattern is common in areas where each person or household lives on a large plot of land. At different scales and with different numbers, this basic pattern appears in many suburbs and many farming and ranching areas.
- In B, people are clustered, or nucleated, in one part of an area. This is a common pattern when people live near a central feature, such as a church, or are concerned about defense.
- In C, people are spread out in a line, known as a linear pattern. This pattern is common for people who live along a river or transit route.

A   Even Distribution   B   Cluster Distribution   C   Linear Distribution

Physiological Population Density

Another measure is **physiological population density**, calculated by dividing population by the amount of **arable** land, or land suitable for growing crops. Egypt (with 2.8 percent arable land), for example, recently had a physiological density of 8,078/sq. mile (3,156/sq. kilometer) compared to an arithmetic density of 226/sq. mile (88/sq. kilometer).

Such a large difference between the arithmetic and physiological densities indicates that a small percentage of a region's land is capable of growing crops. Egypt's high physiological density suggests a need for greater crop yields or for other food sources. The physiological population density is a much more useful measure than the arithmetic density to determine a region's *carrying capacity*— the population it can support without significant environmental deterioration. (See Topic 2.2 for more about carrying capacity.)

A country with a high physiological density indicates that it needs high crop yields, but higher yields are not always possible. Many regions rely on imported food. Egypt and Japan both have physiological densities greater than 8,000 people/sq. mile of arable land. In both countries, growing enough food to feed the nation's population is not practical with current technology. Both supplement crops through the fishing industry and with imported food. Paying for imported food is easier for a developed country, such as Japan, than it is for a less-developed country, such as Egypt.

In the table below, notice the relationship between the percent of arable land in a country and the difference between the arithmetic and physiological densities.

ARITHMETIC AND PHYSIOLOGICAL POPULATION DENSITIES			
Country	Arithmetic Density (people/sq. mi.)	Physiological Density (people/sq. mi.)	Arable Land
Iceland	8	687	1.2%
United States	85	498	16.8%
Egypt	226	8,078	2.8%
Japan	962	8,218	11.7%
Netherlands	1,044	3,505	31.0%
Bangladesh	2,914	4,938	59.0%
Singapore	19,982	2,498,197	0.8%

Egypt is mostly covered by desert with most of its fertile land near the Nile River, while nearly 70 percent of Japan's topography is mountainous. What advantages does the United States have compared to Egypt and Japan in its ability to produce enough food for the nation's population?

Agricultural Population Density

The third type of population density, **agricultural population density**, compares the number of farmers to the area of arable land. This value gives an indication of the efficiency of the region's farmers. Developed countries have lower agricultural densities because farmers have resources and technology to produce large quantities of food with few workers. The agricultural densities in less-developed countries are higher because farmers often cannot afford modern technology, so they depend more upon labor. As a result, farmers in these areas are not able to produce as much food per farm worker.

Compare all three types of population density for Bangladesh and the Netherlands, for example. Both had high arithmetic densities—Bangladesh had 2,914/sq. mi. and the Netherlands had 1,044/sq. mi. Also, both had high physiological densities, with Bangladesh at 4,938/sq. mi. and the Netherlands at 3,505/sq. mi. Yet the countries' agricultural densities are drastically different, as might be expected because of their different levels of economic development. The more economically developed Netherlands has a low agricultural density of 31/sq. mi. This indicates that Dutch farmers can afford technology and produce food more efficiently than farmers in Bangladesh, which has an agricultural population density of 431/sq. mi. Additionally, the Netherlands is highly developed and can import food not be produced by local farmers.

Population Density and Time

Density also varies by time of year and at different scales of analysis. At one scale, the population of warm-weather states, such as Arizona and Florida, become more dense each winter as "snowbirds" from northern states flee the cold weather.

Time also influences population density at a local scale. For example, the population density of the New York City borough of Manhattan changes greatly throughout the day. About 1.5 million people reside there but each weekday when commuters enter the city to work, the population rises to about 3 million. Such variation is a challenge for Manhattan, which provides water, sewer, fire protection, and other services for 3 million people—even though most return home at night. These commuters often live outside of Manhattan and pay taxes that fund public services in other communities.

REFLECT ON THE ESSENTIAL QUESTION

Essential Question: *What are the factors that influence population distribution and what are the impacts of different methods used to calculate population density?*

Factors Influencing Population Distribution	Methods Used to Calculate Population Density

---

KEY TERMS

population distribution	arithmetic population density
population density	physiological population density
midlatitudes	arable
social stratification	agricultural population density

Consequences of Population Distribution

Essential Question: How do population distribution and density affect society and the environment?

Population density is linked to population distribution. At different scales—a country, province, or even city—an uneven distribution results in lower densities in some regions and higher densities in others. Areas with high population densities are referred to as densely settled, and regions with low densities are known as sparsely settled. Whether a place is densely or sparsely inhabited has profound effects on it. In locations with high densities of human population, the impact on the natural environment is usually also high. Conversely, the effects of human activities affect the environment to a lesser degree in areas that are sparsely inhabited.

Implications of Distribution and Density

The distribution of a region's population and its density reflect choices people make. These choices, in turn, reflect their values, such as whether they choose to live in densely settled urban areas and cities or rural areas that are characterized by the presence of farming and agricultural activities.

Economic, Political, and Social Processes

Most economic decisions are based, at least partly, on population distribution and density. Businesses are more likely to earn profits when they are near a large customer base. For manufacturing plants, being close to a large labor force is important. Towns and cities have large concentrated populations that provide customers and workers for businesses, so that is where most businesses locate. People live in cities to take advantage of the economic, social, and educational opportunies found there.

Political processes can be influenced by population distribution and density too. Since population distribution and densities continually change, the Constitution requires adjustments to boundaries every ten years based on census data to maintain similar numbers of voters per district. Rulings by the Supreme Court require state legislatures to create electoral districts of reasonably equal population sizes so each representative serves approximately the same number of people. Because urban areas are continuing to increase in population and the population of rural areas is usually shrinking, these boundary adjustments, called **redistricting** (see Topic 4.6), usually result in physically smaller urban districts and larger rural districts.

The population characteristics of a region can also affect the number of government and private services and the location of these services. Facilities such as schools, police stations, fire stations, social assistance offices, and hospitals are usually positioned close to concentrations of population. Each of these facilities acts as a node, or point of central intersection for the areas they serve. In other words, each of the nodes is surrounded by a functional region. Towns and cities have greater and more concentrated populations than rural areas. Therefore, urban areas have many more of these facilities and their associated and overlapping functional regions than rural areas. Often remote rural areas lack basic services, such as medical care, and residents have to travel long distances or do without the service.

Infrastructure and Urban Services

The term **infrastructure** refers to the facilities and structures that allows people to carry out their typical activities. Included are things such as sewer systems, electrical grids, roads and bridges, etc. The larger a city grows, the more demands it will have on its infrastructure. (See Topic 6.7 for more on infrastructure.)

When people want to live in a particular region—from a country to a neighborhood—they can increase the population density. They can live in high-density housing units rather than single-family homes. Since many people enjoy living in the centers of big cities, these neighborhoods usually feature apartment and condominium buildings that include many households. In Chicago, the population of the central part of downtown, known as the Loop, is about 21,000 people/sq. mi., more than double what it is for many surrounding neighborhoods.

Providing services such as sewer, water, snow removal, and policing is more cost-effective in high-density areas. The cost of installing a mile of sewer pipe is mostly based on the labor required to dig up the land and connect the pipe. Whether it is a large pipe to serve tens of thousands of people in high-rise buildings or a small pipe to several dozen people in single-family houses is not that significant.

However, high-density areas have challenges. For example, contamination of the water supply for a downtown area can make thousands of people ill, and disease that spreads through casual contact is much harder to manage in crowded settings. Similar problems in a rural or suburban area with lower population density would be much less severe.

Environment and Natural Resources

Whether a region experiences **overpopulation**—having more people than it can support—is partially dependent on its population distribution and density. Another factor is the region's **carrying capacity**, the number of people a region can support without damaging the environment. The higher the population density, usually the greater the strain on the environment. A region with good soil, climate, and other resources might be able support many people. Another with less favorable attributes will be unable to support as many people.

The Influence of Time The carrying capacity of a region can change over time. For example, technological changes in agriculture—such as plants that require less water or improved irrigation methods—can increase the carrying capacity of a region.

Changes in climate may also limit or increase the agricultural potential of locations. Locations with variable or marginal climates, such as the Sahel in Africa (the southern fringe of the Sahara), have seen changes in carrying capacity. Areas that were once wetter and had successfully supported the population have experienced drought and exceeded their carrying capacity without help from outside regions.

Influence on Cities Cities could be built on land with low carrying capacity, such as where the soil is not ideal for farming. However, for historical reasons, most of these cities are located on land with the greatest carrying capacity. Throughout history, the original settlers have chosen sites for their settlements on or near land that could support a large population and have remained there.

Signficance of Density In addition to agriculture, many other aspects of the environment are affected as population density increases. High population density can result in environmental problems such as air and water pollution or depletion of resources. Because of factors such as sewage and industrial wastes, many lakes and rivers no longer provide drinkable water. In some areas, water must be purified or piped in from hundreds of miles away. Large cities that face serious water shortages include Cairo, Egypt; Cape Town, South Africa; Moscow, Russia; Bangalore India; Beijing, China; and Jakarta, Indonesia. In the United States, cities such as Los Angeles, Houston, Atlanta, and Miami are among those where too little fresh water threatens economic and population growth.

REFLECT ON THE ESSENTIAL QUESTION

Essential Question: *How do population distribution and density affect society and the environment?*

Population Density's Effects on Social, Political, and Economic Processes	Population Density's Effects on Environment and Natural Resources

---

KEY TERMS

redistricting	overpopulation
infrastructure	carrying capacity

Population Composition

Essential Question: What are elements of population composition, and how are those elements used by geographers to depict and analyze population composition?

Populations have distinct demographic characteristics. A population may be called "young" if it is comprised of an especially large proportion of younger people. The reverse is true if a society has many older people. Most places, especially at larger scales, have approximately the same number of males as females, but this is not always the case. There are places in the world, especially at smaller scales, that have many more females than males and vice versa. The makeup of ages and sexes in a population is known as its composition, and geographers use a unique type of graph to examine it. The composition of a population influences its culture and economic potential.

Population Composition

Identifying the composition of a region's population is crucial to understanding the population of the region's past, present, and future. Understanding a population's composition requires an examination and analysis of the age and sex of the region's people.

Age and Sex

Distribution patterns are related to age and sex of the population. Some regions of a country may have a younger or older average population than others:

- In 2018, Utah had the youngest average age in the United States at 31.0,
- The oldest average age was in Maine at 44.9.

This difference is so significant that it shapes public policy. Officials in Utah have a higher percentage of school-age children for which to provide services. Officials in Maine might be more concerned with the needs of seniors. Similar distinctive patterns and the resulting issues also exist at the scale of cities and towns of all sizes.

Differences in the gender balance can result from wars, migrations, and government policies. At the level of entire communities, mining towns and military training bases often have significantly more males than females. Within a city, a gender imbalance might appear if one neighborhood has a post-secondary institution offering courses that tend to attract more students of one gender.

Population Pyramids

One of the most useful tools to study population is the **age-sex composition graph**, which is commonly called a **population pyramid**. Although this tool is based only on age and gender data, it can provide information on birth rates, death rates, how long people live on average, and economic development. Population pyramids can also give evidence of past events such as environmental hazards, wars, political changes, and epidemics.

Reading a Pyramid

Most pyramids follow the same fundamental structure. However, as with most types of graphics, the format can vary:

- The vertical axis shows age groups, known as **cohorts**. They are often listed in the middle but are sometimes shown on the left or right side.
- Pyramids usually show the male population on the left and the female population on the right.
- The values on the horizontal axis may be percentages or absolute numbers of males and females and amounts increase as one moves further from the center.
- Pyramids are most commonly constructed at a country scale, but they can also be constructed for cities, states, or multicountry regions.

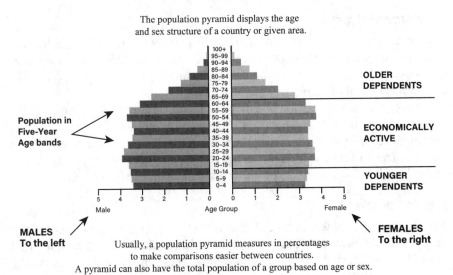

POPULATION PYRAMID STRUCTURE

The population pyramid displays the age and sex structure of a country or given area.

Determining Population Trends

If a population pyramid has a wide base and tapers upward, the region's population is growing. The wide base indicates a large percentage of children (at the bottom of the pyramid) compared to the adults (in the middle) and the older people (at the top). A wide base indicates large families. Populations with a high percentage of large families will grow as the children mature into adults and begin to produce their own families.

NIGER, 2016

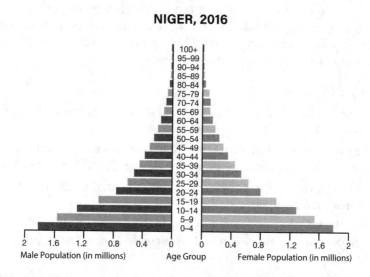

The population pyramid for the African nation of Niger is an example of a pyramid with a wide base. Notice that the three longest bars are at the bottom of the pyramid and represent ages 0 to 14. As these children age, there will be more people in the older categories. There will also likely be a greater number of children born as these people reach childbearing age.

Common Patterns

The Niger pyramid is nearly symmetrical, or balanced, left to right, indicating a balance of males and females until approximately age 65. Since women as a group live longer than men, the lack of symmetry in the upper part of the pyramid is typical of many countries.

Another notable trait on the Niger pyramid is that the changes in the size of the bars from one cohort to the next are gradual. There are no sudden indentations or bulges. Assuming there have been no circumstances such as war, natural disaster, epidemics, or government interference, a population pyramid will be symmetrical and show gradual change between cohorts.

Impact of War

The clearest effect of war on population is that people are killed. Often, half or more of deaths in wartime are civilians, and those deaths affect people of all ages. However, the loss of fighting-age people, traditionally males between the ages of 18 and 40, is most noticeable.

During war, men and women are often separated. Even if they remain together, they may decide to delay a family until the war ends. The bars of the pyramid representing children born during the conflict are often significantly shorter than the bars immediately above and below them. This slowdown of births is called a **birth deficit**.

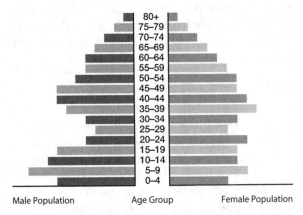

THE GERMAN POPULATION, 1946

Male Population   Age Group   Female Population

The post-World War II pyramid of Germany shows the loss of life of both males and females in the 20 to 40 age cohorts, with a greater loss of men than women. The birth deficit during war is evident in the 0–4 cohort.

Baby Booms, Busts, and Echoes

Once hostilities end and peace resumes, the birth rate often spikes, causing what is known as a **baby boom**. This increase might last a few years or stretch over many years. After World War II, the United States baby boom lasted from 1946 to 1965. Baby booms are usually associated with the end of a war, but booms also occur for other reasons, such as times of economic abundance.

Once the boom ends, birth rates are lower for a number of years. This **baby bust** continues until the boomers reach childbearing age. With a high number of boomers in the population having children, there can be a significant increase in births that shows up as a bulge on a pyramid. Since this increase reflects an earlier baby boom, it is called an **echo**. As of 2015, children in high school were the last of the echo cohorts, and their parents were the last baby boomers.

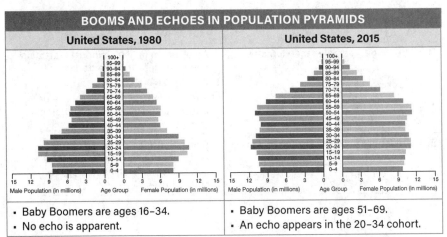

BOOMS AND ECHOES IN POPULATION PYRAMIDS

United States, 1980	United States, 2015
• Baby Boomers are ages 16–34.	• Baby Boomers are ages 51–69.
• No echo is apparent.	• An echo appears in the 20–34 cohort.

Source: U.S. Census Bureau

In 1980, the baby boomers in the United States were ages 16–34. Notice the bulge in the pyramid on the left. By 2015, the Baby Boomers large generation were in their 50s and their children—the "echo"—can be seen between the ages of 20–34 bulge in the pyramid on the right.

Once any anomaly, or unexpected occurrence, appears in a pyramid, it will remain there, moving upward over time until the affected cohort or cohorts disappear from the top of the graph due to death. Notice the upward movement of the baby boom and the echo resulting from World War II in the two U.S. pyramids on the previous page.

Migration and Other Anomalies

Many factors can affect a population pyramid. An asymmetrical pyramid, one with significant differences between cohorts, suggests that something notable happened in the population. The viewer of the pyramid then determines what historical event caused the irregularity. Several anomalies are described in the table below, along with possible explanations. Pyramids with atypical shapes most often represent smaller geographic areas, such as states, cities, or even neighborhoods, where local age-sex differences are more pronounced.

ANOMALIES IN POPULATION PYRAMIDS	
Pyramid Feature	**Possible Reason**
Bars are longer for people ages 18 to 25 than for people younger or older.	• A small city with a large university causes an increase of this age group. • A shortage of school funding causes families to move away when they have children.
Bars are longer for people ages 25 to 50 than for children.	• An economic crisis causes people to decide to have fewer children. • A government policy to slow population growth discourages births. • An epidemic causes many infants to die.
Bars are longer for people over the age of 65.	• A community in a warm climate attracts retirees. • A lack of jobs causes young people to move away.
Bars are longer for males than females.	• An oil boom or fishing industry attracts people for jobs that are traditionally done by men. • A region contains a military base or prison that may have a larger percentage of men.
Bars are longer for females than males.	• A neighborhood contains a large assisted living home with a high percentage of females who typically outlive males.

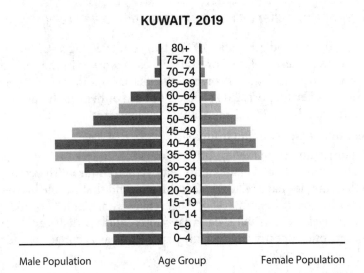

KUWAIT, 2019

Male Population   Age Group   Female Population

80+
75–79
70–74
65–69
60–64
55–59
50–54
45–49
40–44
35–39
30–34
25–29
20–24
15–19
10–14
5–9
0–4

Source: populationpyramid.net

Kuwait is an oil-rich country in the Middle East. Many working-age males migrate to Kuwait to work in the oil fields and related industries.

Dependency Ratio

Demographers, consider people ages 15–64 the **potential workforce**, the group expected to be the society's labor force. Everyone else—people under 15 or over 64—is the **dependent population**, because they are considered too young or too old to work full-time and, therefore, are assumed to rely on the economically active workforce to keep the society running. The comparison between the size of these two groups is called the **dependency ratio**. (See Topic 2.9 for more on dependency ratio.)

REFLECT ON THE ESSENTIAL QUESTION

Essential Question: *What are elements of population composition, and how are those elements used by geographers to depict and analyze population composition?*

Elements of Population Composition	Information Taken from Population Pyramids

---

KEY TERMS

age-sex composition graph	baby boom	dependent population
population pyramid	baby bust	dependency ratio
cohorts	echo	
birth deficit	potential workforce	

GEOGRAPHIC PERSPECTIVES: *INTERPRETING DEPENDENCY NUMBERS*

Comparing the dependency ratios of any two countries suggests differences in how people live in each place. For example, each worker in the United States supports 1.52 people—himself or herself plus an additional .52 people. In Niger, each worker supports 2.08 people—himself or herself plus an additional 1.08 people. (See Topic 2.9 for more on dependency ratio.)

Composition of Dependent Groups

Part of interpreting dependency ratios is knowing more about the dependent groups. The United States includes more seniors than children. This composition reflects that families have relatively few children and that people live relatively long lives. In contrast, families in Niger have more children and people live shorter lives. As a result, Niger has more children than senior citizens. Geographers often specify whether the dependents are younger or older than the working-age population.

Spatial Distribution

The composition of the dependency groups shapes the spatial distribution of the population in each country. In the United States, senior citizens who have retired often choose to move to warm climates, so the populations of Arizona and Florida and other warm-weather states have grown rapidly. In Niger, the high ratio of children means that school density should be high to provide education for them. However, Niger's poverty makes that difficult to achieve.

1. Since Niger has a large youth dependent population (under age 15), describe a potential economic benefit and problem that country could face.

2. Countries like the United States have large dependent population over age 65. Describe a potential economic benefit and problem these countries could face.

3. Why do you think age 65 is used as the age of elderly dependency? Is it an appropriate age for elderly dependency? Explain your response.

THINK AS A GEOGRAPHER: *ONE PLACE MANY DENSITIES*

The concept of population density applies at many scales. A resident of Salt Lake City, Utah, lives in areas with these numbers of people per square mile:

- Salt Lake City—1,387/sq. mi.
- State of Utah—34/sq. mi.
- United States—87/sq. mi.
- the world—130/sq. mi.

1. What does the difference in density between the United States and the world suggest about the United States?

2. Explain why a Salt Lake City, Utah, resident could claim to live in a place of both high and low population density.

CHAPTER 3 REVIEW:
Population Distribution and Composition

Topics 2.1–2.3

MULTIPLE-CHOICE QUESTIONS

Questions 1 and 2 refer to the map below.

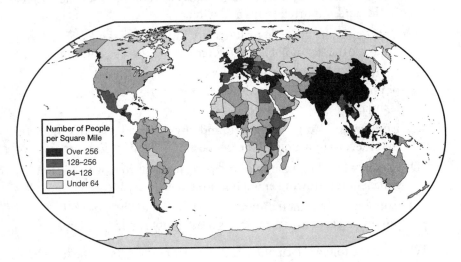

1. Which generalization is best illustrated by the world map above?

   (A) Climate is the primary factor influencing population distribution.

   (B) People are spread out evenly throughout the world.

   (C) The majority of the world's population lives between 20° N and 60° N latitude.

   (D) More people live in the Western Hemisphere than in the Eastern Hemisphere.

   (E) People have preserved fertile land for farming by choosing to settle heavily in areas with poor farmland.

2. Based on the map, which area is most densely populated?

   (A) Eastern Asia

   (B) Northern Europe

   (C) Western North America

   (D) Central South America

   (E) Southern Africa

	Arithmetic Density	Physiological Density	Arable Land Percentage
Country A	226 people/sq. mi.	8,078 people/sq. mi.	2.8
Country B	84 people/sq. mi.	498 people/sq. mi.	16.8

3. According to the table, which country has a greater need for increased crop yields and imported foods and why?

(A) Country A: Its physiological density indicates that its farmers do not have the technological resources to grow crops efficiently.

(B) Country A: The large difference between its arithmetic and physiological densities indicates that it has only a little good farmland.

(C) Country A: Its high arithmetic and physiological densities indicate that it needs to use a high percentage of its land to grow crops.

(D) Country B: It has an arable land percentage of 16.8, which is not sufficient for growing enough food to feed everyone.

(E) Country B: The small difference between its arithmetic and physiological densities indicates it has ample good farmland.

4. Which of the following can be concluded from the data in the table?

(A) Country A has a larger total population than Country B.

(B) Country B has a larger total population than Country A.

(C) Country A has a larger total amount of arable land than Country B.

(D) Country B has a larger total amount of arable land than Country A.

(E) None of the above can be concluded using information in the table.

5. Which country has the lowest arithmetic population density?

(A) Egypt

(B) United States

(C) Australia

(D) India

(E) France

UNITED ARAB EMIRATES, 2016

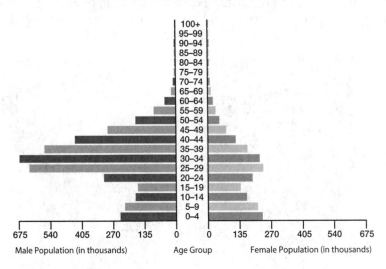

6. Which might explain the asymmetrical aspect of the population pyramid?

   (A) A high death rate among men ages 25–50

   (B) A large guest-worker population

   (C) An overcounting of children during the census

   (D) An epidemic with a high rate of mortality among the elderly

   (E) A major war fought in the years 2006 to 2010

7. Which statement about birth is best supported by the pyramid?

   (A) More occurred in 1956 than in 1966.

   (B) More occurred in 1986 than in 2006.

   (C) The number steadily increased between 1956 and 2016.

   (D) The number steadily decreased between 1956 and 2016.

   (E) Fewer occurred in 2016 than in 2011.

1. The median age is the age at which half of all people are older and half of all people are younger. Changing scale is also an important tool for geographers to use to better understand patterns and processes. Use the map below to answer the questions that follow it.

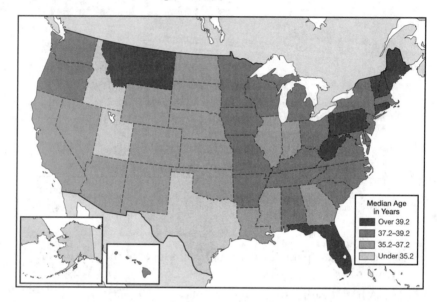

(A) Describe the regional distribution of U.S. residents by median age.

(B) Explain why Florida has a relatively high median age compared to other states and its economic impact on the state of Florida.

(C) Explain ONE age-related issue that affects Texas more than Florida.

(D) Identify the scale in which the data on the map is aggregated.

(E) Using a specific location on the map, describe how changing the aggregated scale of the data could impact the patterns on the map.

(F) Describe ONE additional specific quantitative data source, not shown on the map, that would help explain the patterns on it.

(G) Describe ONE additional specific qualitative data source, not shown on the map, that would help explain the patterns on it.

CHAPTER 4

Population Change

Topics 2.4–2.9

Topic 2.4 Population Dynamics

Learning Objective: Explain factors that account for contemporary and historical trends in population growth and decline. (IMP-2.A)

Topic 2.5 The Demographic Transition Model

Learning Objective: Explain theories of population growth and decline. (IMP-2.B)

Topic 2.6 Malthusian Theory

Learning Objective: Explain theories of population growth and decline. (IMP-2.B)

Topic 2.7 Population Policies

Learning Objective: Explain the intent and effects of various population and immigrant policies on population size and composition. (SPS-2.A)

Topic 2.8 Women and Demographic Change

Learning Objective: Explain how the changing role of females has demographic consequences in different parts of the world. (SPS-2.B)

Topic 2.9 Aging Populations

Learning Objective: Explain the causes and consequences of an aging population. (SPS-2.C)

A finite world can support only a finite population; therefore, population growth must eventually equal zero.
—Garrett Hardin, "The Tragedy of the Commons," 1968

Source: Getty Images

Educating women and children plays an important role in population dynamics. (See Topic 2.8 for the changing role of women.)

Population Dynamics

Essential Question: What are the factors that account for contemporary and historical trends in population growth and decline?

Before the 19th century, the total human population grew very slowly. By making small improvements in farming techniques, clearing forested areas to expand land for crops, and finding new regions of the ocean dense in fish, people became more efficient at extracting energy from the environment. Around 1800, the population reached 1 billion. In the 200-plus years since then, world population has exploded—it is around 7.4 billion today. The United Nations predicts it will reach nearly 11 billion by 2100. What problems—and what opportunities—will this growth present?

WORLD POPULATION GROWTH SINCE 1760

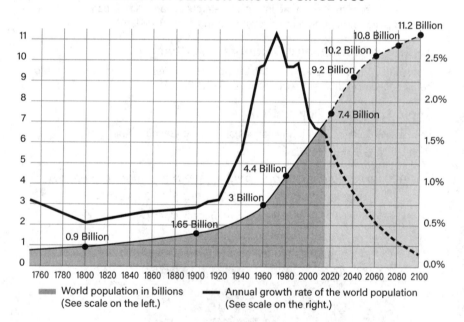

Source: Population projections come from "World Population Prospects: The 2015 Revision," UN Department of Economic and Social Affairs, 2015.

Compare the relationship between the population growth rate and the total population. What does the line representing the total population do when the growth rate line spikes? What is the relationship between the two dotted (predicted) lines after 2060?

Population Change

Populations always change—sometimes they shrink, but more often than not, they grow. For example, the population of the United States has grown steadily since the first census was taken in 1790.

UNITED STATES POPULATION GROWTH	
Year	Population (in millions)
1790	3.9
1900	76.2
2020	332.6

Prior to 1910, U.S. population grew 20 percent to 40 percent per decade, even during the 1860s, which included the American Civil War. Since 1980, it has increased 7 percent to 14 percent per decade.

Measuring and predicting population change over time is key to understanding the world. Geographers use a simple equation, the **demographic balancing equation**, to describe the future population of a region of any scale:

Future population = Current population + (number of births – number of deaths) + (number of immigrants – number of emigrants)

Figuring the demographic balancing equation takes several variables into account. The number of births and deaths are only part of a country's total population change. Migration also plays a part. To calculate a country's total population change, the number of **immigrants**—people who moved into the country—and the number of **emigrants**—people who moved out of the country—must be added to the equation.

The challenge for geographers is to understand and predict births, deaths, immigration, and emigration accurately. This chapter and the next will examine the concepts associated with population change and explore the ways that geographers use them to understand human populations.

Measuring the Number of Births

Geographers commonly use two different statistics to describe the rate at which children are born:

- The **crude birth rate (CBR)** is the number of live births per year for each 1,000 people.
- In contrast, the **total fertility rate (TFR)** focuses on women in their childbearing years of ages 15 to 49. TFR is the average number of children who would be born per woman of that group in a country, assuming every woman lived through her childbearing years.

Of the two statistics, the TFR more accurately reflects cultural norms—such as how people weigh the costs and benefits of having a child and how people perceive the role of women in society. The CBR is simpler to calculate and clearly relects the total population change within a country.

TOTAL FERTILITY RATES

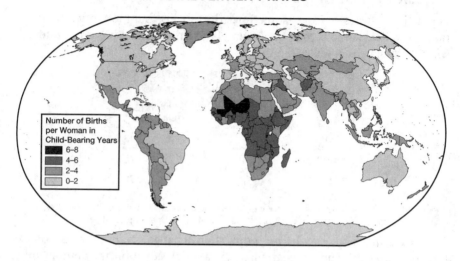

The total fertility rates (TFR) vary widely among different regions of the world. TFR varies among countries and it generally declines as countries become wealthier.

In most of the world, the TFR was higher in the past than it is today. In parts of Europe before 1800, the TFR averaged 6.2 children. In those days, most people lived on farms and having more children meant more people to work the land. However, because so many children died as infants, the average life span was only about 40 years. Despite the high TFR, population growth was slow.

Life Expectancy

Even though the total fertility rate worldwide has been decreasing, the world's population continues to grow. This growth reflects a decrease in the death rate and an increase in how long people live.

Global Population Increase

The most important factor in the increase in global population is the rise in **life expectancy**, the average number of years people live. It is commonly expressed from the time of a person's birth, but it can be calculated at any point in his or her lifetime. A century ago, the global life expectancy was about 34 years at birth; today it is nearly 70 years. In most of Europe, life expectancy at birth is more than 80 years. However, in less-developed areas, such as many sub-Saharan African countries, life expectancy at birth is less than 50 years.

One of the most important factors that affects increasing life expectancy is the drop in the **infant mortality rate**, the number of children who die before their first birthday. For example, in Massachusetts, the infant mortality rate per 1,000 live births dropped from 130 in 1850, to about 4 today.

LIFE EXPECTANCY BY COUNTRY, 2015

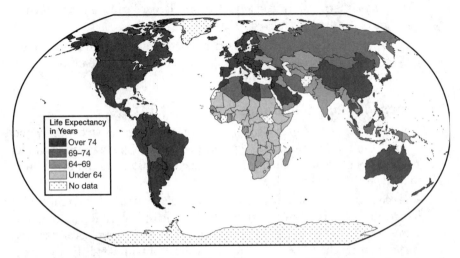

What regions of the world have the highest and lowest life expectancies? What is the scale of analysis used on the map? Note: Some regions on the map have no data because of political instability.

The decrease in infant mortality rate and increase in life expectancy can be explained by economic, political, and technological changes. Economic development has increased wealth and increased the amount and quality of food available to millions of people. Political stability has allowed for improved sanitation infrastructure, and advances in technology have greatly improved healthcare.

Better Food Production and Nutrition

Over the past 250 years, several advances in agriculture have helped increase life expectancy:

- mechanizing food production, such as replacing horses with tractors
- improving seeds, fertilizers, and farming techniques through research by state universities and private companies
- transporting products more efficiently in trucks, trains, and ships, often on roads, rail lines, or canals built with government support

In the United States in 1800, most of the population farmed. Today farmers make up less than 3 percent of the population, yet they produce enough food to feed everyone in the country and export vast quantities. Advances in agriculture such as the following had effects that rippled through society:

- Greater farming efficiency freed people to work in nonfarm industries, easing the transition to industrialization.
- Food security improved around the world. Hunger and famines still occurred because people were too poor to purchase food or because of political issues or distribution problems, not because of food shortage.
- As farms depended less on manual labor, farm families became smaller.

- The use of machinery meant that one person could farm more acres. Many small farms were consolidated into larger farms, and the former owners of those farms moved to urban areas.
- As the population of rural areas decreased, and cars and better roads allowed people to travel farther and more easily, many small towns that had served farmers disappeared.

Advances in Public Sanitation

As early industrial cities grew, so did the problems of large concentrated populations. One problem was the spread of disease. Cholera, for example, was spread through water contaminated by human waste, and the plague was carried by fleas that live on rodents.

Sewer Systems One of the most important advances in reducing mortality was the creation of public sewer systems. Before the Industrial Revolution and in its early years, people in cities dumped human waste into streets and rivers. The waste often reached the water supply, which contaminated the drinking water and made people sick. Children and the elderly were especially vulnerable to disease. Then cities began to install sewer systems, protecting water supplies from contamination and thus increasing life expectancy.

Water and Waste Systems People also learned that boiling water before they used it could prevent transmission of waterborne illnesses. That worked before citizens decided to pay for systems that provide clean water through taxes. Communities began to install water treatment plants that transported clean water to the homes in the cities. Cities also created departments of public sanitation and started to collect garbage and other waste produced by city residents. By doing this, cities reduced the number of rodents that fed on the waste and often carried disease.

Improvements in Healthcare

Improved medical care coincided with improvements in food production and sanitation. The development of vaccines to prevent diseases, antibiotics to cure diseases, and improved medical procedures boosted life expectancy.

Vaccines Prior to the 1800s, smallpox killed as many as 400,000 people each year. However, in the 1700s, British doctor Edward Jenner figured out that if he infected people with cowpox, a much milder disease related to smallpox, those people would be immune to smallpox. Jenner's work led to a smallpox vaccine. Today, efforts by the United Nations, national governments, and private organizations to vaccinate people around the world have been so successful that no case of smallpox has been reported since 1977. Jenner's work was also the basis for vaccines against other serious diseases, such as polio, tuberculosis, and rabies.

Antibiotics While vaccines helped prevent people from getting ill, antibiotics helped cure people who had bacterial infections. The first widely used antibiotic was penicillin, which came into use in the mid-1900s. Before penicillin, deadly bacterial infections killed many people. The deadliest epidemic in history was the plague, which was spread by flea bites. During the mid-1300s, the plague killed about 20 million people in Europe alone—about one-third of the continent's total population. Other common bacterial infections include parasitic infections, strep, and staph—which commonly killed people who got wounded in battle or suffered a deep cut.

Better Medical Care Improved medical procedures have also extended life expectancy. Among these procedures was advancements in surgery, which was often deadly before antibiotics. Now surgery is safe enough that it can help an individual suffering from a heart attack, stroke, cancer, or other ailments. Doctors have also saved the lives of pregnant women and their newborn children through the use of caesarean section surgeries.

RELATIONSHIP BETWEEN INCOME AND LIFE EXPECTANCY
(of selected countries)

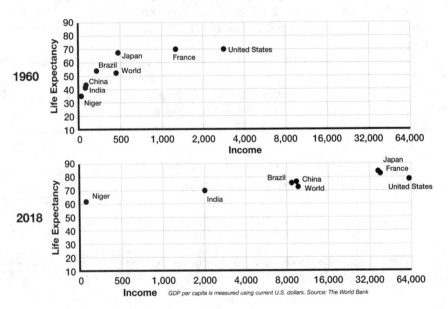

GDP per capita is measured using current U.S. dollars. Source: The World Bank

Rate of Population Increase

The natural increase or natural decrease in a population is measured by subtracting the number of deaths from the number of births. To compare countries of different sizes, demographers use rates rather than total numbers. The crude birth rate (CBR) and the **crude death rate** (CDR) of an area are measured per 1,000 population. The percentage at which a country's population is growing or declining, without the impact of migration, is the **rate of natural increase** (RNI).

Calculate it with this formula: *RNI = (CBR – CDR) ÷ 10*, and then add a percent sign. For the entire world, the CBR is about 20 and the CDR is about 8.

Since $(20 - 8) \div 10$ equals 1.2, the RNI for the world is about 1.2 percent. RNI tends to be less than 1.0 percent in more-developed countries and greater than 1.0 percent in less-developed countries.

Population Doubling Time

Demographers describe population growth in two ways:

- Arithmetic growth is when the increase is a constant number each period. Arithmetic growth by the addition of 1 would be 1, 2, 3, 4, etc. Arithmetic growth by 5 would be 1, 6, 11, 16, etc.

- Exponential growth is when the increase is a constant factor each period. If the factor is 2, then the number doubles each period: 1, 2, 4, 8, etc. Exponential growth by 5 would be 1, 5, 25, 125, etc.

Since the early 1800s, global population has been growing exponentially. For any quantity growing exponentially, the time it takes to double in size, or **population doubling time**, can be estimated using an equation known as the Rule of 70 (some people use the Rule of 72). Assuming the growth rate remains steady, the approximate doubling time in years will be 70 divided by the growth rate per year.

For example, in 2014, the West African country of Ivory Coast had a population growth rate of about 2.0. Since 70 divided by 2 equals 35, and assuming the growth rate remains about 2.0, the population of Ivory Coast will double in 35 years. The United States had a much lower growth rate: 0.77. If the U.S. growth rate remains at 0.77, the U.S. population will double in about 91 years.

REFLECT ON THE ESSENTIAL QUESTION

Essential Question: *What are the factors that account for contemporary and historical trends in population growth and decline?*

Current Trends in Population Growth and Decline	Historic Trends in Population Growth and Decline

---

KEY TERMS

demographic balancing equation	life expectancy
immigrants	infant mortality rate
emigrants	crude death rate (CDR)
crude birth rate (CBR)	rate of natural increase (RNI)
total fertility rate (TFR)	population doubling time

The Demographic Transition Model

Essential Question: How does the demographic transition model explain population growth and decline?

Populations change over time. One way they change is in size, usually growing but sometimes shrinking. Recall that a population pyramid is a type of graph used by geographers to represent the composition of a population. Geographers use another specific tool—a model—to represent and calculate, analyze, and display the change in total population size over time. This is the demographic transition model, which shows how the decline in death rates produced a growth in population and eventually a decline in birth rates.

The Demographic Transition Model

Changes in the birth rate and death rate in a country are shaped by how a country changes from an agrarian to an industrial society. The **demographic transition model** (DTM) shows five typical stages of population change that countries experience as they modernize. Each stage lasts for a period of indeterminate length. The developed countries of the world passed through these stages first, while the underdeveloped areas of the world are still passing through the early and middle stages.

THE DEMOGRAPHIC TRANSITION MODEL AND POPULATION DYNAMICS

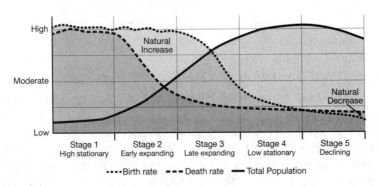

As a country passes through the stages, its total population increases. A country's death rate begins to decrease when it moves into Stage 2. Also, when a country reaches Stage 3, its birth rate starts to drop.

CHARACTERISTICS OF THE DTM STAGES

Factor	1. High Stationary	2. Early Expanding	3. Late Expanding	4. Low Stationary	5. Declining
Birth Rate	High but fluctuating as need for farm labor changes	High but fluctuating to reflect desires for big families	Declining as urbanization decreases the need for child labor	Low but enough to keep the population stable	So low it falls below the death rate
Death Rate	High but fluctuating to reflect diseases and poor sanitation	Rapidly declining as nutrition, sanitation, and medicine improve	Declining but not as fast as in previous stage	Low and stable	Low, sometimes increasing as the population ages
Natural Increase (yearly rate)	0 to .5%	.5 to 4%	4 to .8%	.8 to 0%	0% to (-1%)
Population Change	Very low growth because births and deaths are both high	Rapid growth as death rates fall faster than birth rates	Rapid but slowing growth as birth rates decline	Very low growth because births and deaths are both low	Very low decline as births fall below deaths
Population Structure	Very young	Very young	Young, with rising life expectancy	Balanced, with more aging	Very old
Examples Today	· Scattered isolated groups	· Mali · South Sudan	· Mexico · Turkey · Indonesia	· United States · China	· Japan · Germany
Economy and Society	· Subsistence agriculture · Hunter gathering	· Rural agricultural society · Less developed	· Large movement of people from farms to cities · Emerging/ industrializing economies	· Urbanized service economy · Highly developed · Rising gender equity	· Urbanized service economy · Highly developed

Demographic Transition and Population Pyramids

Only a few isolated groups are in Stage 1 and they are typically subsistence farmers or hunters and gathers. Societies in this stage have high birth rates and high fluctuating death rates based on Stages 2 to 5 of the Demographic Transition Model. Each tend to produce a different-shaped population pyramid.

Stage 2 Niger represents a Stage 2 country with an expansive population pyramid, one with a high birth rate—which produces a wide base—and a low life expectancy—which leads to narrowing in the upper years. Because the younger generations are larger than the older ones, the result is rapid population growth. This is typical of a less-developed region.

NIGER, 2016

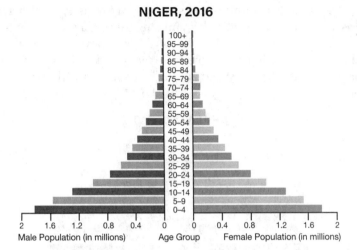

It is common to see population pyramids with either percentages or total population as above. Using percentages makes it easier to see differences between cohorts while using total population allows a better understanding of the number of people in a cohort of a certain age group.

Stage 3 Turkey represents an urbanizing Stage 3 nation with a declining birth rate and a more slowly declining death rate. Notice that the majority of the population is under the age of 34. The society is still young, but the percentage of elderly is increasing as life expectancy goes up. The transition from Stage 2 to Stage 3 has the fastest population growth. Countries attempt to navigate through Stage 3 as quickly as possible to avoid long-term exponential population growth. As countries transition from early Stage 3 into Stage 4, population will continue to grow for at least one generation because of **demographic momentum**. This process occurs because even though fertility rates have declined, people are living longer, and this results in population continuing to grow for another 20–40 years.

TURKEY, 2016

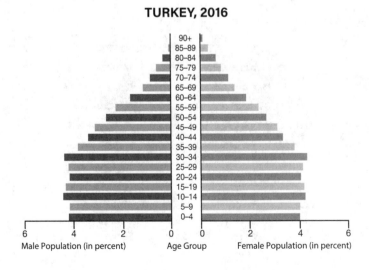

Stage 4 France's pyramid, representing Stage 4, is typical of the shape known as a stationary population pyramid. It indicates a population that is not significantly growing or shrinking. The birth rate is low but steady. The death rate is also low, indicating a high life expectancy and an increased percentage of older people. This graph shape is usually associated with more-developed countries.

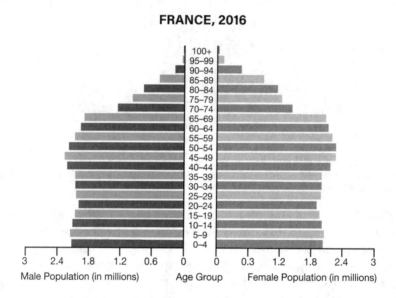

FRANCE, 2016

Stage 5 Japan's pyramid represents Stage 5. The narrow base reflects a decreasing birth rate. The population is aging and declining slightly overall. The largest age group is 65–69.

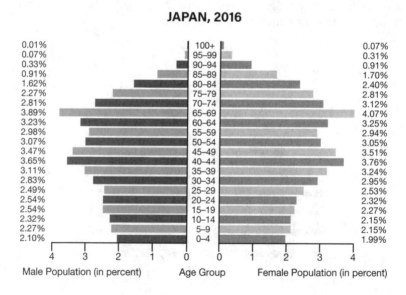

JAPAN, 2016

Policy Implications

As countries move from stage to stage, they face different challenges. A country in Stage 2 or 3, with a relatively high percentage of young people, often lacks the resources to educate all children. A country in Stage 4 or 5, with a relatively high percentage of old people, often faces problems funding healthcare. However, since the elderly can vote while children cannot, the elderly often have more political influence.

DTM at Different Scales of Analysis

Just as population pyramids can be created to illustrate the population of an entire country or a smaller portion of the population (like a province, state, or city), the demographic transition model can be used to analyze changes at a smaller scale. For example, birth rates and death rates of a particular region or subregion within a country, can differ from that of the larger society. They can also change at a different rate or in a different way. This will indicate a stage of demographic transition for the region that is different from that of the total population of the country.

Evaluation of the Demographic Transition Model

The demographic transition model helps explain, describe, and predict spatial activity and phenomena related to population increase and decline. It explains well the experiences of Western Europe, the United States, and Japan, mostly because it is based on these countries' experiences. However, it is less useful in explaining the experiences of all countries, particularly the less-developed countries of the world today:

- Citizens of countries in Stage 2 and 3 do not have as many options to migrate out of the country to help release some of the population pressure.
- Governments often place severe restrictions and limitations on migration.
- Today, birth control and government policies play a much larger role in reducing birth rates than previously.
- Economic changes in less-developed countries today are much different than the experiences of the United States and Western Europe in the past.

The DTM is a population change model and changes in the economy or society can have multiple reasons that cause the changes to occur. Just because changes in demographics and the economy occur at similar stages does not mean that they necessarily are the cause of the change. However, the DTM does assume that urbanization and industrial development help propel countries through each stage.

Each stage has demographic challenges and benefits, and the model is designed to help gain insight to those. Countries in later stages of the model are not necessarily more successful than countries in earlier stages; they simply have different demographic characteristics.

Epidemiological Transition Model

The world's countries develop industrially and economically at their own pace, so there is a large discrepancy in the types of diseases found across the world. In the early 1970s, epidemiologist Abdel Omran identified predictable stages in disease and life expectancy that countries experience as they develop. Omran's work is known as the **epidemiological transition model**. This model is an extension of the demographic transition model and explains the changing death rates and more common causes of death within societies.

EPIDEMIOLOGICAL TRANSITION MODEL

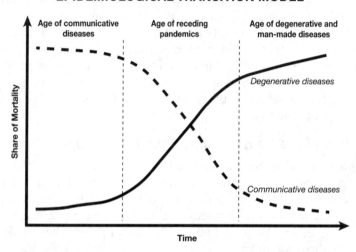

EPIDEMIOLOGICAL TRANSITION MODEL STAGES		
Stage	**Description**	**Effects on Population**
1. Disease and Famine	Parasitic or infectious diseases, accidents, animal attacks, or human conflicts cause most deaths. Food insecurity makes famine more common and more devastating.	A high death rate and low life expectancy.
2. Receding Pandemics	The number of pandemics (widespread diseases that affect large populations) declines as a result of improved sanitation, nutrition, and medicine.	A decreasing death rate and increasing life expectancy.
3. Degenerative and Human-Created Diseases	Infectious and parasitic diseases continue to decrease, but diseases associated with aging—such as heart disease and types of cancer—increase as people live longer.	Death rate stabilizes at a low level and life expectancy increases.
4. Delayed Degenerative Diseases	Stage 4 is an extension of Stage 3, but the age-related diseases are put off as medical procedures delay the onset of these diseases through advanced procedures. Diseases such as Alzheimer's and dementia increase.	Death rate reaches its lowest level and life expectancy reaches a peak.

EPIDEMIOLOGICAL TRANSITION MODEL STAGES		
Stage	Description	Effects on Population
5. Reemergence of Infectious and Parasitic Diseases	Infectious and parasitic diseases increase as some bacteria and parasites become resistant to antibiotics and vaccines.	Life expectancy decreases.

The COVID-19 pandemic in 2020 challenged some of the theories of the epidemiological transition model. Pandemics are usually a part of Stage 1 or 2, but as the world becomes more urbanized and globally connected, the threat of pandemics seems to be increasing. The model assumes that pandemics will decrease as countries develop economically. The extensive consequences of the virus illustrate the importance of studying and understanding the spread of diseases. According to Johns Hopkins University, by March 2021, approximately 120 million people were infected and more than 2.6 million people worldwide died from COVID-19. A factor supporting the effectiveness of the model is that advanced medicine and science limited the impacts as compared to historic pandemics, such as the 1918 influenza outbreak.

One criticism of the model is that it does not take into account the impact of lifestyle choices nor local environmental factors in extending or shortening life expectancy. Eating healthier food, drinking less alcohol, and exercising more have enabled many people to live longer and more active lives. One of the biggest lifestyle changes has been in smoking. In the United States, the percentage of adults who smoke has declined in the last five decades from approximately 40 percent to under 15 percent, which partly explains an increase in life expectancy in the United States. In some regions of the world, high levels of industrial pollution or exposure to pesticides and chemicals has resulted in localized higher death rates that are not captured in the model.

REFLECT ON THE ESSENTIAL QUESTION

Essential Question: *How does the demographic transition model explain population growth and decline?*

Demographic Transition Model's Explanation of Population Change	Epidemiological Transition Model's Explanation of Changing Death Rates

KEY TERMS

demographic transition model   epidemiological transition model
demographic momentum

Malthusian Theory

Essential Question: How does Malthusian theory explain population growth and decline?

In 1798, Thomas Malthus published one of the most provocative books on population growth ever written, *An Essay on the Principle of Population*. Malthus, a member of the clergy and an early economist, focused on one of the underlying concerns of geography: the relationship between people and the earth.

Food Production and Population Growth

Malthus lived during a period when people were optimistic that new technology would make life better—but Malthus feared it would not. He analyzed the relationship between natural resource use, particularly agricultural output, and the growing population and concluded that society was on a path toward massive starvation. Geographers and other social scientists have debated the usefulness of Malthus's ideas about population growth, known as **Malthusian theory**, since he first published them.

He believed that food production would increase arithmetically—growing steadily by a similar amount each generation. In contrast, he believed that people would not limit the number of children they had, so the population would increase exponentially—growing steadily by a similar percentage each generation. Since population would grow faster than food production, the world's population would soon be unsupportable or referred to by Malthus as **overpopulation**. If people could not limit population growth voluntarily, Malthus believed famine, or widespread and massive starvation, would limit population growth. Additionally, he argued that the likelihood of war, plagues, and economic struggles would increase.

MALTHUSIAN THEORY

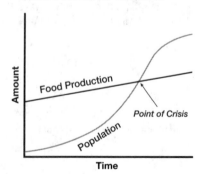

The j-shaped population curve grows faster than resources. At the point of crisis, the population exceeds carrying capacity. What types of challenges does exceeding carrying capacity create for a region?

Alternative Views

The famines predicted by Malthus did not and have not occurred for several reasons. The first is that food production increased dramatically faster than he predicted. Malthus did not live to see the dramatic improvements in agricultural technologies that have revolutionized food production. Also, Malthus was incorrect in his prediction that population would continue on its steady growth path. In the years since he wrote his essay, fertility rates have dropped in all regions of the world.

Additionally, some scientists believed that an increasing population could improve the situation. In contrast to Malthus, Ester Boserup (1910–1999), a Danish economist, emphasized the positive aspects of a large population. In simple terms, the **Boserup theory** suggested that the more people there are, the more hands there are to work, rather than just more mouths to feed. Boserup also argued that as population increases, more pressure is placed on the existing agricultural system, which stimulates invention resulting in more food production.

BOSERUP AND MALTHUSIAN THEORIES

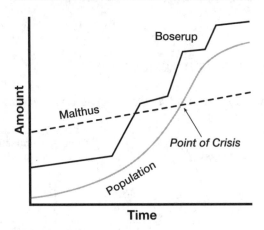

Malthusian Theory Today

The widespread starvation that Malthus feared has not happened. Yet, there are those who still accept his fundamental premise as correct today, they are known as **neo-Malthusians**. They argue that population growth is a serious problem currently and an even greater threat for the future. On a regional scale, places like the Sahel region in Africa, the transition between the Sahara and the grasslands, could represent a Malthusian scenario. The region's population is expected to triple over the next 30 years and is suffering with political instability, poverty, food shortages, and dramatic climate change.

Neo-Malthusians point out continued population growth will lead to the depletion of nonrenewable resources such as petroleum and metals, pollution of air and water, and shortages of food. These issues could lead to social, political, economic, and environmental catastrophe.

SAHEL REGION OF AFRICA WITH NATURAL INCREASE RATES, 2020

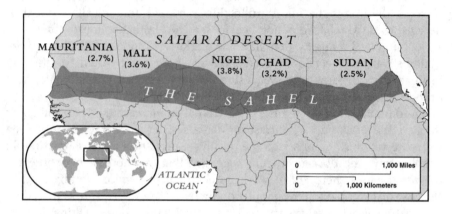

Source: PRB.org

The natural increase rates of the countries of the Sahel indicate what stage of the demographic transition model? How could countries of the Sahel region avoid a Malthusian crisis?

REFLECT ON THE ESSENTIAL QUESTION

Essential Question: *How does Malthusian theory explain population growth and decline?*

Malthus's Concerns About Population Growth	Checks or Impacts at the Point of Crisis

KEY TERMS

Malthusian theory
overpopulation

Boserup theory
neo-Malthusians

Population Policies

Essential Question: What are the intent and the effects of population and immigration policies on population size and composition?

Population growth rates can also be influenced by political factors. Many countries in the world today have adopted national policies intended to either slow the growth of their populations or to increase it.

Government Programs to Reduce Population Growth

Concerns about population growth have led to **antinatalist policies**. These policies attempt to decrease the number of births in a country and are often used by developing countries.

The Chinese government introduced two different antinatalist policies in the 1970s. The first, known as "later, longer, fewer," was introduced in 1972. It encouraged parents to get married later in life, wait longer between children, and as a result, have fewer children.

The impact of the "later, longer, fewer" policy can be seen in China's pyramid for 2016 in the relatively shorter bars for the 40–44 and 35–39 cohorts. The expansion in births in the 25–29 and 30–34 cohorts is the result of the large number of women who entered childbearing age in the mid-1980s.

CHINA, 2016

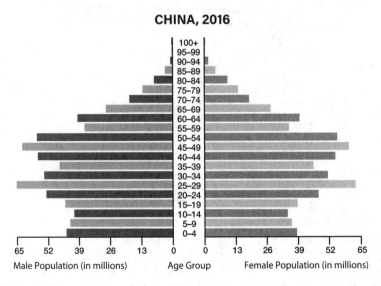

Review the 5-year cohorts for 24 years and under. Describe the pattern of boys compared to girls using quantitative data.

"Later, longer, fewer" resulted in reduced fertility but not as quickly as officials wanted. In response, China instituted its One-child policy in 1979. Parents who had more than one child were subject to fines, although the law made exceptions for rural couples and ethnic minorities. The policy remained in effect until 2016. During that period, China's fertility rate decreased. However, researchers disagree on how much of the decline resulted from the policy and how much from other factors, such as increased education for women.

Gender Preference Chinese culture has long preferred male children over females, so the One-child policy contributed to an unbalanced gender ratio. By 2010, China had 118 males born for every 100 females. The gender imbalance was so great that Chinese leaders feared it would lead to greater crime and civil unrest among young men who felt they had no prospects to get married and have children.

Gender preference is not unique to just China. Many countries have unbalanced gender ratios at birth, such as India, which has a similar sex ratio to China. Demographers estimate that upwards of 100 million Indian girls are missing from the population because of a gender preference for males. Sons are required economically to care for their elderly parents, while girls are viewed as a financial burden with less economic potential than boys. According to the World Health Organization changing structural elements of gender inequality by promoting equal education and pay, allowing women to own property, and changing attitudes about gender roles are essential to increase the perceived value of girls.

CHINA'S MALE AND FEMALE POPULATIONS

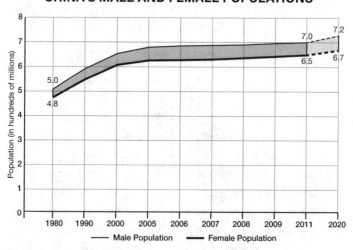

Source: United Nations Development Programme

Males outnumber females in the total world population. China's antinatalist policy is the reason for about half of these "extra" males. Why might a couple have had a preference for a male child to be their first?

Revision of One-Child Policy One effect of China's One-child policy was a change in the dependency ratio. Chinese government officials reevaluated the policy because of concerns that, in the future, the economically active workforce will not be large enough to sustain economic growth and support the elderly. In 2016, the Chinese government modified the controversial program and allowed families to have two children.

While China's One-child policy was the most comprehensive population-control plan, other countries used more targeted programs. In European nations, birth-education decreased teenage pregnancy. In parts of Africa and South Asia, laws banning child marriage raised the average marriage age and the average age that a woman had her first child.

Policies to Encourage Population Growth

Throughout history, some governments have encouraged large families. Those governments believed that a growing population stimulated economic growth and increased military power.

In recent decades, a variation of this reasoning has emerged in some highly developed countries. As fertility rates dropped but people lived longer, the percentage of elderly people increased. To keep the economy vibrant, countries such as France, Sweden, and Japan instituted **pronatalist policies**, or programs designed to increase the fertility rate. For example, they have provided paid time off from jobs held by mothers, free childcare, and family discounts on government services. Other countries like Denmark, Singapore, Russia, and Italy have advertising campaigns to encourage families to have more children and express family and national pride. These campaigns have had mixed results.

The island city-state of Singapore has engaged in both pronatalist and antinatalist policies. In 1966, the official policy was "Stop at Two" and "Boy or Girl, Two is Enough," and by 1987, the policy changed to "Have Three or More, If You Can Afford It." In 2000, "Work-Life Harmony" and "Family-Friendly Work" were added as new policies. Policies included paid leave, cash bonuses, and tax rebates for working mothers who had a baby.

Restricting or encouraging immigration through national policies is another political tool that a country can use to promote or discourage population growth. Remember that the **demographic balancing equation** includes both immigration and emigration when predicting future populations.

REFLECT ON THE ESSENTIAL QUESTION

Essential Question: *What are the intent and the effects of population and immigration policies on population size and composition?*

Policies Encouraging Population Growth	Policies Discouraging Population Growth

---

KEY TERMS

antinatalist policies	pronatalist policies

Women and Demographic Change

Essential Question: What are the demographic consequences due to the changing role of women in different parts of the world?

The changing roles of females has had profound effects on the demographics worldwide. The goals, responsibilities, and opportunities of women are different today than in the past. The effects of these changes can be seen in both the developing and the developed world.

Changes in Fertility

Beginning in the mid-18th century, Europeans began having fewer children. Part of the lower fertility rate was unintentional. During this time, countries began keeping larger standing armies, so more men were away from home for longer periods.

However, most of it was intentional. With the Industrial Revolution (see Topic 7.1), people began to rely more on machines than on human labor to produce goods, so couples felt they needed fewer children to support their families. Additionally, people were migrating from rural agricultural regions into more urban city centers where an increasing number of jobs were located. In cities, raising children was often more expensive, further reducing the fertility rate. Yet, industrialization contributed to a lower death rate and also enabled people to live longer. So even though total fertility rate (TFR) declined, population growth increased. **Total fertility rate** is the average number of children who would be born per woman of that group in a country, assuming every woman lived through her childbearing years.

Role of Women in Society

Cultural, economic, political, and environmental realities have always shaped decisions about whether to have children. Since these conditions have varied across time and cultures, so have birth rates. The changing way that people view the role of women in a society has been a particularly important factor influencing TFR.

Over the past 250 years, as countries industrialized, people moved from rural areas to urban areas and found work in factories. Many women found work in textile mills, so they often began families later and sometimes not at all. Families lived in small apartments or small houses in cities, which were more suitable for small families.

As the number of factories grew in the early 19th century, children worked there alongside adults. Later that century, governments passed laws prohibiting child labor and began opening public schools. As young women obtained more schooling, they began to expand their work opportunities. The longer they stayed in school, the fewer children they had—a trend that continues to the present day, as the chart on Ghana shows.

TFR AND SCHOOLING FOR GIRLS IN GHANA		
Years of Schooling	TFR, 1990	TFR, 2007
0	7.0	6.1
4	6.4	5.0
8	5.6	3.7
12	2.7	2.0

Source: worldbank.org

What are the differences in the trends of TFR and schooling for girls from 1990 and 2007? What are some possible causes for the differences?

In Ghana, between 1990 and 2007, as young women gained more education, the number of children they had decreased. This suggests that young women who spent more time in school chose to delay marriage and childbirth.

The United States showed a similar pattern of delayed marriage. As educational opportunities increased for women between 1950 and 2010, the median marriage age of women increased from just over 20 years of age to nearly 27. As a result, the average age at which women gave birth to their first child increased as well.

Family Planning

Throughout the 20th century, the spread of family planning information and changes in technology aided people who wanted to choose the number of children they had. In countries with wide access to family planning methods, including the United States and many countries in Europe, couples gave birth to their first child later in life, had fewer children, had fewer unintended pregnancies, and had larger intervals between having children. In these places, the total fertility rate continued a decline that began with the Industrial Revolution.

Religious and cultural values also shape attitudes toward having children. Some religious traditions oppose certain forms of family planning. Women who follow traditional religious beliefs have higher fertility rates than those who do not. These women are less likely to use birth control and less likely to be employed outside the home. The combination of access to family planning, educational attainment of girls, and the resulting gains in economic wealth for women, is powerful in reducing total fertility rates.

Political Changes

Women have been expanding their participation in politics and government across the world in the last 50 years. Although females are still underrepresented in government positions, their presence and involvement there has never been greater. These political changes have coincided with the expanded opportunities for women to gain education, access jobs and leadership roles, and make decisions about family size. Family planning is a political topic in many countries, including the United States, and the voice of women in prominent political and cultural positions can have significant influence.

NUMBER OF COUNTRIES WITH A WOMAN IN THE HIGHEST GOVERNMENT POSITION, 1960 TO 2020

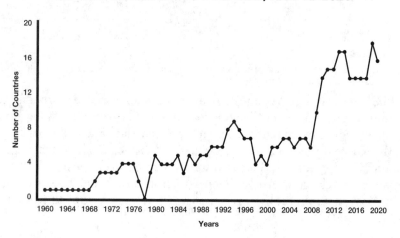

Source: statista.com

The graph shows changes from 1960 to 2020. In 2021, only 12 of the 193 countries (6 percent) in the United Nations had a woman as leader.

REFLECT ON THE ESSENTIAL QUESTION

Essential Question: *What are the demographic consequences due to the changing role of women in different parts of the world?*

Reasons for Reduced Fertility Rates	Effect of Social, Economic, and Political Roles for Women

---

KEY TERM

total fertility rate (TFR)

Aging Populations

Essential Question: What are the causes and consequences of an aging population?

Across the world, the populations are getting older. This is most evident in highly seveloped countries such as Japan and much of Europe. However, the processes that cause the average age of a population to increase are occurring in all parts of the world. There are numerous significant effects on a society with an aging population.

Causes of Aging Populations

There are two primary reasons for the increasing average ages in populations: longer life expectancy and lower crude birth rates.

Improvements in healthcare and eldercare have allowed for life expectancies to increase in developed countries. In many of these countries, people routinely live well into retirement.

In less-developed societies, life expectancies have also been increasing due to much simpler, but effective, improvements. Building better sewage treatment facilities and improving drinking water quality have helped tremendously. Mitigation of diseases such as malaria, dysentery, AIDS, and influenza have greatly improved chances of living not only to adulthood but into old age. The presence of basic medical services, trained midwives, and available antibiotics are now much more common in many countries and have resulted in increasing life expectancies worldwide.

Crude birth rates are also dropping as a result of changes attitudes about family size. (See Topic 2.4.) When fewer children are born, there will eventually be fewer adults to create families. In many places, this process has tended to reinforce itself with each successive generation becoming slightly smaller than the one that proceeded it. Consequently, as the percentage of younger people in a population decreases and the number of people living into old age increases, the average age of a population increases.

Effects of Aging Populations

As populations age, their needs change. Japan's population has an average age of 49 years and has different priorities than Iraq where the average age is 21 years. The average age in the United States in 2020 was 40 years, but in 2000, it was only 35.

Political Impacts

Older people may vote differently than younger people. Many older people are on a fixed income and may not support tax increases for things such as parks that they won't likely use and may not be able to afford the taxes to support. Potentially political tensions can rise over differing political issues and age-specific viewpoints, such as increasing the retirement age or changing funding levels for education or Social Security.

Retirees are very likely to vote, and as the percentage of elderly rise, they have become a powerful voting bloc. The importance of the senior voting bloc is partly because of the number of seniors, but even more because of the willingness to vote. Between 1986 and 2018, voter turnout among people over the age of 60 was consistently about 30 percent higher than among people 18 to 29 years old.

Social Impacts

Traditionally, in many countries, families lived in multigenerational homes with children and aging parents. Increasingly, married couples have moved away from the region where they were raised to seek jobs and opportunities. As people live longer, families face increasing social and economic challenges to care for elderly members. Positive impacts include retired grandparents assisting in raising grandchildren and maintaining a strong family unit for working parents.

Economic Impacts

An aging country will often invest in additional services for the elderly, which might result in a reduction of spending in other areas or tax increases. One of the great challenges is the increased economic expense of caring for the elderly, especially the cost of medical care and retirement income. Increasingly as a society ages, these costs are being incurred by the government and paid for by the younger generation who are working. In Stage 4 and 5 countries, like the United States and Japan, there are decreasing numbers of young people compared to retirees.

The economic benefits of a graying society are numerous. If the aging population stays healthy, they often will volunteer, continue working, and spend money in the economy, resulting in increased jobs and services for other workers. Additionally, many jobs are created in healthcare and caring for the elderly.

Dependency Ratio

Another result of an aging population is a change in the **dependency ratio** (DR), a value comparing the working to the nonworking parts of a population. Demographers consider people ages 15–64 the potential workforce, the group expected to be the society's labor force. Everyone else—people under 15 or over 64—are the **dependent population**, because they are considered too young or too old to work full-time. Put simply, the dependency ratio is a consideration of the number of people in a population who are economically supporting the rest of the population. Dividing the potential workforce by the dependent population results in the dependency ratio. Remember, however, that because many people who are 15 to 64 do not work for pay and since many people under 15 and over 64 do work, this number is only a rough estimate. Nevertheless, it is an important reality for aging populations that fewer people will inevitably be supporting more people. (See Geographic Perspectives on page 70 for more on interpreting dependency ratio.)

CALCULATING DEPENDENCY RATIO			
Country	Population by Age Group	Dependent Population (under 15 + over 64)	Dependency Ratio Calculation
United States	• under 15: 19% • 15 to 64: 66% • over 64: 15%	34%	$\dfrac{19 + 15}{66} = 0.52$
Niger	• under 15: 49% • 15 to 64: 48% • over 64: 3%	52%	$\dfrac{49 + 3}{48} = 1.08$

REFLECT ON THE ESSENTIAL QUESTION

Essential Question: *What are the causes and consequences of an aging population?*

Causes for Population Aging	Political, Economic, and Social Consequences of an Aging Population

KEY TERMS

dependency ratio

dependent population

GEOGRAPHIC PERSPECTIVES: *CHANGING THE PERCEPTION OF GIRLS*

Many countries have engaged in policies to decrease population growth and to highlight the value of a having a girl. As discussed in Topic 2.7, many countries have a gender gap in their overall population primarily because some cultures believe that boys are more valuable than girls. One of the strategies that countries employ to counter this belief is to use advertisement campaigns and create posters that illustrate the benefits of girls. The images often have visuals and symbols that represent the benefits of girls to society and to families. Visually showing people the benefits and the potential opportunities of girls is a necessity in many communities to change the perception that many people have about girls. Use the photos below to complete the directions that follow.

| China | Jordan | India |

Sources: pbs.org, Wikimedia Commons

China-English translation: "It's better to marry and have children at a mature age." The poster is from the Shanghai Center of Communication and Education for Family Planning.

Jordan-A photo of young girls reading at a government primary school in Amman, Jordan, from 2011.

India-English translation: "Why only a boy? Are these not girls?" The image was created by India Directorate of Family Welfare in 1993.

1. Using the images from China, describe three benefits of having a girl.
2. Using the image from Jordan, describe why showing young girls reading is an effective strategy to improve the value of girls in society.
3. Using the image from India, explain the main point that the poster conveys about girls.
4. Explain the social factors that make it necessary to show the value of girls.

THINK AS A GEOGRAPHER: *PREDICTING POPULATION CHANGE*

Geographers study patterns and trends to help them make predictions about the future. This often has very practical uses. For example, knowing where people will be living in 30 years helps communities plan their investments in roads and schools. But making predictions is very difficult because they are always based on assumptions about how much the future will look like the past.

Use data from this unit and from this chart to answer the questions that follow about how much the world population will grow.

EXAMPLES OF POPULATION GROWTH AND DECLINE			
Region	**Time Period**	**Important Event or Trend**	**Population Change**
World	1800 to 2000	Industrialization	Total increase of about 600 percent
Europe	Late 14th century	Disease epidemic	Total decrease of about 25 percent
Americas	1492 to late 1800s	Disease epidemic	Total decrease among indigenous population of 70 to 90 percent
Russia	1987 to 1999	Political turmoil	Birthrate decrease of about 45 percent
United States	1929 to 1941	Economic depression	Birthrate decrease of about 30 percent
World	2000 to 2019	Globalization	Birthrate decrease

1. What evidence from this unit supports a prediction that the world population will increase at a decreasing rate for the next 100 years and then level out?

2. What evidence from the chart above supports a prediction that the growth of the world population will slow in the future?

3. How does evidence in the chart both support and disprove Malthus's theory?

CHAPTER 4 REVIEW:
Population Change

Topics 2.4–2.9

MULTIPLE-CHOICE QUESTIONS

Questions 1 through 3 refer to the population pyramid below.

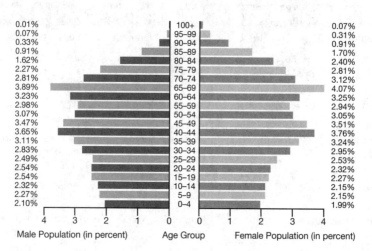

Male Population (in percent)	Age Group	Female Population (in percent)
0.01%	100+	0.07%
0.07%	95–99	0.31%
0.33%	90–94	0.91%
0.91%	85–89	1.70%
1.62%	80–84	2.40%
2.27%	75–79	2.81%
2.81%	70–74	3.12%
3.89%	65–69	4.07%
3.23%	60–64	3.25%
2.98%	55–59	2.94%
3.07%	50–54	3.05%
3.47%	45–49	3.51%
3.65%	40–44	3.76%
3.11%	35–39	3.24%
2.83%	30–34	2.95%
2.49%	25–29	2.53%
2.54%	20–24	2.32%
2.54%	15–19	2.27%
2.32%	10–14	2.15%
2.27%	5–9	2.15%
2.10%	0–4	1.99%

1. Which stage of the demographic transition model does the population pyramid represent?

   (A) Stage 1

   (B) Stage 2

   (C) Stage 3

   (D) Stage 4

   (E) Stage 5

2. Which is most likely a bigger concern for the country represented in the pyramid than for countries in other DTM stages?

   (A) A greater demand for government spending on pensions and healthcare for the elderly

   (B) A greater demand for government spending on education and daycare for children

   (C) A higher rate of unemployment among people of working age

   (D) A higher rate of emigration by people in search of jobs

   (E) A faster overall population growth than in previous decades

3. What concept is illustrated by the graph's "peaks" at ages 40–44 and 65–69?

   (A) An unbalanced dependency ratio

   (B) Increasing crude birth rates over time

   (C) Increasing life expectancy

   (D) A baby boom and echo

   (E) A need for more effective family planning in certain years

4. Which change most reduced fertility rates in less-developed countries?

   (A) Building hospitals and healthcare facilities

   (B) Providing more education for girls

   (C) Implementing pronatalist policies

   (D) Discouraging the use of birth control

   (E) Promoting fundamentalist religious values

5. How do the concerns of an aging population differ from those of a population with a younger average age?

   (A) Increased concern with childcare

   (B) Increased need for pharmacies and care facilities

   (C) Less worry about a higher dependency ratio

   (D) Less worry about the need for health services

   (E) Increased need for family planning

Questions 6 and 7 refer to the chart below.

BIRTH RATES AND DEATH RATES BY LEVEL OF DEVELOPMENT			
Country	Level of Development	Crude Birth Rate/ 1,000 People	Crude Death Rate/ 1,000 People
Niger	Less developed	45.5	12.4
Bangladesh	Less developed	20.0	5.7
Mexico	Developing	18.8	5.3
Australia	More developed	13.2	6.4
France	More developed	12.4	9.2

6. Which country's population has the highest rate of natural increase?

   (A) Niger

   (B) Bangladesh

   (C) Mexico

   (D) Australia

   (E) France

7. France's crude death rate is higher than Bangladesh's because

(A) France is involved in more wars

(B) France has more natural disasters

(C) France has a higher percentage of elderly people

(D) Bangladesh has a better healthcare system

(E) Bangladesh has a higher life expectancy

FREE-RESPONSE QUESTION

POPULATION GROWTH AND DEVELOPMENT, 1950–2050

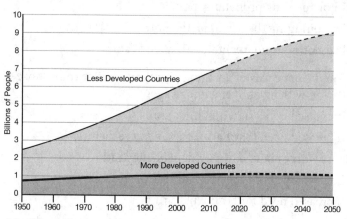

Source: Population Reference Bureau

1. Since 1950, population has grown fastest in less-developed countries, and the total fertility rate is an important indicator of population growth. Use the graph above and the map about total fertility rates on page 78 to answer the following questions.

(A) Describe the population growth patterns of more-developed countries shown on the graph.

(B) Explain ONE reason why the pattern in A is occurring.

(C) Using both sources, explain ONE reason why population is growing faster in less-developed countries than in more-developed countries.

(D) Explain ONE social consequence of uneven population growth between less- and more-developed countries.

(E) Explain ONE economic consequences of uneven population growth between less- and more-developed countries.

(F) Explain ONE political way that countries have attempted to lower their total fertility rate.

(G) Describe ONE unintended consequence of the political policy in F.

CHAPTER 5

Migration

Topics 2.10–2.12

Topic 2.10 Causes of Migration

Learning Objective: Explain how different causal factors encourage migration. (IMP-2.C)

Topic 2.11 Forced and Voluntary Migration

Learning Objective: Describe types of forced and voluntary migration. (IMP-2.D)

Topic 2.12 Effects of Migration

Learning Objective: Explain historical and contemporary geographic effects of migration. (IMP-2.E)

More than any other nation on Earth, America has constantly drawn strength and spirit from wave after wave of immigrants. In each generation, they have proved to be the most restless, the most adventurous, the most innovative, the most industrious of people.

—President Bill Clinton, speech at Portland State University, 1998

Source: Wikimedia Commons

Somalian refugees fled to Kenya to escape drought and conflict in 2011. (See Topic 2.11 for more on forced migration and refugees.)

Causes of Migration

Essential Question: How have different causal factors encouraged migration?

In his 1998 commencement address at Portland State University (see previous page), President Bill Clinton highlighted the ongoing impact of immigrants coming to the United States. The United States is the most populous immigrant country in the world. Like many countries in the Americas and Australia, most residents are either immigrants or descendants of immigrants. United States culture, institutions, and population are the products of five centuries of immigration.

Migration's Push and Pull Factors

World history is a story of constant movement. **Migration** is the permanent or semipermanent relocation of people from one place to another. Since the first humans lived in eastern Africa, people have been on the move. Early humans were very mobile, searching for nuts, seeds, and fruits, and hunting for animals to eat. As agriculture developed, people moved less in search of food and urban settlements began. However, people continued to move, from rural to urban areas, and from settlement to settlement.

Most people who move do so in search of a better life. They are part of a **voluntary migration**, or a movement made by choice. The choice usually combines a decision to move away from someplace with a decision to move toward someplace else:

- Geographers classify the reasons that people migrate *to* a specific location. People generally decide to move because of **push factors**, which are negative circumstances, events, or conditions present where they live that compels a person to leave.

- Once migrants decide to leave, they usually choose a destination based on its positive conditions and circumstances, or **pull factors**.

- From the perspective of a receiving country, an **immigrant** is a person who migrates across an international border with the intention of staying permanently.

- From the perspective of the country the migrant is leaving, the person is viewed as an **emigrant**. When people migrate away from somewhere, they **emigrate**.

Economic Push and Pull Factors

The most common reason people migrate is that they lack jobs and economic opportunities. These migrants go to areas offering greater chances for economic prosperity.

EXAMPLES OF ECONOMIC PUSH AND PULL FACTORS		
Group and Place of Origin	**Push Factors**	**Pull Factors**
Factory workers in the U.S. Rust Belt states, beginning in the 1970s	Unemployment rose among factory workers, particularly in traditional manufacturing states such as Michigan and Pennsylvania.	Many factory workers moved to southern states such as Kentucky and Tennessee, as manufacturers opened new factories there.
Farmers in rural China, beginning around 1950	Increased use of machines and consolidation of small farms into fewer large farms reduced the number of farmers needed to raise crops.	Farmers moved to China's large cities, increasing the urban population from 64 million in 1950 to 850 million by 2020.

Social Push and Pull Factors

People will often migrate when they experience discrimination and persecution because of their ethnicity, race, gender, or religion. They move to locations where they can practice their culture safely. People are often influenced by kinship links, or ties with relatives who have already settled in a place.

EXAMPLES OF SOCIAL PUSH AND PULL FACTORS		
Group and Place of Origin	**Push Factors**	**Pull Factors**
Mormon migration, 1845–1857	Anti-Mormon violence in Illinois and Missouri resulted in dozens of deaths, including that of leader Joseph Smith.	Approximately 70,000 Mormons migrated to the Great Salt Lake area, a place chosen for its isolation and agricultural opportunities.
Hindus and Muslims during and after the partition of India, 1947–1957	Violence resulted in around 1 million deaths.	More than 14 million people migrated in hopes of finding safety in a new country.

Political Push and Pull Factors

People who oppose the policies of a government often migrate because they face discrimination, arrest, and persecution. Such political migrants move to countries where they feel safe and have protection from the danger they faced in their home country.

EXAMPLES OF POLITICAL PUSH AND PULL FACTORS		
Group and Place of Origin	Push Factors	Pull Factors
Anti-communist Cubans after Fidel Castro's Communist takeover in 1959	Opponents of Castro were jailed or killed if they spoke out against Castro's government.	Opponents of Castro fled to the United States, where they were protected.
The Dalai Lama and Tibetan government officials, after China's takeover of Tibet in 1950	The Chinese persecuted, arrested, and killed many Tibetans who opposed the takeover.	The Dalai Lama and his supporters fled Tibet to India in 1959, which allowed them to set up a government in exile.

Environmental Push and Pull Factors

People often migrate to escape harm from natural disasters, drought, and other unfavorable environmental conditions. Such migrants move to areas that are not under the same environmental stresses.

EXAMPLES OF ENVIRONMENTAL PUSH AND PULL FACTORS		
Group and Place of Origin	Push Factors	Pull Factors
Farmers from Colorado, Kansas, Oklahoma, and Texas, 1930s	A severe drought caused thousands to lose their farms.	Farmers moved to California hoping to find work.
Residents living near the Fukushima Nuclear Power Plant in Japan, 2011	An earthquake and tsunami damaged nuclear reactors, releasing radioactive materials.	Residents near the power plant resettled to cities around Japan.

Demographic Push and Pull Factors

Some countries are unbalanced demographically. For example, in the case of a gender imbalance, young adults may not find someone to marry. Or if the population is too young, the country may eventually become overpopulated.

Geographers, such as Wilbur Zelinsky, saw a connection between migration patterns and the demographic transition model. (See Topic 2.5.) Zelinsky's theory, called the **migration transition model**, argues that countries in Stages 2 and 3 of the demographic transition model experience rapid population growth and overcrowding. This overcrowding limits the economic opportunities of the people and acts as a push factor. Thus, they migrate to less-crowded Stage 4 or 5 countries, which offer greater economic opportunities with growing economies and aging populations.

EXAMPLES OF DEMOGRAPHIC PUSH AND PULL FACTORS		
Group and Place of Origin	Push Factors	Pull Factors
Farmers in Europe, 1800s	The population of industrial countries increased, while land became scarce.	European migrants came to the United States, in part because the Homestead Act gave them plots of land.
Young educated people in less-developed countries in Latin America, North Africa, the Middle East, and Asia	Many people in less-developed countries live in areas where population is growing very quickly and unemployment and underemployment is high.	Developed countries in North America and Europe with aging populations need workers for difficult jobs, so they attract immigrants from less-developed countries.

Intervening Obstacles and Opportunities

Migration consists of more than just push and pull factors. Geographer Everett Lee introduced the idea in 1966 that migrants may encounter **intervening obstacles,** barriers that make reaching their desired destination more difficult. These obstacles might be political, such as laws restricting immigration and border patrols. They could be environmental, such as deserts or oceans for migrants to cross. Walls and fences that constructed at borders would be considered both political and environmental (physical) barriers or obstacles. Migrants can face economic obstacles in the form of costs incurred in migration.

Migrants may also encounter opportunities en route that disrupt their original migration plan. These are known as **intervening opportunities.** For example, a migrant might find a job along the way.

LEE'S MODEL OF MIGRATION

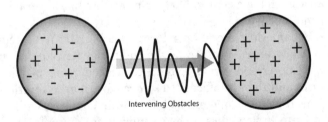

Intervening Obstacles

INTERVENING OBSTACLES	
Type of Obstacle	Example
Economic	A migrant lacks enough money to reach a destination.
Social	A migrant gets married to someone who lives along the migration route and settles in that person's community.
Political	A migrant cannot get a visa needed to pass through a country to get to his or her final destination.
Environmental	A migrant cannot cross a sea, desert, or mountain range.

Ravenstein's Laws of Migration

In the 1880s, German geographer E.G. Ravenstein observed patterns—sometimes referred to as laws—about migration tendencies and demographics. They still form the basis for migration theory today.

Short Distances Most migrants travel only a short distance. The further apart two places are, the less likely it is that people will migrate between those places. Ravenstein called this phenomenon **distance decay**. In the 1960s, geographers expanded this to time-distance decay, the idea that things near one another are more closely connected than things that are far apart.

Urban Areas Migrants traveling long distances usually settle in large urban areas. This is mainly because migrants believe that a larger city will have more opportunities than a smaller city.

In the 1970s, geographers used Ravenstein's laws to develop the **gravity model of migration**. The model assumes that the size and distance between two cities or countries will influence the amount of interactions that include migration, travel, and economic activity. The larger the population of a city or country, the more pull the location will have with migrants seeking economic opportunities. However, as the distance between two locations increases, the pull, or gravity, weakens and the person may choose a closer place to migrate.

One demonstration of the model is the Cuban migration to the United States following Fidel Castro's successful overthrow of the government in 1959. Most people settled in Florida, the state closest to Cuba. And most settled in large cities, such as Miami. Today, more than two-thirds of Cuban Americans in the United States live in Florida. More than half of all Cuban Americans live in Miami.

Multiple Steps Most migration occurs through **step migration**, a process in which migrants reach their eventual destination through a series of smaller moves. For example, in a common pattern in rural-to-urban migration, a migrant from a small town is most likely to move first to a larger town, later to a small city, and finally to a large city.

Rural to Urban Most migration in history has been from rural agricultural areas to urban city areas. Because of the Industrial Revolution, rural areas needed fewer laborers on farms, and cities needed more people to work, first in factories and then in offices. This **rural-to-urban migration** remains common today. It includes migrations both within countries—rural residents of India moving to Indian cities such as Mumbai, for example—and between countries—rural residents of Syria moving to cities in Germany.

Counter Migration Each migration flow produces a movement in the opposite direction, called **counter migration**. For example, in the 1990s and early 2000s, as many Mexican migrants were moving to the United States, a counter migration of people moved from the United States to Mexico. Some were part of a **return migration**, immigrants moving back to their former home. Others were retirees from the United States who had never lived in Mexico but were attracted by its warm weather and lower cost of living. One result of counter migration is that neighborhoods of former U.S. residents are found scattered throughout Mexico. Today, about 1 million retired U.S. citizens live in Mexico.

AGE-SEX PYRAMID OF INTERNATIONAL MIGRANTS, 2019
NORTHERN AFRICA AND WESTERN ASIA

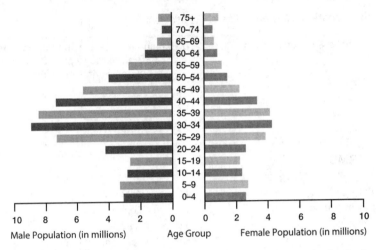

Using the graph, identify one pattern of migration related to age and one pattern related to gender. Explain reasons why the patterns occurs.

Youth Most migrants are younger adults, between ages 20 and 45. People in that age group are usually not as established with jobs, homes, and families as older groups, so they are more likely to move to improve their fortunes.

Gender Patterns Most international migrants are young males, while more internal migrants are female. Men are more likely to move outside of the country looking for work. For example, several countries in the Middle East have guest-worker programs where young men are recruited from South and Southeast Asia to work in the oil and construction industries.

Women are more likely to move within a country. One reason is that many women living in traditional societies move in with their husbands and husbands' families. However, today women comprise nearly half of the international migrants. The female migration pattern is changing for a variety of reasons:

- An increasing demand in destination countries and markets for jobs typically done by women, including employment in medical care, home and domestic work, and labor-intensive factories.

- Increasing female education is opening up employment opportunities.

- More women are becoming the primary income earner in their family.

- Although this trend is slowing, family reunification with husbands and children still occurs.

- An emerging trend is women migrating from countries with gender inequality to more gender-equal countries. However, this trend is being slowed by laws in sending countries that block women from migrating out of the country.

REFLECT ON THE ESSENTIAL QUESTION

Essential Question: *How have different causal factors encouraged migration?*

Push and Pull Factors	Explanation of Push and Pull Factors as Cultural, Demographic, Economic, Environmental, or Political

KEY TERMS

migration
voluntary migration
push factor
pull factor
immigrant
emigrant
emigrate
migration transition model

intervening obstacles
intervening opportunity
distance decay
gravity model of migration
step migration
rural-to-urban migration
counter migration
return migration

Forced and Voluntary Migration

Essential Question: What are the types of forced and voluntary migration?

Geographers classify migration and migrants as either forced or voluntary depending on the reason for which people move. Ideally, people would only move because they wanted to. That is often the case. However, throughout history and continuing into the present, millions of migrants have moved unwillingly. There are economic, cultural, political, and environmental push and pull factors behind both the voluntary and involuntary migration patterns.

Forced Migration

Migration that is involuntary, meaning migrants have no choice but to move, is **forced migration**. Today, the largest number of forced migrants are fleeing natural disasters, war, political persecution, or ethnic and cultural problems in their homelands.

Slave Trade

Throughout history, millions of people have migrated unwillingly. The largest forced migration in history is that of the African slave trade. From the 15th through the 19th centuries, about 12.5 million Africans were captured, enslaved, and forcibly moved from their homes in Africa to North America, the Caribbean, South America, and the Middle East.

Internally Displaced Persons and Refugees

Forced migration can result from political events and policies or environmental crises such as floods, earthquakes, or famines that threaten peoples' lives. Such migrants must usually flee quickly in order to stay alive and cannot bring many items with them. Most intend to return to their homes once the danger has passed. If these migrants move to another part of the same country, they are classified as **internally displaced persons (IDPs)**. If they cross international borders, they are **refugees**.

An example of forced migration is the Syrian Civil War, which began in 2011 and forced about half the population to flee their towns and villages. The result was the creation of more than 6 million internally displaced persons and more than 4 million refugees. Most of these refugees fled to neighboring or nearby countries such as Turkey and Greece. It is typical for refugees to be relocated to neighboring countries, which has resulted in a clustering of refugees.

Source: Wikimedia Commons

Refugees of the 2011 Syrian Civil War fled to neighboring countries. In the image, Syrian refugees jump from a boat off the coast of Greece to reach safety. Why would refugees risk their lives to take such a dangerous journey?

REFUGEES, 2016

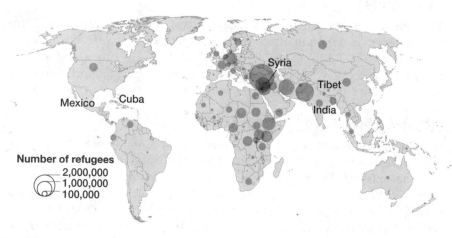

Source: unhcr.org

What are several geographic distribution patterns of refugees in 2016?

Some political refugees apply for **asylum** when they arrive in their country of destination. Asylum is protection granted by one country to an immigrant from another country who has a legitimate fear of harm or death if he or she returns. If granted, asylum-seekers receive protection and special status from the government of the receiving country.

EXAMPLES OF DISPLACED PERSONS AND REFUGEES		
Category	Internally Displaced Persons	Refugees
Political	Many Afghan people moved to safer areas during the war between the United States and the Taliban in the early 2000s.	Jews fled Nazi Germany in the 1930s and 1940s, hoping to find safety in other countries.
Environmental	Thousands of Louisianans fled to neighboring states after Hurricane Katrina in 2005.	Thousands of Haitians relocated to neighboring countries after earthquakes in 2010.

Voluntary Migration

Unlike forced migration, **voluntary migration** occurs when people choose to relocate. The term **internal migration** is used to describe movement that occurs within a country. One of the most important phenomena reshaping our world today is rural-to-urban migration. (See Topic 2.10.) Millions of people who leave villages and small towns every year for opportunities in cities and more densely settled areas. In less-developed countries, such as Kenya and India, migration is the most important factor driving urban growth.

Often internal migration, including rural-to-urban, operates in the process of step migration (see Topic 2.10), where people make a series of intermediate moves. Many people move to more urbanized areas gradually, step-by-step, toward their final destination. Internal migration does not have to be exclusively voluntary. Internally displaced persons are also an example of internal migrants. The country of Ethiopia is divided into ten regions. Civil strife in several of these regions has forced local populations to seek better circumstances in neighboring regions without leaving the country. These migrants are examples of both IDPs and internal migration.

Transnational migration is when people move from one country to another, or internationally rather than internally. For example, a person migrates from Mexico to the United States. When people migrate to and settle in a new country, they often decide to locate in a city or community where others from their home country, family members, friends, or those from thier culture group have previously settled. This process of **chain migration** explains many patterns of migration and helps migrants transition into the receiving country.

Guest workers are also transnational migrants who relocate to a new country to provide labor that isn't available locally. Most are unskilled jobs such as agricultural work or manual labor. Countries in the Persian Gulf are notable for having large percentages of the total populations made up of foreign migrants. In Bahrain, Kuwait, Qatar, and the United Arab Emirates, migrants constitute more than half the population. Most of these migrants work in some part of the petroleum industry. Many also work in the service industry to support tourism, which has boomed in the region.

Most migratory workers do not intend to make a permanent move. Often, they intend to return home or are given permission to stay for only a finite period of time. However, guest workers frequently decide to stay in the host country permanently, and thus become migrants.

The process of herders moving with their animals to different pastures during different seasons is **transhumance**. In mountainous regions, herders move their animals to higher areas in the summer and lower elevations during the winter. This ancient practice still takes place in Italy, Greece, and Turkey, where it is an example of internal migration. In parts of the Sahara in North Africa, herders move their animals across international boundaries as seasons change to find food for their animals.

PATTERNS OF HUMAN MIGRATION

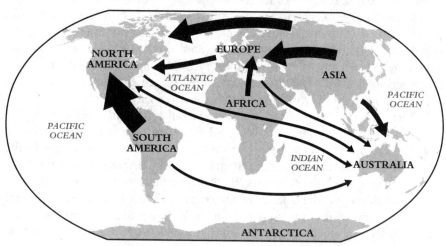

Which region is the source of most international migrants? Which regions are most common destinations for immigrants? What push and pull factors are driving this global pattern of movement?

Migration Trends

Since the mid-20th century, international migration flows have changed. Europe, once a region people were leaving, has become a destination for migrants from around the world. Many come from former European colonies in the Middle East, South Asia, and Africa. The immigrants are usually seeking jobs, unifying with family or escaping war and conflict. This pattern has continued into the 21st century.

COUNTRIES WITH THE HIGHEST NET EMIGRATION AND NET IMMIGRATION, 2010-2020			
Net Emigrants (in thousands)		**Net Immigrants** (in thousands)	
Syria	-752	United States	974
India	-501	Germany	466
Bangladesh	-415	Turkey	318
Venezuala	-329	Russia	271
China	-225	United Kingdom	260
Pakistan	-225	Canada	245
Nepal	-183	Saudi Arabia	240
Myanmar	-134	Italy	238
Zimbabwe	-121	Australia	178
Philippines	-117	South Africa	165

The United States has experienced several trends in immigration and forced migration from other countries. Between 1500 and 1700, European countries raced to colonize North America. By 1700, North America had been claimed primarily by England, France, and Spain. However, major sources of migrants (both voluntary and forced) entering the United States have shifted over time:

- 1600s to 1808: northern and western European colonizers and enslaved Africans
- 1808 to 1890: northern and western Europe immigrants
- 1890 to 1914: southern and eastern Europe immigrants
- 1945 to the present: Latin America and Asia immigrants

Since 1950, the United States and Canada together have received the highest number of immigrants, but recently countries in the Middle East and Europe have increased rates. Government policies have influenced migration trends and will be discussed in Topic 2.12.

REFLECT ON THE ESSENTIAL QUESTION

Essential Question: *What are the types of forced and voluntary migration?*

Examples of Forced Migrations	Examples of Voluntary Migrations

KEY TERMS

forced migration	asylum	chain migration
internally displaced persons (IDPs)	voluntary migration	guest workers
	internal migration	transhumance
refugee	transnational migration	

Effects of Migration

Essential Question: What are historical and contemporary geographic effects of migration?

The number and characteristics of migrants can have profound political, economic, and cultural effects on both the places they leave and the places they move to. Movements of people, though, are often controversial, particularly when people are moving from one country to another.

Migration Policies and Their Consequences

While countries have encouraged immigrants, others have restricted them, Political policies attempt to regulate migration both internal and international.

Policies Encouraging Immigration

Before the 1880s, the U.S. government placed few restrictions on immigration. The ratio of farmland to the number of people to work it was high, so immigrants were often welcomed. In addition, most Americans recalled their own immigrant heritage with pride.

Homestead Act One policy that attracted immigrants was the Homestead Act (1862), a program in which the U.S. government gave land to settlers willing to stay and farm it for five years. Most of the people who benefited from this program were White settlers, who eventually became the property owners. In recent years, the U.S. government offered visas to well-educated people with hopes they would remain in the country.

Current Immigration Policies Today, many governments regulate the flow of workers into their country. For example, the Persian Gulf countries of Bahrain, Kuwait, Oman, Qatar, Saudi Arabia, and the United Arab Emirates formed an organization called the Gulf Cooperation Council, and through it they set **guest-worker policies.** These regulate the number of workers who can temporarily enter each country to work in specific industries for a defined amount of time. Once the work visa has expired, workers are expected to either renew or return to their sending country. Some guest workers are highly skilled engineers, programmers, or teachers. Others find employment as domestic and home care workers and manual laborers in agriculture or manufacturing.

Most countries have **family reunification** policies that allow migrants to sponsor family members who migrate to the country. Other policies allow refugees to migrate quickly in emergencies and allow foreign college students an easy pathway to becoming permanent residents after they graduate.

Policies Discouraging Immigration

Countries may also pass laws to restrict immigration. They can make entering the country difficult by establishing educational standards for immigrants or by restricting the type of work immigrants can do. Countries can also simply set a quota to limit the number of people allowed to enter the country legally.

Some restrictions reflect **xenophobia**, a strong dislike of people of another culture. Other restrictions reflect economic concern that immigrants will take away jobs from citizens. For example, in the United States, xenophobia and economic fears combined to prompt Congress to pass the Chinese Exclusion Act that banned immigration from China between 1882 and 1943.

Countries sometimes restrict immigration primarily in an attempt to preserve their own cultural homogeneity, or cultural sameness. For example, the people of Japan form one of the most ethnically similar countries in the world. Japan maintains this homogeneity by strictly limiting immigration.

Economic and Cultural Effects of Migration

There are several effects, both positive and negative, that migration has on the countries of origin as well as on the destination countries. Effects include ones that are demographic, economic, cultural, and political.

Effects on Countries of Origin

One benefit on the countries of origin is relief from overcrowding. According to Zelinsky's migration transition model, when countries are heavily populated, opportunities are scarce. Migrants who leave reduce the competition for jobs and resources. The demographic transition model helps explain this effect. People from countries in Stage 2 and 3 seeking jobs, where population growth is high, will migrate to countries in Stage 4 or 5, where jobs are available.

Benefits of Migration Since immigrants generally move from poorer regions to wealthier ones, they often can afford to make **remittances**—money sent to their family and friends in the country they left. Remittances help the individuals receiving them, and account for nearly 40 percent of the income of some small countries, such as the Central Asian countries of Tajikistan and Kyrgyzstan.

Costs of Migration Migration can also have negative effects on the places people are leaving. When working-age people leave an area, it is left with a population skewed toward the elderly and children, creating a dependency ratio problem. This occurred during China's rural-to-urban migration, which was the largest internal migration in history. Additionally, when a family member leaves, a disruption can be caused in traditional roles and social structures of the family.

When migration out of a country is made up of many highly skilled people, it is called a **brain drain**. Today, students from around the world enter the United States or Great Britain to study medicine, engineering, or other fields and often decide to stay, rather than return to the land of their birth. This creates a brain drain on their countries of origin. A recent United Nations report found that about 11 percent of Africans with graduate or professional degrees were living in the United States, Europe, or other developed countries.

Effects on Receiving Countries

Countries receiving immigrants usually benefit greatly. Immigrants make important cultural contributions to their new countries, including new foods, new words and languages, diverse forms of entertainment, and a variety of religious traditions. **Ethnic enclaves**, or neighborhoods filled primarily with people of the same ethnic group, such as "Little Italy" or "Chinatown," add to the cultural richness of the countries in which they develop.

In addition, because most immigrants want to better their economic situations, they are highly motivated to get an education, work hard, and succeed. Many start businesses. Immigrants often start small, labor-intensive businesses such as restaurants, nail salons, and other service-oriented enterprises, but not all of these businesses stay small. Nearly 200 of the 500 largest businesses in the world were started by immigrants or their children.

Conflicts sometimes arise between immigrants and native-born citizens in receiving countries. The two groups might clash over religious beliefs, cultural practices, or access to jobs. Countries sometimes pass laws, and businesses follow practices that discriminate against immigrants.

Signs expressing prejudice against the Irish appeared in the United States in the early 1900s.

REFLECT ON THE ESSENTIAL QUESTION

Essential Question: *What are historical and contemporary geographic effects of migration?*

Policies Influencing Migration	Effects of Migration

KEY TERMS

guest-worker policies	xenophobia	brain drain
family reunification	remittances	ethnic enclaves

A Nation of Immigrants

The United States has experienced trends in immigration during different periods of the country's history. Prior to 1820, most people entering the United States came from Europe and Africa. However, there has been a shift in places of origin of migrants to the United States in the last two centuries.

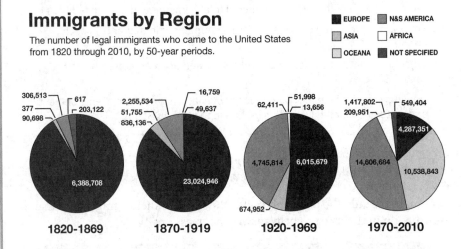

Immigrants by Region

The number of legal immigrants who came to the United States from 1820 through 2010, by 50-year periods.

EUROPE   N&S AMERICA
ASIA   AFRICA
OCEANA   NOT SPECIFIED

1820-1869 | **1870-1919** | **1920-1969** | **1970-2010**

Source: U.S. Dept. of Homeland Security

Migration Within the United States

Significant events in U.S. history caused people to move within the country. This was evident during and after both world wars.

The Great Migration from the South

Starting with the entry of the United States into World War I in 1917, millions of Americans migrated from the South to cities in the rest of the country. This movement is known as the Great Migration. The major pull factor was employment since factory jobs were plentiful in cities. With reduced immigration from Europe because of World War I, opportunities for laborers increased. In addition to the pull of jobs, African Americans left the south in large numbers to escape severe racial discrimination, violence, and poverty. The migration continued throughout the 20th century in response to the rapid industrialization in the North and on the Pacific coast.

The Migration to the South

A second large migration still shaping the modern United States is from the Northeast and Midwest to the South and Southwest. After World War II, government policies—the construction of a fast-moving national highway system and tax subsidies for buying new homes—made moving anywhere easier. But the development of air conditioning made life in hot climates more pleasant, and the expansion of defense industry jobs in the South and Southwest pulled many people to the band of states from southern California to Florida. These migrants felt pushed out of the North and Northwest by harsh winters and the decline in job opportunities because of factory automation. In addition, stable benefits for retirees and lower costs of living in the Sun Belt encouraged migration causing retirement communities to flourish. Between 1950 and 2020, Arizona's population grew from 750,000 to over 7,000,000.

1. Which period had the largest number of total immigrants to the United States?

2. From which world region were the largest number of immigrants in each period?

3. What effect have crises, such as world wars, had on migration within the United States?

4. How have each of the following types of pull factors—economic, environmental, and cultural—affected internal migration in the United States?

THINK AS A GEOGRAPHER: *INFLUENCES ON MIGRATION*

Geographers study the push and pull factors that influence migration. Use the information in the chart to help answer the questions.

INFLUENCES ON MEXICAN MIGRATION TO THE UNITED STATES	
Year or Period	**Event or Trend**
1970 to 2010	The TFR for women in Mexico falls from 7 to 2.
1979 to 1982	Worldwide oil demand creates a boom in Mexico.
1982	An economic crisis hits Mexico.
2000	The election of a new leader in Mexico creates hope.
2000 to 2010	The United States increases the number of agricultural work visas from 29,000 to 52,000.
2006 to 2020	A new president begins a powerful new resistance against drug lords and gangs in Mexico that results in violence, death, and widespread fear.
2016 to 2020	The United States increased deportation of undocumented workers and reduced the number of work visas for legal immigrants.

1. Identify one statement from the chart that was a push factor for Mexicans to migrate. Identify one that reduced the push.

2. Identify and explain how one statement from above acted as a pull factor for Mexican immigrants to the United States.

3. Choose one of the statements above and explain how it reflects the global influence on Mexico.

CHAPTER 5 REVIEW:
Migration

Topics 2.10–2.12

MULTIPLE-CHOICE QUESTIONS

Question 1 refers to the diagram below.

1. Which best summarizes the migration process represented by the diagram?

   (A) With European colonization and migration, positive aspects of European culture spread across the globe in spite of obstacles.

   (B) In the process known as step migration, migrants move from rural to urban areas through a series of smaller moves, or steps.

   (C) Each migration produces a counter migration of people returning to their country of origin.

   (D) The gravity model predicts that most migrants will move to the closest metropolitan area in search of economic opportunities.

   (E) Migrants leave their homelands because of push factors and move to places with pull factors, but they often face barriers.

2. Which statement best summarizes Zelinsky's model of migration in relation to the demographic transition model (DTM)?

   (A) High unemployment in countries in Stages 4 and 5 pushes migrants to Stage 2 and 3 countries in search of economic opportunity.

   (B) Overcrowding in countries in Stages 2 and 3 pushes migrants to Stage 4 and 5 countries in search of economic opportunity.

   (C) Overcrowding in countries in Stages 4 and 5 pushes migrants to Stage 2 and 3 countries in search of economic opportunity.

   (D) A gender imbalance in countries in Stages 4 and 5 pushes migrants to Stage 2 and 3 countries to find mates and start families.

   (E) Overcrowding in countries in Stages 4 and 5 pushes migrants to Stage 2 countries in a counter migration as large as the original migration.

3. According to the gravity model of migration, in which state and city of the United States would Mexican migrants be most likely to live?

(A) Florida and Philadelphia

(B) Texas and Los Angeles

(C) North Carolina and Chicago

(D) Georgia and Memphis

(E) Alabama and Washington, DC

4. The most common impact of emigration on the country of origin is

(A) an increase in unemployment rates

(B) a decline in the crowded conditions of urban areas

(C) a loss of farmers resulting in smaller food supply

(D) a loss of working age population to another country

(E) an increase in the number of abandoned and homeless children

Question 5 refers to the diagram below.

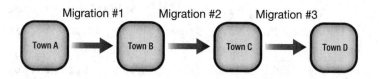

5. A person living in Town A moves three times, as shown in the diagram, and settles in Town D. This is an example of

(A) chain migration

(B) step migration

(C) distance decay

(D) intervening obstacle

(E) intervening opportunity

6. Which best illustrates counter migration?

(A) Chinese farmers migrating from a village to a small city and then to Beijing

(B) Ethiopians migrating to Turkey and then to Germany

(C) Italians migrating to France at the same time some French are migrating to Italy

(D) Nigerians migrating to Ghana and then migrating back to Nigeria

(E) Enslaved Africans being taken by force to Brazil and then voluntarily migrating to Argentina

7. Which pair of phrases best describes asylum-seekers?

(A) Voluntary migration, internal migrants

(B) Voluntary migration, transnational migrants

(C) Forced migration, transnational migrants

(D) Forced migration, internal migrants

(E) Forced migration, rural-to-urban migrants

FREE-RESPONSE QUESTION

1. Use the distance decay model of migration and the map of global migration flows to answer the questions below.

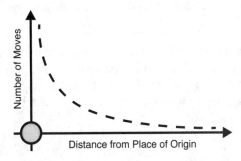

LARGE-SCALE MIGRATIONS

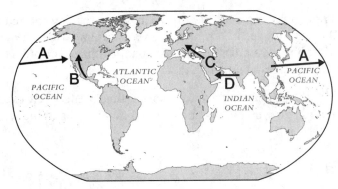

(A) Define the concept of distance decay shown in the graph.

(B) Using both visuals, explain how a specific migration trend from the map illustrates the concept of distance decay.

(C) Explain the difference between push and pull factors.

(D) Using the map, identify ONE economic pull factor.

(E) Using the map, identify ONE political push factor.

(F) Describe ONE positive result for countries receiving migrants.

(G) Describe ONE positive result for countries sending migrants.

UNIT 2 REVIEW:
Connecting Course Skills and Content

APPLYING GEOGRAPHIC SKILLS

Applying geographic skills is critical for success on the AP® Exam. For each skill listed, write a one-paragraph response that illustrates your understanding of that course skill. Support your response with specific examples and evidence. Refer to the Unit 1 introduction (pages 3–7) for tips on how to apply geographic skills.

1B Explain the importance of either the demographic transition model or Malthusian theory as it relates to explaining population growth or decline.

2B Explain how the spatial interaction measured by migration is likely impacted if a less-developed region or country is experiencing rapid population growth while a neighboring highly developed economic region is experiencing an aging and zero population growth demographic scenario.

3F Use the map in Topic 2.4 that shows and life expectancy for countries of the world. Explain possible limitations of the data shown on the map.

4D Using the three visual images from Changing the Perception of Girls in Chapter 4 (page 102) compare patterns of similarities in the images and describe the similar conclusion that the images' creators likely want the viewers to understand.

5D Explain the degree to which Malthusian theory effectively explains population growth and decline across different geographic scales.

WRITE AS A GEOGRAPHER: *PLAN THE ANSWER*

Before writing an answer to a free-response question, plan what claims you want to make and can support. Think about what you want to say, the order you want to say it in, and how your points fit together. Students often begin to plan by making notes about what they know: concepts, facts, and examples. And if the question includes an exhibit, they add information from the map, diagram, chart, or other type of source.

Next, students plan how to transform this list of content into a coherent answer. A good answer is a narrative—not simply a list of points. It states a clear response to the question rather than simply stating information that might be related to the question.

The response does not need to begin with an introductory paragraph, and answers are not graded on grammar or style. And no extra points are given for extraneous information. One challenge many students face is to keep their answer focused. They tend to wander off, inserting interesting facts they know that are not relevant to the question.

For each part of the following question, plan a possible answer. Describe the information you would use and how you would organize it.

1. People migrate as a result of push and pull factors, and their movement affects both the places they leave and the places they arrive.

   (A) Describe TWO pull factors that might cause someone to migrate to the United States.

   (B) Describe TWO push factors that might cause someone to migrate away from the United States.

   (C) Give a detailed account of THREE consequences of migration to or from the United States.

UNIT 3

Cultural Patterns and Processes

Chapter 6 *Cultural Landscapes, Patterns, and Diffusion*
Chapter 7 *Historical and Contemporary Processes of Diffusion*

Unit Overview

While some human attributes, such as hair color, are heavily influenced by biological inheritance, most are not. In general, how people think and act is shaped, formally and informally, by what they learn from other people. All of the practices, attitudes, and behaviors that people learn from others are part of their culture.

Behaviors People Share

Areas where many people share an element of culture—such as speaking a particular language—form **cultural regions**. Geographers use maps, from small to large scale—to show the boundaries of these regions.

When people of different cultures meet, they sometimes have conflicts, but they always adjust to each other. For example, if they speak different languages, one group might adopt the other's language over time. Or people might blend the two languages to create a new one (creolized language). Improvements in transportation and communication have increased the interaction of cultures throughout history. Culture spreads (diffusion) as people move from one place to another and as people interact and learn from each other. In 1500, the region where most people spoke English was a small area on the northwest corner of Europe. Today, English is the most widely spoken language around the world.

Variations in Culture

Culture changes over time and so do the spatial patterns and processes. Geographers use maps to show regions and spatial patterns, such as where specific languages are spoken. Additionally, they utilize various types of charts and diagrams to show relationships and changes among the elements of culture. For example, a tree diagram can show how several languages, including French and Spanish, are branches that diverge from a common ancestor, Latin.

ENDURING UNDERSTANDINGS

PSO-3: Cultural practices vary across geographical locations because of physical geography and available resources.

IMP-3: The interaction of people contributes to the spread of cultural practices.

SPS-3: Cultural ideas, practices, and innovations change or disappear over time.

Source: *AP® Human Geography Course and Exam Description.* Effective Fall 2020. (College Board).

CHAPTER 6

Cultural Landscapes, Patterns, and Diffusion
Topics 3.1–3.4

Topic 3.1 Introduction to Culture

Learning Objective: Define the characteristics, attitudes, and traits that influence geographers when they study culture. (PSO-3.A)

Topic 3.2 Cultural Landscapes

Learning Objectives: Describe the characteristics of cultural landscapes. (PSO-3.B)

Explain how landscape features and land and resource use reflect cultural beliefs and identities. (PSO-3.C)

Topic 3.3 Cultural Patterns

Learning Objective: Explain patterns and landscapers of language, religion, ethnicity, and gender. (PSO-3.D)

Topic 3.4 Types of Diffusion

Learning Objective: Define the types of diffusion. (IMP-3.A)

The Buffalo was part of us, his flesh and blood being absorbed by us until it became our own flesh and blood. Our clothing, our tipis, everything we needed for life came from the buffalo's body. It was hard to say where the animals ended and the human began.

— John (Fire) Lame Deer, *Lame Deer, Seeker of Visions*, 1972

Source: Getty Images

Diffusion and migration influence the cultural landscape of Chinatown in San Francisco. (See Topic 3.2 for characteristics of the cultural landscape.)

Introduction to Culture

Essential Question: What are the characteristics, attitudes, and traits that influence geographers when they study culture?

To the Lakota, and other indigenous people on North America's Great Plains, the bison was an essential part of their culture (expressed in the quote on the previous page). The bison provided meat for nutrition, a hide for clothing and shelter, bones for tools, and fat for soap. The bison was also central to their religious beliefs. So, when European settlers hunted the bison nearly to extinction, Lakota culture suffered.

Culture is central to a society and the identity of its people, as well as its continued existence. Therefore, geographers study culture as a way to understand similarities and differences among societies across the world, and in some cases, to help preserve these societies.

Analyzing Culture

All of a group's learned behaviors, actions, beliefs, and objects are a part of **culture**. It is a *visible* force seen in a group's actions, possessions, and influence on the landscape. For example, in a large city you can see people working in offices, factories, and stores, and living in high-rise apartments or suburban homes. You might observe them attending movies, concerts, or sporting events.

Culture is also an *invisible* force guiding people through shared belief systems, customs, and traditions. Culture is learned, in that it develops through experiences, and not merely transmitted through genetics. For example, many people in the United States have developed a strong sense of competitiveness in school and business, and believe that hard work is a key to success. These types of elements, visible and invisible, are **cultural traits**. A series of interrelated traits make up a **cultural complex**, such as the process of steps and acceptable behaviors related to greeting a person in different cultures. A single cultural artifact, such as an automobile, may represent many different values, beliefs, behaviors and traditions and be representative of a cultural complex.

Since culture is learned there are many ways that one generation passes its culture to the next. Children and adults learn traits three ways:

- imitation, as when learning a language by repeating sounds or behaviors from a person or television
- informal instruction, as when a parent reminds a child to say "please"
- formal instruction, as when students learn history in school

CULTURAL COMPLEX OF THE AUTOMOBILE

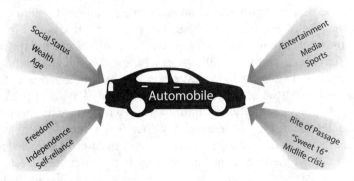

The automobile provides much more than just transportation, as it reflects many values that are central to American culture.

Origins of Culture

The area in which a unique culture or a specific trait develops is a **culture hearth**. Classical Greece was a culture hearth for democracy more than 2,000 years ago. New York City was a culture hearth for rap music in the 1970s. Geographers study how cultures develop in hearths and **diffuse**—or spread—to other places.

Geographers also study **taboos**, behaviors heavily discouraged by a culture. For example, many cultures have taboos against eating certain foods, such as pork or insects. What is considered taboo changes over time. In the United States, marriages between Protestants and Catholics were once taboo, but they are not widely opposed now.

Traditional, Folk, and Indigenous Cultures

With the beginning of the Industrial Revolution in the late 18th century, modern transportation and communication connected people as never before and led to extensive cultural mixing, especially as cities have grown. The world prior to this time was very different; however, remnants of the past are still evident in our modern cultures. Traditional, folk, and indigenous cultures share some important characteristics and are often grouped together, but they do have some subtle differences.

Traditional Culture Recently, the meanings of traditional, folk, and indigenous culture have begun to merge, causing geographers to debate when each should be used. Increasingly, the term **traditional culture** is used to encompass all three cultural designations. All three types share the function of passing down long-held beliefs, values, and practices and are generally resistant to rapid changes in their culture.

Folk Culture The beliefs and practices of small, homogenous groups of people, often living in rural areas that are relatively isolated and slow to change, are known as **folk cultures**. Like all cultures, they demonstrate the diverse ways that people have adapted to a physical environment. For example, people around the world learned to make shelters out of available resources, whether it was snow or mud bricks or wood. However, people used similar resources such as wood differently. In Scandinavia, people used trees to build cabins. In the American Midwest, people processed trees into boards, built a frame, and attached the boards to it. Many traits of folk culture continue today. Corn was first grown in Mexico around 10,000 years ago, and it is still grown there today.

While many elements of folk culture exist side by side with modern culture, there are people whose societies have changed little, if at all, from long ago. These people practice traditional cultures, those which have not been affected by modern technology or influences. They often live in remote regions, such as some small tribes in the Amazon rainforest, and have scant knowledge of the outside world. As the lines continue blurring between cultural designations, the Amish of Pennsylvania are often referenced as both folk and traditional culture.

Indigenous Culture When members of an ethnic group reside in their ancestral lands, and typically possess unique cultural traits, such as speaking their own exclusive language, they are considered an **indigenous culture**. Some indigenous peoples have been displaced from their native lands, but still practice their indigenous culture. Native Americans in the United States, such as the Navajo, have kept indigenous cultural practices. First Nations of Canada, such as the Inuit, have also retained their indigenous culture.

Globalization and Popular Culture

As a result of the Industrial Revolution, improvements in transportation and communication have shortened the time required for movement, trade, or other forms of interaction between two places. This development, known as *space-time compression* (see Topics 1.4 and 3.6), has accelerated culture change around the world. In 1817, a freight shipment from Cincinnati needed 52 days to reach New York City. By 1850, because of canals and railroads, it took half that long. And by 1852, it took only 7 days. Today, an airplane flight takes only a few hours, and digital information takes seconds or less.

Similar change has occurred on the global scale. People travel freely across the world in a matter of hours, and communication has advanced to a point where people share information instantaneously across the globe. The increased global interaction has had a profound impact on cultures, from spreading English across the world to instant sharing of news, events and music.

Globalization specifically refers to the increased integration of the world economy since the 1970s. The process of intensified interaction among peoples, governments, and companies of different countries around the globe has had profound impacts on culture.

The culture of the United States is intertwined with globalization. Through the influence of its corporations, Hollywood movies, and government, the United States exerts widespread influence in other countries. But other countries also shape American culture. For example, in 2019, the National Basketball Association included players from 38 countries or territories.

When cultural traits—such as clothing, music, movies, and types of businesses—spread quickly over a large area and are adopted by various groups, they become part of **popular culture**. Elements of popular culture often begin in urban areas and diffuse quickly through globalization processes such as the media and Internet.

These elements can quickly be adopted worldwide, making them part of **global culture**. People around the world follow European soccer, Indian Bollywood movies, and Japanese animation known as *anime*. With people in many nations wearing similar clothes, listening to similar music, and eating similar food, popular cultural traits often promote uniformity in beliefs, values, and the cultural landscape across many places The **cultural landscape**, also known as the built environment (see Topic 3.2), is the modification of the environment by a group and is a visible reflection of that group's cultural beliefs and values.

Traditional Culture to Popular Culture

Popular culture emphasizes trying what is new rather than preserving what is traditional. Many people, especially older generations or those who follow a folk culture, openly resist the adoption of popular cultural traits. They do this by preserving traditional languages, religions, values, and foods. While older generations often resist the adoption of popular culture, they seldom are successful in keeping their traditional cultures from changing, especially among the young people of their society.

One clash between popular and traditional culture is occurring in Brazil. As the population expands to the interior of the rain forest, many indigenous cultures, like the Yanamamo tribe, have more contact with outside groups. Remaining isolated by the forest is becoming increasingly difficult as many young people from the indigenous cultures become exposed to popular culture and begin to integrate into the larger Brazilian society. As the young people leave their communities, they are more likely to accept popular culture at the expense of their indigenous cultural heritage, which threatens the very existence of their folk culture.

Traditional culture typically exhibits *horizontal diversity*, meaning each traditional culture has its own customs and language that makes it distinct from other culture groups. Yet, people people within each group are usually homogeneous, or very similar to each other.

By contrast, popular culture typically exhibits *vertical diversity*, meaning that modern urban societies are usually heterogeneous, or exhibiting differences, within the society and usually contain numerous multiethnic neighborhoods. However, on a global scale popular cultures are relatively similar with the same type of malls, shops, fast food, and clothing. Urban global culture centers are not identical, yet, global cities often do not have as much horizontal diversity across space as folk cultures.

COMPARING TRADITIONAL AND POPULAR CULTURE		
Trait	**Traditional Culture**	**Popular or Global Culture**
Society	• Rural and isolated location • Homogeneous and indigenous population • Most people speak an indigenous or ethnic local language • Horizontal diversity	• Urban and connected location • Diverse and multiethnic population • Many people speak a global language such as English or Arabic • Vertical diversity
Social Structure	• Emphasis on community and conformity • Families live close to each other • Well-defined gender roles	• Emphasis on individualism and making choices • Dispersed families • Weakly defined gender roles
Diffusion	• Relatively slow and limited • Primarily through relocation • Oral traditions and stories	• Relatively rapid and extensive • Often hierarchical • Social media and mass media
Buildings and Housing	• Materials produced locally, such as stone or grass • Built by community or owner • Similar style for community • Different between cultures • Traditional architecture	• Materials produced in distant factories, such as steel or glass • Built by a business • Variety of architectural styles • Similar between cities • Postmodern / contemporary architecture
Food	• Locally produced • Choices limited by tradition • Prepared by the family or community	• Often imported • Wide range of choice • Purchased in restaurants
Spatial Focus	• Local and regional	• National and global

Artifacts, Mentifacts, and Sociofacts

Whether a cultural attribute is considered traditional, folk, indigenous, or popular in nature, it is valuable to differentiate between elements of culture that can be seen and those that can not. There are **artifacts** that comprise the **material culture**, which consists of tangible things, or those that can be experienced by the senses. Art, clothing, food, music, sports, and housing types are all tangible elements of culture. Another element of the study of artifacts is understanding the techniques to use or build a specific artifact. Artifacts can be unique to a particular culture, or can be shared. For example, people of all cultures need to communicate through language, yet there are many groups that possess languages unique to their culture. The ability to read, write and understand the English language is an artifact of importance for much of popular global culture.

Mentifacts comprise a group's **nonmaterial culture** and consist of intangible concepts, or those not having a physical presence. Beliefs, values, practices, and aesthetics (pleasing in appearance) determine what a cultural group views as acceptable and desirable. Mentifacts can also be unique or shared. People of many cultures possess an belief in one or many deities, and often the deities are unique to that culture. The belief in a god is a mentifact—the religious building or symbols are artifacts.

Cultural groups also possess **sociofacts**, which are the ways people organize their society and relate to one another. Taken altogether, people tend to see the whole of their culture as greater than the sum of its individual parts. Sociofacts are embodied through families, governments, sports teams, religious organizations, education systems, and other social constructs. As with artifacts and mentifacts, sociofacts may also be unique or similar to other societies. Families are the foundations of most societies, yet what constitutes the structure of a family may vary widely between cultural groups. For example, Western cultures tend to view the nuclear family, consisting of the parents and their children as the basic family unit. By contrast, in many Western African cultures the norm is the extended family, consisting of several generations and other family members such as cousins living under one roof.

REFLECT ON THE ESSENTIAL QUESTION

Essential Question: *What characteristics, attitudes, and traits influence geographers when they study culture?*

Influences on Geographers	Explanation of Influences on Geographers

KEY TERMS

culture	globalization
cultural traits	popular culture
cultural complex	global culture
culture hearths	cultural landscape
diffuse	artifacts
taboos	material culture
traditional culture	mentifacts
folk culture	nonmaterial culture
indigenous culture	sociofacts

Cultural Landscapes

Essential Question: What are the characteristics of cultural landscapes and how do those characteristics, land use, and resource use reflect cultural beliefs and identities?

A cross the world, the physical landscape changes with almost immeasurable variability. In the United States, the beaches of Florida, mountains of Colorado, and plains of Oklahoma are only a few of the many landscapes throughout the country. However, condos on the shores in Florida, ski lifts on the slopes in Colorado, and wheat fields in Oklahoma illustrate the numerous ways humans adjust and adapt to the environment.

While the modern cultural landscape is extremely diverse, it may also exhibit striking similarities from location to location. In the 1986 film *Ferris Bueller's Day Off*, the exploits of three teenagers skipping school took place in Chicago, Illinois, and its surrounding suburbs. However, a great deal of the filming took place in California—the suburbs of Long Beach and South Pasadena. Although separated by more than 2,000 miles, the suburbs in Illinois often look remarkably similar to those in California because of comparable incomes, a common American culture, similar architecture, related socioeconomic status, and other related factors. This phenomenon is known as **placelessness**, in which many modern cultural landscapes exhibit a great deal of homogeneity.

Characteristics of Cultural Landscapes

The boundaries of a region reflect the human imprint on the environment. This is called the **cultural landscape**—the visible reflection of a culture—or the built environment. This concept encompasses any human alteration to the landscape, whether as obvious as a skyscraper or as subtle as a cleared field.

EXAMPLES OF CULTURAL LANDSCAPES		
Element	**Area**	**Significance**
Protected Wilderness Area	United States	Land set aside from development reflects the desire to preserve unique environments.
Signage	Quebec	Bilingual signs in French and English reflect the desire of French Canadians to retain their heritage.
Schools	Pakistan	Gender-segregated schools reflect attitudes toward male and female roles.
Office Buildings	Shanghai	Massive skyscrapers reflect economic power and a desire to have a prestigious location.

An observant traveler can notice changes in the cultural landscape while driving along a highway. For example, travelers on Interstate 25 going from Wyoming to New Mexico see a definite change, both in toponyms, or place names, and in the built environment. Names change from Anglo words to Spanish names. Wooden buildings are replaced by adobe buildings. Architectural styles shift from looking like those in England to looking like structures in Spain.

CULTURAL CHANGE ALONG INTERSTATE 25

Buildings in Santa Fe, New Mexico, reflect a blend of the styles of Native American pueblos and Spanish missions. What do the map and photo tell you about the groups of people who lived in the I-25 region?

The Built Landscape

The word environment is often used in reference to nature. Plants, the air, water, and animals are all part of the natural environment. Human geographers often refer to the **built environment**, by which they mean the physical artifacts that humans have created and that form part of the landscape. Buildings, roads, signs, and fences are examples of the built environment.

The architectural style of buildings varies from place to place. Think of typical homes and buildings in China, and then think of homes and buildings in Germany. These differences occur because people with different cultures who live in different physical landscapes construct the buildings, roads, and other elements to create a unique built environment. Anything built by humans is part of the cultural landscape.

Traditional vs. Postmodern Architecture

Traditional architecture style reflects a local culture's history, beliefs, values, and community adaptations to the environment, and typically utilizes locally available materials. Examples would include Spanish adobe (mud) homes common in the southwestern United States or the colonial homes that were wood-constructed with a steep-pitched roof from New England. Many traditional architectural styles have now been adopted by popular culture and are mass produced within many communities, but they are still considered traditional architecture. Traditional architecture is usually built with the utility to people and community as a central focus.

Postmodern architecture developed after the 1960s. It is a movement away from boxy, mostly concrete or brick structures toward high rise structures made from large amounts of steel and glass siding. Most of the skyscapers in the United States today are considered postmodern architectural style. Postmodernism has evolved to also include more use of curves, bright colors, and large glass atriums that bring light into spaces.

During the 21st century, a new style called **contemporary architecture** has emerged as an extension of postmodern architecture. This style uses multiple advances to create buildings that rotate, curve, and stretch the limits of size and height. Postmodernism and contemporary downtown skylines reflect businesses and corporations, and the towering height often is considered a reflection of a city's wealth and power. Both styles of architecture are known for the drama and large-scale beauty of the structures but often are criticized for a lack of an approachable human scale interaction. Both styles can create a steel and glass canyon feel when viewing from the street level. Postmodern and contemporary architecture are associated with globalized popular culture.

Source: Wikimedia Commons

Postmodern architecture of the 1983 Bank of America Center in Houston, Texas, (left) and contemporary architecture of the 2015 Shanghai Tower in China (right).

Ethnic Enclaves

Ethnicity refers to membership within a group of people who have common experiences and share similar characteristics such as ancestry, language, customs, and history.

The neighborhood or subregional scale of the cultural landscape might include **ethnic enclaves**—clusters of people of the same culture—that are often surrounded by people of the dominant culture in the region. Ethnic enclaves sometimes reflect the desire of people to remain apart from the larger society. Other times, they reflect a dominant culture's desire to segregate a minority culture. Inside these enclaves are often stores and religious institutions that are supported by the ethnic group, signs in their traditional language, and architecture that reflects the group's place of origin. These enclaves can provide a buffer against discrimination by the dominant culture or a network of people to help with employment and cultural integration. Examples would include "Chinatown" in San Francisco or "Little Mogadishu," a Somali enclave in Minneapolis.

Geography of Gender

The geography of gender has become an increasingly important topic for geographers in recent decades. In folk cultures, people often have clearly defined gender-specific roles. Women usually handle the domestic responsibilities, such as farming, educating children, and caring for family members. Men often work outside the house earning money and serving as leaders in religion and politics.

In popular culture, traditional gender-specific roles are challenged. Women in popular culture tend to have more access to education which leads to more opportunities to work outside of the home. In turn, this gives women more economic power and opportunities to serve as leaders.

The concept of gendered spaces or gendered landscapes clarifies the importance of cultural values on the distribution of power in societies. Throughout history and in many cultures, certain behaviors have been acceptable for only one gender, and often only in certain spaces. Men have commonly operated more freely than women in public spaces, while certain private spaces have been reserved for women. These differences might appear in the etiquette of visiting someone's home. The host might welcome men in the public areas on the main level but feel comfortable only with women visiting the more private rooms on the upper level.

In Iran and India, some restaurants and parks are designated "men only" or "women only". Many women view these "women only" areas as a safe place to gather and discuss issues, while others view them as discriminatory.

Cultural Regions

Cultural regions are usually determined based on characteristics such as religion, language, and ethnicity. Unless regions are defined by clear features, such as a mountain range, a transition zone often exists. In these zones, two cultures mix and people exhibit traits of both. Cultural regions do not always follow political borders. The border between the United States and Mexico clearly illustrates this pattern. People who live in border communities such as El Paso, Texas, are often fluent in both Spanish and English, and have cultural ties to both Mexico and the United States.

Realms

Geographers also identify larger areas, **culture realms**, that include several regions. Cultures within a cultural realm have a few traits that they all share, such as language families, religious traditions, food preferences, architecture, or a shared history. Some geographers view realms simply as very large regions.

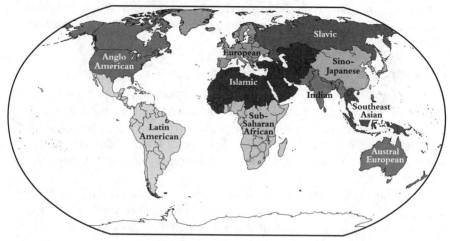

TEN MAJOR CULTURE REALMS

Each realm is made up of several subregions that may have great diversity of culture, languages, religions, and traditions. Choose a culture realm from the map and describe the similarities and differences within that realm.

Religion and the Landscape

Like all human activities, religion influences the organization and use of space. This appears in both how people think about natural features and what people build.

Sacred Space

Many specific places and natural features have religious significance and are known as **sacred places** or sites. Some sites are sacred spaces where deities dwell. For example, followers of Shinto view certain mountains and rocks as the homes of spirits. Other sacred sites are important for what occurred there. Mt. Sinai is honored by Jews, Christians, and Muslims because they believe it is where God handed the Ten Commandments to Moses. Some entire cities have special religious meanings, such as Jerusalem (Israel), Mecca (Saudi Arabia), and Lhasa (Tibet).

Religious Cultural Landscapes

Sacred physical features are important, but rare. More commonly, people express their beliefs through the cultural landscapes they create:

- Memorial spaces to the dead, such as cemeteries, are traditionally located close to worship spaces.

- Restaurants and food markets often cater to particular religious groups by offering religiously approved food.

- Signs often are written in the language and sometimes the alphabet that reflects the ethnic heritage of the group.

The most obvious example of the cultural landscape shaped by religion is in architecture. Each major faith provides examples of this.

Christianity Christian churches often feature a tall steeple topped with a cross, as Christians believe Jesus was resurrected after dying on a cross. Churches also demonstrate how the origin of the architectural style was often influenced by the environment. The hearths of that faith are more likely to resemble the original architecture. Christian churches closer to the eastern Mediterranean tend to have dome-shaped roofs that reflect the traditional style of architecture popular with the Romans, while churches in northern Europe have steep-pitched roofs designed for snow to slide off in the winter. This was an environmental adaptation, as the build-up of snow on a flat roof can cause it to cave in. Cultural influences similarly shape the preferred and available materials to build such structures.

One similarity among Christians is in treatment of the deceased. In most parts of the world, Christians bury the dead in cemeteries, although types of cemeteries may vary greatly. Most burials are underground, but in New Orleans, where the water table is high, cemeteries are above ground.

The Protestant Christian church on the left, in Norway, shows the style of churches farther from the hearth. The Orthodox Christian church on the right, in Greece, illustrates the dome-shaped roofs of the eastern Mediterranean region.

Hinduism Hindu temples often have elaborately carved exteriors with multiple manifestations of deities or significant characters. Thousands of shrines and temples dot the landscape in India since devout Hindus believe the construction of these religious structures will reflect well on them. Sacred sites, such as the Ganges River, provide pilgrims a place to bathe for the purpose of purification. Many Hindu shrines and temples are located near rivers and streams for this very purpose.

Source: Wikimedia Commons

Meenakshi Temple on Tamil Nadu, India, represents a common design for Hindu architecture. A Hindu woman prays in the River Ganges near the holy city of Varanasi.

Hindus practice cremation, the ritual burning of a dead body, as an act of purification as well. However, in some regions, a shortage of wood has made cremation very expensive. The ashes of the deceased are often spread in the Ganges River.

Source: Wikimedia Commons

A Buddha statue sits in front of a stupa-style temple in Java, Indonesia. Stupas are often plaster, stone, white, or gold.

Buddhism The practice of Buddhism differs widely from place to place and from ethnic group to ethnic group. However, most Buddhists emphasize meditating and living in harmony with nature. These features of Buddhism are represented in stupas, structures to store important relics and memorialize important events and beliefs. Stupas were often built to symbolize the five aspects of nature—earth, water, fire, air, and space. Pagodas are also a common architectural style that developed from stupas, but unlike stupas, they are used as temples and people can enter into larger pagodas. Believers often meditate near both sacred spaces.

Among Buddhists, the decision to cremate or to bury the dead is a personal choice and consequently the imprint on the cultural landscape differs. Burial sites for Buddhists are often marked with memorials of individuals or families and often serve as a sacred quiet space to meditate.

Source: Getty Images

A Jewish synagogue in Buenos Aires, Argentina

Judaism Jews worship in synagogues or temples. Once concentrated in the Middle East, Jews spread throughout the world because of exile or persecution, or through voluntary migration. This scattering is known as *the Diaspora*. A **diaspora** occurs when one group of people is dispersed to various locations. Synagogues vary in size based on the number of Jews in an area. Burial of the dead customarily occurs before sundown on the day following the death.

The Putra Mosque in Putrajaya, Indonesia

Islam In places where Islam is widely practiced, the mosque is the most prominent structure on the landscape and is usually located in the center of town. Mosques have domes surrounded by a few minarets (Arabic for *beacon*) from which daily prayer is called. Burial of the dead is to be done as soon as possible, and burials are in cemeteries.

Shinto Shinto, whose cultural hearth is Japan, emphasizes honoring one's ancestors and the relationship between people and nature. One common landscape feature of Shinto shrines is an impressive gateway, or torii, to mark the transition from the outside world to a sacred space.

A torii is a traditional gate usually found in front of or within a Shinto shrine.

How Religion and Ethnicity Shape Space

The first group to establish cultural and religious customs in a space is known as the **charter group**. Native Americans were the charter group in the Americas. Their influence appears in many places, such as in place names from Mt. Denali in Alaska to Miami, Florida. Often, the cultural landscape of charter groups shows their heritage. For example, English settlements in colonial America resembled the settlements they migrated away from in England, and names such as Plymouth and Jamestown reflect this heritage. The layout of these towns would often have a centrally located church, which also served as a meeting hall for the community.

Ethnic Landscape

Ethnic groups that arrive after the charter group may choose to bypass the already established cultural location and create a distinctive space with their own customs. In urban areas, these enclaves become ethnic neighborhoods.

Rural Areas In rural areas, ethnic concentrations form **ethnic islands**. Their cultural imprints revolve around housing types and agricultural dwellings that reflect their heritage. Because ethnic islands are in rural areas and have less interaction with other groups than groups in cities, they maintain a strong and long-lasting sense of cohesion. Today, Germanic ethnic islands of people who fled religious persecution in the past continue to exist in the United States (the Pennsylvania Dutch and the Amish), Canada (Mennonites in Alberta), and in scattered locations in the Balkan region of southeastern Europe.

Urban Ethnic Neighborhoods Ethnic neighborhoods in urban settings are often occupied by migrants who settle in a charter group's former space. The charter group has already shaped much of the landscape, but new arrivals create their own influence as well. Dozens of cities around the world—Melbourne, Australia; Gachsaren, Iran; Liverpool, England; San Francisco—have neighborhoods known as "Chinatown." The name tends to live on even if the original occupants have moved out or assimilated, and the neighborhood primarily caters to tourists.

Frequently, members of a particular ethnic group cluster in particular regions. Group members might choose to live close together for cultural reasons. This is often true of immigrants or some religious groups. Some ethnic clusters have specific needs requiring special funding, such as funds to help preserve distinctive architecture or to provide English language training.

Discrimination may limit the housing choices for members of a particular group. The most notable example of this were the practices in many cities that limited the neighborhoods where African Americans could live in the United States. As the maps below show, the distribution of African Americans varies based on scale. At the national scale, African Americans are concentrated in the southeast United States. At the state scale, they are often clustered in large cities. And at the city scale, African Americans are often clustered in particular neighborhoods.

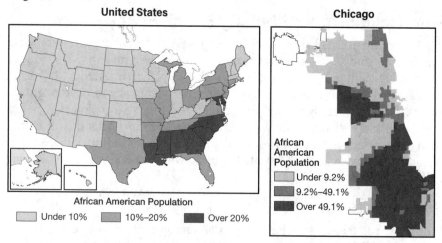

The map shows the African American population in the United States and Chicago. What does changing scales of analysis reveal about the distributions of African Americans in the United States?

New Cultural Influences

Ethnic groups move in and out of neighborhoods and create new cultural imprints on the landscape in a process geographers call **sequent occupancy**. In Chicago, the Pilsen neighborhood is heavily populated by Hispanics today, but its name recalls a history as a home for German and Czech immigrants. In New York City, the neighborhood of Harlem has been home to many ethnic groups: Jews from Eastern Europe starting in the late 1800s, African Americans from the southern United States starting in the 1910s, and Puerto Ricans starting in the late 1900s. As a result of sequent occupancy, Harlem's cultural landscape includes former Jewish synagogues, public spaces named for African American leaders such as Marcus Garvey Park, and street names honoring Puerto Rican leaders such as Luis Muñoz Marin Boulevard.

Reactions to New Residents When new groups move into a neighborhood the process of change can be well received and result in positive changes. However, the evolution and changing occupancy of neighborhoods can create cultural, economic and political tension. Tension often increases when the incoming group changes or destroys the cultural landscape without considering the people already living in the space. Conversely, existing residents can exhibit prejudices or resentment toward the group moving in. (See Topic 6.10.)

Assertions of Identity As a result of global culture and changing occupancy patterns, the ideas, traditions, and history of communities can erode. Sometimes people respond with **neolocalism**, the process of re-embracing the uniqueness and authenticity of a place. For example, a neighborhood in a large city might hold a festival to honor the cuisine, religion, and history of the migrants who settled the community.

REFLECT ON THE ESSENTIAL QUESTION

Essential Question: *What are the characteristics of cultural landscapes and how do those characteristics, land use, and resource use reflect cultural beliefs and identities?*

Characteristics of Cultural Landscapes	Reflection of Cultural Identities in Land and Resource Use

---

KEY TERMS

placelessness	ethnicity	diaspora
cultural landscape	ethnic enclaves	charter group
built environment	cultural regions	ethnic islands
traditional architecture	cultural realms	sequent occupancy
postmodern architecture	sacred place	neolocalism
contemporary architecture		

Cultural Patterns

Essential Question: What are the patterns and landscapes of language, religion, ethnicity, and gender?

Cultural patterns consist of related sets of cultural traits and complexes that create similar behaviors across space. Geographers are particularly interested in understanding cultural patterns across time and space, specifically, patterns of cultural components such as religions, ethnicities, and nationalities. The diverse tapestry of cultures creates a rich local and global cultural landscape that enhances placemaking. The effects of these patterns have the power to bring people together or tear them apart. Patterns are powerful.

Religious Patterns and Distributions

Developing strong mental maps of the origins, diffusion, and distribution of major religions and their divisions is one of the most valuable ways to understand culture. Geographers start by mapping a **culture hearth**, where a religion or ethnicity began, and then track its movement and predict its future direction. Religions, like other elements of culture, often diffuse outward from their hearths in various ways. The spread of religious settlements, both locally and globally, contributes to the sense of place and of belonging for each religious group and greatly shapes the cultural landscape.

LARGEST RELIGION BY COUNTRY

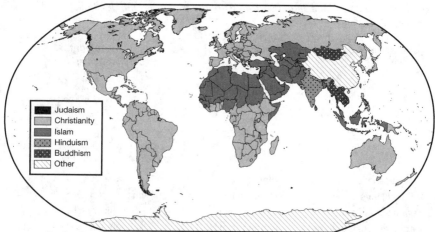

The choropleth map shown is very small scale and at the global level. However, the scale of analysis is at the state, or country, level. Among many other notable observations, Christianity is the most widespread religion by territory, and in China, most people identify no religious affiliation.

Geographers analyze maps, charts, and other data to understand the growth, decline, movement, and cultural landscapes of the world's religions. They have traced the geographic patterns of each major world religion, including the religion's hearth, the geographic spread of the religion, and practices that can influence both the culture and the cultural landscape.

Regional Patterns in U.S. Religion

The distribution of ethnic and religious groups in the United States reflects historical patterns:

- Congregationalists are still strong in New England, where their English ancestors settled in the 1600s.
- Baptists and Methodists are most common in the Southeast, where these denominations were spread by traveling preachers in the 1800s.
- Lutherans live mostly in the Midwest, where their German or Scandinavian ancestors, who immigrated in the late 1800s, could find good farmland.
- Many Mormons live in or near Utah, where their founders settled in the mid-1800s after religious persecution drove them out of Missouri and Illinois.
- Roman Catholics are most common in urban areas in the Northeast and throughout the Southwest.
- Jews, Muslims, and Hindus live most often in urban areas, the traditional home to immigrants.

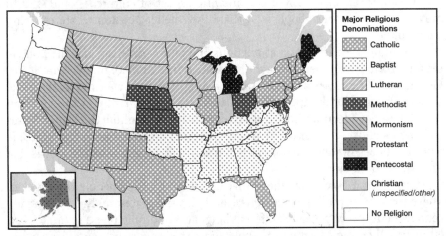

Cultural Variation by Place and Region

Patterns and landscapes of religious and ethnic groups vary by place and region at different scales. The world map above shows that the United States is mostly Christian; however, the scale of the data hides the fact that the United States has great religious diversity. The map above does show data aggregated by state and can show the breakdown and spatial patterns of other religions. For example, the world map doesn't show the breakdown of Roman Catholics and Protestant

Christians. Additionally, at the regional level within the United States, Baptists are the most common religious group in the Southeast, but this cannot be seen on the world map.

Religion, Ethnicity, and Nationality

Religion is often closely linked to **ethnicity**, or membership in a group of people who share characteristics such as ancestry, language, customs, history, and common experiences. Most geographers distinguish between **nationality**—based on people's connection to a particular country—and ethnicity—based upon group cultural traits. For example, Russian Jews make up a different ethnicity than Russians in general.

Geographers often study ethnic groups as minorities within a greater population. To do so, they focus on mapping and analysis to trace the movement of ethnic groups and investigate their spatial dimensions and cultural landscapes. People often identify with both their ethnicity and nationality but the order of identification is a very personal process. In the United States, many Hispanics identify their nationality as American first, and then ethnically as Hispanic; others reverse the order.

Centripetal and Centrifugal Forces

Understanding cultural patterns requires consideration of centripetal and centrifugal forces. **Centripetal forces** are those that unify a group of people or a region. These forces may include a common language and religion, a shared heritage and history, ethnic unity and tolerance, a just and fair legal system, a charismatic leader, or any other unifying aspect of culture. People tend to gravitate toward other people who share their beliefs, customs, interests, and background.

The United States has great religious and ethnic diversity, but the holiday season from November through December has unified many Americans. German and Scandinavian immigrants, among others, enjoyed the camaraderie of shared values and experiences, of holidays like Christmas. The German cultural trait of adorning Christmas trees diffused throughout the United States and has established itself as a part of American culture Today, many people who do not celebrate Christmas as a holy day still consider the Christmas tree as a part of their culture.

Centrifugal forces are those that divide a group of people or a region. These forces can pull apart societies, nations, and states, and are essentially centripetal forces in reverse. Different languages and religions, a separate past, ethnic conflict, racism, unequal application of laws, or dictatorial leadership are just a few of the many cultural attributes that can sow division within a society.

Centrifugal forces can be especially harmful toward national cohesion in *multicultural states*, those which possess more than one distinct cultural identity or ethnic group within its borders. Ireland was historically Catholic since the 5th century. However, as England became Anglican—a Protestant denomination—this cultural influence extended into Northern Ireland through invasion and migration. While Catholics and Anglicans are both Christians, the competition over territory, political power, and cultural influence drove the region into repeated violence over centuries.

In Iraq, Islam is dominant. However, there are regional divisions between the Shiite majority in the east and the Sunnis in the west. Ethnically, the majority of Iraqis are of Arabic heritage, yet there is a significant concentration of Kurds throughout northern regions of Iraq. (See Topic 4.3.) While cultural differences may lead to friction between groups, the competition for land, resources, and the desire for greater autonomy has also occasionally erupted into violence.

Religion's Impact on Laws and Customs

Since religious traditions predate current governments, they are often the source for many present-day laws and punishments by the government. Some religions have strict systems of laws that have been adopted fully by governments. An example of this is **Sharia**, or the legal framework of a country derived from Islamic edicts taken from their holy book, the Qur'an. Sharia has been adopted by some fundamentalist religious groups, such as the Taliban in Afghanistan, as the law of the land.

While no highly industrialized countries have fully adopted religious laws, their legal codes often show clear influence of religion. In the United States, many communities have **blue laws**, laws that restrict certain activities, such as the sale of alcohol, on Sunday. In Colorado and some other states, car dealerships must be closed on Sunday as well.

In most countries, religious beliefs are more influential as guides to personal behavior than as state-sponsored laws. For example, many faiths include guidelines on the choices people make about what clothes they wear and how they cut their hair. Most faiths include some food taboos, prohibitions against eating and drinking certain items. For example, many Hindus do not eat beef, and many Jews and Muslims do not eat pork.

Religion is also the source of many daily, weekly, or annual practices for adherents:

- Many Muslims pray five times a day, and many Buddhists and Hindus engage in daily meditation.
- Most religions have weekly religious services for worship or instruction. For example, Muslims usually gather on Friday, Jews on Friday evening or Saturday morning, and Christians on Sunday.
- Many people celebrate important religious holy days, such as Holi—a festival of light for Hindus—and Vesak—which commemorates the birth of Buddha.

In addition, many days that people now commonly treat as secularized holidays have their roots in religious practices. Valentine's Day, St. Patrick's Day, and Mardi Gras all originated as Christian holy days.

Religious Fundamentalism

The degree of adherence to tradition varies within each religion. Every religion includes followers who practice **fundamentalism**, an attempt to follow a literal interpretation of a religious faith. Fundamentalists believe that people should live traditional lifestyles similar to those prescribed in the faith's holy writings. In some traditions, this means that women are likely to leave school at a young age, to live in an arranged marriage, and to avoid working outside the home. Fundamentalists are more likely than others in their faith to enforce strict standards of dress and personal behavior, often through laws.

The strength of fundamentalism often diminishes with greater distance from the religious hearth, which is known as distance decay. (See Topic 1.4.) For example, the hearth of Islam is the Arabian Peninsula, and where Islamic fundamentalism has long been strongest. Fundamentalism is less prevalent in Muslim-majority countries farther from the hearth, such as Malaysia and Indonesia. One way to measure fundamentalism in Islam is by the role of Sharia. In countries where Sharia dominates, there is no separation between religious law and civil law. Sharia is strongest in countries of the Arabian Peninsula such as Saudi Arabia and Yemen.

Some fundamentalist countries, such as Iran, are **theocracies**, countries whose governments are run by religious leaders through the use of religious laws. Iran follows Sharia and the nation's leader, the Supreme Leadership Authority, is not only the political head of the state, but concurrently its highest religious authority. Fundamentalists often clash, sometimes violently, with those who wish to follow religious traditions more loosely or to live a more secular lifestyle. All major religions of the world—including Christianity, Buddhism, Hinduism, and Judaism—have a history of theocracy and each have some adherents who are fundamentalists.

Cultural Ethnocentrism and Relativism

Most states are multiethnic in that they possess a significant number of people who do not identify with the national majority as their own ethnic group. If people are more **ethnocentric**, they believe their own cultural group is more important and superior to other cultures. In many cases, they see others by means of generalizations and stereotypes, and often do not seek to understand different customs or cultural norms. While loyalty and pride in one's own culture is common and understandable, ethnocentric views typically lead to misinterpretations of others and the value they give certain artifacts and mentifacts.

Without consciously pursuing an understanding of other cultures, a "we" versus "them" mentality can grow. Ethnocentrism may lead to centrifugal forces within a state, such as discrimination, intolerance, violence, and mass killings. The same attitude may lead to issues with other states, including misunderstandings, increased tension, or even war.

A counter to ethnocentric views has been **cultural relativism**, which is the concept that a person's or group's beliefs, values, norms, and practices should be understood from the perspective of the other group's culture. Groups have developed their identities often through years—if not centuries—of environmental adaptation, interaction with other cultures, changing internal attitudes, and technological innovation. For example, many Americans are disgusted when some cultures eat fried insects. Applying cultural relativism, a geographer would attempt to understand why some communities may eat bugs. They would learn that other sources of protein were not available. This available food source was essential to survival and became ingrained in the community's culture over time.

Cultural appropriation is the action of adopting traits, icons, or other elements of another culture. The greatest concern is when the trait is adopted by the majority culture from a minority, or oppressed, cultural group. Concern increases if the trait is used out of context (not understanding the meaning of trait) or in an inappropriate or disrespectful way. An example would be naming sports teams after indigenous people or dressing up in costumes that propagate racial or cultural stereotypes. There is debate about where the boundaries of appropriation should be drawn. Not everyone agrees, with some arguing that people are too sensitive and that borrowing traits is a sign of respect and admiration, while others view it as a sign of oppression and discrimination.

Understanding other cultures from the inside affords everyone the opportunity to foster communication that leads to empathy and mutual respect. The culture-relativist perspective generally leads to centripetal forces within multiethnic societies and to vastly improved relations between states.

REFLECT ON THE ESSENTIAL QUESTION

Essential Question: *What are the patterns and landscapes of language, religion, ethnicity, and gender?*

Religious Patterns That Shape the Global Landscape	Factors That Create Centripetal and Centrifugal Forces

---

KEY TERMS

cultural patterns	blue laws
culture hearth	fundamentalism
ethnicity	theocracies
nationality	ethnocentrism
centripetal forces	cultural relativism
centrifugal forces	cultural appropriation
Sharia	

Types of Diffusion

Essential Question: What are the types of diffusion and when does each occur?

People study deadly diseases in many ways. Doctors focus on treating patients. Economists focus on the supply for medicines. Geographers focus on spatial distribution, including how a disease diffuses outward from its hearth. The influenza outbreak of 1918–1919, immediately after World War I, diffused in the United States from east coast cities. Troops returning from Europe either carried the virus or contracted it in a port. Then, as troops traveled home, they spread the disease throughout the country. The virus killed more than 50 million people worldwide, more than double the battle deaths in the war.

Types of Diffusion

The spread of information, ideas, behaviors, and other aspects of culture from their hearths to wider areas is known as **diffusion**. The two major forms of cultural diffusion come through exchanges between people. Some exchanges occur when people migrate from one place to another. Others result more indirectly, as people share ideas.

The spread of disease is one example of diffusion. Outbreaks of Ebola in West Africa in 2013, the Zika virus in South America in 2015, and COVID-19 in 2020 threatened death and serious illness. However, using geospatial medical data and geographic reasoning, scientists had learned how to combat diffusion of diseases. Coordinated global and national public health efforts prevented death on the scale of the 1918–1919 flu outbreak.

Relocation Diffusion

One main type of diffusion is **relocation diffusion**, the spread of culture and/or cultural traits by people who migrate and carry their cultural traits with them. A small-scale example is the spread of pizza, which Italian immigrants brought to the United States in the late 19th century. A large-scale example is the spread of European culture around the world starting in the 1500s.

At times, the areas where migrants settle continue a trait after it has lost its influence in its hearth. The people in the modern world who pronounce English most like Shakespeare did in the 1500s live in Appalachia (from southern New York to northern Alabama), not in England. Disco music evolved in the United States in the 1970s but remained popular in Egypt long after its popularity faded in the United States.

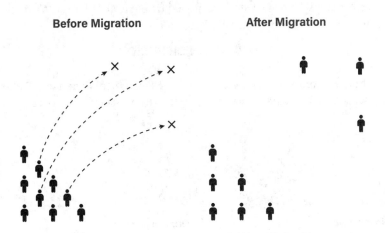

RELOCATION DIFFUSION

Before Migration   After Migration

Expansion Diffusion

The spread of cultural traits outward through exchange without migration is called **expansion diffusion**. Unlike relocation diffusion, expansion diffusion requires a different person to adopt the trait. It occurs in many ways.

Contagious diffusion occurs when a cultural trait spreads continuously outward from its hearth through contact among people. For example, the hearth for blues music is the southern United States. As musicians outside the hearth heard the music, they began to play it themselves. Blues slowly spread northward and reached cities such as St. Louis, Chicago, and New York.

Hierarchical diffusion is the spread of culture outward from the most interconnected places or from centers of wealth and influence. Cultural traits spread first from one powerful person, city, or powerful class to another powerful person, city, or social class. Eventually the trait could be shared with other people, smaller cities, different social classes, or less-developed countries. Unlike contagious diffusion, hierarchical diffusion may skip some places while moving on to others. Most popular culture, such as music, fashion, and fads, follows the hierarchical diffusion path.

Cell phone technology demonstrates how hierarchical diffusion works. When cell phones first appeared in the 1980s, they were expensive. Only wealthy people in large cities in developed countries owned them. As cell phone networks grew and cell phones became mass-produced, they eventually spread to a wider market. Today, cell phones have diffused throughout the world.

At times, a trait diffuses from a group of lower status to a group of higher status, in a process called **reverse hierarchical diffusion**. For example, in the United States in the 1940s through the 1960s, people commonly considered tattoos to be a symbol of low social status. Tattoos were associated with three types of places: seaport towns (among dockworkers and sailors), military bases, and prisons. Since the 1970s, the custom of getting tattoos has diffused throughout many segments of society and geographic areas.

Some reverse hierarchical diffusion goes from small, rural communities to larger urban areas. Walmart stores diffused from rural Arkansas to small cities and now nearly every city in the United States.

EXPANSION DIFFUSION

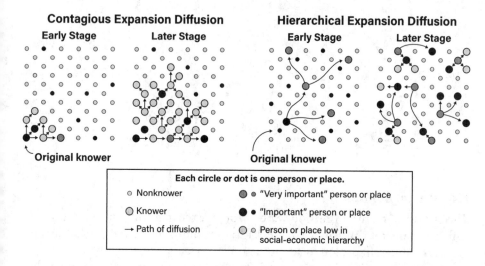

The process of **stimulus diffusion** is when an underlying idea from a culture hearth is adopted by another culture but the adopting group modifies or rejects one trait.

STIMULUS DIFFUSION

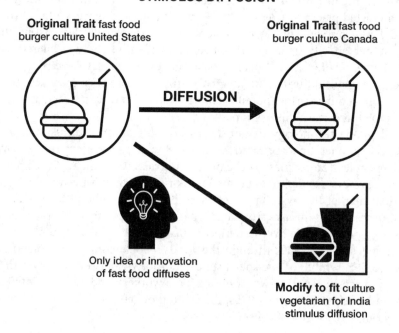

For example, Hindus in India adopted the practice of eating fast food, but they rejected eating beef because doing so would violate their Hindu beliefs. So, they adapted the custom by making vegetarian and other non-beef types of burgers. Five centuries ago, Europeans adopted the use of lightweight, beautifully decorated porcelain dishes that they obtained from China, but they rejected the high cost of importing the dishes. So, when people in Germany found deposits of the right type of clay to make their own porcelain, they modified the process of obtaining porcelain by making it in Europe.

REFLECT ON THE ESSENTIAL QUESTION

Essential Question: *What are the types of diffusion and when does each occur?*

Types of Diffusion	Examples of Types of Diffusion

KEY TERMS

diffusion	contagious diffusion	reverse hierarchical
relocation diffusion	hierarchical diffusion	diffusion
expansion diffusion		stimulus diffusion

GEOGRAPHIC PERSPECTIVES: *MUSLIMS OF THE UNITED STATES*

Muslims have been living in the Americas since the days of Columbus. Geographers have studied the patterns in the diffusion of Muslims in the Americas, including the reasons behind their involuntary or voluntary migrations and where they have been concentrated.

Muslims Among Enslaved Africans

The first concentration of Muslims was in what is now the southeastern United States. As many as 15 percent of the enslaved Africans brought to the Americas were followers of Islam.

Migrants to Industrial Cities

Then, between 1890 and 1917, a new wave of Muslim immigrants entered the United States. Most came from Bosnia, Turkey, Syria, and other lands in the Middle East. Pulled by the lure of industrial jobs, most settled in the growing cities of the North and Midwest.

Industrial cities in the 1920s and 1930s also attracted millions of African Americans from the rural South. Some African Americans joined a distinctive movement within Islam, known as the Black Muslims. They were concentrated in New York, Detroit, and Chicago. Today, about one-fifth of American Muslims are African Americans.

Diverse Immigrants

In recent decades, Muslim immigrants have come from around the world. While many come from the Middle East and South Asia, others migrate from Nigeria, Indonesia, and other countries. Again, they commonly settled in large urban areas, but increasingly in suburban communities, such as Dearborn, Michigan. Today, Muslims constitute about 1 percent of the total population.

1. What type of migration is represented when Muslim slaves were brought to the United States?

2. What are the benefits for Muslims to concentrate together in small communities in cities or small towns?

THINK AS A GEOGRAPHER: *RELIGIOUS SPACES AT DIFFERENT SCALES*

The distribution of religious elements on the landscape reflects the importance of religion in society's values. How each religion distributes its elements across the landscape depends on its beliefs. The impact of religion is clearly seen on the landscape at several scales from small areas within homes to entire communities.

Explain how the concept of scale applies to the three following religious landscapes.

1. Hindu home shrine in India

2. Vatican City, Italy

3. Buddhist five-story pagoda, Japan

1. How does the location of the Hindu shrine reflect the religious traditions in Hinduism?

2. What scale of analysis does the photograph of Vatican City represent?

3. How does the photograph of the pagoda suggest a regional scale of analysis?

CHAPTER 6 REVIEW:
Cultural Landscapes, Patterns, and Diffusion
Topics 3.1–3.4

MULTIPLE-CHOICE QUESTIONS

Question 1 refers to the diagram below.

CULTURAL COMPLEX OF THE AUTOMOBILE IN THE UNITED STATES

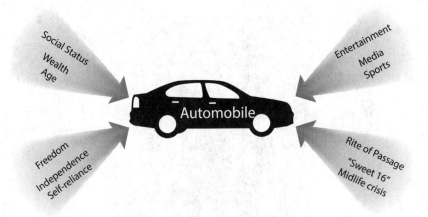

1. According to the cultural complex described in the diagram, auto ownership provides transportation but also

   (A) represents a set of American cultural traits, such as self-reliance and independence

   (B) provides greater likelihood that its owner will attain American values such as wealth

   (C) represents one American cultural trait, depending on the values of the auto's owner

   (D) comes about as a result of possession of a particular American trait, such as wealth

   (E) helps identify the owner's cultural landscape, region, realm, and level of freedom

2. Which of the following best demonstrates the concept of a culture hearth?

(A) The Middle East, where many cultures share the religion of Islam

(B) Latin America, which consists of several distinct but related cultures

(C) The places in the world where material and nonmaterial traits emerged

(D) The buildings, roads, and other elements built by humans

(E) An area within a city where people share a common culture distinct from the surrounding culture

Question 3 refers to the image below.

3. The architecture style of Saint Basil Eastern Orthodox Cathedral in Moscow, Russia, is most clearly an example of the city's cultural

(A) barriers

(B) enclaves

(C) realm

(D) landscape

(E) borders

4. A family that immigrates from China to the United States and chooses to live in an ethnic enclave is probably hoping to
   (A) expose their children to people of many other cultures
   (B) assimilate their family into American culture as quickly as possible
   (C) find a buffer against discrimination while they seek new opportunities
   (D) find more religious and language diversity than in most communities
   (E) separate itself from its Chinese culture rapidly and completely

5. Which of the following best describes an artifact?
   (A) The territory in which people reside including valleys and rivers
   (B) The nonmaterial culture consisting of intangible things such as beliefs and values
   (C) A way in which people organize their society such as through families and government
   (D) The material culture consisting of tangible things, such as food and clothing
   (E) The interaction between different groups including trading and negotiating

6. Amish residents of Lancaster, Pennsylvania, who are descendants of immigrants from Switzerland in the 1700s, live without the benefits of electricity. This choice is an example of
   (A) an adherence to traditional culture
   (B) a longstanding indigenous culture
   (C) a dominant national identity
   (D) acclimation to their new environment
   (E) an adaptation of popular culture

7. Which pattern is more typical of folk/traditional cultures than other types of cultures?
   (A) Welcoming in new practices from other cultures
   (B) Promoting a high level of religious diversity
   (C) Taking steps to transform rural areas into urban areas
   (D) Emphasizing the value of customs
   (E) Establishing flexible gender roles

Shibuya Crossing in Tokyo, Japan

1. Cultural values and traditions help people develop a sense of place where they live. As globalization increases, various cultures come in contact with each other, resulting in a variety of processes and impacts.

(A) Define the concept of cultural landscape.

(B) Define the concept of globalization.

(C) Using the image of Tokyo, Japan, describe an element of the photo that illustrates globalization.

(D) Explain the diffusion of popular culture using the concept of hierarchical diffusion.

(E) Explain how traditional cultures most commonly diffuse.

(F) Describe how global culture is threatening to traditional folk cultures.

(G) Identify the scale of analysis of the image shown and describe a limitation of the image related to scale.

CHAPTER 7

Historical and Contemporary Processes of Diffusion

Topics 3.5–3.8

Topic 3.5 Historical Causes of Diffusion

Learning Objective: Explain how historical processes impact current cultural patterns. (SPS-3.A)

Topic 3.6 Contemporary Causes of Diffusion

Learning Objective: Explain how historical processes impact current cultural patterns. (SPS-3.A)

Topic 3.7 Diffusion of Religion and Language

Learning Objective: Explain what factors led to the diffusion of universalizing and ethnic religions. (IMP-3.B)

Topic 3.8 Effects of Diffusion

Learning Objective: Explain how the process of diffusion results in changes to the cultural landscape. (SPS-3.B)

In 1979, [schools on the Navajo reservation had about] 80 percent of students speaking Navajo – ten years later, 5 percent. There's just too much English influence to really be effective in keeping our language. [If the Navajo language is lost] we will not be a unique people. We will have no culture; we will have no prayers.

—Marilyn Begay, 5th grade teacher, The Navajo Language
Immersion School, Navajo Nation reservation, Arizona

A bilingual stop sign in Quebec, Canada. (See Topic 3.7 for more about cultural landscape.)

Historical Causes of Diffusion

Essential Question: How do historical processes impact current cultural patterns?

Today, few formal colonies remain in the world, but the practices left behind by the European powers are present in their former colonies. The afternoon break for tea, a British tradition, is still practiced in Kenya and India. Christianity and the legacy of colonial languages are still widespread in many former colonies.

Influences of Colonialism, Imperialism, and Trade

Colonialism, imperialism, and trade have played a powerful role in spreading religion and culture. Historians often divide European colonialism into two separate waves. From the 16th through the 18th centuries, Europeans colonized the Americas and South Asia. Then, during the next two centuries, European powers expanded colonization into most of Africa, Southwest Asia, and other coastal regions of East and Southeast Asia.

Imperialism and colonialism are related ideas, but they are not the same. **Imperialism** is a broader concept that includes a variety of ways of influencing another country or group of people by direct conquest, economic control, or cultural dominance. **Colonialism** is a particular type of imperialism in which people move into and settle on the land of another country. Examples of imperialism and colonialism can be found throughout history and all over the world, but modern European imperialism and colonialism are the most relevant to the current political map because they strongly influenced the diffusion of language and religion.

European colonizers imposed their cultural traits on the local populations. For example, before European colonization, most religions practiced by the native indigenous people of Africa and North America were forms of **animism**, the belief that non-living objects, such as rivers or mountains, possess spirits. Europeans forced many of their colonial subjects to adopt the Christian faith. The Spanish and French spread Roman Catholicism throughout Latin America and North America. The English and Dutch spread forms of Protestantism in their North American colonies.

Diffusion of Languages

Languages commonly spread through both relocation and expansion diffusion. As people migrated and colonized to new locations, they brought their culture and language with them via relocation diffusion. Additionally, via political control a colonial language would be imposed hierarchically as the language of trade, business, and politics. People wanting to benefit financially would connect to these networks of power and influence by learning and speaking colonial languages resulting in an expansion of language. Some languages spread over wide areas of the world and often follow a mixture of types of diffusion. The major globalized languages of the world—English, French, Spanish, and Arabic—spread from their hearths largely because of conquest and colonialism. In the case of Arabic, its use as the standard religious language in Islam contributed to its success and facilitated an expansion of adherents.

Widely Diffused Languages Trade has aided the spread of languages because ships, railroads, and other forms of transportation built and strengthened connections between places. Trade, conquest, and colonialism have so widely spread some languages that more people speak it outside its hearth than within it. For example, the largest population of speakers of Portuguese are in Brazil, not Portugal. The same is true for English, Spanish, and French—the highest population of speakers for each of those languages are not in the hearth.

MOST SPOKEN LANGUAGES IN THE WORLD IN ORDER OF TOTAL SPEAKERS			
Language	Language Hearth	Total Population of Hearth 2019	Total Speakers Worldwide 2019 (native and second language)
English	England	55 million	Over 1.5 billion
Mandarin (Chinese)	China	1.4 billion	Over 1.2 billion
Hindi	India	1.3 billion	Over 615 million
Spanish	Spain	47 million	Over 570 million
French	France	67 million	Over 300 million
Arabic	Arabian Peninsula	78 million	Over 270 million

Chart appears in order of total speakers worldwide. Which languages have not diffused extensively from their hearth? What are reasons why they did not diffuse widely?

Limited Diffusion of Manadrin Some languages have never diffused widely. Mandarin Chinese, though the second-most commonly spoken language in the world, did not spread globally. China has been among the most powerful and innovative countries in the world for much of the past 2,000 years, and its merchants settled in various parts of Asia and locations in the Pacific Ocean. Yet China never established colonies outside of Asia and, as a result, Chinese speakers have always been concentrated in China and port cities in Asia.

Mandarin does have the most **native speakers**, those who use the language learned from birth, with over 900 million native speakers. The Chinese government wants to increase the number of Mandarin speakers and has been using government policies and its economic influence to encourage the use of Mandarin throughout Asia and across the world.

English as a Lingua Franca

Unlike Chinese, English has a wide spatial distribution. English is the most widely used language in the world, with over 1.5 billion speakers. Native speakers (380 million) are concentrated in lands colonized by Great Britain such as the United States, Canada, South Africa, India, and Australia.

However, most speakers of English do not use it as their primary language. Rather, they use it as a **lingua franca**, a common language used by people who do not share the same native language. For example, Nigerians commonly speak one of 500 indigenous languages at home, but they learn English to communicate with everyone who does not speak their language. Globalization and new technology explain why English is often used as a lingua franca:

- U.S. and British multinational corporations made English the common language for international business.
- Scientists and other scholars, airline pilots, and journalists have used English to communicate with others across the globe.
- English evolved as the lingua franca of the Internet and is widely used in social media.
- English is often spoken by actors in television shows and movies which are shown around the world.

The wide use of English has made communication among people around the world easier. However, it has also sparked resentment in some who feel that the intrusion of American English language and western culture delegitimizes their own unique linguistic and cultural practices.

Creating New Words and Languages

Many new words begin as **slang**, words used informally by a segment of the population. As the world has become more globalized, certain words have spread dramatically and their meaning has changed. For example, the word *brunch* was slang before it became standard. Slang used in video gaming chats such as "w00t," to express excitement or victory, has diffused to common language today as woot.

Pidgin Languages

When speakers of two different languages have extensive contact with each other, often because of trade, they sometimes develop a **pidgin language**, a simplified mixture of two languages. A pidgin language has fewer grammar rules and a smaller vocabulary than either language but is not the native language of either group. In Papua New Guinea, the pidgin combines English and Papuan languages.

Creole Languages

Over time, two or more separate languages can mix and develop a more formal structure and vocabulary so that they are no longer a pidgin language. They create a new combined language, known as a **creole language**. Afrikaans is a creole language spoken in South Africa that combines Dutch with several European and African languages.

On the islands of the Caribbean, creole languages are common. Africans captured and enslaved in the Americas between the 1500s and the 1800s were unable to transplant their languages. Stolen from their communities, they were forced onto ships with captives from various regions in Africa. With no common language among the groups of captives, communication was difficult. Most groups lost their languages after a generation in the Americas because of this linguistic isolation. Yet they were able to create creole languages by combining parts of their African languages with the European colonizers' languages of English, Spanish, French, or Portuguese.

The most widely used creole language in the Americas is found in Haiti. Haitian Creole is derived mostly from French with influences from numerous languages of West Africa. It has become an official language of Haiti and a source of national pride and cultural identity.

Swahili in East Africa

Another example of language mixing occurred in East Africa. As early as the 8th century, trade between Arab-speaking merchants and Bantu-speaking residents resulted in the development of Swahili. Swahili is estimated to be spoken by some 50 to 100 million people in Africa and is an official language of five African nations—Kenya, Uganda, Rwanda, Tanzania, and the Democratic Republic of the Congo. Many proponents believe that using Swahili as the common language of Africa would help promote unity within the continent. They also feel it would help Africans overcome the legacy of colonialism. Using Swahili would help erase the notion that speaking European languages is prestigious and critical for advancement while using native languages is viewed as an obstacle to advancements in social, economic, and political spheres.

REFLECT ON THE ESSENTIAL QUESTION

Essential Question: *How do historical processes impact current cultural patterns?*

Historical Processes That Have Shaped Culture	Resulting Cultural Patterns

---

KEY TERMS

imperialism	native speakers	pidgin language
colonialism	lingua franca	creole language
animism	slang	

Contemporary Causes of Diffusion

Essential Question: How do contemporary processes impact cultural patterns?

Cultural ideas and practices are socially constructed and change through both small-scale and large-scale processes such as urbanization and globalization. **Social constructs** are ideas, concepts, or perceptions that have been created and accepted by people in a society or social group and are not created by nature. These processes influences culture through media, technological change, politics, economics, and social relationships. In the past, technology has facilitated the spread of multiple languages. However, contemporary communication technologies have encouraged the use of fewer languages, especially English, Chinese, and Spanish. Globalization has further encouraged this phenomena because of the fundamental need for a lingua franca to communicate across cultures.

Communication Technologies

Communication technologies have allowed for the globalization of popular culture through multiple methods of spatial diffusion. Music, video games, TV shows, cars, and clothing are heavily influenced by mass media, the Internet, and traditional and online publishing.

Due to historical processes such as colonialism, conquest, and trade, the English language diffused around the world. More recent developments in the ease of use and access to many of these technologies have served to strengthen the use of American English around the world. The elite hierarchies, or most influential creators of popular or global culture, continue to concentrate in the usual major cities—New York City, Los Angeles, London, and Tokyo. Major news networks, publishers, and multinational corporations have driven popular culture creation over the last 75 years.

However, access to social media, search engines, and entertainment on the web is challenging traditional corporate sources of popular culture. The rise of social media allows for individuals or small groups of people to promote their own self-produced forms of entertainment (TikTok and YouTube, for example), eSports, fashion, and other products, creating influencers who challenge the status quo and how culture is created and diffused.

As a result of technological changes, the rate of diffusion has increased dramatically and the patterns of diffusion have taken on new and interesting forms. Social media at its heart is a form of expansion and contagious diffusion. However, hierarchical diffusion is shown via the connections that people have with influencers and the vast networks of their followers. The hierarchical diffusion graphic below also illustrates a nodal, or functional regional pattern.

Technology can be a global equalizing force by helping to provide access to information and economic opportunity. However, if a person does not have access to the Internet, the world is still a very unequal place.

HIERARCHICAL DIFFUSION VIA SOCIAL MEDIA INFLUENCERS

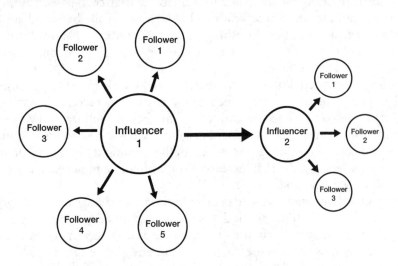

The size of the circles indicates the number of followers. Arrows indicate sharing of information. Each follower would also have their own network of connection. What could be added to this graphic/model to make it a more complete representation of how diffusion works on the Internet and social media? Defend your response with evidence or examples.

Time-Space Convergence

The greater interconnection between places that results from improvements in transportation is called **time-space convergence**. It often makes places less culturally distinct. For example, in 1492 it took Christopher Columbus 36 days to cross the Atlantic Ocean on a wind-powered ship. By 1907, that time was reduced to 4.5 days due to the invention of the steam engine. Modern commercial aviation replaced ocean liners as the dominant mode of transatlantic transportation. A commercial airplane makes the transatlantic journey from Europe to North America in about 7 hours. Modern communication technologies have caused a similar change in the amount of time needed for information to travel.

Time-space convergence provides another way of thinking about geography as not just physical space but also of relative distance. While transportation and communication changes do not actually "shrink" the earth, the time and cost of movement between places have greatly decreased, making the earth feel smaller. This demonstrates how a person's sense of time and space vary based upon cultural, economic, and social factors.

Cultural Convergence and Divergence

As the relative distance between places shrinks, the interactions among cultures increases. Some argue that globalization is resulting in **cultural convergence**—cultures are becoming similar to each other and sharing more cultural traits, ideas, and beliefs. This cultural homogenization, or becoming more alike, is a concern for many societies and is met with resistance by some people. (See Topic 3.8.) These interactions often result in cultural change. For example, people around the world wear jeans and t-shirts on a daily basis and are less likely to wear the traditional clothing of their ancestors or parents. In many instances, cultural convergence can cause indigenous or traditional cultures and languages to become extinct.

Occasionally, people use new technologies and social media to help preserve local or threatened languages. Technology is used to record and preserve languages that could become extinct in the face of cultural convergence. Communities of speakers use social media to discuss and share their cultural beliefs and language with other members of the community who are separated from or have left an area. That increases the likelihood of preservation of some elements of language and culture.

Cultural divergence is the idea that a culture may change over time as the elements of distance, time, physical separation, and modern technology create divisions and changes. A culture's isolation because of absorbing barriers of physical geography, such as mountains, oceans, or distance, can halt diffusion. The longer a group is isolated, the more slowly its culture will change or diverge from the original culture. Today, most barriers are permeable, which means that part of an idea or trait may reach a cultural group but usually not enough to rapidly change the entire culture. As new ideas seep into the culture, the pace and changes can occur more quickly, especially if a person moves away from their home and into a city or new region.

REFLECT ON THE ESSENTIAL QUESTION

Essential Question: *How do contemporary processes impact cultural patterns?*

Methods of Contemporary Diffusion	How Methods Diffuse Culture

---

KEY TERMS

social constructs	cultural convergence
time-space convergence	cultural divergence

Diffusion of Religion and Language

Essential Question: What factors lead to the diffusion of universalizing and ethnic religions?

The Navajo, a Native American group of the Southwest United States, face many of the same problems as indigenous people across the world—the loss of their native language and culture in the context of globalization. Currently there are approximately 7,000 languages that people around the world speak. But by the end of the century, about half of those languages will be gone. Most of the languages are spoken by small, isolated groups. As these groups become integrated into the larger society, the people often learn the language of the majority. The traditional language falls into disuse and becomes extinct. Since language is the key element in communication, with this loss of the language comes a loss of a central part of a group's history, ethnicity, and cultural identity.

Relationships Among Languages

As the Navajo example illustrates, language is essential to a group's culture. It creates a sense of place and a cultural landscape. The Navajos' experience shows that today's communication technologies are reshaping cultures and bringing drastic changes to languages. Some of these changes can contribute to destroying age-old practices and languages.

Yet language, like all elements of culture, has always been changing. The earliest languages spread from their culture hearths and faced a multitude of local, international, and global forces. These global forces include conquest, colonialism, imperialism, trade, and the widespread instant communication of the present day.

Origins of Language

Currently, **linguists**, scientists who study languages, have differing theories as to when humans first began communicating through spoken sounds. Some claim first communication began as recently as tens of thousands of years ago to as long ago as a few hundred thousand years. They are also unsure how language diffused:

- Was it through the dispersion of people, who carried language with them as they spread across the planet?
- Was it through transmission, as people learned language from their neighbors?
- Was it through conquest, with one people imposing language on others?

Language Families

Linguists also are uncertain whether all languages descended from one original language. They do agree that nearly all of the languages spoken today can be grouped into about 15 language families. The relationship among these language families is often shown on a **language tree** because it suggests how several languages are related to each other, as well as how one language grows out of another.

The distribution of languages reflects human migrations. For example, the migration of Huns from central Asia to central Europe around 1,500 years ago explains why the languages most like Hungarian are found nearly 3,000 miles east of Hungary.

Indo-European Languages

One of the 15 major language families is the **Indo-European language family**, a large group of languages that might have descended from a language spoken around 6,000 years ago. Nearly half of the world's population speaks one of the languages of the Indo-European language family. This family includes about 2.8 billion native speakers of between 400 and 500 languages.

EXAMPLES OF INDO-EUROPEAN LANGUAGES

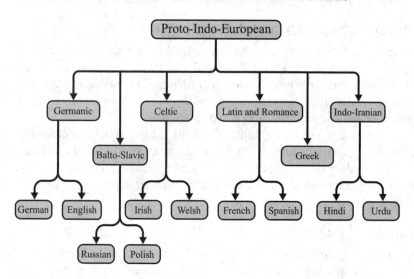

The British Isles were settled by waves of Germanic speaking peoples over millennia. In 1066 French was introduced to the islands when England was conquered by William the Conqueror of Normandy.

One of the branches of the Indo-European language tree is Latin, and its history shows the difficulties in the study of language. Languages are challenging to study because they constantly evolve as people move away from the languages' cultural hearths, have contact with other languages, or are isolated from other languages.

Two thousand years ago, when the Roman Empire dominated much of what is present-day Europe, people there spoke Latin. However, as the empire dissolved, starting in the 5th century, transportation became more dangerous and trade declined. As a result, Latin speakers became geographically isolated from each other. The unifying language of Latin diverged into dozens of distinct regional languages, known as **Romance languages**. Most of these later vanished, but Portuguese, Spanish, French, Italian, and Romanian, among others survived and grew. The historical connection among these languages is evident in their similar words.

LATIN WORDS RELATED TO WORDS IN OTHER LANGUAGES					
Latin (meaning in English)	Pater (father)	Mater (mother)	Panis (bread)	Lupus (wolf)	Die (day)
Portuguese	Pai	Mae	Pao	Lobo	Dia
Spanish	Padre	Madre	Pan	Lobo	Dia
French	Pere	Mere	Pain	Loup	Jour
Italian	Padre	Madre	Pane	Lupo	Giorno
Romanian	Tata	Mama	Paine	Lup	Zi

What patterns of similarity do you notice between words in each of the Latin-based languages? What does this tell us about the different languages' development?

Note that English words such as *father* and *mother* are similar to Latin words, but words such as *bread* and *wolf* are not. This suggests that English is not a direct descendant of Latin. English evolved from a Germanic language but has been heavily influenced by Romance languages such as French.

Accents and Dialects

Languages can be further divided into smaller categories by other traits. One is by accent, how words sound when pronounced. Accents often reflect social class or geographic region. The boundaries between variations in pronunciations or word usage are called **isoglosses**. For example, as you move from east to west in Texas, the term "dry creek bed" used near Dallas is replaced by the Spanish word "arroyo." This isogloss represents the boundary between southern dialect and a Texan variation.

Variations in accent, grammar, usage, and spelling create **dialects**, or regional variations of a language. Variations between dialects are large enough that most speakers notice them, but small enough that speakers can understand each other easily. Often, the dialect spoken by the most influential group in a country is considered the standard, and others are modifications of it. "Hello, everyone" is standard. "Hi, y'all" and "Hi, you guys" are dialectical variations.

Dialects often include distinct **adages**, or sayings that attempt to express a truth about life, such as "the early bird gets the worm." Additionally, dialects are geographic and create formal regions of a country or the world. Within dialects are subdialects. For example, in the United States, a native of Texas is likely to speak a different dialect than a native of New York City.

Often, dialects are the legacy of differences in the past, but they can also be a first step in the evolution of a new language. Just as the Romance languages emerged as regional variations of Latin, new languages are developing today. For example, if the differences between British English and American English increased so much that speakers could not easily communicate with each other, the two would be classified as different languages instead of dialects of one.

The following chart shows differences between two dialects of English—American and British.

DIALECTS OF AMERICAN ENGLISH AND BRITISH ENGLISH		
Category	American English	British English
Vocabulary	• Elevator • Apartment • Parking lot • Trunk (of a car) • Gas (for a car)	• Lift • Flat • Car park • Boot • Petrol
Pronunciation	• Lieutenant (loo-TEN-uhnt) • Schedule (SKED-juhl)	• Lieutenant (lef-TEN-uhnt) • Schedule (SCHEDZH-uhl)
Spelling	• Meter • Color • Tire • Center • Theater	• Metre • Colour • Tyre • Centre • Theatre
Common Phrases	• "I'm tired." • "I'll call you."	• "I'm knackered." • "I'll ring you."

Language Policies and Cultural Landscape

Language is important to a group's cultural identity. Because a culture occupies a certain spatial area, its language becomes intertwined with that place and its landscape. For example, native Hawaiians, whose economy relies on fishing, have five dozen words for fishing nets. In addition, signs can create a cultural landscape as they reflect the people's linguistic heritage and tie them to that place—from the single-language signs in France to bilingual signs in places such as Belgium, Quebec, or Wales.

Toponyms

Toponyms, or the names of places (see Topic 1.4), can provide insights into the physical geography, the history, or the culture of a location or region. Closely reviewing maps or listening to how people in a region refer to specific places helps geographers gain insight into the historical, cultural, ethnic, religious, and linguistic story of a location. For example, in 657 B.C.E., the Greeks founded a colony that they named Byzantium, after a leader named Byzas. When the city fell under Roman control, it was remained Constantinople, after the Roman emperor Constantine. When the Turks seized the city in 1453, they started to call it Istanbul, which means "to the city." Geographers look for clues as to why a place may have multiple names depending on who you ask and the point in history.

Official Languages

While the United States does not have an **official language**, one designated by law to be the language of government, some countries do. These countries can be grouped into three categories:

- Some countries are **homogeneous**, or made up largely of ethnically similar people, such as in Iceland, Japan, or Slovenia.
- Some countries use language to discourage people from maintaining a traditional culture. English colonizers did this in Ireland, Scotland, and Wales to promote quick assimilation.
- Some countries include several large ethnic groups. These countries want to honor all groups equally. For example, Zimbabwe is home to several large ethnic groups, so it has 16 official languages. People use English as a lingua franca to make communication easier.

English is the most common official language in the world with 64 countries, followed by French (32), Arabic (27), Spanish (23), and Portuguese (10). Official language does not necessarily mean the most spoken language in a country.

EXAMPLES OF OFFICIAL LANGUAGES IN AFRICA

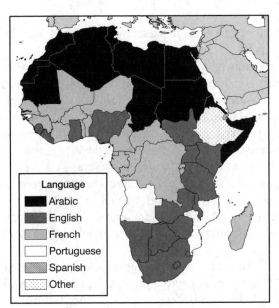

Language
- Arabic
- English
- French
- Portuguese
- Spanish
- Other

The map above represents some but not all official languages in Africa. Using the map describe the distribution pattern of each language shown. What does Ethiopia having an "Other" language tell you about its political history?

Ethnic and Universalizing Religious

Religion is intertwined with all other aspects of history and geography because, compared to other aspects of culture, it is relatively resistant to decay over time and distance. For example, descendants of immigrants often adopt a new language but continue to practice the faith of their ancestors and remain **adherents**, or believers in their faith. Developing strong mental maps of the origins, diffusion, and distribution of major religions and their divisions is one of the most valuable ways to understand culture.

Ethnic religions are belief traditions that emphasize strong cultural characteristics among their followers. In most cases, adherents of an ethnic religion are born or adopted into it. Members have a shared historical experience or struggle that creates strong bonds. Ethnic religions rarely recruit new followers actively. Rather, they spread as a result of relocation diffusion. Hinduism and Judaism are the world's two most widespread ethnic religions. The Jewish Diaspora and global migration of Hindus from India are examples of such relocation diffusion.

In contrast to an ethnic religion, a **universal religion** actively seeks converts to its faith regardless of their ethnic backgrounds. Universalizing religions are open to all people regardless of their ethnicity, language, social status or nationality. The major universalizing religions of the world are Christianity, Islam, and Buddhism. Sikhism is also considered universalizing but has a much more limited geographic diffusion. Universalizing religions have spread far from their original hearths because existing members feel a mandate to spread their beliefs to others. To carry out this mandate, members of universalizing religions often serve as missionaries who both perform charitable works and convert non-believers.

Eastern Religions

Several belief systems have developed in Asia. Of these, two developed in India and have diffused to other places from there.

Hinduism   Classified as an ethnic religion, Hinduism includes the worship of many deities, so most scholars consider it **polytheistic**, which means having many gods. However, Hindus consider all deities as manifestations of one god, so it can be considered **monotheistic**, which means having one god. Hindus believe in **karma**—the idea that behaviors have consequences in the present life or a future life—and in dharma—which means the righteous path. For part of its history, Hinduism worked closely with a **caste system**, a rigid class structure, that shaped Indian society. The concept of reincarnation or rebirth based on the quality of life a person lived is a central belief of most Hindus. A soul would spiritually advance enough to become liberated from this cycle of death and rebirth. Rivers are considered sacred and symbolic of life and purification of sin.

Buddhism   Buddhism grew out of the teachings of a prince named Siddhartha who lived around 600 B.C.E. Accepting many beliefs of Hinduism but rejecting the caste system, Siddhartha became known as the Buddha, or "enlightened one." According to Buddhist traditions, Siddhartha had been meditating for several days underneath a bodhi tree when he finally understood the cause of suffering and how to end it. Buddhist doctrines became summarized in the Four Noble Truths, which sought to eliminate desire and suffering by following the Eightfold Path. Siddhartha advised followers to escape the cycle of suffering through "right" views, hopes, speech, conduct, livelihood, effort, mindfulness, and meditation. This path requires an individual to meditate, reflect, and refrain from excessive earthly pleasures. The goal is, over time, to achieve enlightenment and the peaceful bliss known as nirvana, which would end the cycle of reincarnation.

THE SPREAD OF BUDDHISM

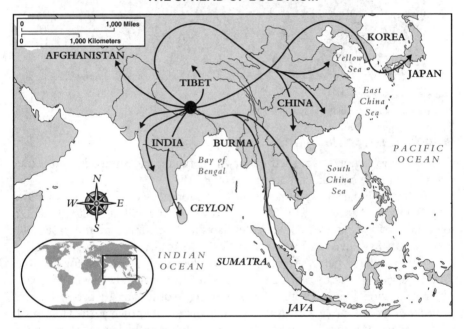

The hearth and diffusion routes of Buddhism

Sikhism A relatively new universalizing monotheistic faith, Sikhism was founded by Guru Nanak in the Punjab region that crosses the border of India and Pakistan during the 16th century. Most Sikhs live on the Indian side of the border and enjoy more religious freedom than those of other religions in the area. The faith stresses serving others, honesty, hard work, and generosity rather than rituals. All men who are baptized add the name Singh (lion) and women add the name Kaur (princess). This practice was adopted to break down the influence of family names and the caste system in India in order to create a more equal society. A Sikh's place of worship is called a **gurdwara** and followers usually attend a service once a week. All gurdwaras have a worship gathering space and contain a food kitchen that serves meals to people of all faiths. The most holy place is the Golden Temple in Amritsar, India.

Source: Wikimedia Commons

Sikh pilgrim at the Harmandir Sahib (Golden Temple) in Amritsar, India

Middle Eastern Religions

Three major religions trace their history to Abraham. He was a religious leader who lived in the Middle East around 1800 B.C.E.

Judaism Judaism was among the first monotheistic faiths. Jews believe that the writing known as the Torah expresses divine will. It is supplemented by other writings as well as unwritten laws and customs. For the past 2,000 years, most Jews lived in Europe and North Africa. Always a small minority, they often suffered persecution. In the late 1800s, Jews searching for religious liberty began efforts to establish a homeland in the Middle East and began their migration to the United States. During World War II, the systematic murder of six million Jews by Nazi Germany, an event known as the Holocaust, strengthened the movement to create a predominantly Jewish state in the Middle East. In 1948, the country of Israel was formed. Jews from around the world migrated there.

Christianity Christianity began when followers of a Jewish teacher, Jesus (c. 4 B.C.E. to c. 30 C.E.), evolved into their own religion based on the belief that Jesus was the son of God and the savior of humans. He emphasized the importance of faith, love, and peace. Christianity spread outward from the Middle East to become the dominant religion in Europe, and then to America and other parts of the world.

There are three main branches of Christianity—Roman Catholic, Protestant and Eastern Orthodox—with hundreds of further subdivisions. Strong patterns associated with language help to explain in part the geographic distribution of both religion and language. Many Catholics trace their heritage or colonial history to regions that spoke Romance languages such as French, Spanish, or

Portuguese. Protestants often have a similar history with northern European and Germanic languages like English. And many Eastern European countries have a complex religious history related to a mix of Eastern Orthodox, Judaism, and Islam. While Christianity diffused primarily west, north, and east from its hearth in Israel, in one unique case it diffused south. In Ethiopia, Christianity attracted many adherents.

Islam Islam is the religion followed by Muslims. Muslims believe that Allah—the Arabic word for God—revealed his teachings to humans through a series of prophets. The last of these was Muhammad, who lived in what is now Saudi Arabia in the 6th and 7th centuries C.E.

Muslims believe that Allah communicated his teachings to Muhammad, who shared them with people in the book of holy writings known as the Quran. The core principles of the Quran became known as the Five Pillars of Islam:

- belief in one god—Allah
- ritual prayer
- almsgiving (giving of wealth or volunteering for charitable causes)
- fasting (abstaining from food or drink)
- pilgrimage to Mecca

Muslims evolved a law code based on the Quran, called sharia, to regulate religious and civic behavior. Sharia made no distinction between religious and civil law and countries that operate under it are considered theocracies. (See Topic 3.3.)

The two major subdivisions of Islam are the Sunni (90 percent of adherents) and Shia (10 percent of adherents). Countries with the highest Shia populations are Iran, India, Pakistan, Iraq, Yemen, and other countries in the Middle East and Africa.

Diffusion and Pilgrimage The two largest universalizing religions are Christianity and Islam. Each spread from their hearths partially through conquest and colonization.

Christianity, which was found mostly in Europe in the 15th century, added millions of followers when Christian missionaries accompanied European explorers and conquerors to the Western Hemisphere, southern Africa, and Australia. As Europeans expanded their empires, they converted people to Christianity, sometimes forcefully.

Islam spread in much the same way, through the Middle East, North Africa, and Asia. Today, Islam is the fastest growing religion in the world based on natural increase.

In many faith traditions, followers feel called to go on a **pilgrimage**, a religious journey taken by a person to a sacred place of his or her religion. Each year, over 20 million Hindus journey to the Ganges River, millions of Muslims travel to Mecca (a pilgrimage known as a *hajj*), and many Muslims, Jews, and Christians visit Jerusalem's many holy sites.

RELIGIOUS HEARTHS AND DIFFUSION

Religion (number of adherents)	Hearth	Type of Diffusion
Hinduism (1.1 billion)	Along Indus River in present-day Pakistan	• Expansion diffusion across Indian subcontinent • Relocation diffusion in recent decades to Europe and the United States
Buddhism (500 million)	South Asia in present-day Nepal	• Contagious diffusion as teachings spread throughout East and Southeast Asia along land and water trading routes • Relocation diffusion throughout the world
Sikhism (20 million)	Punjab (crosses border of India and Pakistan)	• Contagious diffusion via conversion • Relocation diffusion mostly within the former British Empire and the United States
Judaism (15 million)	Eastern Mediterranean and southwestern Asia; present-day Israel	• Relocation diffusion throughout North Africa and Europe forced by the Romans beginning around 70 C.E. • Relocation diffusion to the United States and other countries including return migration to Israel post-1948
Christianity (2.3 billion)	Eastern Mediterranean and southwestern Asia	• Contagious diffusion via conversion and missionaries through the Middle East, Europe, and Central Asia • Hierarchical diffusion through conversion of rulers, who then forced their followers to adopt the faith • Expansion and relocation diffusion throughout the world via imperialism and colonialism
Islam (1.8 billion)	Southwest Asia	• Contagious diffusion by trade and conquest to Spain, Africa, and much of Asia • Relocation diffusion throughout the world

DIFFUSION OF RELIGIONS

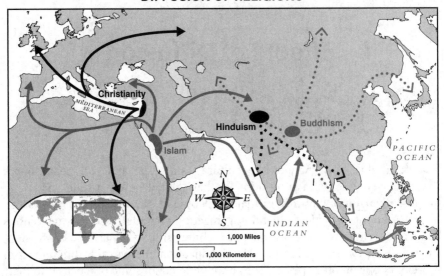

The map above show the historical diffusion of the four largest religions. The map does not show the global spread of Christianity during the European Imperialism and Colonialism period.

REFLECT ON THE ESSENTIAL QUESTION

Essential Question: *What factors led to the diffusion of universalizing and ethnic religions?*

Universalizing and Ethnic Religions	Types of Diffusion

KEY TERMS

linguists	Hinduism
language tree	polytheistic
Indo-European language family	monotheistic
Romance languages	karma
isoglosses	caste system
dialects	Buddhism
adages	Sikhism
toponyms	gurdwara
official language	Judaism
homogeneous	Christianity
adherents	Islam
ethnic religions	pilgrimage
universal religion	

3.8

Effects of Diffusion

Essential Question: How does the process of diffusion change the cultural landscape?

Cultural diffusion changes the cultural landscape and can be a source of controversy. One assumption is that globalization would result in **homogenization** of cultures, or making people of different places more alike. Theories about the effects of homogenization include losses of indigenous languages, religious practices, unique architectural styles, artistic expression, etc. People in some places respond to globalization in ways quite different from those of people in other places. They adopt and adapt some practices into their local culture while rejecting other aspects.

Smartphones and texting provide a good example of local adaptations. Texters in different countries have developed different shortcuts to lessen the number of keystrokes or to express emotions. For example, someone in the United States might use :) to represent a smiling face, while a person in Korea would use ^^.

Contact Between Cultures

Diffusion describes the ways cultures spread. As they spread, they come into contact with other cultures. The interaction of cultures is one of the driving forces in human history, and it can have several types of results, ranging from a person fully adopting the culture to picking up several cultural traits to acquiring no traits.

Acculturation

Often, an ethnic or immigrant group moving to a new area adopts the values and practices of the larger group that has received them, while still maintaining valuable elements of their own culture. This is called **acculturation**. For example, in the 1880s, the Syndergaard family migrated from Denmark to the United States, settling in a Danish enclave in Iowa. The mother and father gave most of their ten children common Danish names, such as Inger and Niels. They commonly ate Danish foods, including spherical pancakes called *abelskivver*. Within three generations, their descendants still ate abelskivver, but they had names common in U.S. culture, such as Susan, Jim, and Dave.

Another example of acculturation occurs when children or families speak Spanish or another native language at home but at school or work, they speak English. Acculturation is one reason why so many immigrants are multilingual.

Assimilation

Unlike acculturation, assimilation happens when an ethnic group can no longer be distinguished from the receiving group. This often occurs as ethnic groups become more affluent and leave their ethnic areas. Complete assimilation rarely happens, though. Usually, the one trait that is retained the longest is religion. For example, the grandchildren of immigrants from India might no longer speak Hindi or eat traditional Indian cuisine daily, but they might still practice their Hindu faith. Commonly, the third and fourth generations of an ethnic group display a resurgence in ethnic pride by organizing festivals, learning their ethnic language, and revitalizing ethnic neighborhoods.

Syncretism

The fusion or blending of two distinctive cultural traits into a unique new hybrid trait is called syncretism. This process results in new practices, beliefs, innovations, and traits within a society and ultimately results in changes to culture. This process is most likely to occur when different cultures are in proximity to each other and can occur via immigration, marriage between two groups, conquest, or simple creativity. One example is the blending of American fast food with cuisine from another culture, such as Taco Bell or Panda Express. Another example is the blending of snow skiing with inspiration from skateboarding and surfing, resulting in snowboarding. Holidays, such as Christmas, are a blending of a German tradition (decorating a tree), a Turkish belief (St. Nick—Santa Claus), a Christian doctrine (birth of Jesus), and American commercialism.

Most religions and languages are modified or blended as groups of people interact and create new meanings and traditions that reflect elements of multiple cultures. Additionally, music styles are often syncretic. Contemporary hip-hop freestyle rapping was influenced by Black jazz musicians of the 1930s and 1940s. Their willingness to improvise and create new rhythmic beats freely while playing allowed creativity and expression of culture and emotion. Hip-hop rappers incorporated this jazz freestyle rhythm and on-the-fly rhyming into their stories and poetic songs to express their views of inner-city America.

Glocalization is a form of syncretism that involves the creation of products or services for the global market by adapting them to local cultures. An example would be how McDonald's created the McCafé idea of designer coffees and pastries to attract customers in France. This blended model of fast food and coffee was so successful it diffused back to the United States market.

Multiculturalism

Without full assimilation, most receiving societies, such as the United States, are characterized by multiculturalism, the coexistence of several cultures in one society with the ideal of all cultures being valued and worthy of study. A major idea of multiculturalism is that the interaction of cultures enriches the lives of all.

Foods commonly eaten in the United States demonstrate the benefits of multiculturalism. Many foods introduced by one specific cultural group became common in the diet of people of all cultural groups:

- Corn, tomatoes, and potatoes come from indigenous American groups.
- Peanuts were first grown in South America and rice was first grown in China, but both entered the North American diet by way of Africa.
- Bagels were first made by Jews in Eastern Europe.

Nativism

However, coexistence of cultures can also bring conflicts, as people and groups with different values, beliefs, and customs often clash. Minority groups can face prejudice and discrimination. Refugees hoping to settle in the United States after fleeing Syria at the outbreak of the 2011 civil war faced opposition from Americans who feared that some refugees might be terrorists.

In some cases, the conflict between two cultures becomes harsh. **Nativist**, or anti-immigrant, attitudes may form among the cultural majority, sometimes bringing violence and government actions against the immigrant or minority group. Often, nativist attitudes are directed toward one particular group. For example, from the mid-1800s through the early 1900s, many native-born Protestants in the United state were strongly opposed to Roman Catholic immigrant from Ireland, Italy, Poland, and other countries. Mexican Americans and other immigrant from Spanish-speaking countries have often faced oppostion from nativist groups.

Other times, nativism reflects a general dislike of people from other countries, or xenophobia. A more contemporary example is the poor reception that Syrian refugees experienced in some European countries. Many Europeans feared the introduction of non-European languages, religions, and cultural practices of the largely Muslim Syrian refugee population.

REFLECT ON THE ESSENTIAL QUESTION

Essential Question: *How does the process of diffusion change the cultural landscape?*

List of the Effects of Diffusion of Culture	Explanation of the Effects of Diffusion of Culture

---

KEY TERMS

homogenization	glocalization
acculturation	multiculturalism
assimilation	nativist
syncretism	

What defines the region of the United States where Spanish is widely spoken? Geographers answer this question using various tools, such as census data, surveys, and the cultural landscape. They have found that the Spanish-speaking region changes depending on the level of analysis.

Spanish at the Country and U.S. State Scale

The United States includes more than 41 million people who grew up speaking primarily Spanish, and another 11 million bilingual people. On a cartogram showing the total number of Spanish speakers in a country, the United States would be the second-largest country in the world; only Mexico would be larger.

ENGLISH-LANGUAGE SPEAKERS AMONG U.S. HISPANICS		
Age Group	**2000**	**2014**
5 to 17		
18 to 33		

Percentage of U.S. Hispanics who speak English very well or speak only English

Source: Pew Research Center of data from the 2014 American Community Survey and the 2000 Census (IPUMS).

At the state level, the answer is slightly more complex. States vary, generally according to history and relative location. States with the highest percentages of Spanish-speaking Americans were all once colonies of Spain and are located close to Latin America: California, Nevada, Arizona, New Mexico, Texas, and Florida.

Spanish at the Local Scale

At the county level, the issue becomes even more complex. Large cities throughout the country have large populations of residents who speak Spanish as either a first or second language. The Chicago metropolitan area has more Spanish speakers than the entire populations of either New Mexico or Arizona. In addition, scattered counties around the country, from southern Idaho to eastern North Carolina, each have at least 7 percent of their population who speak Spanish.

1. Using the concept of scale, explain how the United States is labeled on a map as a majority English-speaking country but is still the country with the second-most Spanish speakers in the world.

2. What are trends related to the change in English-language speakers among Hispanics in the United States?

THINK AS A GEOGRAPHER: *LANGUAGE CONNECTIONS IN NEW YORK*

The connection between language and culture is often very close. However, it is often not identical. When immigrants come to the United States, they often lose their ancestral language but keep elements of their ancestral culture. The reverse can also occur: people might continue to worship in their traditional language, such as Arabic, Hebrew, or Greek, but also speak English, watch baseball, and eat apple pie.

New York City, a magnet for immigrants from around the world, includes native speakers of every major language. These speakers form networks among each other and with overseas communities. English and Spanish are widely spoken, but neighborhoods are often pockets of speakers of other languages. Look at the data in the chart below.

NEW YORK CITY LANGUAGES	
Language	**Number of Speakers in New York City**
English	3,700,000
Spanish	1,870,000
Chinese	419,000
South Asian Languages (Hindi, Urdu, and Others)	200,000
Russian	186,000
French Creole	106,000
Yiddish	85,000
French	81,000

1. Based on the languages spoken in other parts of the world, with which parts would New York City have the strongest network?

2. Explain how English creates a network in New York City by serving as a lingua franca.

3. What evidence would you look for in the cultural landscape to see whether you were in a neighborhood where a language other than English is widely used?

CHAPTER 7 REVIEW:
Historical and Contemporary Processes of Diffusion

Topics 3.5–3.8

MULTIPLE-CHOICE QUESTIONS

1. Some countries have several official languages because they want to

   (A) make international diplomacy easier

   (B) foster political cooperation with neighboring countries

   (C) make government operate more efficiently

   (D) prepare students to participate in the global economy

   (E) give recognition to different groups within the country

2. Which statement best describes the most common reason groups wish to preserve their traditional languages?

   (A) Language is central to cultural identity, so preserving a language helps preserve a culture.

   (B) Language is used in religious services, so preserving a language is primarily a religious obligation.

   (C) Language is used for trade, so preserving language is one way to keep a group economically prosperous.

   (D) Language change is a politically disruptive force, so preserving a language is one way to keep stability.

   (E) Language preservation passes on a group's history, so preserving a language is the only way to record history accurately.

3. The Arabic language spread from its hearth and became one of the major global languages mainly through

   (A) increased use of communication technology in Arab nations

   (B) spread of Middle Eastern multinational oil corporations

   (C) worldwide colonization beginning around 600 C.E.

   (D) conquest and its use as a standard religious language

   (E) resisting colonization by European nations and the United States

Question 4 refers to the map below.

DIFFUSION OF BUDDHISM OUT OF INDIA

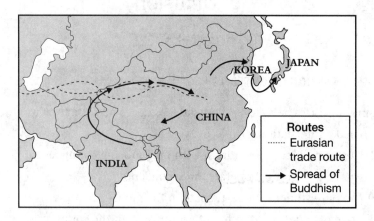

4. Which general conclusion about the expansion diffusion of the religion does the map most strongly support?

   (A) It requires mass migrations of people over long distances.

   (B) It usually moves in an eastward direction.

   (C) It is aided by the presence of a major trade route.

   (D) It occurs more in Asia than on other continents.

   (E) It experiences strong fundamentalism at its hearth.

5. Which was the most common religious change among Africans as a result of contact with people from Europe and the Middle East?

   (A) Animism to a universalizing religion

   (B) An ethnic religion to animism

   (C) A universalizing religion to an ethnic religion

   (D) Monotheism to polytheism

   (E) Polytheism to an ethnic religion

6. Which type of influence has been most significant in shaping the distribution of religious groups in the United States?

   (A) Climate and landforms

   (B) Immigration patterns

   (C) Federal government policies

   (D) Economic development

   (E) Shifts in agriculture

7. Which of the following is NOT a factor that has encouraged globalization?

(A) Technological advances in communication and transportation

(B) Increased business costs

(C) The quest for global markets associated with capitalism

(D) An increase in the flows of financial capital

(E) Governmental policies

FREE-RESPONSE QUESTION

1. Two major religious hearths in the world are Southwest Asia and South Asia. Religions diffused from these regions to many others. Use the map below to answer the questions that follow.

THE DIFFUSION OF FOUR RELIGIONS

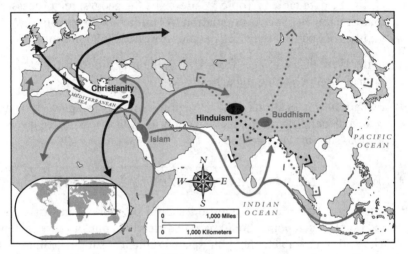

(A) Identify ONE religion that originated in Southwest Asia and a country today where the majority of people follow the religion.

(B) Identify ONE religion that originated in South Asia and a country in the world today where the majority of people follow the religion.

(C) Describe the difference between universalizing and ethnic religions.

(D) Explain how hierarchical diffusion helped the spread of Christianity.

(E) Describe how relocation diffusion explains the spread of either Hinduism or Judaism.

(F) Identify the scale of analysis of the map shown and describe ONE limitation of the map.

(G) Describe ONE specific way that when a religion diffuses to a new area it can change the cultural landscape.

UNIT 3 REVIEW:
Connecting Course Skills and Content

APPLYING GEOGRAPHIC SKILLS

Applying geographic skills is critical for success on the AP® Exam. For each skill listed, write a one-paragraph response that illustrates your understanding of it. Support your response with specific examples and evidence. Refer to the Unit 1 introduction (pages 3–7) for tips on how to apply geographic skills.

1C Compare and contrast the three types of expansion diffusion.

2A Describe the spatial patterns, networks, and relationships of a major language and religion.

3E Using the data table in Topic 3.5, describe the geographic processes that explain why Spain's population (47 million) differs from the number of Spanish-speaking people worldwide (570 million).

4A Using three visual images from Unit 3, identify different types of information presented in each source.

5B Explain how a location's cultural region (language, religion etc.) can change depending on the scale of analysis. Cite at least three levels of scale to support your response.

 WRITE AS A GEOGRAPHER: *WRITE IN COMPLETE THOUGHTS*

A response to a free-response question should be more than just a list of unrelated points. Each point should be stated clearly in one or more sentences that each express a complete thought. Related sentences should be linked with words such as "for example," "as a result," and "in the next stage" that make the relationship between ideas clear. Together, all of the sentences should work together to form a larger complete thought that answers the question.

For each word, write one or two sentences that demonstrate how that word might be used in answering a free-response question about categories of religion.

1. monotheistic
2. polytheistic
3. fundamentalism
4. ethnic
5. universal
6. theocracies

Write a sentence that includes each pair of words or phrases and states a clear relationship between the concepts.

7. Jewish Diaspora; relocation diffusion
8. sharia; religious law
9. universalizing religions; members feel a mandate
10. Mecca, Jerusalem, Lhasa (Tibet); sacred space

UNIT 4

Political Patterns and Processes

Chapter 8 Political Processes and Power

Chapter 9 Political Boundaries and Forms of Governance

Chapter 10 Challenges in the Modern State

Unit Overview

Today's political map consists mostly of independent states in which all territory is connected, and most people share a language and other cultural traits. This was not true in the past. Many states were sprawling, diverse empires, such as the Ottoman Empire in the Middle East or the British Empire that included people of many cultures. At the same time, many cultural groups were divided into several states, such as the hundreds of small German states in central Europe or the various groups of nomads in central Asia.

Political Power Over a Territory

A government demonstrates its power over a geographic area by enforcing laws that govern individual behavior and affect how resources are used. Boundaries separate territories at various scales, from those that divide the world into countries to those that determine where students attend school.

Political power can be divided in several ways. In a country, it can be centralized in one national government or divided between the national government and local governments. In the United States, local power can be centralized under regional or county governments or divided into a patchwork of cities, school districts, and other types of districts.

Challenges for States

Independent states face challenges from globalization. Transnational corporations, international organizations, and global environmental problems make the boundaries around a state less important than in the past. States also face challenges from within. Regions with distinctive cultural groups, such as Quebec and Nunavut in Canada, have successfully argued for more autonomy.

ENDURING UNDERSTANDINGS

PSO-1: The political organization of space results from historical and current processes, events, and ideas.

IMP-4: Political boundaries and divisions of governance, between states and within them, reflect balances of power that have been negotiated or imposed.

SPS-4: Political, economic, cultural, or technological changes can challenge state sovereignty.

Source: *AP® Human Geography Course and Exam Description.* Effective Fall 2020. (College Board).

CHAPTER 8

Political Processes and Power

Topics 4.1–4.3

Topic 4.1 Introduction to Political Geography

Learning Objective: For world political maps:

a. Define the different types of political entities.

b. Identify a contemporary example of political entities. (PSO-4.A)

Topic 4.2 Political Processes

Learning Objective: Explain the processes that have shaped contemporary political geography. (PSO-4.B)

Topic 4.3 Political Power and Territoriality

Learning Objective: Describe the concepts of political power and territoriality as used by geographers. (PSO-4.C)

[Soviet] General Secretary Gorbachev, if you seek peace, if you seek prosperity for the Soviet Union and Eastern Europe, if you seek liberalization, come here to this gate. Mr. Gorbachev, open this gate! Mr. Gorbachev, tear down this wall!

—President Ronald Reagan, speech, 1987

Source: David Palmer

The Berlin Wall has mostly been torn down after the unification of East and West Germany in 1989. Parts of the wall have been preserved to express messages of unification and remembrance. (See Topic 4.2 for how political processes shape boundaries.)

Introduction to Political Geography

Essential Question: What are the different types of political entities, with current examples, on a world map?

Empires and kingdoms were common in most of the world for the past 2,000 years. However, global forces, wars, and changing ideas about political power, economics, and self-rule have reshaped the world map over the last few centuries.

The Structure of the Contemporary Political Map

People often use the words *country, state,* and *nation* to mean the same thing. But they have different meanings. *Country* is the most general term. It is often used to describe any political entity that is independent from the control of any other entity. *State* and *nation* have more precise meanings.

Independent States as Building Blocks

Political units exist at various scales. In the United States, for example, a person resides in several political units at once: maybe a town or city, a county, a state, and finally, in the country as a whole. The term *state* can be confusing because it can be used in two different ways. In this example, it refers to one of the 50 states that make up the United States. But in international relations, a **state** is the largest political unit, the formal term for a country. To be defined as a state, several criteria must be met:

- has a defined boundary
- contains a permanent population
- maintains sovereignty (defined below) over its domestic and international affairs
- is recognized by other states

The United States recognizes 195 states based on these criteria, but the number can vary depending on which government or international organization makes the list. These four requirements are easily defined, but in the geopolitical arena, they can be difficult to recognize.

Understanding Sovereignty The power of a political unit, or government, to rule over its own affairs is known as **sovereignty.** It is a key principle in understanding how governments function. In order for a political unit to have legitimacy over its domestic and international affairs, it must maintain sovereignty over its own land. In the modern world, a territory must have defined borders that have been legally established. No political unit can exist or claim sovereignty without a permanent population within its borders. In most cases, the people of a state have lived in a territory for generations, if not centuries. However, most states are multinational, or made up of several ethnicities and nationalities.

The Example of China Consider the complicated relationship between the People's Republic of China and the nearby island of Taiwan (the Republic of China). In 1949, China ended a long civil war. The victorious communist forces led by Mao Zedong established their capital in Beijing. More than 2 million supporters of the losing side, known as nationalists, retreated to Taiwan. China was divided between two governments, one on the mainland and one in Taiwan, and each considered itself China's legitimate ruler. The government on the mainland never gave up its claim on Taiwan, and Taiwan never declared independence.

Today, the government in Beijing rules more than 1.4 billion residents. Taiwan rules about 24 million, but it manages its own affairs and has diplomatic relations with about 20 countries.

China's claim that Taiwan is nothing more than a renegade province is a direct challenge to Taiwan's sovereignty. And since Taiwan is recognized by so few other states, it seems to be an effective challenge. Largely because of China's opposition, Taiwan is not a member of the United Nations (UN), and the case can be made that Taiwan does not fully meet the third and fourth criteria to be recognized as a state listed on the previous page.

Types of Political Entities

Often the term *nation* is interchangeably used with *country*; however, the terms are not identical. In general, a **nation** is a group of people who have certain things in common:

- a common cultural heritage
- a set of beliefs and values that unify them
- a traditional claim to a particular space as their homeland
- a desire to establish their own state or express self-rule in another way

Depending on how tightly one applies these standards, the number of nations ranges from a few hundred to several thousand. Many political entities combine aspects of nationhood and statehood.

Nation-States A nation of people who fulfill the qualifications of a state form a **nation-state**. Among the best examples of nation-states are Iceland and Japan. Icelanders make up 94 percent of its total population of 360,000. Scandinavian settlers founded Iceland on an island that had no indigenous population. Japanese account for 99 percent of the total population of its 128 million permanent residents. A strong national identity coupled with strict immigration policies have maintained Japan as a nation-state.

DISTINGUISHING NATIONS AND STATES

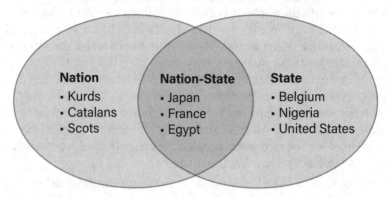

Nation	Nation-State	State
• Kurds	• Japan	• Belgium
• Catalans	• France	• Nigeria
• Scots	• Egypt	• United States

Multinational States A **multinational state** is a country that contains more than one nation. Most countries in the world today are multinational states that consist of one dominant nation and other smaller ones. The dominant nation controls most of the political power, but the smaller ones can have a significant impact.

Numerous multinational states fit these criteria, including Canada. While the English-language culture dominates, about 25 percent of Canadians speak French primarily. Most live in the province of Quebec. In an effort to prevent Quebec from demanding independence, the national government passed legislation making Canada a bilingual state and gave the province increased local autonomy in government and education.

Similarly, the Canadian government granted more autonomy over local affairs and natural resources to the indigenous nations. As part of this effort, it created the territory of Nunavut in 1999. Nunavut is in the far north of Canada. Over 80 percent of the population consider themselves Inuit, a culturally similar group of indigenous people in the Arctic. South of this region, Canada has designated over 600 indigenous governments and tribes as First Nations. This label has granted these people legal status as designated groups, providing them with certain legal rights and privileges. These privileges usually include hunting and fishing rights, as well as more control over local affairs.

Autonomous Regions A defined area within a state that has a high degree of self-government and freedom from its parent state is sometimes known as an **autonomous region**. States often grant this authority to geographically, ethnically, or culturally distinct areas.

For example, Åland is a group of islands in the Baltic Sea. It is part of Finland but lies near Sweden. Most residents are ethnically Swedish and speak that language. The people of Åland submitted a request to the League of Nations, a body similar to today's United Nations, to join Sweden after World War I ended in 1918. The League ruled that Åland should remain part of Finland, but as a nonmilitarized, largely self-governing entity, which it still is today.

Semiautonomous Regions A state that has a degree of, but not complete self-rule, is a **semiautonomous region**. Straddling the Four Corners region of the United States (where the borders of Arizona, Utah, Colorado, and New Mexico meet) is one of the largest American Indian nations, the Navajo. With more than 300,000 tribal members, they claim exclusive rights to over 27,000 square miles for their reservation, which is a federally recognized territory for Native Americans. Reservations, like the one controlled by the Navajo, possess tribal sovereignty, providing them exclusive rights, such as local self-government, and exemption from some state and federal taxes. However, the United States does not recognize complete sovereignty or independence of the Navajo or other Native American reservations.

Stateless Nations The Navajo are an example of a **stateless nation**, a cultural group that has no independent political entity. Since the world includes more nations than states, many stateless nations exist. Two that have sought to become independent states in recent decades are the Palestinians who live primarily in the Israeli-controlled territories of the Gaza Strip and the West Bank, and the Basques who live near the Spanish-French border.

The largest stateless nation belongs to the Kurdish people. Spread among six states in southwest Asia—Turkey, Armenia, Iraq, Iran, Azerbaijan, and Syria—the Kurds number between 25 million and 30 million people in an area called Kurdistan. As states such as Syria and Iraq became destabilized in the 2000s, ethnic Kurds intensified their push for their own independent country.

THE KURDISTAN REGION

In which countries do the Kurds currently live? Since the Kurds live in numerous countries, what challenges might this create for Kurdish independence?

Multistate Nations A **multistate nation** occurs when a nation has a state of its own but stretches across borders of other states. For example, most Hungarians live in Hungary, but many live in the Transylvania region of Romania. The Korean nation is divided primarily between two states—the Democratic People's Republic of Korea—North Korea—and the Republic of Korea—South Korea—but with large numbers in China and the United States.

REFLECT ON THE ESSENTIAL QUESTION

Essential Question: *What are the different types of political entities, with current examples, on a world map?*

Political Entity	Description of Entity

KEY TERMS

state

sovereignty

nation

nation-state

multinational state

autonomous region

semiautonomous region

stateless nation

multistate nation

Political Processes

Essential Question: What are the processes that have shaped contemporary political geography?

How many states are there in the world? While there are criteria for defining and describing the different types of states (see Topic 4.1), there is no unifying consensus as to how many countries actually exist. The United Nations officially recognizes 195 member states and has also granted permanent non-member observer status to non-states, such as the Holy See (the political body of the Vatican) and the State of Palestine. Additionally, other territories claim sovereignty but have not achieved full statehood, such as Taiwan (off the coast of China) and Kosovo (claimed by Serbia).

To understand why a seemingly straightforward question about the number of countries in the world is complex, a look at history is needed. The modern world map is a mosaic of borders, states, and nations that have been created and changed throughout history.

Evolution of the Contemporary Political Map

Today's world map includes nations without states, nations in multiple states, and states containing multiple nations. This mixture of situations reflects the distribution of cultures and the evolution of politics, economics, and warfare over the last 600 years.

The Modern Nation-State Concept

For most of European history, no relation existed between the language people spoke and the state to which they belonged. For example, most people who paid allegiance to the king of France in the 1500s did not speak French. Rather, they spoke a regional language. And people who spoke various forms of Italian in the 1600s did not assume that they should all be part of the same state. By the 1700s, the idea that people should live in nation-states had caught hold in some areas, beginning in France and England. However, the map of Europe was still a patchwork of tiny states and a few large multiethnic empires—Russian Empire, Ottoman Empire, etc.

The 1800s saw an explosion of nationalism in Europe. On one hand, groups rebelled against being part of large empires that were controlled by another culture. On the other hand, divided groups wanted to consolidate into unified countries. Between 1858 and 1871, eight separate states in southern Europe combine to form the modern country of Italy.

THE EIGHT INDEPENDENT ITALIAN STATES IN 1858

Forces Unifying and Breaking Apart Countries

One definition of **nationalism** is a nation's desire to create and maintain a state of its own. Since nationalism unifies people, it is an example of a **centripetal force**, one that helps to unify people within a country. There are other centripetal forces that unite people:

- a shared religion—Roman Catholicism unites Mexicans
- external threats—Estonians are united by fear of Russia
- a common language—Japanese share the same language

A counter to centripetal forces would be a **centrifugal force**. This is a force that tends to divide people, break states apart, or even prevent states from forming. For example, religion and language divide the people of Belgium. Most people in the north speak a Dutch language called Flemish and are historically Protestants, while people in the southern regions of Belgium speak French and tend to be Roman Catholics. The capital region of Brussels is officially bilingual in an attempt to foster centripetal forces that unify the people of both regions.

Imperialism and Colonialism

Imperialism and colonialism are related ideas, but they are not the same. **Imperialism** is a broader concept that includes a variety of ways of influencing another country or group of people by direct conquest, economic control, or cultural dominance. **Colonialism** is a particular type of imperialism in which people move into and settle on the land of another country. Examples of imperialism and colonialism can be found throughout history and all over the world, but modern European imperialism and colonialism are relevant to the current political map because the boundaries of most countries were created by these forces. European imperialism occurred in two distinct waves.

Early Colonialism The first wave of European colonialism was led by Spain and Portugal, and then by France and Britain. These countries established large empires in the Americas, and they were motivated by "God, gold, and glory." They wanted:

- religious influence by spreading their form of Christianity
- economic wealth from exploiting land, labor, and capital to enrich the home country
- political power by expanding their influence throughout the world

The European powers justified their conquests through the legal concept of *terra nullius,* a Latin phrase meaning "land belonging to no one." According to this concept, they could legitimately seize "uncivilized land." The result was the dispossession of indigenous people and the impact of this is still being redressed throughout parts of the world today.

Wars among empires influenced colonial claims. In the Seven Years' War (1756–1763), known in North America as the French and Indian War, the British won control of Canada from France. However, the strain of paying for the war led to conflicts between Britain and its colonies, soon resulting in the American Revolution. U.S. independence then inspired similar movements in other colonies. By 1833, most of Latin America was free from European rule, and nationalism was spreading through the region.

Later Colonialism During the 19th century, the influence of Spanish and Portuguese empires declined, which allowed other European countries to launch a second wave of colonization. The competition to claim resources (to feed factories) and new markets (to sell goods) resulted in Great Britain, France, the Netherlands, Belgium, Italy, and Germany seizing control of lands in Africa and Asia.

In 1884 and 1885, representatives from the major empires of Europe met in the German capital of Berlin to lay out claims made on the continent of Africa. The **Berlin Conference** (see Topic 4.5), sometimes known as the Congo Conference, used these claims to form state boundaries in Africa. These boundaries showed little regard to the existing ethno-linguistic, cultural, and political boundaries. As a result, one colony might include a patchwork of rival cultural groups, and another cultural group might be divided among multiple colonies.

The modern country of Nigeria has several major languages and more than 500 individual languages are spoken within its borders. Hausa is widely spoken in the Muslim-dominated regions of the north, while Igbo and Yoruba are regionally spoken farther south where Christianity mixes with traditional religions. As a former British colony, Nigeria's official language is English, which acts a centripetal force for such a diverse population.

Geopolitical Forces Influencing Today's Map

While the European colonies in Africa and Asia did not last long, their legacy was strong. It can be seen in contemporary maps and the links among countries.

Modern Colonial Independence Movements

Colonists, inspired by nationalism, resisted the rule of Europeans, sometimes with violence. People in these European colonies wanted several types of influence:

- economic control over natural resources such as petroleum and precious metals
- political power through free elections
- social changes such as racial equality and religious freedom

However, subject people in colonies wanted **self-determination**, the right to choose their own sovereign government without external influence. With the support of the United Nations, created in 1945, they were slowly successful. Within a century of the Berlin Conference, all European colonial territories had won independence. This process is known as **decolonization**, the undoing of colonization, in which indigenous people reclaim sovereignty over their territory.

While many former colonies gained political independence, they remained in a state of economic dependence. A new form of colonization, *neocolonialism* (see Topic 4.3), emerged in which control over developing countries was exerted through indirect means, whether economic, political, or even cultural power.

Civil Wars in the Developing World

From 1960 through 1970, 32 colonial territories in Africa gained independence. However, since independence was won by colonies rather than by cultural groups, the boundaries imposed by Europe remained in the newly independent states. As a result, cultural boundaries and political boundaries often did not match. Cultural conflicts within countries led to many civil wars. Then, because cultural groups spanned political borders, conflicts in one country often spilled over into other countries.

Among the worst of these wars was in Rwanda in 1994, which led to **genocide**, organized mass killing, in which people are targeted because of their race, religion, ethnicity, or nationality. Before colonization by Belgium, two rival ethnic groups, the Hutu and Tutsi, had competed for control of territory and resources. In 1961, Rwanda won independence. The Hutu majority won elections to govern the country, but the rivalry with the Tutsi continued. In April 1994, the Rwandan president, a Hutu, died when his plane was shot down. Although no one knew then who was responsible, Hutus exacted revenge by killing Tutsis and moderate Hutus on a vast scale. Within just a few months, more than 800,000 Rwandans were killed and nearly 2 million migrated as refugees to neighboring countries.

This pattern of independence followed by civil wars and regional conflicts is nothing new to the political landscape. Serious problems result when national and ethnic rivals are forced to share political space because of boundaries drawn by outside powers. And in many cases, one ethnicity may be spread over several states, so a conflict in one state quickly escalates into a regional one. Today, many of the geopolitical "hotspots" in Africa and the Middle East are difficult to solve because of borders established long ago.

THE SPREAD OF INDEPENDENCE, 1945 TO 2015

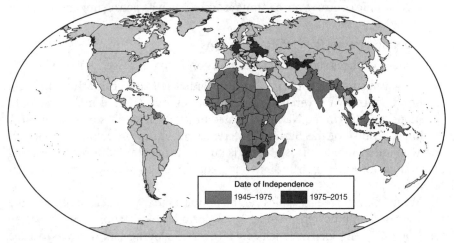

Identify three regions where numerous countries gained independence from 1945 to 1975 and from 1975 to 2015.

The Cold War and Devolution

The **Cold War** was a period of diplomatic, political, and military rivalry between the United States and the Union of Soviet Socialist Republics (USSR or Soviet Union), a confederation of 15 republics, including Russia. It started at the end of World War II (1945), continued through the collapse of the Berlin Wall (1989), and ended with the breakup of the Soviet Union (1991).

Although the United States and the Soviet Union did not fight a direct war against each other, they fought several proxy wars—by providing military and financial support to the countries involved—in Africa, Latin America, and Asia. For the United States, the largest of these conflicts were in Korea, Vietnam, and Afghanistan. The superpowers wanted to extend their spheres of influence, or the areas over which they had some degree of control. This meant winning allies in other countries and thwarting their rival from doing the same. The American-Soviet contest often influenced the newly independent states emerging out of colonialism.

After World War II, the frontline for the Cold War was Europe, where a tenuous peace divided the continent between East and West. Eastern European countries were liberated from Nazi Germany and later occupied by the Soviet army, became Soviet **satellite states**, or a state dominated by another politically and economically. Attempts by Hungary in 1956 and Czechoslovakia in 1968 to break away from Soviet domination were put down with overwhelming force.

Germany's status was complicated. Its territory and its capital city (Berlin) were split between the democratic and capitalist-friendly West Germany and West Berlin and the Communist Soviet Union-dominated East Germany and East Berlin. In 1961, to prevent people from defecting from the Soviet sphere of influence, the Berlin Wall was constructed by East Germany, physically demarcating and ideologically representing the deep divide between the two worlds.

COLD WAR BLOCS, c. 1960

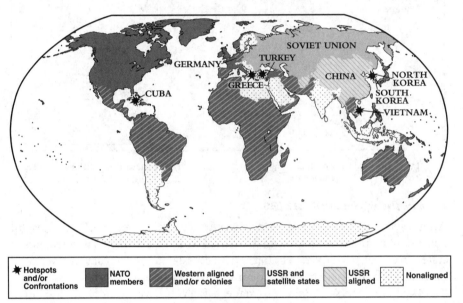

The Collapse of Communism

In the late 1980s, new leadership in the Soviet Union began to relax its grip over satellite states in Eastern Europe. Finally, in November 1989, citizens of East and West Germany brought down the wall that had long divided the city of Berlin. Within two years, Germany had reunited and former satellite states of Eastern Europe were holding free elections without Soviet influence. Some states experienced a relatively peaceful transition, such as Poland with the Solidarity movement led by Lech Walesa. However, others endured more violence. In Romania, a 1989 revolution resulted in the execution of the dictator Nicolae Ceausescu and his wife. But change in Europe did not end there.

The Soviet Union began to collapse as well. Under extreme economic duress, and significant social and political division within the Soviet Union, the 15 republics were granted more autonomy and self-rule. This process in which one or more regions are given increased autonomy by the central political unit is known as **devolution**.

FORMER REPUBLICS OF THE SOVIET UNION

Each of the former republics became an independent state. Identify three states that gained independence in Eastern Europe and in Central Asia.

Newly Independent States

After 1990, the political boundaries were once again altered. The collapse of communism and the Soviet Union resulted in the creation of 15 independent states from former Soviet republics, with Russia as the largest. This series of events significantly altered the modern map of Europe and Asia.

Many former *satellite states* made a peaceful transition into the post-communist world. For example, in 1993, Czechoslovakia divided into the Czech Republic and the Republic of Slovakia, predominantly along ethnolinguistic lines. This event has been called the "Velvet Divorce," since the transition was so smooth.

However, the breakup of Yugoslavia in 1991 was complicated and violent. Long-standing ethnic tensions erupted. Hundreds of thousands died in clashes between Serbs, Bosnians, and others before a handful of independent countries emerged. Many died because of *ethnic cleansing* (see Topic 4.8), the forced removal of a minority ethnic group from a territory. Geographically, this region was a *shatterbelt* (see Topic 4.5), a place that suffers instability because it is located between two very different and contentious regions.

Changes in the Balance of Power

The collapse of communism and the Soviet Union drastically changed the balance of power in Europe and throughout the world. Some former communist countries of Eastern Europe, as well as some independent states, joined the European Union and the North Atlantic Treaty Organization (NATO)—the

Western military alliance, formed in 1949 to oppose Soviet military power in Europe. (See Topic 4.9.) By the early 21st century, the balance of economic, political, and military power tilted toward Western Europe and the United States.

This power shift frightened Russian leaders. They reacted by providing military support to pro-Russian groups. For example, in 2008 a border dispute developed between the Republic of Georgia and Russia over land known as South Ossetia. Involvement of the Russian military led to a five-day war. As a result of this short conflict, Russia asserted its influence and dominance beyond its borders.

Russia also set its sights on Crimea in 2014. The Crimean Peninsula lies on the northern edge of the Black Sea and existed as a *semiautonomous republic* (see Topic 4.1) within the borders of Ukraine after the Soviet Union's downfall. However, shortly after the Winter Olympic Games in Russia in 2014, Russian troops took over several sites around Crimea. Many countries, including Ukraine, vehemently condemned this annexation as a violation of international law. However, Russia defended this action under the principle of self-determination. Russia claimed part of Crimea, yet a majority of states still regarded the region as an integral part of Ukraine. (See Topic 4.3 for more on the strategic importance of Crimea.)

REFLECT ON THE ESSENTIAL QUESTION

Essential Question: *What are the processes that have shaped contemporary political geography?*

Process	Impact on Political Geography

KEY TERMS

nationalism	self-determination
centripetal force	decolonization
centrifugal force	genocide
imperialism	Cold War
colonialism	satellite states
Berlin Conference	devolution

Political Power and Territoriality

Essential Question: What are the concepts of political power and territoriality as used by geographers?

The concepts of power, territoriality, and boundaries are often intertwined and dependent on one another. Economic systems, cultural patterns and processes, and political systems have shaped various theories of how power is distributed on the political landscape. Physical geography and the natural landscape impact the distribution of power within and between political units, as well as the form and function of boundaries. The forms of governance on international, national, regional, and local scales are products of the human and physical landscapes.

Concepts of Political Power and Territoriality

Geopolitics is the study of the effects of geography on politics and relations among states. More than just political power, geopolitics also relates to trade, resource management, and the environment on a global scale. A key concept in geopolitics is **territoriality**, or a willingness by a person or a group of people to defend space they claim. People express their territoriality when they influence others or shape events by asserting control over a space. At the local scale, for example, towns and cities lay claim to municipal districts. At the national scale, states administer and defend their borders, especially those that lie adjacent to neighboring countries. States also extend their territoriality into the oceans and bodies of water within their jurisdictions (see Topic 4.5 for more on the Law of the Sea). However, states maintain sovereignty within their borders through the consent of the people who reside there, in addition to the government's ability to negotiate at the international level.

Territoriality Connects Culture and Economy

Defining territoriality may be relatively easy, but applying it is complex. Under the influence of cultural forces and economic interests, people often disagree on how to allocate control of territories. Maps that show the boundaries of a state as clear, precise lines might suggest those boundaries are well defined. However, people might hotly disagree over the boundaries, or simply ignore them in reality. Similarly, a state's sovereignty might be well established on paper, but people might not fully accept it.

Religious Conflicts One example of the connection of territoriality to culture is the relationship between Sunni and Shia Muslims. These two branches of Islam divided on the question of who should succeed Muhammad after his death in 632. They have remained divided ever since, a division that has sometimes contributed to violence.

In recent years, the conflict within Islam has been clearest in the rivalry between Sunni-dominated Saudi Arabia and Shia-dominated Iran. Adding to the religious conflict between the countries is an ethnic difference: the Saudis are Arabs and the Iranians are Persians. Not only are these people devoted to their cultures and beliefs, but they also feel attached to the lands where their ancestors lived and where they now inhabit. Each country has tried to expand its power over territory, which has led to tension and instability.

SHIA REGIONS IN THE MIDDLE EAST

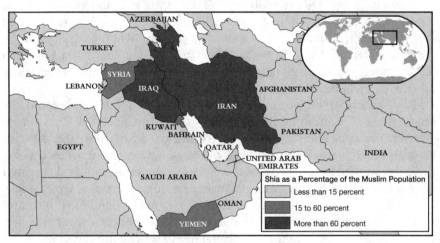

Identify countries that have over 15 percent Shia population.

Economic Conflicts Territoriality has always been closely connected to economic issues. In recent years, the Philippines, Malaysia, Brunei, Vietnam, Taiwan, and China have claimed sovereignty over the Spratly Islands—an isolated group of islands in the South China Sea. Tensions run high on the subject in the region. But why are these countries seemingly willing to risk conflict over a group of islands, islets, and reefs? The answers are, in large part, economic:

- Experts believe that significant, but unconfirmed, petroleum reserves exist in the area.
- The region's fishing grounds supply work and food for many throughout the entire region.
- Major international shipping lanes pass through the area.

At times, each of the countries involved (except Brunei) occupied at least part of the island group. China attempted to expand the size of its holdings through dredging and land reclamation—by building up small reefs into full-fledged islands—from which to better push for and enforce its claims of sovereignty.

Neocolonialism

In the aftermath of World War I and accelerating after World War II, worldwide decolonization occurred. (See Topic 4.2.) Exacerbated by high tariffs (taxes on trade) and wartime devastation, as well as economic uncertainty during the Great Depression (1929–1939), the profitability of European colonial possessions was drastically reduced. Scores of new countries gained independence across Asia and Africa. By 1975, virtually all former colonies had achieved self-determination. Gaining political independence was sometimes a long and arduous process, often with violent events involved. For example, bloodshed occurred during India's split from Britain and Algeria's break from France.

Economic Self-Determination Gaining economic independence was equally challenging. Many of these newly independent nations had focused on exporting one or perhaps only a few cash crops or light industrial products when they were colonies. In turn, these nations relied heavily on European manufactured goods, which resulted in the value of their imports being greater than that of their exports.

Additionally, these former colonies were culturally influenced by longstanding European traditions and often manipulated by foreign governments even after achieving independence. Apart from the previous direct control of these territories, in many cases, a new system of colonialism, or **neocolonialism,** emerged. In this system, economic, political, or even cultural control was indirectly exerted over developing countries. For example, transnational corporations based in European countries continued to control the extraction of natural resources through mining and the export of coffee, cacao, bananas, and other crops on plantations in developing countries.

Modern Globalization After World War II and the establishment of the United Nations (UN), trade barriers were dramatically lowered, and a new era of globalization emerged. Many people and companies in the former colonies benefited from increased access to regional and global markets. While the UN and many non-governmental organizations (NGOs) provided food and economic aid for these countries, several European states and the United States offered conditional aid. Many newly independent states had developed powerful central governments that maintained tight controls over domestic businesses and international commerce, which, at times, had a negative effect on economic growth. The United States and countries of Europe offered loans to many of these developing countries, if they reduced regulations and opened up to more free trade.

While some have praised policies like these in helping the new states modernize their economies, others have decried the effect of leading these countries toward dependence and subservience. Despite efforts to maintain territoriality, some less-developed countries (LDCs) have experienced massive debt obligations that have spiraled out of their control and, as a result, have been politically dominated by richer nations. Neocolonialism promotes a similar type of imbalanced relationship found in traditional colonialism.

Choke Points

A **choke point** is a place of physical congestion between wider regions of movement and interaction. Land-based choke points can be natural valleys or bridges. However, the most vital choke points in the world today are predominantly water-based, such as straits and canals. Around 90 percent, or $8 trillion annually, of all global goods are transported by sea.

Since the onset of the industrial age—beginning in the 18th century—and especially in modern times, power and wealth is increasingly derived from controlling strategic maritime areas of the world. The most densely populated cities and regions reside along coastal areas that are crucial to the global movement and distribution of resources. Geopolitically, countries that claim jurisdiction over these choke points often wield an inordinate amount of international clout and can benefit economically from these locations through fees and taxes, such as tolls, tariffs, and customs duties.

Bab el-Mandeb ("Gate of Tears") strait is a choke point that connects the Red Sea to the Gulf of Aden north of the Horn of Africa. It is vital to the flow of goods and traffic and has garnered international attention by nations attempting to control the area. The United States has several military bases around the Bab el-Mandeb, including a naval base in Djibouti, which demonstrates the geopolitical and economic importance of locations such as these. Many other countries also possess military bases in strategic areas, and they have gone to great lengths to ensure that shipping and travel can continue unimpeded.

Arguably, the world's most important choke point is the Strait of Hormuz, lying between the Gulf of Oman and the Persian Gulf. Around one-third of the world's natural gas and around one-quarter of the world's oil passes through this narrow waterway.

ARABIAN PENINSULA CHOKEPOINTS

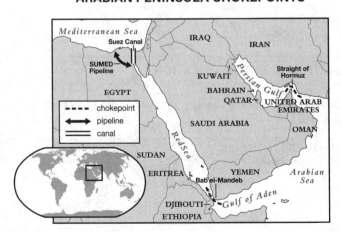

Source: eia.gov

Three of the world's most strategically important choke points, the Suez Canal, the Strait of Hormuz, and Bab el-Mandeb are around the Arabian Peninsula. Protecting free and open access to these waterways is vital in maintaining the global flow of goods and people.

At the north end of the Black Sea, Crimea affords Russia even greater proximity to a key choke point, the Turkish Straits. In 2014, Russia claimed Crimea, which had been within the borders of Ukraine since 1992. (See Topic 4.2.) Aside from the demographics, in which around two-thirds of the population is ethnically Russian, Crimea boasts a geographic advantage for Russia. These narrow waterways allow access to the Aegean and Mediterranean seas and, more importantly, increased access for global commerce. Oil and natural gas account for around two-thirds of Russia's exports and almost one-third of its gross domestic product (GDP). The Crimea enables Russian petrochemical corporations increased accessibility to the Turkish Straits. Despite the protestations of Ukraine, and the bulk of the international community decrying Russia's actions as illegal, Russia has maintained control of the area.

WORLD OIL CHOKE POINTS

Oil Transit Volumes Through Select Maritime Routes, 2016

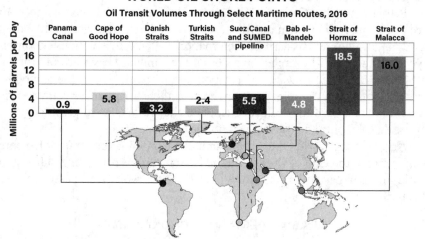

Source: US Energy Information Administration

Explain the importance of choke points for oil and other globally-traded goods.

REFLECT ON THE ESSENTIAL QUESTION

Essential Question: *What are the concepts of political power and territoriality as used by geographers?*

Political Power and Territoriality Concepts	Descriptions

KEY TERMS

geopolitics	neocolonialism
territoriality	choke point

The United States has been roughly the same size since 1867 when the country purchased Alaska. Since then, the United States has added important islands, including Hawaii and Puerto Rico, but all additions have been small in size. However, there is no guarantee that this stability will continue into the future.

Better Communication and Transportation

One of the forces that might reshape the political map of the United States is technology. Computers, the Internet, and cell phones have increased the connections among people across space. Technology could be a centripetal force. As people communicate more closely across long distances, variations from region to region might diminish. The United States might become a more tightly united country, with less cultural variation than in the past.

After World War II, the United States built an interstate highway system that was designed to connect the country. Many rural communities became more connected to cities as people traveled via highway across the country. Later, jet air travel created faster connections between cities. A negative of air travel was that people flew from city to city, often flying over rural regions, decreasing the connectivity of these areas.

Or the technology could be a centrifugal force. As Americans find people with whom they share interests and values in other places in the country, they could relate more to them than to the neighbors in their community. Place might become less important.

Movement of People

Migrations of people could also have mixed results for American political unity. The migration of people from one region to another could reduce regional variation in politics. For example, in most presidential elections in the past century, states in the Northeast and the Southeast have voted for opposing candidates. Will continued migration from the Northeast to the Southeast change this? Will the two regions become more similar politically, either because the migrants take their voting behavior with them or because the migrants adapt to the behavior of their new neighbors?

1. What challenges does the large size of the United States pose for the unity of the country?

2. How can communication technology act as both a centripetal and centrifugal force within a country?

3. What impact could internal migration have on the political landscape of the United States?

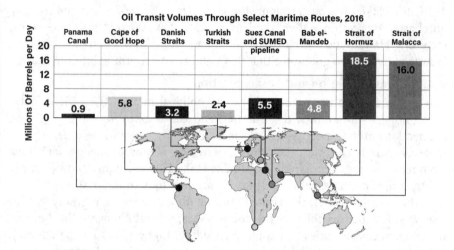

Oil Transit Volumes Through Select Maritime Routes, 2016

Many choke points have the words "strait" or "canal" as part of their toponyms. This represents a key intersection where human geography meets physical geography. The study of geopolitics helps us better understand the complex relationship between people, places, and power.

Three of the choke points regarding petroleum transit have been discussed already—Bab el-Mandeb, the Strait of Hormuz, and the Turkish Straits.

1. Describe the locations of the choke points using the concepts of countries and regions.

2. Explain the importance of each of the following choke points:

   A. Panama Canal

   B. Cape of Good Hope

   C. Danish Straits

   D. Suez Canal

   E. Strait of Malacca

CHAPTER 8 REVIEW:
Political Processes and Power

Topics 4.1–4.3

MULTIPLE-CHOICE QUESTIONS

1. Which of the following is NOT a necessary criterion for a state?
   (A) Sovereignty
   (B) Defined boundary
   (C) Common culture and identity
   (D) Recognition by other states
   (E) Permanent population

Questions 2 and 3 refer to the map and table about Slovakia.

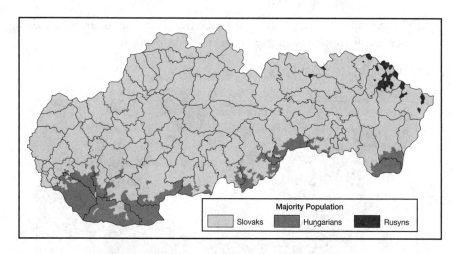

ETHNIC GROUPS IN SLOVAKIA	
Group	Percentage of the Population
Slovak	81%
Romani	9%
Hungarian	8%
Other	2%

2. Which term best describes Slovakia?

(A) Stateless nation

(B) Multinational state

(C) Empire

(D) Dependent territory

(E) Autonomous region

3. Which of the following best explains why the Romani ethnic group is identified on the chart but does not appear on the map?

(A) The scale of analysis of the data reflects that the Romani are a large minority group but are not a majority in any region.

(B) The map shows only the nodal regions in Slovakia.

(C) The friction of distance limits what information can be shown in each type of source.

(D) The data in the chart is not reliable because Slovakia is a former satellite state of the USSR.

(E) The map uses qualitative data while the chart uses quantitative data, creating an inconsistency between the information.

Question 4 refers to the map below.

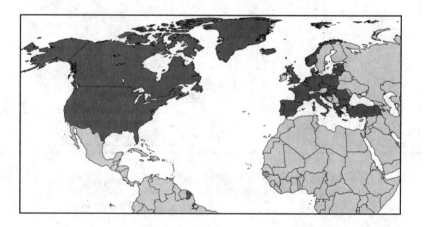

4. Countries highlighted in the darker shade in the map above represent most or all of the members which of the following organizations?

(A) North Atlantic Treaty Organization

(B) Warsaw Pact

(C) United Nations

(D) League of Nations

(E) European Union

Questions 5 and 6 refer to the chart below.

ETHNIC GROUPS IN MYANMAR (BURMA)		
Group	**Percentage of the Population**	**Traits**
Burmans	68%	• Spread throughout the center of the country • Speak the dominant language of the country
Shan	9%	• Concentrated in eastern region • Speak their own language
Kachin	7%	• Concentrated in northeast region • Speak their own language • Desire independence
Other	16%	• Government recognizes more than 130 ethnic groups • Many desire independence

5. Based on the information in the chart, Myanmar is a
   (A) nation
   (B) nation-state
   (C) multinational state
   (D) stateless nation
   (E) multistate nation

6. Based on the information in the chart, the lands of the Kachin can be considered
   (A) a multistate nation
   (B) an autonomous region
   (C) a nation-state
   (D) a stateless nation
   (E) a newly independent state

7. Which of the following would describe a positive development for a state that became independent through decolonization?
   (A) Establishing territoriality by claiming sovereignty over its lands
   (B) Maintaining economic neocolonial ties with its former mother country
   (C) Engaging in ethnic cleansing of a minority group within its borders
   (D) Existing along a shatterbelt between two powerful states
   (E) Experiencing centrifugal forces due to multiple ethnicities

1. After 1945 many of the countries in Africa won their independence. Today, independent states are the primary building block of not just Africa but the entire world. Use the map to answer the questions that follow.

AFRICA TODAY

(A) Identify TWO characteristics of a state.

(B) Explain the difference between a nation and a state.

(C) Explain the role that imperialism played in creating the borders of modern Africa.

(D) Identify a country in Africa that had a civil war after 1945, and explain ONE centrifugal force that caused the conflict. (2 points)

(E) Define the concept of stateless nation and provide a real-world geographic example.

(F) Describe ONE example of a multistate nation.

CHAPTER 9

Political Boundaries and Forms of Governance

Topics 4.4–4.7

Topic 4.4 Defining Political Boundaries

Learning Objective: Define types of political boundaries used by geographers. (IMP-4.A)

Topic 4.5 The Functions of Political Boundaries

Learning Objective: Explain the nature and function of international and internal boundaries. (IMP-4.B)

Topic 4.6 Internal Boundaries

Learning Objective: Explain the nature and function of international and internal boundaries. (IMP-4.B)

Topic 4.7 Forms of Governance

Learning Objectives: Define federal and unitary states. (IMP-4.C)
Explain how federal and unitary states affect spatial organization. (IMP-4.D)

Who rules East Europe commands the Heartland; Who rules the Heartland commands the World-Island; Who rules the World-Island commands the world.

—Sir Halford John Mackinder, *British geographer*, 1919

Depicted is the Korean Demilitarized Zone (DMZ). Despite the name, it is the militarized boundary between the Democratic People's Republic of Korea (DPRK) and the Republic of Korea (ROK). (See Topic 4.4 for more about militarized boundaries.)

Defining Political Boundaries

Essential Question: What are the types of political boundaries used by geographers?

The most common type of map used is a reference map, in which physical and cultural features are shown and usually identified. One expects a map, at any scale, to include boundaries that have been clearly delimited. Whether at the local, regional, or national scale, boundaries are an integral part of our lives. Some are invisible to the eye and others are clearly demarcated, yet all serve some political or functional purpose.

In essence, any contemporary political boundary can be categorized in one of two ways, physical or cultural. **Physical geographic boundaries** are natural barriers between areas such as oceans, deserts, and mountains. For example, the Missouri River divides Iowa and Nebraska, and the Himalayan Mountains separate India and China.

By contrast, **cultural boundaries** divide people according to some cultural division, such as language, religion, or ethnicity. A cultural boundary may exist in the midst of a gradual change over space. For example, in China, cuisine was once divided into two regions: wheat-based in the north and rice-based in the south. However, no exact line has ever divided the two regions sharply. A boundary can be classified as possessing both physical and cultural attributes.

Classifications of Boundaries

While classifying political boundaries as physical or cultural enables us to identify what a border is, geographers have developed a more in-depth classification system that provides greater context on how borders develop over time.

Genetic Classification of Boundaries

There are four genetic types (classified as to how they were generated) of political boundaries: antecedent, subsequent, superimposed, and relic.

Antecedent Boundary This type of boundary preceded the development of the cultural landscape. For boundaries, significant physical obstacles—such as oceans or mountains—possess a static aspect in that they feature a relatively unpopulated zone between populated areas. They also possess a kinetic aspect in that they hinder connections and interactions between people in adjacent regions. An example includes the straight-line boundaries for states across the western frontier of the emerging United States. Political boundaries like these were established before a large population was present and remained in place as people increasingly occupied these regions.

Antecedent boundaries are typically based on physical features. Since humans are terrestrial beings and need to live on land for survival, the unpopulated oceans such as the Atlantic and Pacific make for logical antecedent boundaries. The Andes Mountains form the long-reaching eastern boundary of Chile, naturally separating it from Bolivia and Argentina. However, antecedent boundaries that do not present a significant physical obstacle, such as small hills or rivers, tend to make less effective political boundaries.

While rivers possess a static benefit in that they maintain an unpopulated zone between populated areas, they tend to facilitate more connections and interactions. Transboundary freshwater sources, such as the Jordan River, have resulted in competing claims among Israel, Lebanon, Jordan, and Palestine. Just because an antecedent boundary exists, it does not necessarily mean it is effective.

Subsequent Boundary This boundary is typically created while the cultural landscape is evolving and is subject to change over time. These boundaries are characteristically **ethnographic** in nature, meaning they are usually related to cultural phenomena. They may be drawn to accommodate ethnic, religious, linguistic, or economic differences among groups. Subsequent boundaries are often altered as a result of non-cultural developments such as governmental negotiations or war. Beginning in the mid-16th century, the monarch of Scotland and England encouraged emigration to Ireland, which was then under English rule. Many Scots and English Protestants settled in the northern region of predominantly Roman Catholic Ireland. Over the years, resentment and violence broke out between the groups over internal borders and political influence in the region. In 1921, Northern Ireland officially became part of the United Kingdom, separating from the southern portion of the island—the Republic of Ireland. A commission was formed to draw the new border based on the religious and political cultural landscape.

Superimposed Boundary This type of boundary is drawn by outside powers and may have ignored existing cultural patterns. These boundaries often lack conformity to natural features and, therefore, were superimposed on the landscape. Between 1884 and 1885, the **Berlin Conference** paved the way for colonization of Africa or what Europeans regarded as "effective occupation" of the continent. At the time of the conference, only some coastal areas were colonized by the Europeans and around 80 percent of the continent was under traditional and local control. As a result of the conference, a series of superimposed boundaries were established, initially with little knowledge of the terrain or the cultural borders.

One of the legacies of this "Scramble for Africa" was the creation of around 50 irregularly shaped countries out of the more than 1,000 indigenous cultures that inhabited the continent. Of the 54 current African countries, 17 are **landlocked states**, or without territory connected to an ocean. The increased cost of importing and exporting goods through neighboring countries presents these states with a perpetual geographic and political disadvantage. Governments of landlocked states are inherently dealing from a weakened position and struggle to effectively negotiate with neighboring countries. While landlocked states, such as Botswana and Rwanda, have recently prospered through effective business growth policies, many landlocked states area among the most-impoverished and least-developed countries in the world.

LANDLOCKED COUNTRIES OF THE WORLD

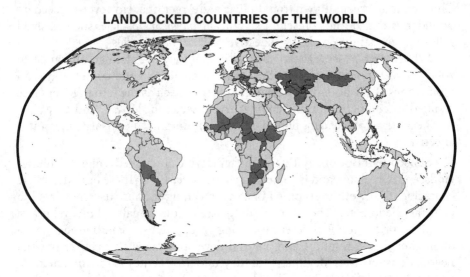

Source: Wikimedia Commons

Which regions of the world have the most landlocked states? Describe an economic and political challenge that landlocked states face.

Relic Boundary This is a boundary that has been abandoned for political purposes, but evidence of it still exists on the landscape. These boundaries are nonfunctional in the political sense but are sometimes preserved for historic purposes. Constructed in 1961, the Berlin Wall that divided East and West Berlin was famously torn down in 1989. Toward the end of the Cold War, East and West Germany reunited, but portions of the Berlin Wall are still upright, maintained as a tourist attraction and symbol of a past age. The Great Wall of China is also a relic boundary, serving no political separation between states, but still very visible on the landscape.

Geometric and Consequent Boundaries

In addition to classifying boundaries by how they were generated, geographers classify boundaries by what they follow. Do they conform to existing cultural boundaries or do they conform to physical features on the landscape?

In contrast to a physical boundary, a **geometric boundary** is a straight line or arc drawn by people that does not closely follow any physical feature. Historically, many boundaries have fallen upon lines of latitude or longitude, and since the surface of the earth is rounded, extended boundaries may more accurately form arcs. The majority of the boundary between the United States and Canada follows along the 49th parallel (latitude). After World War II,

North and South Korea were divided along the 38th parallel. Many geometric boundaries are created as internal divisions within a state or territory, such as the political boundaries of Colorado and Wyoming.

A type of subsequent border that takes into account already-existing cultural or physical landscapes is a **consequent boundary**. A border that is drawn taking into account language, ethnicity, religion, or other cultural traits it is a **cultural consequent boundary**. Also, these boundaries are created with the cultural landscape as a primary consideration. Political boundaries of this nature would be consequent upon an already-existing cultural phenomenon, such as the partition of the British colony of India in 1947, creating a Hindu-majority India and a Muslim-majority Pakistan.

Unlike geometric borders, a division that uses already-existing natural features that divide a territory such as rivers, deserts, or mountains is a **physical consequent boundary**. An example would be the Pyrenees Mountains that run across the northern edge of the Iberian Peninsula, separating Spain from France, and completely surrounding the country of Andorra.

CLASSIFICATIONS OF BOUNDARIES		
Type	**Definition**	**Example**
Antecedent	A boundary established before a large population was present	The boundary of the Pyranees Mountains established between Spain and France
Subsequent (Ethnographic)	A boundary drawn to accommodate religious, ethnic, linguistic, or economic differences	The boundary between Northern Ireland (part of the United Kingdom) and the Republic of Ireland
Superimposed	A boundary drawn by outside powers	The boundary between Mali and Mauritania (common throughout Africa and Southwest Asia)
Relic	A boundary that no longer exists, but is still evident on the landscape	The boundary between East and West Germany (states that are now combined)
Geometric	A straight line or arc drawn by people that does not closely follow any physical feature	The boundary between the United States and Canada along the 49th parallel
Consequent	A type of subsequent boundary that takes into account existing cultural or physical landscapes	The boundary between India and Pakistan created for religious reasons

Protection of Boundaries

Accurately defining and describing political boundaries are important tasks for geographers in understanding the complex structure of states and the interaction between them. There are many ways to define boundaries and, furthermore, a single border can possess the attributes of several types. For instance, most superimposed boundaries are geometric. Additionally, there are other border terms that deal with the protective nature of borders and can meet some of the previously discussed classifications.

An **open boundary** is unguarded and people can cross it easily, with little or no political intervention. These borders only occur between countries that have maintained friendly relations with each other over long periods of time. Most states within the European Union (EU) fit this category. In 1985, the Schengen Agreement abolished most border checks between member states (of the then European Economic Community)—making most of the continent effectively borderless. With goods and people flowing freely from one country to another, people seemed less willing to turn to violence to settle disputes.

A **militarized boundary** is one that is heavily guarded and discourages crossing. While many of these borders only have a limited military presence, others are fortified, using a constructed barrier to prevent the flow of people. In 1989, when the Berlin Wall fell, there were 15 border walls in the entire world. As of 2020, there were five times that number. For example, India has constructed a guarded 1,700-mile barbed wire fence along its border with Bangladesh to curb immigration and smuggling.

One of the most well-known barriers in the world today is the Korean DMZ (demilitarized zone) that separates North and South Korea. The 160-mile long, 2.5-mile wide strip of land serves as a buffer zone between the rival states. It was established in 1953 after the cease-fire that ended the Korean War. In 2020, the United States had more than 28,000 troops stationed in South Korea along the DMZ, a deterrent to any potential aggression by North Korea. The DMZ almost completely blocks the flow of trade and people.

REFLECT ON THE ESSENTIAL QUESTION

Essential Question: *What are the types of political boundaries used by geographers?*

Type of Boundary	Function of Boundary

KEY TERMS

physical geographic boundaries	superimposed boundary	cultural consequent boundary
cultural boundaries	Berlin Conference	physical consequent boundary
antecedent boundary	landlocked states	open boundary
subsequent boundary	relic boundary	militarized boundary
ethnographic	geometric boundary	
	consequent boundary	

The Function of Political Boundaries

Essential Question: What are the nature and function of international boundaries?

When most people think of a boundary, they focus on what is represented on the surface of the earth. However, boundaries are actually vertical planes that cut through the subsoil below, rise into the airspace above, and even extend into outer space.

Political borders serve a vital function as dividing lines between countries, states, provinces, territories, counties, cities, towns, villages, and municipalities. Political borders also exist to separate bodies of water, especially those that possess multiple claims to the same areas. To fully comprehend the complex interactions between political entities, an understanding is needed of boundary formations and functions, as well as why disputes erupt around them.

International and Internal Boundaries

In theory, boundaries of all kinds exist to add clarity. Boundaries signal where one political entity begins and another ends. This helps people know what territory is theirs to administer and what belongs to another country. But when neighbors disagree on where the line that separates them should be, boundaries become the subject of conflict. Throughout history, uncertain boundaries have been a frequent cause of bloodshed and war.

Formation of Boundaries

Boundaries represent changes in the use of space from one political entity to another. Crossing a boundary implies that some rules, expectations, or behaviors change. When moving across a formal political boundary, these rules are called laws. Boundaries can be identified in various ways:

- A **defined boundary** is established by a legal document, such as a treaty, that divides one entity from another (invisible line). The entity could range from a country—in which points of latitude and longitude are specified—to a single plot of real estate—in which points in the landscape are described.
- A **delimited boundary** is drawn on a map by a cartographer to show the limits of a space.
- A **demarcated boundary** is one identified by physical objects placed on the landscape. The demarcation may be as simple as a sign or as complex as a set of fences and walls.

Some very influential boundaries are not set formally. Informal boundaries include ones marking the spheres of influence by powerful countries at the regional scale, such as the Monroe Doctrine. In 1821, President James Monroe warned Europeans that the United States would oppose any attempts they made to expand their influence in the Americas. Informal boundaries also exist at the local level, such as those dividing the neighborhoods controlled by various street gangs.

International Boundary Disputes

As the number of states has increased over the last century, so too have international boundary disputes. There are four main categories of boundary disputes: definitional, locational (territorial), operational (function), and allocational (resource).

A **definitional boundary dispute** occurs when two or more parties disagree over how to interpret the legal documents or maps that identify the boundary. These types of disputes often occur with antecedent boundaries. (See Topic 4.4.) One example is the boundary between Chile and Argentina. The elevated crests of the Andes Mountains serve as the boundary, but since most of the southern lands were neither settled nor accurately mapped, control of this territory lies in dispute.

Boundary disputes that center on where a boundary should be, how it is *delimited* (mapped), or *demarcated* are known as **locational boundary disputes**. These disputes are also called **territorial disputes** because of the fundamental question of who possesses the land. An example of a locational dispute was the post-World War I boundary between Germany and Poland. Germans disputed the location because it controlled the land prior to the war, but the border drawn after the war left many ethnically German people on the Polish side. This led to **irredentism**, a type of expansionism when one country seeks to annex territory where it has cultural ties to part of the population or historical claims to the land. Many groups are divided between countries by a border. When this occurs a desire to unify their nation is a common national goal and can lead to irredentist feelings but not always action.

An **operational boundary dispute,** or **functional dispute,** centers not on where a boundary is but how it functions. Disagreements can arise related to trade, transportation, or migration. As refugees fled Syria and attempted to enter Europe during the 2011 civil war, Europeans viewed their national boundaries differently. Refugees began migrating from southern Europe to the interior seeking safe haven. Interior countries of Europe often viewed the countries to the south and east as responsible for stopping migrants, while others felt the boundaries should stay open in order to help the refugees. Additional operational boundaries can occur with rivers and choke points that serve as boundaries. Questions related to who controls the transportation and shipping on a river or choke point can cause disagreements.

When a boundary separates natural resources that may be used by both countries, it is referred to as an **allocational boundary dispute**, or **resource**

dispute. When it comes to natural resources, boundaries serve as vertical planes that extend both up into the sky and down into the earth. The extraction of subterranean resources extending on both sides of the boundary may become complicated and lead to conflict. In 1990, Iraq invaded Kuwait because it claimed that the Kuwaitis were drilling too many wells using directional drilling, thus breaking the vertical plane and extracting oil on the Iraqi side of the boundary. Other resources that are often at the center of disputes include fresh water, minerals, and fishing rights.

DIRECTIONAL DRILLING

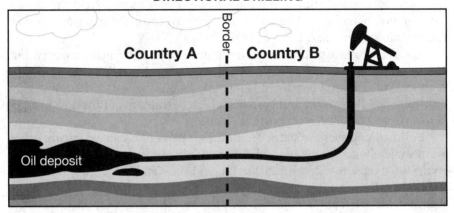

If a country uses directional drilling to access oil or gas and crosses an international border, this can lead to a resource dispute.

Demarcation and Functions of Boundaries

How a border is labeled on the physical landscape such as with a fence, wall, stones or signs is called *demarcation*. This process can indicate the type of relationship that exists between countries and be a clue to how the border functions. Many borders in the world are not demarcated at all because they are in vast wilderness areas with no one living there or the relationships between the two states is cordial, open, and peaceful. Additionally, most boundaries are not demarcated as the process tends to be protracted and expensive.

How a boundary will be maintained, how it will function, and what goods and people will be allowed to cross are important aspects of an **administered boundary**. As relations change between countries, and also between entities within a state, the means by which a boundary is demarcated and administered may change significantly. The Israeli-West Bank barrier separates Israel's claims from those of the Palestinians through a multi-layered fence system. From Israel's standpoint, it is necessary to prevent terrorism, while the Palestinians argue that it promotes racial segregation. Begun in 2000, during a period of increased tension and violence, the militarized border remains an ever-present point of contention.

Recently, because of the Syrian refugee crisis and the COVID pandemic, many of the borders between EU states have become much more restrictive and less open. Boundaries that have checkpoints where a passport or visa are required to enter the country are called **controlled boundary**. These boundaries allow some people and goods to traverse the border while denying entry to others. In 2020, the United Kingdom left the EU (Brexit), potentially creating a more controlled border between the island state and mainland Europe.

Unique Boundaries: Exclaves and Enclaves

As a result of migration, trade deals, devolution, conflicts, and other reasons, pockets of isolated national groups sometimes find themselves separated from their homeland. **Exclaves** are territories that are part of a state, yet geographically separated from the main state by one or more countries. For example, Alaska is separated from the lower 48 United States by Canada. Nakhchivan, an autonomous republic of Azerbaijan, is separated from the main territory of Azerbaijan by Armenia.

Exclaves may help to reunite ethnic groups with the main country, but communication and transportation challenges often exist. Kaliningrad Oblast is an exclave of Russia because it is separated from the rest of the country by Lithuania and Belarus. Kaliningrad has a high percentage of Russians (over 85 percent) and is an important port for Russia.

Political enclaves are states, territories or parts of a state or territory that are completely surrounded by the territory of another state. At the national level, the sovereign states of San Marino and the Vatican City are completely engulfed by Italy making them political enclaves. Autonomy, national identity, and self-rule are often a benefit of an enclave. Challenges for enclaves often include maintaining positive relationships with the surrounding country and transportation accessibility.

LESOTHO

Source: Wikimedia Commons

Lesotho is totally surrounded by South Africa, making it a political enclave and landlocked. Describe the challenges of exclaves and enclaves.

Indian reservations within the United States may be considered enclaves as they possess tribal sovereignty and are recognized as independent nations. At the local level, informal *ethnic enclaves* (see Topic 3.2) exist in a number of cities and municipalities.

The Effects of Boundaries

A boundary is more than a line between two political entities. It has effects that stretch well beyond simple questions of space and into political, cultural, and economic regions that affect various populations in many ways.

Shatterbelts

Political boundaries often do not follow cultural and economic landscapes, which can cause a region to become a political **shatterbelt**, a place located between two very different and contentious regions. These places are under consistent stress and may suffer instability or fragmentation due to external aggression. Sometimes boundaries separate people who speak the same language, practice the same religion, or share other traits. (See Topic 4.9 for more information of Yugoslavia as a shatterbelt.)

Eastern Europe has historically been a shatterbelt between Western Europe and Russia. While Western Europe has historically been Roman Catholic or Protestant, Russia has been Orthodox. For most of the 20th century, Western Europe was generally capitalist and Russia was communist.

Another shatterbelt is the Caucasus, a mountainous region between the Black Sea and Caspian Sea that includes the states of Armenia, Azerbaijan, and Georgia. After the fall of the Soviet Union, many ethnically distinct territories gained autonomy. However, these independence movements were often violent, and territorial claims are still in flux in many places. Nagorno-Karabakh is a semi-autonomous region but is predominantly recognized as part of Azerbaijan. (See Topic 4.8.) Many Orthodox Christian Armenians live in the region but the surrounding land is home to mostly Muslim Azerbaijanis. After a destructive war between the two states from 1988 to 1994, disputes over sovereign territory and national rights persisted, and a new clash erupted again in 2020.

Language and Religion

As people move and boundaries change, language changes also. The language often changes because people separated by boundaries develop distinct dialects. When boundaries are placed in an attempt to unite people who have distinct dialects, the unification process proves to be difficult, as was the case with Italy. Italy did not become a unified state until the 1860s. Before unification, people spoke a variety of languages depending on where they lived. From the Alps in the north to Sicily in the south, no single language united everyone. Even after 160 years as a single state, people in Italy remain only loosely bound together.

Religion and boundaries can make for a volatile mixture. Within the boundaries of India, the majority of the people are Hindus, but a significant minority are Muslims. This division creates tension that sometimes leads to violence. However, countries such as the United States and South Korea demonstrate that people of different faiths can live in harmony.

The division of Ireland demonstrates how complicated religion and boundaries can become. In the mid-20th century, most of Ireland won its independence from the United Kingdom and formed the Republic of Ireland, which was 95 percent Roman Catholic. However, a small area in the north, known as Northern Ireland, remained part of the United Kingdom. This area was only 35 percent Catholic and mostly Protestant.

The boundary between the Republic of Ireland and Northern Ireland created two problems. On one hand, it divided the Catholics of both places who wanted to be together in one country. On the other hand, the boundary united Catholics and Protestants into one political entity, Northern Ireland. There, Catholic-Protestant tensions—which included economic and political conflicts as well as religious ones—led to three decades of violence starting in 1968. Before peace was restored, about 3,000 people were killed in bombings and shootings.

Ethnicity, Nationality, and Economy

Boundaries that are superimposed, or enforced by a dominant nation or ethnic group, can create conflict for nations occupying the same space. Sri Lanka, a large island off the southern tip of India, is home to two groups that see themselves as ethnically distinct from the other:

- the Sinhalese are the majority, mostly Buddhist, and live in the southern part of the country
- the Tamil are the minority, mostly Hindus, and live in the northern and eastern parts of the island

The Tamils long felt they were treated as second-class citizens by the Sinhalese. Hoping to win an independent homeland, Tamil rebels began fighting in the 1980s. They were defeated in 2009, but around 75,000 Sri Lankans had died in the fighting.

The Law of the Sea

Countries generally agree that a vertical plane extends through borders, defining space above and below the land. However, how far horizontally out into the ocean should a country's influence spread? Conflicts over the use of the ocean have been common in modern history. Only in the last half of the 20th century were water boundaries addressed systematically. Between 1973 and 1982, the **United Nations Convention on the Law of the Sea** was signed by more than 150 countries. It defined four zones:

1. **Territorial sea:** This area extends up to 12 nautical miles of sovereignty where commercial vessels may pass, but noncommercial vessels may be challenged. A nautical mile is equal to 1.15 land-measured miles.

2. **Contiguous zone:** Coastal states have limited sovereignty for up to 24 nautical miles where they can enforce laws on customs, immigration, and sanitation.

3. **Exclusive economic zone (EEZ):** Coastal states can explore, extract minerals, and manage natural resources up to 200 nautical miles.

4. **High seas:** Water beyond any country's EEZ that is open to all states.

UNITED NATIONS CONVENTION AND THE LAW OF THE SEA (UNCLOS)

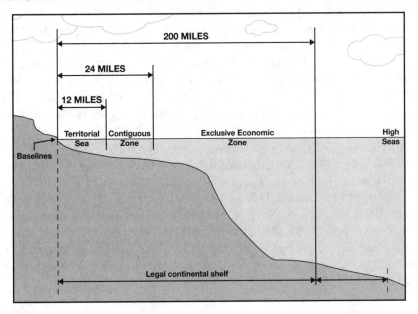

Source: United Nations

UNCLOS is an international treaty that defines the rights and responsibilities of nations related to the sea. The United States abides by the treaty but has not signed it.

If two coastal states share a waterway and are less than 24 nautical miles apart, then the distance between the two coasts is divided by half. For example, if only 20 miles of water separated two countries, then each would be entitled to 10 miles of territorial sea.

The Value of Islands States that have islands have been granted vast areas of space. For example, if a country's farthest island extends several hundred miles from the mainland, then the EEZ of that outward island extends that country's claims by another 200 miles. For example, near Alaska, where islands extend far out in the Bering Sea, the EEZ of the United States is huge. The United States' EEZ covers more area than any other country—3.4 million square miles. That is almost as much as the total land area of the United States (3.8 million square miles).

The 200-mile EEZ is very valuable economically to the many **small island developing states (SIDS)** in the world's oceans. SIDS control nearly 30 percent of all oceans and seas and their EEZs are much larger than their landmass. Tuvalu's EEZ in the South Pacific is 27,000 times the size of its land, but its EEZ contains valuable minerals, natural gas and fishing stocks, and the prospect of tourism. These new economic opportunities based on the ocean for SIDS have been given the term *blue economy*.

Artic Opportunities The Arctic Ocean is a region where challenges are being made related to land, deep water natural resources, and sea passages for ships. As the ice in the Arctic Ocean melts, countries in the region such as

Russia, Canada, the United States, Norway, and Denmark see new economic opportunities in the region.

South China Sea In 2011, a territorial dispute in the South China Sea emerged related to the Spratly Islands, a series of small islands and coral reefs. The region is a rich fishing ground, important trade route, and a source of potential natural gas and oil reserves. China, Vietnam, and other neighboring countries are in the midst of a tension-filled dispute. China has made claims to large parts of the sea and has built artificial islands on the reef to solidify its territorial claims and expand its 200-mile EEZ.

Challenging a Zone Disputes over territorial control in coastal waters can turn violent. In 1973, Libyan dictator Muammar Gaddafi extended his 12-mile territorial sea to include the entire Gulf of Sidra. He created a "line of death" that was not to be crossed. U.S. leaders considered the line a violation of the Law of the Sea, and U.S. Navy ships challenged the line by sailing through the gulf. In August 1981, while flying inside the line of death but outside the 12-mile limit, U.S. F-14 fighter jets engaged and shot down two Libyan fighter jets. Similar incidents between the United States and Libya occurred in 1986 and 1989.

REFLECT ON THE ESSENTIAL QUESTION

Essential Question: *What are the nature and function of international boundaries?*

Type of Boundary	Function of Boundary

KEY TERMS

defined boundary	controlled borders
delimited boundary	exclaves
demarcated boundary	political enclaves
definitional boundary dispute	shatterbelt
locational boundary disputes	United Nations Convention
(territorial disputes)	on the Law of the Sea (UNCLOS)
irredentism	territorial sea
operational boundary dispute	contiguous zone
(functional dispute)	exclusive economic zone (EEZ)
allocational boundary dispute	high seas
(resource dispute)	small island developing
administered boundary	state (SIDS)

Internal Boundaries

Essential Question: What are the nature and function of internal boundaries?

International boundaries create borders between countries, but **internal boundaries** are used at the subnational scale to divide countries into smaller units. These units, such as states, counties, cities, and local districts, break up territory into more manageable units of governance. Internal boundaries fall within the jurisdiction of the government, and therefore state and local governments can change these boundaries as needed.

Types of Internal Boundary Spaces

Some subdivisions, such as states, serve multiple purposes such as maintaining roads and operating hospitals. Others, such as park districts, are specialized. In the United States, these subdivisions are part of *federalism*, the sharing of power between the national and local governments. That's why some laws and policies apply to just a local area and others apply throughout the country.

Electoral Geography

Using spatial thinking techniques and tools to analyze elections and voting patterns is called **electoral geography**. Internal boundaries that divide a country's electorate into subnational regions are called **voting districts** and exist at multiple scales. People of a country who are eligible to vote, known as the **electorate,** vote for leaders in each district to govern on their behalf.

In the United States, the Constitution requires the federal government to take a **census**, a count of the population, every 10 years, to ensure the national congressional districts have approximately the same number of people. After the results of the census have been calculated, the national government determines each state's number of representatives in the House of Representatives through **reapportionment**, changing the number of representatives granted to each state so it reflects the state's population. State legislatures or state committees then redraw district boundaries so that each district contains roughly the same number of people. This process is known as **redistricting**.

The total number of representatives in the U.S. House of Representatives has been fixed at 435 since 1912. Regardless of reapportionment results, each state is guaranteed at least one representative in the House, along with its two members in the Senate. As people in the United States have moved south and west, states in these regions have gained representation and states in the Midwest and Northeast have lost seats in Congress.

Gerrymandering

Some states try to create districts that are contiguous (connected), and compact, and based on existing city and county boundaries. Traditionally, though, political maneuvering shapes redistricting. **Gerrymandering** is the drawing of boundaries for political districts by the party in power to protect or increase its power. The term is derived in part from Massachusetts Governor Elbridge Gerry (1744–1814). He influenced the drawing of districts in Massachusetts to benefit his own political party. A newspaper editor noted that an oddly shaped district resembled a salamander and coined the term *gerrymander*.

NORTH CAROLINA'S "I-85 DISTRICT"

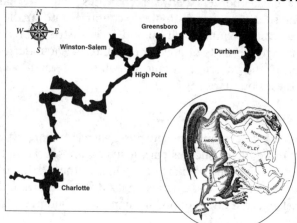

Source: Wikimedia Commons

In 2011, North Carolina District 12 was redrawn to follow the I-85 corridor which gave an advantage to the party in power. The redrawn district was compared to the Massachusetts redistricting (shown in the cartoon inset) supported by governor Elbridge Gerry in 1812.

Results of Gerrymandering By carefully drawing district boundaries, politicians can create "safe seats" that are highly likely to elect members of their own party. As a result, most races in legislative districts are not competitive. Further, gerrymandering can enable one party that regularly loses statewide elections for president, sentor, and governor to still win a solid majority of the district-wide races for the state legislature and Congress. They can do this using the techniques shown in the chart below.

TYPES OF GERRYMANDERING	
Type	**Definition**
Cracking	Dispersing a group into several districts to prevent a majority
Packing	Combining like-minded voters into one district to prevent them from affecting elections in other districts
Stacking	Diluting a minority-populated district with majority populations
Hijacking	Redrawing two districts in order to force two elected representatives of the same party to run against each other
Kidnapping	Moving an area where an elected representative has support to an area where he or she does not have support

Discrimination Gerrymandering has often been used to reduce representation of African Americans and other minorities in government. The 1965 Voting Rights Act attempted to end these discriminatory practices. As a result, minority representation in Congress increased. In 2013, the Supreme Court ruled that the law had succeeded in remedying the racial disparity in representation so key provisions of the act were no longer needed.

Alternatives To prevent gerrymandering, some states have adopted procedures to make redistricting less partisan. Some states use bipartisan committees with equal members of each party, plus independents to draw the boundaries. For example, in 1980, Iowa created a nonpartisan agency to redraw congressional and legislative voting districts after each U.S. census.

LOUISIANA CONGRESSIONAL DISTRICTS, 2018

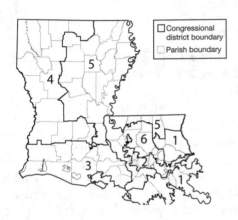

☐ Congressional district boundary
☐ Parish boundary

The map shows the congressional districts in Louisiana. District 1 is not contiguous and several districts cross parish boundaries. District 2 has a majority of African American and Democratic-leaning residents, while Districts 1 and 6 have a majority of white and Republican-leaning residents. What form of gerrymandering technique would be used to describe this example?

REFLECT ON THE ESSENTIAL QUESTION

Essential Question: *What are the nature and function of internal boundaries?*

Concepts That Influence Internal Boundaries	Effects of Concepts

---

KEY TERMS

internal boundaries	reapportionment	packing
electoral geography	redistricting	stacking
voting districts	gerrymandering	hijacking
electorate	cracking	kidnapping
census		

Forms of Governance

Essential Question: What are federal and unitary states, and how do they affect spatial organization?

Governments attempt to unify the people under their jurisdiction by defining the country's boundaries, exerting control over the territory, and blending the nationalites within those boundaries. The structure of the national government and its internal political geography can impact state unity.

Different Forms of Governance

Countries are governed on more than one level. But different forms of governance allocate power in different ways, affecting how much authority is available at both the national and local levels.

Federal and Unitary States

Two main types of political spatial organizations are federal and unitary systems of governance. Both systems administer the day-to-day operations of governance with sovereignty, and the national government is the final authority. A **federal state** unites separate political entities into an overarching system that allows each entity to maintain some degree of sovereignty. This power sharing is vertical with the different functions and responsibilities of government found at the national, provincial/state, and local level. Examples of federal states include Germany, the United States, and Nigeria.

In contrast, in a **unitary state**, most or all of the governing power is held by the national government. All local governments in a unitary system are subject to the authority of the national government. Countries with unitary systems of government include France, Japan, and Kenya. The differences between federal and unitary states are outlined in the chart on the following page.

Local Powers Vary by Government Type

In both federal and unitary states, local divisions of governance have some degree of power. But the amount of that power depends on the level of power exercised by the national government. Large landmass countries—such as the United States, Canada, and Russia—tend to be federal states. In contrast, smaller landmass countries—such as Japan, Egypt, and Spain—tend to be unitary states. These patterns have exceptions. China is a large country with a unitary and very centralized government. Belgium is a small country that is a federal state, which reflects the ethnic divide between its Walloon and Flemish citizens.

States that use federal governance often do so to placate various cultural groups. Allowing local governments to manage their own affairs, such as education, promotes peace. Nigeria is an example of how this works, depending on the mixture of religious faiths of the people of each province:

- Provinces in northern Nigeria, where Islam is common or dominant, have enacted some or all of sharia, the Islamic legal framework.
- Provinces in the southern Nigeria, where Christianity or traditional religious practices are more common, do not use sharia.

Unitary states have strong centralized governments that control almost all matters of governance. Provincial and local governments, in most cases, are simply extensions of the national government. Unitary states can be either non-democratic—such as China and Saudi Arabia—or fairly democratic—such as France and Indonesia.

FEDERAL VS. UNITARY STATES		
Trait	Federal	Unitary
Authority of the Government	Shared between the central government and provincial, state, and local governments	Held primarily by the central government with very little power given to local governments
Hierarchy of Power	Multiple levels of power diffused throughout federal, state, and local governments	No hierarchy of sovereign powers
Type of Country Where Commonly Used	Multiple ethnic groups with significant minority populations	Few cultural differences and small minority populations
Strengths	• Often represents needs of local and regional areas, not just national issues • Can be quicker to address and more representative of local and regional issues • Power is spread across the country, not consolidated in the core area	• One set of laws and policies • Clarity of national policies to other governments and the people • Can be cheaper to run since there is only one level of government
Weaknesses	• Contradictory laws can exist between levels of government • Often slower and more difficult to gain consensus and respond to national issues	• Laws and policies often overlook minority, local, regional, or periphery issues • Power and benefits are often concentrated in core areas of a country

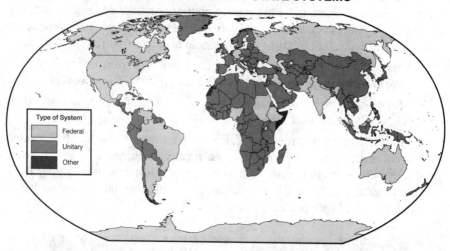

Patterns of Local and Metropolitan Governance

Local and metropolitan forms of governance, such as municipalities and regional planning commissions, are subnational political units that have varying degrees of local control.

Most people in the world are under the rule of overlapping levels of government. The U.S. government is a hierarchy with the federal government at the top and many local and special purpose districts at the bottom. Special purpose districts include transportation, fire, police, library, water, and school districts, to name a few. Each level of government has authority in distinct areas but some of the powers are shared.

LEVELS OF GOVERNMENT IN THE UNITED STATES

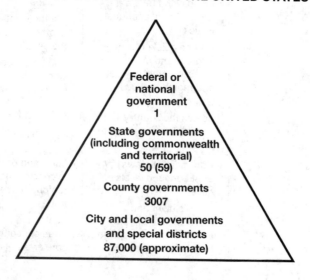

The number of units of government changes from year to year. One way this happens is that a city will add outlying territory to its domain to increase its individual and commercial tax bases. **Annexation** is the process of legally adding territory to a city. However, residents of a new residential development on what had been farmland might prefer to create their own town rather than being annexed by an existing city. This leads to a new city government—and increased competition for services, business, and taxes.

REFLECT ON THE ESSENTIAL QUESTION

Essential Question: *What are federal and unitary states and how do they affect spatial organization?*

Effects of Federal States on Spatial Organization	Effects of Unitary States on Spatial Organization

---

KEY TERMS

federal state   unitary state   annexation

GEOGRAPHIC PERSPECTIVES: *UNITS OF GOVERNMENT*

Geographers study how political power is distributed across space at different scales:

- At the global scale, power is distributed among countries.
- At the national scale, power is distributed among units such as provinces or states.
- At the local scale, power can be distributed among several types of units: counties, cities, school districts, and others.

Diverse Local Districts

Some local districts have very specialized functions. They might fund fire protection or a public library. Illinois includes several mosquito abatement districts. The Des Plaines Valley Mosquito Abatement District includes 77 square miles in the western suburbs of Chicago. It has about five full-time employees and hires another two dozen or so workers seasonally.

Mosquito abatement districts are one reason that Illinois leads all other states in the number of units of local government. In 2017, Illinois had 6,918 units of government. A typical resident lived with six or more layers of local government. In second place was Texas with 5,343 units. However, the population of Texas was more than double that of Illinois.

How to Distribute Power

Mosquito abatement districts highlight the issue of the best way to distribute power spatially. Many problems, such as mosquitoes and the diseases they spread, drug trafficking, and pollution, pay no attention to political boundaries. One response to these types of problems is to create special districts to address them. Another is to build cooperation among existing units of government. A third is to refer the problem to a higher level of government such as a state or national agency. Deciding where to locate the power to respond to these problems is a constant issue for debate.

1. Identify an entity that has power at each scale: global, national and local.
2. Explain why special districts are often used at the local scale.

THINK AS A GEOGRAPHER: *DEMARCATION AND FUNCTION OF BORDERS*

How a border is demarcated or marked indicates a great deal about the relationships that exist between states or regions. For each image, use clues from the image and background information to answer the following questions:

Top: Utah-Wyoming border, Left: Israel-Palestine border, Right: United States-Canada border
Source: Wikimedia Commons

1. Identify each border as controlled, open, or militarized.
2. Describe what the border's demarcation shows about the relationships between the political entities in each image.
3. Explain the purpose of controlling a country's border.

CHAPTER 9 REVIEW:
Political Boundaries and Forms of Governance

Topics 4.4–4.7

MULTIPLE-CHOICE QUESTIONS

Question 1 refers to the following photograph.

1. Which type of boundary is most clearly shown in the image above?
   (A) Defined
   (B) Delimited
   (C) Natural
   (D) Open
   (E) Demarcated

2. When Germany invaded Poland in 1939, it said it wanted to reunite the German minority living in Poland with Germany. This is an example of
   (A) nationalism
   (B) irredentism
   (C) supranationalism
   (D) an allocational dispute
   (E) an operational dispute

Question 3 refers to the following map.

THE U.S.-CANADA BOUNDARY

3. The 49th parallel between the United States and Canada is

(A) a relic boundary

(B) a superimposed boundary

(C) an antecedent boundary

(D) a subsequent/ethnographic boundary

(E) an open boundary

Question 4 refers to the map on page 233 and the chart below. The voter index indicates how strongly a district leans toward a party.

PARTY LEANINGS IN LOUISIANA DISTRICTS	
Congressional District	**Voter Index**
1	Republican, +24
2	Democrat, +25
3	Republican, +20
4	Republican, +13
5	Republican, +15
6	Republican, +19

4. Which gerrymandering strategies do Districts 1 and 2 best show?

(A) Stacking

(B) Packing

(C) Hijacking

(D) Kidnapping

(E) Scaling

5. Uruguay's national government sets policies that are administered by local governments. This system of government is best described as

(A) federal

(B) unitary

(C) reapportioned

(D) communist

(E) compact

6. The formation of India and Pakistan in 1947 led to a new boundary between the two states. This boundary is best described as

(A) an antecedent boundary because the two countries fought over scarce water resources

(B) a controlled boundary because the border was placed by a foreign power without negotiation

(C) an open boundary because it was unguarded and could be easily traversed

(D) a consequent boundary because the border was made along an already-existing cultural division

(E) a relic boundary because it no longer exists but was still visible on the landscape

7. The Syrian Civil War erupted in 2011 and forced millions of refugees to flee into Turkey. The Turkish government was sympathetic to the refugees but became concerned about how many Syrians were crossing Turkey's border. Which type of border dispute describes this scenario?

(A) Definitional

(B) Locational

(C) Allocational

(D) Operational

(E) Territorial

FREE-RESPONSE QUESTION

1. Boundaries serve a variety of purposes and exist at the international, national and local scale. Territoriality is the willingness of a person, group, or country to defend their claimed space. Often claims of space can cause disagreements or even conflict. The United Nations Convention on the Law of the Sea (UNCLOS) defines the rights and responsibilities of nations. Use the two maps on the next page to answer the questions that follow.

LAND CLAIMS IN THE SOUTH CHINA SEA

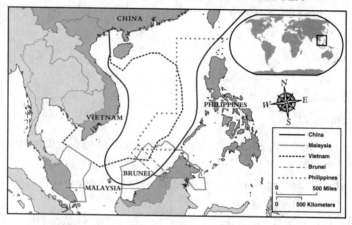

LAND CLAIMS IN THE ARCTIC OCEAN

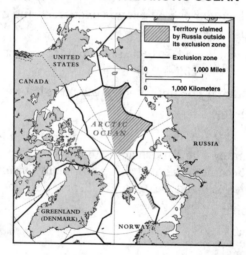

(A) Define the concept of Territorial Seas as used in UNCLOS.

(B) Describe what activities can occur in the Exclusive Economic Zone (EEZ) as used in UNCLOS.

(C) Using one of the maps, identify TWO countries that have competing claims in the Arctic or South China Sea.

(D) Describe TWO economic reasons that explain the importance of the claims in the South China Sea or Arctic Ocean.

(E) Describe ONE environmental concern affecting the oceans.

(F) Describe ONE economic or environmental benefit of the Arctic Ocean for any country not shown on the map.

(G) Briefly explain why choke points are politically or economically important.

CHAPTER 10

Challenges in the Modern State

Topics 4.8–4.10

Topic 4.8 Defining Devolutionary Factors

Learning Objective: Define factors that lead to the devolution of states. (SPS-4.A)

Topic 4.9 Challenges to Sovereignty

Learning Objective: Explain how political, economic, cultural, and technological changes challenge state sovereignty. (SPS-4.B)

Topic 4.10 Consequences of Centrifugal and Centripetal Forces

Learning Objective: Explain how the concepts of centrifugal and centripetal forces apply at the state scale. (SPS-4.C)

Geography cannot solve all of the world's problems; but no problem can be solved without geography.

—Dr. Joseph Manzo, Professor of Geography, Concord University

Source: Wikimedia Commons

The Arab Spring was a series of democratic protests seeking government reform in 2011. The photo shows protests in Yemen. (See Topic 4.9 for challenges to sovereignty.)

Defining Devolutionary Factors

Essential Question: What factors lead to the devolution of states?

Modern states and the political map of the world are dynamic and can change over time and space. Numerous factors influence the changing nature and relationships both among and within states. Independence movements, civil wars, colonialism, economic development, physical isolation, ethnicity, and lack of representation can all put pressure on national and international relationships.

Governments and other political entities, such as the United Nations, often responds to tensions in order to maintain peace and order. These tensions can result in changes in borders, power, and governments, or even the creation of new countries. Geographers study these forces and the changes that result on global, national, and subnational levels.

Forces Leading to Devolution

Within a country, groups or regions can feel disconnected and disempowered, leading to a lack of national pride. In these cases, groups often feel that local or regional issues are being ignored by the central government, causing anger and distrust toward the government to arise. If the feelings are strong and sustained, demands for changes in the political system can increase. This tension can lead to demands from the popluation ranging from more control in political affairs to complete separation.

One response that countries will use to keep a country united but still grant some powers is the process of **devolution**, the transfer of some political power from the central government to subnational levels of government. The powers within a government—administrative, judicial, and legislative—are divided among the national government and subnational levels. This division varies among countries and is influenced by whether the state has a unitary or federal system. (See Topic 4.7.) Federalism by its nature is an example of devolution because provinces and states have power. Forces that lead to or accelerate devolution within a country are physical geography, ethno-linguistic divisions, terrorism, economic factors, and social conditions.

Physical Geography

While globalization and improved technology promote connections, the physical geography of a region can cause isolation, decrease connections, and increase the likelihood of devolution. Many states that are very large in size (Russia, India, the United States) or those that are made up of thousands of islands (Indonesia and the Philippines) can face challenges of communication and connectivity within their borders. Other physical features that have reduced contact among groups of people include deserts, plateaus, mountain ranges, and large bodies of water. These challenges can be overcome but as distance from the political power center increases, identification with and trust in the government can often decrease.

The Kashmir region of northern India and northern Pakistan has been and still is a region of conflict and border disputes. The Pir Panjal and Himalayan mountain ranges cause isolation among people in these regions. Areas claimed by India, China, and Pakistan have had some local autonomy because of the geographical isolation caused by these mountain ranges. Each country is unwilling to release its claims on the Kashmir because of the wealth of fresh water and natural resources in the region.

Ethnic Separatism

Many ethnic separatist movements throughout the world take place within specific regional lines within states. **Ethnic separatism** is the advocacy of full political separation (or secession) from the larger group along cultural, ethnic, tribal, or governmental lines. Ethnic groups and minorities are often concentrated in specific regions, which can lead to independence movements. In order to maintain unity, the central government will often grant more authority to these ethnic regions via devolution.

For example, Spain has two culturally and linguistically distinct groups within its border, the Basques and Catalans, in addition to the Spanish. The Basque Country was granted semiautonomy in 1979 by the Spanish government. Groups in Catalan are still seeking separation on the grounds of cultural differences and lack of power in the Spanish government. However, the intensity of their separatism is tied to actions by the central government of Spain. For example, if the national government imposes more restrictions throughout the country, then the Basques and Catalans may intensify their desire for independence. If the national government allows more local autonomy, it hopes that the desire for independence will decrease.

ETHNIC SEPARATISM IN SPAIN

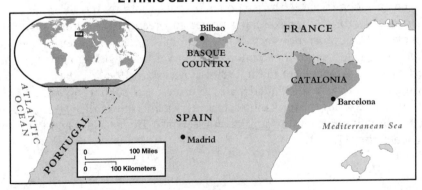

Groups in both the Basque Country and Catalonia are examples of ethnic separatism. Although the processes for these groups has been different, each sought separation from Spain.

Ethnic Cleansing

Ethnic groups may seek separatism because of how they are treated within a country. Certain ethnic groups may be persecuted or not have equal status from the government. In extreme cases, acts of genocide and/or ethnic cleansing attempt to eliminate a group of people from a country. The United Nations Commission of Experts described **ethnic cleansing** as "a purposeful policy designed by one ethnic or religious group to remove by violent or terror-inspiring means the civilian population of another ethnic or religious group from certain geographic areas." Coercive tactics that have been used in ethnic cleansing include destruction of property, attacks on civilians, arbitrary arrest, rape, torture, and murder.

The concept is grounded in the desire to create an ethnically homogeneous nation-state. The term arose out of the conflict in the former Yugoslavia in the 1990s. Examples from earlier in history include European colonists in North America who killed or drove away Native Americans, Hitler's attempt to eliminate all Jews from Germany, and Poles who forced Germans to leave Poland after World War II. More recent examples have been carried out by Russians against the Chechens in the Caucasus Mountains, Indonesians against the people of East Timor, and the Sudanese against people in Darfur, In each of these, hundreds of thousands of people were killed or forced to flee their homes.

Terrorism

Terrorism is organized violence aimed at government and civilian targets to create fear for the advancement of political goals. It is most commonly used by non-governmental groups that do not have an army.

Ethnic separatists sometimes employ terrorist tactics in hopes of achieving devolution. Since its inception in 1959, the Basque nationalist/separatist group Euskadi Ta Askatasuna (ETA) has fought for independence from Spain. Increased frustration spurred ETA to wage a campaign of violence beginning in 1968. After more than 820 deaths, ETA declared a permanent cessation of armed activities in 2011. However, ETA continued to seek independence of the Basque region from Spain.

On a global scale, terrorism often has its roots in specific regions or countries. Terrorist groups seeking power and recognition within a country can expand their operations across international borders and even on a global scale. Al Qaeda has its roots among Sunni Muslims fighting against Soviet occupation of Afghanistan in the 1980s. However, in 1996, Al Qaeda directed its aggression toward the United States to protest U.S. support of Saudi Arabia and Israel. A series of attacks in eastern Africa and the Arabian Peninsula in the 1990s culminated in the attacks on the World Trade Center and Pentagon on September 11, 2001.

Economics

Control of natural resources, such as mineral deposits, can prompt regions of countries to advocate for devolution. People in one region might want to use locally produced wealth for local benefits, such as better schools, infrastructure, and healthcare—or simply to lower taxes. The central government might argue that these resources should benefit the entire country.

Many tribal groups in the Amazon River basin of Brazil object to the extraction of resources and the development of the rainforest without local communities benefiting and being a part of the decision-making process. In Scotland, revenues from North Sea oil helped fuel talk of independence from the United Kingdom. In 2014, Scotland narrowly voted to remain part of the United Kingdom.

Social Issues

Social devolution often follows geographic divisions between religious, linguistic, and historical regions. Countries experiencing social devolution usually have concentrated pockets of a specific religion or distinct spoken language by the local inhabitants. Federal systems, as in the United States and Canada, allow local governments to maintain their distinct languages and religions.

The situation in Belgium, in northwestern Europe, is quite different. As the bilingual sign below reflects, the country is split into the Flemish-speaking north, called Flanders, and the French-speaking south, called Wallonia. As a result of linguistic, cultural, and economic differences, the country is sharply divided. Each region has its own institutions and many people identify themselves as Flemish or Walloon rather than Belgian. The future of Belgium as a single country is in doubt.

A bilingual sign showing direction to a police station in Belgium. It uses both the French term, *police,* and the Flemish term, *politie.*

Irredentism

As mentioned in Topic 4.5, **irredentism** is a movement to unite people who share a language or other cultural elements but are divided by a national boundary. One example of irredentism comes from the Caucasus Mountains region. Under the Soviet Union, Nagorno-Karabakh was an Armenian-majority region within Azerbaijan. However, when the Soviet Union collapsed in 1991, Armenians in Nagorno-Karabakh demanded that they be allowed to join the country of Armenia, which supported their demands. Azerbaijan refused, and war broke out. It is estimated that 30,000 people died before a cease-fire in 1994. In theory, a new state was created, the Nagorno-Karabakh Republic. In practice, the new state became part of the country of Armenia. In the fall of 2020, the conflict reignited, and as a result, Armenia will return the territories to Azerbaijan that it occupied after the 1994 cease-fire.

NAGORNO-KARABAKH REGION

The conflict between Azerbaijan and Armenia is a territorial and cultural dispute. Armenia is mostly Christian and Azebaijan is mostly Muslim. Describe challenges drawing borders based on culture.

REFLECT ON THE ESSENTIAL QUESTION

Essential Question: *What factors lead to the devolution of states?*

Factor	Impact on Devolution

KEY TERMS

devolution	terrorism
ethnic separatism	irredentism
ethnic cleansing	

Challenges to Sovereignty

Essential Question: How do political, economic, cultural, and technological changes challenge state sovereignty?

Major events in history have dramatically changed the world political map and countries face challenges to their sovereignty, and sometimes their very existence. Since 1960, 104 countries have been born. During the 1960s, many of the new countries were in Africa and most had been former European colonies. During the 1990s, numerous countries were created, most as a result of the collapse of the Soviet Union. Between 2000 and 2020, five more countries were created, including Southern Sudan in 2011.

Devolution and Fragmentation

As previously stated, devolution is the transfer of power from the central government to lower levels of government. However, devolved powers can lead to regional autonomy and increased desire for independence, causing fragmentatioin of the state. When this fragmentation occurs, the state fractures along regional lines.

Autonomous Regions

Autonomous regions have their own local and legislative bodies to govern a region with a population that is an ethnic minority within the entire country. Though these regions handle their own day-to-day governance, they are not fully independent from the state in which they are located. Many of these regions, such as the Navajo Nation in the United States, reflect the heritage of an indigenous population. Some, such as the Jewish Autonomous Oblast in far eastern Russia, are based on religion. Jews began settling in the area in the 1920s. Both federal states, such as India, and unitary states, such as China, include autonomous regions.

Subnationalism

People in autonomous regions usually have a great deal of local power but give their primary allegiance to the national state. In contrast, **subnationalism** describes people who have a primary allegiance to a traditional group or ethnicity. Many French-speaking people in the province of Quebec, Canada, are subnationalists. They feel a stronger loyalty to Quebec than to Canada. In 1995, advocates of independence for Quebec narrowly lost a popular vote on the issue. Quebec remained part of Canada. In Nigeria, each of the country's

36 states chooses its own legal system. The 12 northern states of Nigeria, where Islam is the predominant religion, have sharia (legal systems based on traditional Islamic laws). The 24 southern states, where Christianity and animism are more common, use more secular legal systems. Sharia in the north is applied only to Muslims, not Christians or animists.

Many countries include several subnational groups as a result of wars, shifting borders, and movement of people. The concept of subnationalism can evolve into a stateless nation (see Topic 4.1) if the group seeks to separate and create an independent country. These groups have had various types of goals:

- Equality: In France, citizens of North African ancestry have fought for changes in laws that they argue discriminate against them.

- Independence: In far western China, some members of the Uyghur ethnic group have advocated seceding from China to form a new country, East Turkestan.

- Changing countries: In eastern Ukraine, many Russian-speaking citizens felt closer ties to Russia than to the rest of Ukraine. Russia invaded and claimed control of this region in 2014 based on irredentism. Several thousand people died in the fighting. Additionally, Crimea, a part of Ukraine, was invaded and annexed by Russia. Ukraine and NATO did not recognize the annexation. (See Topics 4.2 and 4.3 for more on Crimea.)

PRO-RUSSIAN UNREST IN UKRAINE, 2014

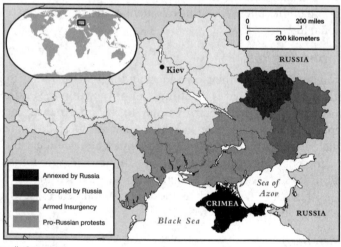

Source: Wikimedia Commons

The southern and eastern portions of Ukraine are where the conflicts occurred. Explain the importance of Crimea to Russia.

Numerous other groups have fought for independence and caused the fragmentation or disintegration of a country. Timor is an island on the eastern end of Indonesia, a predominately Islamic country. The eastern end of the island was settled by the Portuguese, and today is nearly 100 percent Roman Catholic. Timor-Leste (East Timor) won its independence from Indonesia in a brief war in 2002. East Timor has rich oil reserves off of its coast and recently applied to join ASEAN, the Association of Southeast Asian Nations.

Balkanization

Sometimes an entire country or region explodes in ethnic conflict, as the Balkan Mountains region in southeastern Europe did in the early 1900s and again in the 1990s. The rugged mountains of the area made communication difficult, so the region developed a high density of distinct cultural groups—Serbs, Croats, Slovenes, Bulgars, Romanians, and others. In the early 1900s, several of these groups demanded independence from the Austrian and Ottoman empires that controlled the region.

In 1918, several of these Balkan ethnic groups that felt threatened by the Communist victory in the Russia Revolution joined together to form Yugoslavia. However, when the Soviet Union collapsed in 1990, tensions and ethnic cleansing once again fractured the region into multiple countries. Today, **balkanization** means the fragmentation of a state or region into smaller, often hostile, units along ethno-linguistic lines. Areas that suffer from balkanization are also known as *shatterbelts*. (See Topic 4.5.)

BALKANIZATION OF YUGOSLAVIA

Other regions have suffered from balkanization. The country of Sudan was one of the largest countries in Africa when it gained its independence in 1956 from Britain and Egypt. Sudan has a history of numerous civil wars and strife. The southern regions of Sudan are non-Arab, Christian, and animist, while the north is Arab and Muslim. People of the southern regions felt persecuted and marginalized by those in the north. After a long and bloody civil war, with approximately 1.5 million deaths, the country of Southern Sudan was granted independence in 2011. Southern Sudan is very culturally diverse and is experiencing increasing internal disputes recently.

In 1962, after 30 years of internal conflict, Ethiopia annexed the coastal country of Eritrea to gain access to the Red Sea. In 1993, Eritrea declared its independence from Ethiopia and in 2000 the two countries signed a peace agreement to resolve boundary issues over land claimed by both countries. Eritrea claims separate nationality based on ethnic, linguistic, and cultural differences. Both countries signed a formal peace agreement in 2018 that ended the hostilities. In December 2020, the northern province of Ethiopia, Tigray, erupted into conflict and attempted to gain independence which further destabilized the region and country.

Globalization Challenges State Sovereignty

The world is full of networks in transportation, communication, trade, social media, beliefs and values, and politics. **Globalization** is the integration of markets, states, communication, and trade on a worldwide scale. While these forces have brought people and systems closer, they have also put a strain on the sovereignty of states. This in turn has led to a race to create special alliances. Globalization has created the necessity for alliances for collective benefits on a worldwide and regional scale. In addition, economic networks between consumers and producers have changed dramatically as a result of globalization.

The sovereignty of states in the modern age of globalization has been challenged in many ways. Political borders have become less significant as ideas flow more rapidly among most countries, trade in goods is freer than in the past, and even people can travel easily in areas such as Europe. However, the challenges of COVID-19 forced many countries to reassert their control of borders and close country borders and limit in-person interactions in order to slow the spread of the disease. The state system has attempted to adapt to these changes, but the speed at which these changes occur often outpaces states' attempts to keep up. Similarly, social, economic, and environmental forces have had difficulty in maintaining pace with the forces of globalization.

The Arab Spring, a movement of pro-democracy demonstrations and rebellions that began in late 2010, provides a good example of how rapidly ideas can spread. It began with antigovernment demonstrations in Tunisia. But, aided by social media, protests spread quickly throughout North Africa and the Middle East, leading to turmoil throughout the region. The Black Lives Matter movement that started in the United States also spread in 2020 via social and mass media, with protests across the world demanding equality and changes in government and police policies.

Supranationalism

At times, countries sacrifice a degree of sovereignty by joining with other countries for a shared goal. The practice of multiple countries forming an organization for the benenfit of all members is **supranationalism**. These organizations are often formed to create a military alliance, promote trade, or combat an environmental problem. Among the first modern supranational organizations was the League of Nations, founded after World War I. Without the United States as a member, and without strong support from other large countries, the League failed. However, it provided the inspiration for a more effective organization, the United Nations, founded after World War II.

SUPRANATIONAL ORGANIZATIONS			
Organization	**Members States**	**Mission**	**Headquarters**
United Nations (UN), 1945	193: most countries of the world and two others as non-member observer states	To promote peace, security and human rights	• New York City
North Atlantic Treaty Organization (NATO), 1949	30: United States, Canada, Iceland, most countries in western and central Europe, and Turkey	To provide mutual defense of member states	• Brussels, Belgium
European Union (EU), 1993	27: mostly countries in western and central Europe	To integrate member states politically and economically	• Brussels, Belgium
United States-Mexico-Canada Agreement (USMCA), 2020 formerly NAFTA (1994–2019)	3: United States, Mexico, and Canada	To stimulate free trade among members	• Washington, DC • Mexico City • Ottawa, Canada
Association of Southeast Asian Nations (ASEAN), 1967	10: countries from SE Asia	To advance economic growth, peace, social progress, and cultural and economic development in the region	• Jakarta, Indonesia
Arctic Council, 1996	8: only countries with territory in the Arctic—Canada, Russia, the United States, and countries of northern Europe	To foster cooperation, coordination, and interaction among the Arctic states with participation of Arctic indigenous communities	• Tromsø, Norway
African Union, 2002	55: all countries in Africa	To advocate peace, security, and stability on the continent through greater cooperation, economic development, and global integration	• Addis Ababa, Ethiopia • Johannesburg, South Africa

Economic Supranationalism

The most common reason for multiple states to participate in a collective cause is economics. The most significant economic benefits are increased trade members and regulations that consider the interest of all countries involved.

World Trade Organization (WTO) One of the largest and most influential supranational organizations is the World Trade Organization (WTO). The goal of the WTO is to have countries agree to a set of fair and non-discriminatory guidelines for international trade. A secondary goal of the WTO is to ensure that trade flows smoothly, freely, and predictibly.

Organization of the Petroleum Exporting Countries (OPEC) focuses on the production of oil, or petroleum. Its mission is to coordinate and unify its members' petroleum policies in order to stabilize oil markets. Membership spans three continents, including countries such as Saudi Arabia, Kuwait, Indonesia, Venezuela, Nigeria, and Iran. Ensuring a steady income for its members influences the quantity of oil supplied to the global market. Sometimes conflicts arise between the members. For example, one country may want to curtail production in order to drive prices up, while another member may want to increase production to generate more jobs.

Association of Southeast Asian Nations (ASEAN) Seeking mutually beneficial trade agreements has fostered economic growth and peace for member states of ASEAN. For example, the nations of ASEAN had rapidly growing economies—well ahead of regional powerhouses such as Japan, South Korea, India, and Australia.

European Union In the years following World War II, European leaders hoped to create stronger economic and cultural ties that would bring peace to a region ravaged by war for centuries. European countries began to eliminate national barriers to trade and travel on the continent. They reduced tariffs (taxes on trade), established a common set of regulations on products to replace individual national regulations, and coordinated labor policies. The two major steps to overcome nationalism were the formation of the European Union (EU) in 1993 and establishment of a common currency (the Euro) in 1999.

The EU is a political and economic union of 27 democratic European states that has a single-market free-trade zone and movement toward a standardized system of laws. The borders between member states were opened and the movement of people and goods increased. For example, products made in Germany could now be sold and transported to Spain without additional fees or taxes. Nineteen countries in Europe adopted the Euro as their currency. A unified currency within this Eurozone increased efficiency and reduced the cost of trade.

The result of these changes provided European corporations with easy access to a large market—one that included far more people than the U.S. market—in which to sell their products. Success in Europe helped EU-based companies compete in the global marketplace.

THE EUROPEAN UNION, 2021

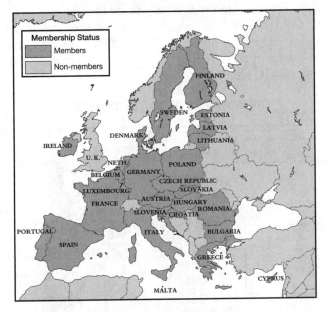

Membership Status
- Members
- Non-members

United Kingdom withdrew in 2020 (Brexit). There are currently five countries seeking admission: Albania, Montenegro, North Macedonia, Serbia, and Turkey.

United States-Mexico-Canada Agreement The success of the European Union inspired the creation of other regional, economic supranational organizations such as the North American Free Trade Agreement (NAFTA). In 1993, the governments of the United States, Canada, and Mexico signed this economic treaty in order to compete in a rapidly changing and extremely competitive global market. In 2020, the treaty was renegotiated and is now called the United States-Mexico-Canada Agreement (USMCA).

Transnational Corporations The rise of **transnational corporations**, companies that conduct business on a global scale, has dramatically weakened state sovereignty. In contrast to corporations based in a single country, transnationals have no strong connection to any one place. As a result, they can move jobs from one country to another in order to take advantage of lower wages, lower taxes, or weaker laws on worker safety and environmental protection. Their ability to move operations around the world gives any single country less influence over them. Some members of the EU are concerned with countries losing their cultural identity as people of different backgrounds move to other countries within the EU, resulting in a changing cultural landscape.

Military and Strategic Supranationalism

Another example of supranationalism is military cooperation through mutual defense alliances. One such alliance, the North Atlantic Treaty Organization (NATO), was created in 1949 by the United States and its allies in response to tensions with the Soviet Union. NATO is the largest military alliance in the world. While NATO did not confront the Soviet military directly, it did use its power to stabilize conflicts in the Balkans during the 1990s.

After the Cold War ended, several former allies of the Soviet Union in Central and Eastern Europe joined NATO. The first were the Czech Republic, Hungary, and Poland in 1999. Their strategic shift angered Russia, and renewed tension between NATO and Russia.

THE GROWTH OF NATO, 1949–2020

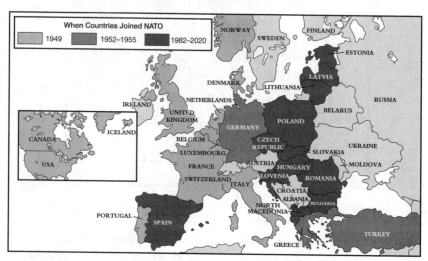

Supranationalism and the Environment

As the 21st century progresses, worldwide concern for the environment has become one of the biggest challenges facing states, supranational organizations, and transnational corporations. Most transnational corporations are based in the economic core—the countries of the developed world. However, much of the production and manufacturing occurs in the economic periphery—countries of the developing world—in order to minimize labor, land, and resource costs. This creates tension.

In wealthy countries such as the United States, workers resent corporations sending their jobs overseas. In poorer countries, people have different concerns. The government of a poorer country, more in need of jobs and development than a wealthy country, might be more willing to accept an environmentally damaging facility. Countries make different economic decisions based on the options they have.

As a result of lax environmental regulations in periphery countries, transnational corporations often pollute the air, water, and soil. To further exacerbate this problem, neighboring states are subject to this pollution as well. The largest supranational organization, the United Nations, has attempted to resolve some of these issues through the Food and Agriculture Organization, the United Nations Convention of the Law of the Sea, and the Paris Agreement on climate change.

The Impact of Technology

The Internet, social media, and the ease of jet travel have had varied effects on how people relate to each other around the world:

- promoted globalization by connecting people across boundaries
- weakened globalization by helping subnational groups to organize
- supported **democratization**—the transition from autocratic to more representative forms of politics—by helping reform movements to communicate in China, Iran, Egypt, and other countries
- threatened democratization where the government has tried to limit the spread of information
- created a digital divide between countries with and without access to information for either political or infrastructure reasons
- increased **time-space compression**, the social and psychological effects of faster movement of information over space in a shorter period of time

REFLECT ON THE ESSENTIAL QUESTION

Essential Question: *How do political, economic, cultural, and technological changes challenge state sovereignty?*

Changes	Challenges to Sovereignty

KEY TERMS

autonomous regions
subnationalism
balkanization
globalization
supranationalism
United Nations (UN)
North Atlantic Treaty Organization (NATO)
European Union (EU)
United States-Mexico-Canada Agreement (USMCA)

Association of Southeast Asian Nations (ASEAN)
Arctic Council
African Union
World Trade Organization (WTO)
Organization of Petroleum Exporting Countries (OPEC)
transnational corporations
democratization
time-space compression

Consequences of Centrifugal and Centripetal Forces

Essential Question: How do the concepts of centrifugal and centripetal forces apply at the state scale?

As defined in Topic 3.3, **centrifugal forces** divide the citizenry in a country while **centripetal forces** unite a country's population. Often, an action has potential to be both types of forces at once. For example, a political election can unite people behind a leader or issue—or divide people bitterly. It is uncommon to find a single event or process that can be neatly defined as centrifugal or centripetal.

Geographers study the extent to which these forces contribute to nation-building by examining interaction, scale, timing, and perspective. To unify a state, a government must define, control, and defend its boundaries. Additionally, the government must blend the different groups within its borders into one society.

Centrifugal Forces

Often a minority population is concentrated in various pockets of a state, thus resulting in minority self-awareness and an emerging nationalist movement. **Regionalism** is when loyalty to a distinct portion of a country is more important than loyalty to the entire country. Regionalism can create centrifugal forces.

When a segment of a state's minority population feels underrepresented and lacking political power, it might pursue a path of separation from the larger state. Canada provides a good example. The country's French-speaking population, concentrated in southern Quebec, has pursued more power over local issues, such as education and administrative governance, including its judicial system. However, for some French-speaking Canadians in Quebec, this is not enough; therefore, political centrifugal forces still exist.

On the economic side, globalization has widened the gap between the rich and poor within a state. Uneven development within a country may lead to divisions between the "haves" and the "have-nots." Uneven development results in uneven benefits and the separation and fragmentation of a state. For example, India is an emerging economic power, but it is not a strongly united country. Despite rapid economic growth on a global scale, India still has large segments of its population living in abject poverty. This poverty is divided along regional lines.

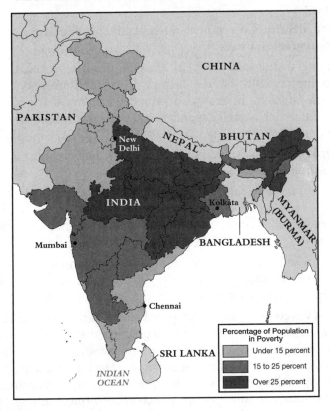

REGIONAL DISTRIBUTION OF POVERTY IN INDIA

Describe the location of regions in India that suffer the highest and lowest percentages of poverty. Explain how high poverty can be a centrifugal force.

Centrifugal cultural forces have intensified as a result of globalization. Declining state sovereignty and economic advances have empowered ethnonational groups to demand more autonomy. **Ethnonationalism** is support for the political interests of a particular ethnic group within a state, especially its national independence or self-determination. For example, fragmentation within Syria and Iraq gave rise to Kurdish independence movements in those countries.

Centripetal Forces

Governments, religious groups, and other institutions use a combination of methods to promote unity in a society. Centripetal forces are often focused on economic development, political identity, and cultural practices.

Economic Development One of the most effective centripetal forces used by governments throughout history has been building infrastructure. Improved infrastructure—such as efficient transportation systems and well-constructed roads and railways—can promote trade, communications, dependence, and other forms of connections among the population within a state. Improvements in transportation are one way to promote unity by increasing interaction among different ethno-linguistic groups. These can increase the overall wealth of the country.

Political Identity Governments attempt to build political unity throughout its population in several ways:

- Unifying institutions, such as schools, promote social cohesion by educating students on the historical accomplishments of the state. Unifying institutions may also promote holidays that are historically significant, such as an independence day or a day to honor veterans.

- **Nationalism**, the strong feelings of patriotism and loyalty one feels toward one's country, promotes a sense of belonging, even if a country's population is an ethnically diverse one.

- The acceptance of rules or laws and the promotion of political equality help to reinforce political centripetal forces. Examples of this are governmental administration practices, such as a fair legal and judicial system and protection of the populace by the government.

- Customs and rituals based on citizenship are a common way to promote a sense of common identity. In the United States, public school students throughout the country often recite the Pledge of Allegiance each day.

Cultural Practices States with a population that is *homogeneous*, one that shares a common trait, likely have cultural practices that function as centripetal forces. For example, in heavily Islamic countries such as Saudi Arabia and Pakistan, Ramadan is a month-long religious observation that helps to unite the overall population. Japan, which has preserved a homogeneous culture by maintaining restrictive immigration policies, has strong cultural centripetal forces such as a common language and a shared sense of history.

FACTORS THAT INFLUENCE CENTRIPETAL AND CENTRIFUGAL FORCES		
	Centripetal Forces	**Centrifugal Forces**
Economic	• Quality transportation and communication infrastructure • Wealth and high quality of life	• Poor transportation and communication infrastructure • Poverty and uneven distribution of wealth
Social	• Acceptance of racial, ethnic, and gender differences	• Practices that discriminate and exclude based on race, ethnicity, or gender
Political	• Just laws that protect all people equally	• Laws that discriminate against different segments of society
Environmental	• Low pollution and access to clean air and water in all regions	• High pollution and unequal access to clean water
Cultural	• Celebration of a national day of importance • Common religion of the majority of country	• Some religions not accepted • Holidays that celebrate controversial individuals or events

Essential Question: *How do the concepts of centrifugal and centripetal forces apply at the state scale?*

Centrifugal Forces and Their Impact	Centripetal Forces and Their Impact

KEY TERMS

centrifugal forces

centripetal forces

regionalism

ethnonationalism

nationalism

GEOGRAPHIC PERSPECTIVES: *UNITED KINGDOM AND EUROPEAN UNION*

In June of 2016, the citizens of the United Kingdom (Britain) voted to leave or exit the European Union (EU), hence the name Brexit. In January of 2021, the United Kingdom and EU reached an agreement of separation and formally split. The United Kingdom and EU will continue to have a free trade zone, but movement of people and products between the two regions will have new restrictions.

The vote to leave demonstrated very clear demographic and geographic patterns. Older, less educated, and unemployed populations were more in favor of leaving the EU, while younger and highly educated voters favored staying in the EU. Young people in the UK had a 65 percent voter turnout rate, while over 90 percent of older populations chose to vote. Scotland, Northern Ireland, and highly populated areas near London voted to remain in the EU. The rural and industrial areas of England and Wales voted heavily to leave.

People who voted to leave the EU were often swayed by concerns about immigration into the UK and a desire to control the United Kingdom's political and financial future without interference from mainland Europe. People who voted to remain were in favor of the open borders and the benefits of economic exchange with mainland Europe. London has many world and European headquarters for transnational companies. Some believe that after Brexit companies may move their headquarters and numerous jobs to cities like Berlin and Paris within the EU.

Scotland and Northern Ireland

Both Scotland and Northern Ireland voted to remain in the EU because they experienced rapid economic growth since joining the EU. Since the Brexit vote, the government of Scotland has increased their desire for independence from the UK in hopes of joining the EU as an independent country. Concerns are high in Scotland and Northern Ireland that numerous jobs will be lost and economic growth will decline.

Residents of Northern Ireland could have a different experience than the rest of the UK. Northern Ireland's citizens have the option of dual citizenship in the UK and Ireland. The country of Ireland is independent and still a member of the EU. If Northern Ireland's citizens choose to get an Ireland passport they can still move freely within the EU and receive all of the benefits of EU citizenship.

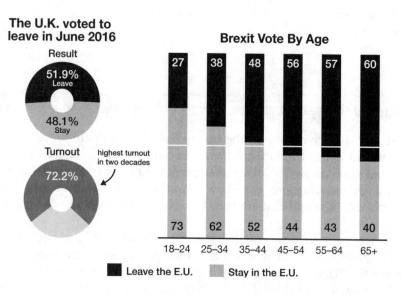

1. Describe the demographic characteristics of people who voted for leaving the EU.

2. Describe the geographic patterns for areas that voted for staying in the EU.

3. Explain how the changing function of borders could influence the United Kingdom.

Various titles of a single map can reflect competing perspectives on geographic relationships. In 1947 the British ended colonial rule in the Indian subcontinent. They divided the colony into two countries, India and Pakistan. (In 1971, the eastern part of Pakistan became the independent country of Bangladesh.) The basis for the separation was religion. Regions where nearly everyone was a Muslim became Pakistan. The rest of the region, with a Hindu majority, became India.

However, people disputed control over the region of Kashmir, in the northern tip of the subcontinent. Most people were Muslims, but the rulers were Hindus, so both Pakistan and India felt a strong claim on it. People failed to agree on a formal boundary. Instead, they accepted a "line of control." Pakistan controls the territory northwest of this line, while India controls the territory southeast of the line. To make the issue more complicated, China claims part of eastern Kashmir. Each country is unwilling to release its claims on the Kashmir because of the wealth of fresh water and natural resources in the region.

The title of a map can influence the point of view or perspective of people viewing a map.

1. If the title of the map was "World's Most Dangerous Boundary Dispute," describe the impact of this title on how you think about the map.

2. If the title of the map was "Indo-Pakistani Boundary Dilemma," describe the impact of this title on how you think about the map.

3. Create a new title for the map that is fair and representative of the dispute.

CHAPTER 10 REVIEW:
Challenges in the Modern State

Topics 4.8–4.10

MULTIPLE-CHOICE QUESTIONS

Question 1 refers to the following diagram.

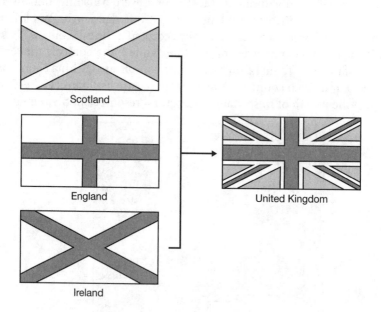

Scotland

England

United Kingdom

Ireland

1. Notice how the crosses in the flags of Scotland, England, and Ireland are combined in the flag of the United Kingdom. Which process does this represent?

(A) The balkanization of the British Isles

(B) The formation of autonomous regions within a state

(C) The process of irredentism in uniting people with the same culture

(D) The creation of a single state out of separate nations

(E) The centrifugal forces pulling a country apart

2. The presence of centrifugal forces within a country has led many central governments to transfer power to regional or local governments. This process is called?

(A) Devolution

(B) Acculturation

(C) Autocratic rule

(D) Imperialism

(E) Capitalism

3. Which of the following terms best applies to what a country experiences when its unity is threatened by inequality or economic problems?

(A) Centrifugal forces

(B) Centripetal forces

(C) Colonialism

(D) Federalism

(E) Supranationalism

4. Which provides the strongest support for the conclusion that Japan has few centrifugal forces?

(A) Japan is an island located off the east coast of China.

(B) Japan is part of the United Nations.

(C) Japan has never colonized another country.

(D) Japan has a high degree of ethnic and linguistic homogeneity.

(E) Japan has one of the largest economies in the world.

5. Which is NOT an example of a centripetal force?

(A) About nine-tenths of Swedes speak Swedish as their first language.

(B) About 95 percent of Iranians belong to the Shia Muslim faith.

(C) The Mindanao region of the Philippines has poor infrastructure and inadequate basic services.

(D) Since the end of World War II, Europe has worked to remove trade and political barriers among countries.

(E) About 96 out of every 100 people in Thailand identify as part of the Thai ethnic group.

6. Which groups have been gaining more local power around the world as a result of devolution?

(A) Indigenous people

(B) French-speaking people

(C) Spanish-speaking people

(D) Recent immigrants from East Asia

(E) Recent immigrants from Syria

7. Which of the following best describes the effect of globalization related to state sovereignty?

(A) States' sovereignty has clearly increased as a result of globalization.

(B) State sovereignty has increased because of the need to defend borders from imperialistic states.

(C) Globalization has not had an effect on state sovereignty.

(D) States have given up some sovereignty in order to join supranationalistic organizations.

(E) The number of sovereign states in the world has declined during the era of globalization.

FREE-RESPONSE QUESTION

1. Political, economic, cultural, or technological changes can challenge a country's ability to self-rule, or its sovereignty. Many boundaries in the world have changed over the past 50 years. Some countries have split into smaller countries and some have joined supranational organizations such as the European Union (EU) or the North Atlantic Treaty Organization (NATO).

EUROPE AND THE FORMER YUGOSLAVIA

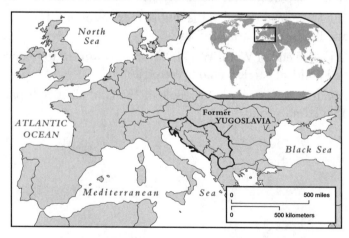

INTERNAL BOUNDARIES IN CANADA

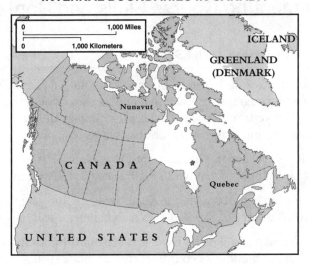

(A) Describe the difference between centripetal and centrifugal forces.

(B) Describe the impact of ONE cultural centrifugal force on the unity of either Canada or the former Yugoslavia.

(C) Explain how federalism might reduce tension within a country.

(D) Explain how nationalism can be both a centripetal and a centrifugal force within a country.

(E) Explain ONE economic reason why many states of Eastern Europe such as Poland, Slovakia, and Romania chose to join the EU.

(F) Explain ONE political reason why many states of Eastern Europe such as Poland, Slovakia, and Romania chose to join NATO.

(G) Describe the role that the Internet or social media has played in fueling subnational protest movements.

UNIT 4 REVIEW:
Connecting Course Skills and Content

APPLYING GEOGRAPHIC SKILLS

Applying geographic skills is critical for success on the AP Exam. For each skill listed write a one-paragraph response that illustrates your understanding of the question. Support your response with specific examples and evidence. Refer to the Unit 1 introduction (pages 3–7) for tips on how to apply geographic skills.

1D Describe TWO geographic concepts, processes, models, or theories in Unit 4 and support them with specific geographic examples.

2C Explain a likely outcome of the Kurds realizing the goal of gaining their own country of Kurdistan. What challenges will they face?

3C Using the map and data in Topic 4.9, explain the patterns and trends related to the number of countries created since 1960.

4B Choose a map from Unit 4 and explain its strengths and limitations.

5A Locate and identify Unit 4 maps, data, and/or images that illustrate the following scales of analysis: global, regional, national, and local.

WRITE AS A GEOGRAPHER: *USE EXAMPLES*

Strong answers to free-response questions usually include specific examples. These examples are one way to show that the writer understands a concept well enough to apply it. They also show that the writer can make distinctions between related concepts such as nation and state, or centripetal and centrifugal.

For each term, list the letter of the example below that best demonstrates it.

1. terrorism
2. subnationalism
3. irredentism
4. supranationalism
5. balkanization
6. devolution

(A) Several dozen countries in Africa form an organization to promote security and economic development throughout the continent.

(B) The national government of France transfers decision-making on building roads and bridges to local and regional governments.

(C) In 1881, a group of Russians attempt to overthrow the government by assassinating the country's leader, Tsar Alexander II.

(D) In early 1861, Robert E. Lee felt more loyalty to his state of Virginia than to his country, the United States.

(E) When the French empire in West Africa collapsed, the region split into eight different countries.

(F) Some Norwegians argue that Norway is the rightful ruler of parts of Sweden that were once part of Norway.

UNIT 5

Agriculture and Rural Land-Use Patterns and Processes

Unit Overview

About 12,000 years ago, people living in Southwest Asia began to intentionally grow crops and raise animals. From the beginning of agriculture in that region, and later in other regions, agriculture diffused throughout the world. The evolution of agriculture has been punctuated by four revolutions that have pushed agriculture and societies forward. Since 1750, mechanization, the use of chemicals, and research have dramatically increased agricultural productivity. Additional advancements have increased productivity and allowed more people to work outside of agriculture, but these advancements have increased stress on the environment.

Physical Geography, Economics, and Settlement Patterns

What people have grown and raised has always been shaped by the climate, soils, and landforms of a place. In addition, the types of agricultural goods that farmers produce, whether dairy or vegetables or grain, are heavily influenced by the nearness of the market. Farmers have also shaped the landscape by cutting down trees, draining wetlands, etc. Improvements in technology have shifted agriculture toward larger enterprises and greater interdependence.

Changes and Opportunities

Changes in technology and society influence how people produce and consume food. Historically, women have often been responsible for cooking, but as more women entered the workforce, more food has been prepared outside the home.

ENDURING UNDERSTANDINGS

1. Availability of resources and cultural practices influence agricultural practices and land-use patterns. (PSO-5)

2. Agriculture has changed over time because of cultural diffusion and advances in technology. (SPS-5)

3. Agricultural production and consumption patterns vary in different locations, presenting different environmental, social, economic, and cultural opportunities and challenges. (IMP-5)

Source: *AP® Human Geography Course and Exam Description.* Effective Fall 2020 (College Board).

CHAPTER 11

Origins, Patterns, and Settlements of Agriculture

Topics 5.1–5.3

Topic 5.1 Introduction to Agriculture

Learning Objective: Explain the connection between physical geography and agricultural practices. (PSO-5.A)

Topic 5.2 Settlement Patterns and Survey Methods

Learning Objective: Identify different rural settlement patterns and methods of surveying rural settlements. (PSO-5.B)

Topic 5.3 Agricultural Origins and Diffusions

Learning Objectives: Identify major centers of domestication of plants and animals. (SPS-5.A)

Explain how plants and animals diffuse globally (SPS-5.B)

> *To most people, this is just dirt. To a farmer, it is potential.*
> —Anonymous

Source: Getty Images

An aerial view of rectangular plots of land in Kansas showing the Public Land Survey System used in the United States. The circular shapes are created by using center-pivot irrigation systems. (See Topic 5.2 for more about survey patterns and Topic 5.10 for more on irrigation systems.)

Introduction to Agriculture

Essential Question: What is the connection between physical geography and agricultural practices?

Two physical elements have always shaped **agriculture**, the process by which humans alter the landscape in order to raise crops and livestock for consumption and trade. One is physical geography, such as soil types and landforms. The other is **climate**, the long-term weather patterns in a region. For example, coffee grows best on hillsides in warm climates, such as in Kenya or Colombia. Olives, grapes, and figs do well in the soil and climate near the Mediterranean Sea. Those foods became dietary staples for people in the region.

Economic factors also impact agriculture. For example, whether consumers want to purchase peaches or plums influences what farmers will grow.

Physical Geography and Agriculture

Agriculture is affected by physical geography in numerous ways. Animals and crops need water. Even cattle herders in the Sahel, a dry region on the southern edge of the Sahara, must have access to water. Nutrient levels in the soil influence what people can grow. For example, cotton needs nutrient-rich soil, while sorghum can grow in nutrient-poor soils, such as those in tropical rainforests.

Landforms also shape agricultural activity. Flat land in large, expansive valleys provides excellent landscapes for agriculture. In contrast, rugged land requires more human labor in order to make the land useful for agriculture.

Humans have altered the physical environment to increase agricultural production. They have used techniques such as irrigation, terrace farming, deforestation, desertification, and the drainage of wetlands. (See Topic 5.10.)

Source: Wikimedia Commons, Raoul Rives

Agricultural activities are dictated by physical constraints as well as the level of economic development of a region. Pictured above are examples of agricultural products and activity in Morocco

Climate and Agriculture

Despite human intervention, environmental and economic factors are often the most important influence on agriculture. They will determine what types of crops will be grown and what types of animals will be raised by farmers in many cases.

Climate Conditions and Agricultural Production

Climate always has and will continue to play a major role in determining what types of agriculture will take place throughout the world. Most of the earth's land surface supports some type of agricultural activity. The few exceptions are those that are considered to be physically extreme. These include land at highest latitudes or highest elevations, and areas with the highest or lowest precipitation. In these areas, population density for most of human history has been low

WET AND ARID AREAS OF THE WORLD

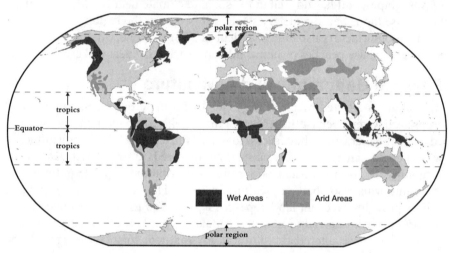

The level of development of a country and its access to modern technology can have a significant influence overcoming climatic obstacles. In the cold climates of Iceland and Greenland, farmers can grow crops in greenhouses. The tomato market, once dominated by sunny and warm U.S. states such as Florida and California, now includes the products of large Canadian indoor growing facilities.

The relationship between climate and cultural traits, such as food preferences, also shapes agricultural activity. The climate of Southwest Asia is fine for raising hogs. However, in a region dominated by Muslims and Jews, most people have religious objections to eating hogs, so farmers choose to raise other animals.

Economic Factors and Agriculture

Climate has a significant influence on agriculture, but economic factors also influence production. Many people across the world are involved in food production, but a significant difference is who consumes the food they produce.

Subsistence Agriculture The primary goal of subsistence agriculture is to grow enough food or raise enough livestock to meet the immediate needs of the farmer and his or her family. A secondary goal is to sell or trade any surplus for income or goods. Most subsistent farmers live in less-developed regions of the world and have small farms of fewer than two acres. Limited land and the expense of advanced agricultural technologies have made it difficult for subsistent farmers to grow excess food to sell or trade.

Commercial Agriculture The primary goal of the commercial farmer is to grow enough crops or raise enough livestock to sell for profit. It exists in all countries but is more common in developed countries. However, it has become increasingly common in semiperiphery countries, such as China, Mexico, and Brazil. To increase yields further, commercial farmers often use the profit from the sale of their products to purchase more land, equipment, and technology, or to pay for training in the newest farming techniques.

The interaction of economic factors and climate influences agricultural activities in many locations. For example, animal herding takes place in drier climates such as North Africa and parts of the United States and Canada. Animal herding practiced by pastoral nomads in North Africa is an example of subsistence agriculture. Their herds are generally smaller in size, and the milk, meat, and hides are used by the farmers and their families, rather than sold for profit. By contrast, cattle raising in the United States and Canada is commercial agriculture. Cattle roam the western prairies and feed on natural vegetation prior to being sold and slaughtered.

Intensive and Extensive Farming Practices

Another factor that influences agriculture is the amount and type of resources used to grow crops or raise animals. **Intensive agricultural** practices are those in which farmers or ranchers use large amounts of inputs, such as energy, fertilizers, labor, or machines, to maximize yields. **Extensive agricultural** practices use fewer amounts of the inputs and typically result in less yields. Every type of agriculture involves labor, resources, and capital. Consider these ideas as part of a continuum, or line, in which each agricultural activity uses resources more or less intensely than the others. (See Topic 5.6.)

Intensive Commercial Agriculture Heavy investments in labor and capital are used in this type of agriculture which often results in high yields and profits. **Capital** is the money invested in land, equipment, and machines. Intensive commercial agriculture is almost always capital intensive but can also be labor intensive. Examples include market gardening, plantations, and large-scale mixed crop and livestock systems.

Intensive Subsistent Agriculture This form of agriculture is often labor and animal intensive. For example, in rice paddies in Southeast Asia, most of the farming is performed using low-paid human labor rather than machines. The seedlings are planted by hand and during the harvesting process, laborers cut the crops and take the outer husks off to expose the grains of rice.

Extensive Commercial Agriculture This type of farming uses low inputs of resources but has the goal of selling the product for profit. Ranching is the most common example and can be found in the western regions of the United States and Canada, Argentina, New Zealand, and Australia. Typically, the human labor required for this type of agricultural activity is extremely low.

Extensive Subsistent Agriculture Few inputs are used in this type of agricultural activity. It is often practiced in areas that have climatic extremes such as tropical, semi-arid, or arid regions. Two examples include nomadic herding and shifting cultivation.

TYPES OF AGRICULTURE				
	Intensive Commercial	**Intensive Subsistent**	**Extensive Commercial**	**Extensive Subsistent**
Location	• Global: core, semiperiphery, and periphery • Regional: near transportation access to urban and global markets	• Global: primarily periphery and semiperiphery • Regional: usually near towns and cities with access to local markets	• Global: core, semiperiphery, and periphery • Regional: transportation access to processing and local, regional, and global markets	• Global: primarily periphery and semiperiphery • Regional: usually in sparsely populated areas with limited access to local markets
Inputs	• Labor: intensive • Capital: intensive	• Labor: intensive • Capital: not intensive	• Labor: not intensive • Capital: intensive	• Labor: intensive • Capital: not intensive
Yield	• Crop productivity: high • Livestock productivity: high	• Crop productivity: low • Livestock productivity: low	• Crop productivity: high • Livestock productivity: low	• Crop productivity: low • Livestock productivity: low

Agricultural Practices and Regions

There are a variety of agricultural practice classifications, and the regions in which they occur are strongly influenced by level of development, climate, and the purpose of the product. American geographer Derwent Whittlesey identified the eleven main agricultural regions in 1936. The following chart summarizes the types of agriculture commonly found in each climate region.

AGRICULTURAL REGIONS		
Agricultural Practice	**Climate**	**Locations**
Pastoral Nomadism	Drylands	• Southwest, Central, and East Asia • North Africa
Shifting Cultivation	Tropical	• Latin America • Sub-Saharan Africa • Southeast Asia
Plantation	Tropical/Sub-Tropical	• Latin America • Sub-Saharan Africa • South and Southeast Asia
Mixed Crop and Livestock	Cold and Warm Mid-Latitude	• Midwest United States and Canada • Central Europe
Grain	Cold Mid-Latitude	• North Central United States • South Central Canada • East Europe
Commercial Gardening	Warm Mid-Latitude	• Southeast United States • Southeast Australia
Dairy	Cold and Warm Mid-Latitude	• Northeast United States • Southeast Canada • Northwest Europe
Mediterranean	Warm Mid-Latitude	• Southern coast of Europe • Northern coast of Africa • Pacific coast of the United States
Livestock Ranching	Drylands	• Western North America • Southeast South America • Central Asia • Southern Africa
Intensive Subsistence	Warm Mid-Latitude	• South, Southeast, and East Asia • Near large populations

Pastoral Nomadism This type of subsistent extensive agriculture is practiced in arid and semi-arid climates throughout the world. Nomads rely on the animals for survival. Animals such as cattle, camels, reindeer, goats, yaks, sheep, and horses provide meat for food and hides for clothing and shelter. Pastoral nomads move their herds to different pastures within their territory and often trade meat for crops with nearby subsistence farmers. Nomads in different regions rely upon different animals, depending on their culture and the climate in which they live:

- In South Central Asia and East Africa, people rely on cattle because they adapt to the hot climate.
- In desert regions of the Middle East, people rely on camels because they can survive without water for long periods.
- In Siberia, people rely on reindeer because they thrive in cold weather.

Shifting Cultivation In this type of subsistent extensive farming, farmers grow crops on a piece of land for a year or two. When the soil loses fertility, they move to another field. Unlike crop rotation, in which farmers change the crops that are grown within a field, shifting cultivation involves using new fields.

A specific type of shifting cultivation used in tropical climate regions is known as slash-and-burn agriculture, or swidden agriculture, because farmers sometimes clear the land by burning vegetation. This process enriches nutrient-poor soil by adding nitrogen to it. On the cleared land, farmers plant and harvest crops for a few growing seasons until the soil becomes less fertile. Then, they move to another area of dense, wild vegetation and repeat the process.

Examples of shifting cultivation including growing rice in Southeast Asia, maize (corn) in South America, and millet and sorghum in Sub-Saharan Africa. Most families grow various food crops in one field for their own consumption. The community or village often owns the land used for shifting cultivation. As population increases and land becomes scarce, this practice is not sustainable.

Shifting cultivation practices are often not sustainable and have negative influences on land, including depletion of nutrients in the soil.

Plantation Agriculture Under colonialism, commerical agriculture often replaced subsistence farming. A **plantation** is a large commercial farm that specializes in one crop. Most plantations are found in the low latitudes with hot, humid climates and substantial rainfall. They are typically labor intensive and often exploit the low-wage labor available in nearby villages and towns.

To reduce the cost of moving bulky crops, some processing occurs near the plantation. The valuable portion of the crop is transported. Common plantation crops include coffee, cocoa, rubber, sugarcane, bananas, tobacco, tea, and cotton. As labor costs rise, plantations become more capital intensive.

Mixed Crop and Livestock Farming Large-scale mixed crop and livestock farming is an intensive commercial integrated system that demonstrates an interdependence between crops and animals. In some cases, one person owns the land on which the crops are grown and the cattle are raised. In other cases, the adjacent parcels of land are owned by different people—one raises crops and the other raises livestock. On these farms, the majority of the crops are grains that are eaten by the livestock—to fatten cattle for slaughter or to feed dairy cows. The animals' manure is, in turn, used to help fertilize the crops.

Mixed crop and livestock farming is common in developed regions, such as Canada, the Midwestern United States, and northern Europe, but it has diffused to parts of the developing world. U.S. farmers often grow corn and soybeans. These crops can be used as animal feed or made into various products.

Grain Farming In regions too dry for mixed crop agriculture, farmers often raise wheat. Consumed mostly by people, wheat is produced in the prairies and plains. China, India, Russia, and the United States are the world's top wheat producers. The type of wheat grown reflects the climate:

- *Spring wheat* is planted in early spring and harvested in early autumn. It is grown in colder regions such as Canada, Montana, and the Dakotas.
- *Winter wheat* is planted in the fall and harvested in early summer. It is grown in warmer regions such as Kansas, Oklahoma, and Europe.

Commercial Gardening Typical fruits and vegetables grown in the United States include lettuce, broccoli, apples, oranges, and tomatoes. Large-scale commercial vegetable gardens and fruit farms are found mostly in California, Arizona, and states of the Southeast. In the winter, the United States imports these types of products from Mexico and Chile. This type of intensive farming is also referred to as truck farming because the products were traditionally driven to local urban markets and sold. Today, however, most trucks are refrigerated which allows farmers to sell their products to distant markets.

The concept of small-scale market gardening is making a resurgence near cities with buy-local food movements. **Market gardening** is when fruits and vegetables are grown near an urban market and sold to local suppliers, stores, restaurants. Today's market gardening in the United States is intensive and usually requires capital investments of greenhouses and fertilizers.

Dairy Farming Traditionally, dairies were local farms that supplied products to customers in a small geographic area. This pattern still exists in many less-developed regions of the world. However, during later 20th century, improvements in refrigeration and transportation expanded the **milk shed**, the geographic distance that milk is delivered. Large corporate dairy operations replaced smaller family-owned farms, which resulted in fewer farms but more production. Most commercial dairy farms in the United States, Canada, and other developed countries are near urban centers and transportation corridors.

In a few countries, such as Argentina and Brazil, demand for dairy products increased faster than the pressure for consolidation. With economic growth and higher incomes, the number of dairy farms increased.

Mediterranean Agriculture Mediterranean agriculture is practiced in regions with hot, dry summers, mild winters, narrow valleys, and often some irrigation. Some of these regions are southern Europe, northern Africa, southwestern Africa, southwestern Asia, southwestern Australia, California, and central Chile. Common crops grown in Mediterranean agriculture include figs, dates, olives, and grapes. Herders in these regions often practice **transhumance**, the seasonal herding of animals from higher elevations in the summer to lower elevations and valleys in the winter. (See Topic 2.11.) Goats and sheep are the principal livestock because of the region's rugged terrain.

Livestock Ranching Livestock ranching is the commercial grazing of animals confined to a specific area. Similar to pastoral nomadism, livestock ranching is found in areas that are too dry to grow crops in large quantities. Ranching is common in the western United States; the pampas of Argentina, Brazil, and Uruguay; parts of Spain and Portugal; China; and central Australia.

REFLECT ON THE ESSENTIAL QUESTION

Essential Question: *What is the connection between physical geography and agricultural practices?*

Elements That Influence Agriculture	Effects on Agriculture

KEY TERMS

agriculture	extensive commercial	grain farming
climate	agriculture	commercial gardening
subsistence agriculture	capital	market gardening
commercial agriculture	extensive subsistent	dairy farming
intensive agriculture	agriculture	milk shed
extensive agriculture	pastoral nomadism	Mediterranean agriculture
intensive commercial	shifting cultivation	transhumance
agriculture	plantation	livestock ranching
intensive subsistent	mixed crop and livestock	
agriculture	farming	

Settlement Patterns and Survey Methods

Essential Question: What are rural settlement patterns and methods of surveying rural settlements?

The study of geography emphasizes a spatial perspective. Learning how people organized themselves spatially in the rural, or agricultural, environment has the same spatial perspective. Population density is less in rural regions compared to urban regions, but how and why humans interact with their environment in rural areas is just as significant. As technology has changed how people interact with the physical environment and the patterns of settlements.

Rural Settlement Patterns

Throughout history, rural residents commonly lived in **clustered,** or **nucleated settlements**. These settlements had groups of homes located near each other in a village and fostered a strong sense of place and often shared of services, such as schools. Villagers raised crops and animals in the fields and pastures around their settlements. Soil types, climate, and labor force influenced the types of crops grown by residents of rural settlements and sold in local markets.

In contrast to many parts of the world, North American farmers usually created **dispersed settlements**, patterns in which farmers lived in homes spread throughout the countryside. In Canada and the United States, the governments promoted westward expansion by giving farmers land—usually 160 acres—if they agreed to reside on it for several years. Settlers moving westward also utilized the wide-open land to raise cattle. Fertile land in the expansive Ohio Valley allowed farmers to grow crops on large farms. As a result, most farmers in North America lived near their fields, and agricultural villages were rare.

Dispersed settlements do occur in other locations, particularly areas that have rugged or challenging environments, such as with limited water or poor soil. Dispersed settlements encourage individual self-sufficiency but make shared services such as schools or defense difficult.

Another rural settlement pattern is a **linear settlement**, in which buildings and human activities are organized close to a body of water or along a transportation route. Linear settlements along a river were common before industrialization because of the need for fresh water to irrigate crops. Today, the desire to be close to a transportation route is even more important. Small communities will sprawl along a railroad track or a metropolitan city will have multiple entry and exit points from an interstate highway.

RURAL SETTLEMENT PATTERNS

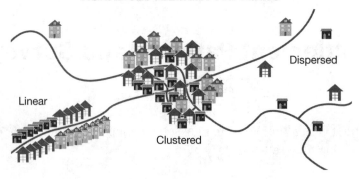

Agricultural Practices Impact Land-Use Patterns

Rural land use evolved as agricultural practices changed, often due to new technology. For example, Cyrus McCormick's invention of the mechanical reaper in 1831 reduced need for human labor since the machine cut and harvested crops. New technology made it easier for more agricultural products to be grown on more land with fewer laborers. Farming techniques, like crop rotation, also improved crop yields and produced a greater variety of foods.

Since new technology allowed more land to be farmed, changes in land ownership followed. The British enclosure movement divided up common land that had been shared by farmers into individual plots. Other European countries did the same, and farm size and production grew across the continent.

Rural land use was further altered by the Green Revolution (see Topic 5.5), which allowed agriculture to be practiced in regions of Mexico, India, and Indonesia, which were previously thought to be incapable of producing food. As agriculture became more commercialized, family farms struggled to compete with large corporate farms and many failed. Each of these changes impacted the size, scope, and organization of land-use patterns.

Source: goegraph.org.uk

Irregularly shaped plots of land created by the metes and bounds system in the United Kingdom.

Establishing Property Boundaries

In England, fields often had irregular shapes that reflected the location of physical features and traditional patterns of use. Plot boundaries were described using the **metes and bounds** system. Metes were used for short distances and often referred to features of specific points, such as "from the oak tree, 100 yards north, to the corner of the barn." Bounds covered larger areas and were based on larger features, such as streams or roads.

The English colonists in America also used metes and bounds. However, beginning in 1785, the United States switched to a system based on surveying rather than landscape features. Surveying involves measuring and recording the distance, elevation, and size of features on the earth's surface. The **Public Land Survey System,** or **township and range system,** created rectangular plots of consistent size. The government organized land into **townships,** areas six miles long and six miles wide. Each square mile, or **section,** consisted of 640 acres, and it could be divided into smaller lots, such as half sections or quarter sections. Because of this system, property boundaries in most of the land the west of the Appalachian Mountains often contain squares or rectangles.

French settlers in North America emphasized the value of access to a river for water and trade. So many farmers could have some river frontage, they developed the **French long-lot system,** in which farms were long, thin sections of land that ran perpendicular to a river. The best examples of this system in North America occur in Quebec and Louisiana.

A positive aspect of the long-lot system is that each landowner had access to water. What are some negative aspects of this system?

REFLECT ON THE ESSENTIAL QUESTION

Essential Question: *What are rural settlement patterns and methods of surveying rural settlements?*

Rural Land-Use Patterns	Rural Land Surveying Methods

KEY TERMS

clustered (nucleated) settlements	metes and bounds	townships
dispersed settlements	Public Land Survey System (township and range system)	section
linear settlement		French long-lot system

Agricultural Origins and Diffusions

Essential Question: What are major centers of domestication of plants and animals and how have plants and animals diffused globally?

Until humans learned to produce a regular, predictable food source, searching for food consumed their time. But as people learned to grow crops, they eventually had time to develop new nonagricultural technologies. The development of agriculture was a gateway to other advances.

Centers of Plant and Animal Domestication

The **First (Neolithic) Agricultural Revolution** was the origin of farming. It was marked by the domestication of plants and animals. Much of the farming that took place during this time was subsistence farming, when farmers consumed the crops that they raised using simple tools and manual labor. The First Agricultural Revolution began in five centers, or hearths. The first hearths were in Southwest Asia, East Asia, South Asia, Africa, and the Americas.

Agricultural Hearths

In the mid-20th century, geographer Carl Sauer was among the first to argue that people in various times and locations developed agricultural hearths independently. He claimed the first hearths were in areas with high biodiversity on the edge of forests. Additional common characteristics of hearths include available fresh water, fertile soils, moderate climates, and skilled residents.

Before humans developed agriculture, they had existed as hunters and gatherers for tens of thousands of years. They lived in small, mobile groups—approximately 30 to 50 people—who could move easily in search of food. Larger groups would have surpassed the carrying capacity of their respective regions. People survived by living in low population density regions.

Animal Domestication Hunters in Central Asia were probably the first people to domesticate animals. They raised dogs and horses for protection, work, transportation, or as a food source. Later, agriculturalists in Southwest Asia kept goats, pigs, sheep, and cattle. People then domesticated cats, horses, camels, donkeys, and llamas, among other animals.

Plant Domestication Growing crops probably began after domestication of animals. People first used vegetative planting, or using parts of the stems or roots of existing plants to grow others. Planting seeds came later. Eventually, people in separate hearths began to trade of crops, animals, and innovations.

MAJOR HEARTHS OF CROP AGRICULTURE			
Time Period	Location	Crops	Early Diffusion Pattern
10,000 to 12,000 years ago	Southwest Asia (Fertile Crescent)	▪ Barley ▪ Wheat ▪ Lentils ▪ Olives	▪ North Africa ▪ Southern Europe ▪ Central Asia
10,000 years ago	Southeast Asia	▪ Mangos ▪ Taro ▪ Coconuts	▪ Southeastern Asia
9,500 to 7,500 years ago	South Asia (Indus Valley)	▪ Barley ▪ Cotton ▪ Wheat ▪ Peas	▪ Indian subcontinent ▪ Southwest Asia
9,500 years ago	East Asia	▪ Rice ▪ Soybeans ▪ Walnuts	▪ North Central Asia ▪ Korean peninsula
7,000 years ago	Sub-Saharan Africa	▪ Yams ▪ Sorghum ▪ Cowpeas ▪ Coffee ▪ African rice	▪ Western Africa ▪ North Africa
5,500 years ago	Mesoamerica	▪ Squash ▪ Peppers ▪ Maize (corn) ▪ Potatos ▪ Cassava	▪ North America ▪ South America

The development of agriculture allowed people to live in permanent, higher-density communities. These communities were usually along rivers, which provided a source of water for people to drink. Rivers also provided a source of food (fish), a means of transporation for trade with other people, and, at times, defense from other groups.

But rivers such as the Nile, the Chang Jiang, and the Indus had another benefit. They flooded regularly, which spread nutrients across the land that contributed to soil fertility. Since this made agriculture more productive, farmers could support denser settlements, and it freed more people to specialize in tasks other than growing food. People could dedicate themselves to building stronger structures in which to live and store products, providing protection from predators and enemies (military), and developing new ideas and products. Increases in agricultural productivity spurred creativity and advances in all areas of human life.

THE FIRST AGRICULTURAL HEARTHS

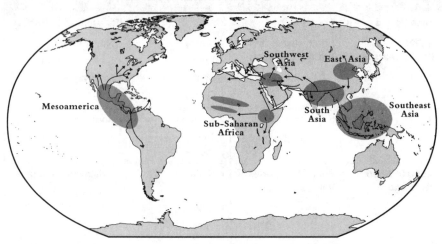

Diffusion of the First Agricultural Revolution

The first major hearth of agriculture is the **Fertile Crescent** in Southwest Asia. The area extends from the eastern coast of the Mediterranean Sea and continues in an arc along the Tigris and Euphrates rivers to the Persian Gulf. Other major hearths existed along large river valleys such as the Chang Jiang (Yangtze) and Huang He (Yellow) valleys in East Asia, the Ganges valley in South Asia, and the Nile valley in northeastern Africa. In each location, people raised a variety of domesticated crops and animals.

In some cases, crops and animals were domesticated in multiple regions with seemingly no interaction among the people. This is called an **independent innovation**. For example, wheat was domesticated independently in Southwest Asia, East Asia, and South Asia. Pigs were domesticated in Southwest Asia, Southeast Asia, and South Asia.

Unique to the hearth of the Americas was the domestication of maize (corn), sweet and white potatoes, and tomatoes. Through diffusion, these products are now important parts of diets throughout most of the world.

Impacts of Hearths and Agriculture

The major hearths of agriculture led to the first urban centers. These first settlements grew into the first civilizations—large societies with cities and powerful states. Civilization brought increased trade, larger empires, and conquest. As societies continued to develop, people had time to specialize in their work and develop new occupations and technologies. This led to the advent of full-time metalworkers, artists, soldiers, weavers, and other specialized jobs.

Over thousands of years, agriculture spread widely and led to increased trade. The diffusion paths in the ancient world were expansive considering the transportation technology of the time. For example, the Roman Empire, which reached its geographic peak around 200 C.E., carried on extensive trade in wheat and other agricultural products with present-day England, Africa, and Southwest Asia. On the Silk Roads, the land and sea routes connecting East Asia to the Middle East and Rome, people traded silk, rice, and other goods.

The Columbian Exchange

One of the most dramatic shifts in agriculture came after the voyage of Christopher Columbus in 1492. The **Columbian Exchange** was the global movement of plants and animals between Afro-Eurasia and the Americas. Europeans brought hundreds of plants and animals west across the Atlantic Ocean to the Americas and took hundreds of plants and animals back east. Crops such as coffee (originally from eastern Africa) and bananas and sugarcane (originally from New Guinea) continue to thrive today in the tropical climates of the Americas. Temperate climate crops such as potatoes (originally from northwest South America) and maize (originally from southern Mexico) are still extensively grown in Europe, Asia, Africa, and the Americas.

Domesticated animals from the Eastern Hemisphere, such as cattle, goats, and horses, were also brought to the Western Hemisphere. The turkey was originally found in the Americas and taken by Europeans back to their respective countries.

In addition to the agricultural exchange, there were many diseases that were also diffused across the Atlantic Ocean to the Americas, including smallpox, influenza, malaria, and measles. All of these had a devastating impact on indigenous populations. Tens of millions of people died, with the total population decreasing as much as 90 percent within a few generations of contact with European diseases.

COLUMBIAN EXCHANGE

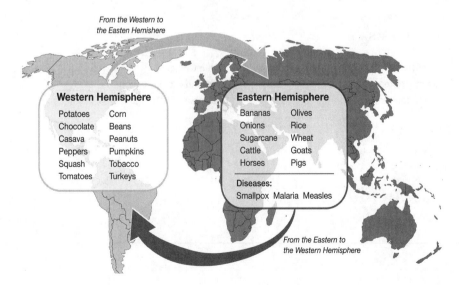

Modern Diffusion

Diffusion of agricultural products, techniques, and technologies continued as civilizations became more advanced. The impact of the Industrial Revolution, which started in Great Britain in the mid-18th century, marked the Second Agricultural Revolution. (See Topic 5.4.) New machines, coupled with scientific discoveries to better preserve food, increased the food supply exponentially. Industrialization diffused across Europe about the same time as it reached the Americas, and ever since, most of Europe, the United States, and Canada have continued to be global leaders in food production and distribution.

By the mid-20th century, Green Revolution (see Topic 5.5) scientists created new crossbred or hybrid seedlings in a laboratory. These seedlings are used in more climatically restrictive regions and allowed people to produce food for themselves. This has helped to support growing populations in the semiperiphery countries of Mexico, India, and Indonesia.

REFLECT ON THE ESSENTIAL QUESTION

Essential Question: *What are major centers of domestication of plants and animals and how have plants and animals diffused globally?*

Agricultural Hearths	Diffusion Patterns from Hearth

KEY TERMS

First (Neolithic) Agricultural Revolution	Fertile Crescent
animal domestication	independent innovation
plant domestication	Columbian Exchange

A modern diet is often rich in food from around the world. Geographers have traced the diffusion of these crops from their hearths and the networks created through trade.

Crops and Locations

Florida oranges, Irish potatoes, Colombian coffee, Swiss chocolate, and Italian tomato sauces are closely associated with specific geographic locations. But each of these items originated in hearths distant from where they are produced today. Similarly, black pepper from India, cinnamon from Sri Lanka, and nutmeg from the Moluccas are among the many non-native luxuries that diffused to the European mainland. The goal of reducing the friction of distance between Europe and these faraway lands in order to improve the variety of peoples' diets was a significant factor in the diffusion of crops from one location to another.

Rate of Adoption

But people are creatures of habit, so it can take centuries for the new crops to be accepted by another culture. For example, when Europeans brought tomatoes from the Americas back to Europe, they became popular in Italy—but only for ornamental purposes. Initially believed to be poisonous, tomatoes did not find their way into conventional Italian cuisine until the 19th century.

Impact of Land and Climate

Successful diffusion depends on more than what people want. Crops are notoriously fickle with respect to the conditions in which they grow best. A slight change in soil conditions, average temperature, growing season, moisture, and latitudinal position can severely hinder the production of a crop.

For instance, natural latex, extracted from rubber trees originating in South America, was first introduced to France in the 18th century. French and British companies then started to plant rubber trees in their colonies in South and Southeast Asia. Today, over 90 percent of its production is concentrated in Southeast Asian countries such as Thailand, Indonesia, and Malaysia. This primarily has to do with the availability of abundant low-paid labor in those regions, as opposed to the Americas. However, this has occurred only because both regions' distances from the equator and relative climates are very similar.

1. Describe a benefit of having access to food from a variety of places around the world.

2. Describe a cultural or social reason why the adoption of food from another location is a slow process.

3. Describe an environmental barrier that slows the spread of new crops growing in different regions.

Global trade has been significantly different ever since Columbus sailed across the Atlantic Ocean in search of India. Even though he did not achieve his goal, lives were changed forever because of the migrations of people, the diffusion of ideas, the introduction of new foods, and the spread of diseases.

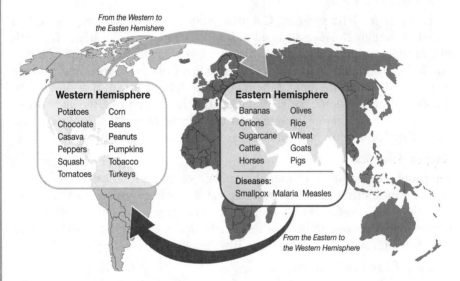

1. Define the Columbian Exchange.

2. Explain ONE positive and ONE negative social consequence of the Columbian Exchange on the Americas.

3. Using the graphic, explain the degree to which you have benefited from the diffusion of foods from Afro-Eurasia to the Americas.

4. Using the graphic, explain to what extent the Columbian Exchange changed the way human beings eat.

CHAPTER 11 REVIEW:
Origins, Patterns, and Settlements of Agriculture

Topics 5.1–5.3

MULTIPLE-CHOICE QUESTIONS

1. As a result of the Columbian Exchange, which crop was transferred from the Americas to Europe and later spread through the world?

   (A) Coffee

   (B) Maize (corn)

   (C) Rice

   (D) Olives

   (E) Wheat

2. An agricultural hearth is a location where

   (A) linear settlements are commonly found

   (B) the Second Agricultural Revolution began

   (C) widespread terracing is used

   (D) plants and animals were first domesticated

   (E) where the Third Agricultural Revolution failed

3. In which state or province is the long-lot land division most common?

   (A) Montana

   (B) Quebec

   (C) Texas

   (D) Iowa

   (E) British Columbia

4. Mediterranean agricultural products are most commonly grown in

   (A) Southern Spain and California

   (B) the American Midwest and the European Highlands

   (C) Northern Italy and the Nordic countries

   (D) Australia and Central Asia

   (E) the Middle East and the Andean Highlands

5. A meal that includes olives, pita bread, cheese, figs, lamb, and wine is most associated with which of the following?

(A) Mexico

(B) United Kingdom

(C) Greece

(D) China

(E) Russia

Question 6 refers to the following image.

6. Using the image above, which of the following is the most important identifier of the Public Land Survey System?

(A) Circular fields

(B) Alternating crops shown with different colors in the fields

(C) Storage structures shown in the top half of image

(D) Square and rectangular fields

(E) Darker fields showing the flow of water

7. Rice and beans are very common ingredients used in Latin American food today. Which of the following scenarios best explains this?

(A) Beans diffused from Europe and were added to meals using rice

(B) Rice and beans diffused from Europe and added to the diets of local people in the Americas

(C) Rice and beans are indigenous foods of the Americas

(D) Rice diffused from China and beans from Spain

(E) Rice diffused from Europe and was added to meals using beans.

Different types of rural settlement patterns developed for specific reasons.

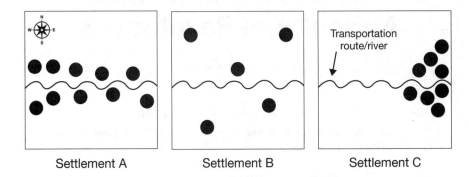

| Settlement A | Settlement B | Settlement C |

(A) Identify the type of rural settlement of A, B, and C.

(B) Describe ONE reason why people settled in permanent rural settlements.

(C) Explain ONE economic reason why people would settle in a pattern that reflects Settlement A.

(D) Describe ONE environmental reason for the settlement pattern on Settlement C.

(E) Using ONE world region explain how technology encouraged the settlement pattern such as in Settlement B.

(F) Explain ONE negative social aspect of the settlement pattern in Settlement B.

(G) Describe ONE limitation of analyzing settlement patterns by using a hypothetical diagram.

CHAPTER 12

The Second and Third Agricultural Revolutions

Topics 5.4–5.5

Topic 5.4 The Second Agricultural Revolution

Learning Objective: Explain the advances and impacts of the Second Agricultural Revolution. (SPS-5.C)

Topic 5.5 The Green Revolution

Learning Objective: Explain the consequences of the Green Revolution on food supply and the environment in the developing world. (SPS-5.D)

Yet food is something that is taken for granted by most world leaders despite the fact that more than half of the population of the world is hungry.

—Norman Borlaug, **Nobel lecture, 1970**

Source: Getty Images

Advanced agricultural techniques and irrigations systems have diffused around the world. This image shows a center-pivot irrigation system in Botswana, Africa. (See Topics 5.4 and 5.5 for irrigation changes during agricultural revolutions.)

The Second Agricultural Revolution

Essential Question: What are the advances and impacts of the Second Agricultural Revolution?

Agriculture underwent a wide-ranging overhaul beginning in the mid-18th century, and the changes have not slowed since. Technological advances of the Industrial Revolution benefited farmers with dramatically better yields and productivity. As a result, the world moved out of the First Agricultural Revolution and into a series of new agricultural revolutions based on innovation and science to meet an increased global demand for food:

- The **Second Agricultural Revolution**, which began in the 1700s, used the advances of the Industrial Revolution to increase food supplies and support population growth. Agriculture benefited from mechanization and improved knowledge of fertilizers, soils, and selective breeding practices for plants and animals.

- The Third Agricultural Revolution (see Topic 5.5), which began in the 1960s, included the Green Revolution and an agribusiness model that controlled the development, planting, processing, and selling of food products.

Impact of the Second Agricultural Revolution

The Second Agricultural Revolution involved the mechanization of agricultural production, advances in transportation, development of large-scale irrigation, and changes to consumption patterns of agricultural goods. Innovations, such as the steel plow and mechanized harvesting, greatly increased food production, particularly in Europe and the United States. The impact of the Second Agricultural Revolution, coupled with discoveries to better preserve food, increased the food supply, especially to countries that participated in global trade networks. The net result was that more people had access to a greater variety of food, which increased life expectancies.

Property Rights and Farming Advances

Paralleling changes in technology were changes in the law. The **Enclosure Acts** were a series of laws enacted by the British government that enabled landowners to purchase and enclose land for their own use. This land had previously been common land shared by peasant farmers. Similar enclosure movements occurred throughout Europe that allowed for larger farms, more efficient production, and crops sold for profit rather than personal consumption.

However, the enclosures came at a high cost. Many farmers were forced off their land and lost their traditional way of life.

Advances in food production technology—in the mid-19th century through the early half of the 20th century—led to better diets, longer life expectancies, and increased population. These factors, combined with many displaced farmers due to the Enclosure Acts, led to a larger potential workforce for growing factories.

Mechanized agricultural technology created a shift in employment as fewer farmers and farm laborers were needed to produce more food. With fewer jobs in farming, workers looked to jobs created in the industrial or manufacturing sector of the economy. Since most of these industrial jobs existed in cities and new factory towns, rural-to-urban migration increased dramatically, which changed the cultural landscape and worldwide population distributions.

Agricultural advancements in sowing (planting) and reaping (harvesting), storage, irrigation, and transportation were made during the 19th century.

EARLY ADVANCES IN MODERN AGRICULTURE		
Advancement	Date	Effect
Iron/Steel Plow	1819	• Reduced human labor • Increased strength to break through harder soils • Increased amounts of crops grown per acre • Increased size of farms
Mechanized Seed Drilling	18th century	• Planted and covered each seed quickly • Resulted in increased yield per acre
McCormick Reaper/ Harvester	1831	• Increased harvest • Reduced human labor • Reduced amount of crops that perished in the field before harvest
Grain Elevator	1849	• Increased storage space and food supply • Protected harvested food from animals and the elements
Barbed Wire	1870s	• Provided inexpensive fencing to keep livestock in grazing areas • Demarcated property
Mixed Nitrogen and Nitric Acid Fertilizer	1903	• Increased crop yields per acre

Farming techniques, like crop rotation and irrigation, increased yields and allowed farmers to produce a greater variety of food products. **Crop rotation** is the technique of planting different crops in a specific sequence on the same plot of land in order to restore nutrients back into the soil. Grains usually extract nitrogen from the soil, while alfalfa puts nitrogen into the soil. A fallow period (ground left unseeded) that allows the land to rest, is also a common technique.

Farmers significantly develped their understand of proper soil management during the Second Agricultural Revolution.

Improved irrigation systems provided a stable and controlled water supply thus increasing yields. **Irrigation** is the process of applying controlled amounts of water to crops using canals, pipes, sprinkler systems, or other human-made devices, rather than to rely on just rainfall.

During the same time period as the Second Agricultural Revolution, transportation infrastructure in Europe, the United States, and core regions improved dramatically with the greater use of roads, canals, ships, steamboats, and railroads. Additional improvements in refrigeration of train cars and trucks further increased the distance goods could be transported, while reducing the time that it took agricultural products to get to domestic urban markets. These transportation infrastructure improvements laid the foundation of a global trade explosion of the Third Agricultural Revolution. (See Topic 5.5.)

Agricultural Changes and Shifting Demographics

The Second Agricultural Revolution resulted in fewer, yet larger and much more productive farms. This change caused a decrease in the number of farm owners and an even greater drop-off in the need for agricultural laborers. By the late 19th century, a large number of displaced farm laborers migrated to U.S. urban centers. The 1920 U.S. Census showed, for the first time in the country's history, that more people lived in urban areas than in rural areas. Only 30 percent of the labor force worked in agriculture, less than half what it was in 1840. Today, only 3.6 percent of the U.S. workforce is involved with farming or related industries.

REFLECT ON THE ESSENTIAL QUESTION

Essential Question: *What are the advances and impacts of the Second Agricultural Revolution?*

Agricultural Advances	Impact on Farming

KEY TERMS

Second Agricultural Revolution	crop rotation
Enclosure Acts	irrigation

The Green Revolution

Essential Question: What are the consequences of the Green Revolution on food supply and the environment in the developing world?

M.S. Swaminatha, an Indian geneticist and a prominent leader in the Green Revolution, once said, "We should look upon agriculture not just as a food-producing machine for the urban population, but as the major source of skilled and remunerative employment and a hub for global outsourcing." Throughout much of human history, farms in rural regions have provided the food necessary for people to survive. However, the Green Revolution introduced a wave of advancement in agricultural technology and its effects on food security, jobs, and the environment are still being realized.

The Third Agricultural Revolution

In the mid-20th century, the **Third Agricultural Revolution** was born out of science, research, and technology, and it continues today. This revolution expanded mechanization of farming, developed new global agricultural systems, and used scientific and information technologies to further previous advances in agricultural production.

Researchers in core countries are responsibile for most of the technological developments of the third revolution, but the benefits and impacts were global. This is most evident in vastly improved varieties of grain facilitated by crossbreeding seedlings in laboratories. These advances are at the heart of the Green Revolution, which is considered the most important aspect of the Third Agricultural Revolution.

The Green Revolution

The advances in plant biology of the mid-20th century are known as the **Green Revolution**. Dr. Norman Borlaug, considered the "Father of the Green Revolution," laid the foundation for scientifically increasing the food supply to meet the demands of an ever-increasing global population. Borlaug's development of higher-yield, more disease-resistant, and faster-growing varities of grain are his most important contribution to the revolution. His work set in motion an entire movement that created hybrid wheat, rice, and corn seedlings. Borlaug's research led to the modern method of plant breeding and eventually earned him a Nobel Peace Prize in 1970.

Borlaug worked specifically on developing a shorter grain of wheat that was both resistant to disease and capable of a growing in harsher climates in Mexico. His work was successful in turning Mexico from a wheat-importing country to one that was self-sufficient and even had a wheat surplus. After his success in Mexico, Borlaug worked with governments in South Asia to deal with food shortages in the face of expanding populations.

Borlaug's work and the resulting transfer of agricultural technology from the United States to Mexico and South Asia would serve as a model for the Green Revolution. Green Revolution scientists also encouraged farmers to *double crop*, or grow more than one crop in a year in the same field (see Topic 5.6), while increasing the use of fertilizer and pesticides.

However, the benefits of increased food production were accompanied by concerns. The increased use of chemical fertilizers and pesticides led to fears about the unforeseen consequences of their use on farm products. Borlaug argued that the alternative of people dying from famine was not acceptable, and his research and methodology are credited with saving millions of lives.

INCREASE IN GRAIN PRODUCTION BY REGION

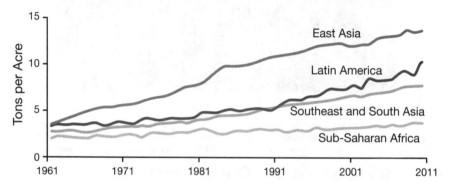

Source: "World Development Report 2013: Jobs," World Bank, 2013.

Based on the graph, which regions increased grain production the most? Why did production in Sub-Saharan Africa lag?

Hybrids Seed **hybridization** is the process of breeding two plants that have desirable characteristics to produce a single seed with both characteristics. For hundreds of years, humans created plant hybrids from local varieties available to them. However, Green Revolution scientists focused their attention on grains. Further, living in an increasingly globalized world, these scientists had a much wider range of plants from which to crossbreed than did local farmers.

Scientists used hybridization to create a new strain of rice in the 1960s. They used long-grain rice from Indonesia and dense-grain dwarf rice of Taiwan to produce a rice grain that was both longer and denser. The hybrid of these two strains was introduced to rice-growing countries in East and Southeast Asia.

Machinery In addition to using hybrids, chemical fertilizers, and pesticides, proponents of the Green Revolution encouraged the transfer of mechanical technology as well. Machinery such as tractors, tillers, broadcast seeders, and grain carts were introduced to countries of the developing world. The introduction of these agricultural technologies assisted in production and challenged traditional labor-intensive farming practices that had been in place for thousands of years.

GMOs Hybridization differs from the production of a **genetically modified organism** (GMO), a process by which humans use engineering techniques to change the DNA of a seed. They have been developed to increase yields, resist diseases, and withstand the chemicals used to kill weeds and pests. (See Topic 5.11 for more about GMOs.)

Source: Wikimedia Commons

A farmer in India uses a tractor to plow his field, while in the background, another farmer does the same with a pair of oxen. The process of accessing Green Revolution and Third Agricultural Revolution technologies is often unevenly distributed across the world and even within the same community.

Positive Impacts of the Green Revolution

During the Green Revolution, global food production increased dramatically. The introduction of new seed technology, mechanization, pesticides, chemical (human-made) fertilizers, and irrigation led to increased yields. More food led to reduced hunger, lower death rates, and growing populations in many parts of the developing world.

Higher Yields

Increased food production in the developing world has prevented millions from starvation. By the mid-1950s, crop yields had increased without cultivating more land. The increased yields have kept up with global population growth, but experts debate whether agricultural production increases or population increases will be greater in the future.

Similar to what occurred in Mexico, India went from being an importer of wheat to harvesting a surplus of wheat within a few decades after World War II. India's increased wheat output helped curb hunger in South Asia. The Green Revolution was also successful in Latin America, East Asia, and Southeast Asia.

The worldwide result of the Green Revolution was higher yields on the same amount of land. Despite rapid population growth in many regions during the mid- to late 20th century, the increased crop output helped to stave off hunger and famine. By the second decade of the 21st century, the World Bank estimated that 80 percent of the developing world's population had an adequate diet. The UN Food and Agriculture Organization (FAO) in Rome, Italy, reported the following yield increases from 1960 to 2000:

- wheat: 208%
- corn: 157%
- rice: 109%
- potatoes: 78%

Money for Research and Business

The Green Revolution helped to create high rates of investment in both the public and private sectors. Research for seed hybridization, fertilizer, and pesticides was funded by governments and universities in developed countries, led by the United States. This research was then used by for-profit corporations to create and market the products farmers used. While the Green Revolution benefited people in poor regions, it also financially benefited universities and corporations in more prosperous regions.

Food Prices

Higher yields and increased production led to falling real food prices, or prices adjusted for inflation. The supply of certain crops, mainly wheat, corn, and rice, grew through the mid- to late 20th century and led to lower prices. More food at affordable prices helped to ease the economic stress of hunger and famine on governments and economic systems in the developing world. However, starting in 2005, global food prices began to rise which triggered large-scale protests in many countries and increased concerns about food insecurity. (See Topic 5.11.)

Negative Consequences of the Green Revolution

Like all large and rapid changes, the Green Revolution had some negative consequences. Some of these were environmental damages, gender inequalities, economic obstacles, and failures in Africa.

Much of the success of the Green Revolution hinged on human-manufactured products such as hybrid seeds, chemical fertilizers, pesticides, and fossil-fuel using equipment. While crop yields increased, they often did so at the expense of the natural environment. The intensive use of land and double or triple cropping, combined with more aggressive irrigation, led to soil erosion and increased environmental pollution. Critics of the Green Revolution argued that it was not a sustainable system.

Farming practices during the Green Revolution increasingly drained the soil of its natural nutrients, which led to more use of and dependecny on human-made fertilizers. The introduction of these chemicals to the environment resulted in potentially hazardous runoff into streams, rivers, and lakes, which posed serious consequences to the local ecosystems, habitats, and communities. Hazards included polluted drinking water, species extinction, and health issues for the population.

The transfer of technology from developed countries to developing countries included machinery such as tractors, tillers, and harvesters. These new technologies required vast amounts of fossil fuels, which increased air, water, and sound pollution. In order for the Green Revolution to succeed, it needed mechanization to keep up with crop production, thus resulting in further environmental stress.

The Green Revolution's Impact on Gender Roles

Many countries in the developing world that participated in the Green Revolution had traditional economies. In a traditional economy, subsistence farming is the cornerstone of economic activity. Even though much of the farming labor is performed by women, men usually dominate socially, politically, and economically based on many societies' traditional beliefs.

When the Green Revolution and its technologies were introduced to these countries, it was often men who benefited and were given decision-making powers. Men owned the land, had access to financial resources, and were educated on newer methods of farming, while women were often excluded from these opportunities. This further marginalized women and limited their role within many societies. (See Topic 5.12 for more about women and agriculture.)

Economic Changes

The initial successes of the Green Revolution were a mixture of private and public investments. The transfer of farming technology heavily relied on private investment by corporations and public support by governments. As the amount of research and production increased, so too did the cost. Machinery, seeds, fertilizers, and pesticides became more expensive and the cost was passed on to farmers in the developing world and the organizations that supported them. As profit margins decreased, many corporations began to curtail further investments in the Green Revolution. Without a clear financial incentive, the motivation to invest waned.

In addition, the labor markets of less-developed countries changed. As with the Second Agricultural Revolution, the Green Revolution allowed, or pushed, people from rural areas to move to urban areas in search of industrial and service sector jobs. Demographers predict that migration from rural to urban areas in the developing world will continue. In the future, the percentage of people living in cities will continue to increase.

People in the developing world had unequal access to Green Revolution technology. Income, accessibility, and government policies played a role in which people and regions of a country had access to or could afford the technologies. The wealthy and transportation-connected core areas have advantages over the outlying, isolated, and poor periphery areas of a country, and resulted in uneven development.

The Green Revolution's Struggles in Africa

Unlike Latin America and Asia, Africa benefited very little from successes of the Green Revolution. The reasons the Green Revolution failed throughout the continent of Africa are environmental, economic, and cultural.

- Africa has a greater diversity of climate and soils than other places. Hence, development of the right fertilizers proved to be very expensive.
- Africa has many regions with harsh environmental conditions. Insects, plants, and viral strains proved to be extremely challenging to the Green Revolution researchers and their technology.
- Africa is large and lacks a well-developed transportation infrastructure, so the costs of investment in research, development, and transportation were very high.
- Africa's staple crops such as sorghum, millet, cassava, yams, cowpeas, and peanuts were not always included in research for seed-hybridization programs.

During the Green Revolution, the world's population more than doubled. Most of this growth was in poor countries on the periphery of the global economy. From the mid-20th into the 21st centuries, Africa had the highest population growth rate of any continent. Since that is where the Green Revolution had the least impact, hunger remains a greater problem there than elsewhere. Today, nearly 30 percent of Africa's population has been affected by food insecurity.

In response to the ongoing food problems in Africa, private foundations and governments are working together. They hope to develop a new Green Revolution there, using updated technology.

REFLECT ON THE ESSENTIAL QUESTION

Essential Question: *What are the consequences of the Green Revolution on food supply and the environment in the developing world?*

Green Revolution's Consequences on Food Supply	Green Revolution's Consequences on the Environment

---

KEY TERMS

Third Agricultural Revolution	hybridization
Green Revolution	genetically modified organism (GMO)

Dr. Norman Borlaug contributed to the advancement of humanity by researching and developing methods to expand the food supply, thereby reducing the possibility of famine around the world. His work, and the subsequent Green Revolution, had many positive impacts on the world, but there are also negative consequences.

The Food and Agricultural Organization (FAO), a specialized agency of the United Nations, believes that providing safe drinking water to people is among its most important functions. Because the Green Revolution occurred as rapidly as it did, it had the unintended consequence of pollution. Agricultural pollution can be defined as contamination of the environment because of the process of farming or raising livestock. One of the most obvious and critical concerns related to agricultural pollution is the contamination of the water supply by chemical pesticides and fertilizers.

The FAO believes that population growth has put undue pressures on countries to produce enough food that, in some cases, regulatory short cuts have been taken in order to achieve food production needs. Chemical contamination of surface and ground water not only endangers the marine life in the water, but also potentially pollutes the supply of drinking water for people. Contaminated water can cause immediate illnesses or long-term diseases, such as cancer or birth defects.

Another concern of the FAO is that surface water can be contaminated because of industrial waste or poor water treatment processes. If surface water reservoirs are used to help irrigate farmland, and there are pollutants in those sources of water, disease can spread from the water supply to the crops, and in some cases, even to the agricultural workers themselves.

Human beings continue to try to understand the implications, both positive and negative, of their policies and actions regarding agriculture. Agricultural pollution was an unintended consequence of the Green Revolution and remains a concern in the 21st century.

1. What is the FAO's concern about water use and agriculture?

2. Describe two unintended negative consequences of the Green Revolution.

3. Explain the danger of water pollution to people and the environment.

THINK AS A GEOGRAPHER: *COMPARE THE SECOND AGRICULTURAL REVOLUTION TO THE GREEN REVOLUTION*

Understanding how to compare two ideas, concepts, images, or sets of data is critical for geographers. The skill of comparing requires looking for both similarities and differences. Similarities are things the two concepts have in common, while differences are what make each concept unique. When making a comparison, geographers must take into account that the experiences in one country or region may be different than another and even the experiences of people in the same community can be different. Looking for and describing these subtle distinctions with precision is an important skill for geographers to master.

1. On your own paper, create a Venn diagram like the one below. List characteristics that are individual to the Second Agricultural Revolution and the Green Revolution in the outside portion of each circle. List similarities shared by both revolutions in the center of the circles, where they overlap.

2. After you complete your list, circle or highlight those which you consider the most important similarities and differences.

3. Deepen your comparison. Using your most important similarity and difference, find facts, data, details, or examples to support your answers.

4. Explain how your answers could change if you use different regions, countries, or communities of the world to support your answers.

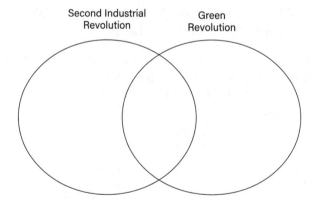

Second Industrial Revolution

Green Revolution

CHAPTER 12 REVIEW:
The Second and Third Agricultural Revolutions
Topics 5.4–5.5

MULTIPLE-CHOICE QUESTIONS

1. Which of the following is NOT considered to be a negative consequence of the Green Revolution?

   (A) Air pollution from farm equipment that use fossil fuels increased.

   (B) Overfertilization resulted in soil pollution.

   (C) Gender income inequality worsened as women were frequently not allowed to operate or own farm equipment.

   (D) Family farms disappeared because they could not compete with the corporate farms and the increased costs of farming.

   (E) Agricultural yields increased and food prices dropped until 2005.

2. Which statement best explains a result of crop rotation?

   (A) Maintains soil fertility by restoring nutrients

   (B) Increases reliance on synthetic fertilizers

   (C) Extracts nitrogen making fields more fertile

   (D) Increases the need to mechanize farms and develop new seeds

   (E) Increases migration of people to cities in search of jobs

3. Though the research and scientific discovery that fueled the Green Revolution occurred mostly in the United States, which of the following regions benefited the most from the Green Revolution?

   (A) Western Europe

   (B) Russia

   (C) South Asia

   (D) Sub-Saharan Africa

   (E) North America

4. The greatest impact of the Second Agricultural Revolution was

   (A) an increase in farm jobs

   (B) an increase in available food supplies

   (C) an increase in global conflicts over control of natural resources

   (D) a decrease in life expectancy

   (E) a decrease in factory jobs

Question 5 refers to the following graph.

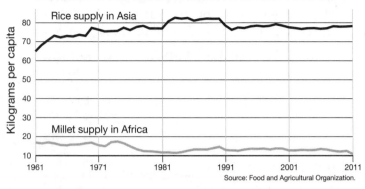

CHANGES IN FOOD SUPPLY IN ASIA AND AFRICA

Source: Food and Agricultural Organization.

5. Which statement about 1961 to 2011 is best supported by the graph?

   (A) Food security improved in both Asia and Africa.

   (B) Green Revolution techniques worked better in Asia than in Africa.

   (C) Population growth was higher in Africa than in Asia.

   (D) Green Revolution techniques worked well in both regions but slowed down dramatically.

   (E) Millet and rice are not very important food sources for either region, indicating that a conclusion about food security is invalid.

6. Which is a characteristic of the Second Agricultural Revolution?

   (A) Domestication of wheat and rice

   (B) Increased mechanization of farming

   (C) Increased number of woman farmers as compared to men

   (D) Rapid development of genetically modified crops (GMO)

   (E) Higher percentage of farming jobs in a country's economy

7. Which of the following is most accurate about agriculture today?

   (A) Agricultural resources are equally distributed among developed and developing countries.

   (B) A higher percentage of the population is works in agriculture than the 1800's.

   (C) Productivity of land is increasing as are concerns about sustainability.

   (D) Less land is used for farming and productivity is declining.

   (E) A much smaller percentage of women are involved in farming compared to the 1900s.

1. The Second Agricultural Revolution (mid-1800s and early 1900s) benefitted mostly developed countries. The Green Revolution (1961 to 2011) dramatically changed agriculture in developing countries.

INCREASE IN GRAIN PRODUCTION BY REGION

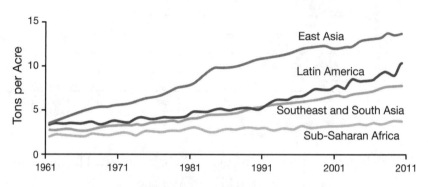

Source: "World Development Report 2013: Jobs," World Bank, 2013.

(A) Using the graph, identify the region that had the largest increase in grain production between 1961 and 2011.

(B) Explain ONE environmental reason why Sub-Saharan Africa's grain production did not increase as much as other regions.

(C) Explain ONE economic reason why Sub-Saharan Africa's grain production did not increase as much as other regions.

(D) Describe ONE technological change that occurred in agriculture as a result of the Green Revolution.

(E) Describe ONE technological change that occurred in agriculture as a result of the Second Agricultural Revolution.

(F) Compare ONE demographic impact that occurred as a result of the Second Agricultural and Green Revolutions.

(G) Describe ONE environmental impact of the Second Agricultural Revolution.

CHAPTER 13

Spatial Arrangement of Agriculture

Topics 5.6–5.9

Topic 5.6 Agricultural Production Regions

Learning Objective: Explain how economic forces influence agricultural practices. (PSO-5.C)

Topic 5.7 Spatial Organization of Agriculture

Learning Objective: Explain how economic forces influence agricultural practices. (PSO-5.C)

Topic 5.8 Von Thünen Model

Learning Objective: Describe how the von Thünen model is used to explain patterns of agricultural production at various scales. (PSO-5.D)

Topic 5.9 The Global System of Agriculture

Learning Objective: Explain the interdependence among regions of agricultural production and consumption. (PSO-5.E)

Without agriculture it is not possible to have a city, stock market, banks, university, church, or army. Agriculture is the foundation of civilization and any stable economy.

—Allan Savory, biologist and farmer, Zimbabwe

Source: Getty Images

High-density cattle feedlots often contain a mill to produce feed which increases the efficiency of beef production. (See Topic 5.6 for how feedlots and other agricultural practices are shaped by economic factors.)

Agricultural Production Regions

Essential Question: How do economic forces influence agricultural practices?

Residents of every continent, except Antarctica, practice agriculture. There are differences in agricultural practices in various regions of the world, and even within individual continents. These differences include the crops or animals raised, level of technology, methods for production, percentage of the population working in agriculture, importance of agriculture to the economy, and gender roles in farming. These variables are important considerations in farmers' decisions about agricultural practices and land use.

Influence of Economic Forces

Among the many factors that influence farmers' decisions are available capital and the relative costs of land and labor. Because of these different costs, farmers balance the use of their resources differently. If land is plentiful and costs little, they use it extensively. If land is scarce and expensive, they use it intensely. In reality, not every farm fits perfectly into one of these two categories.

Geographers often refer to the **bid-rent theory** when discussing land costs for different types of agricultural activities. There is usually a distance-decay relationship between proximity to the urban market and the value of the land, meaning the closer the land is to an urban center, the more valuable it is. The farmer willing to pay the highest price will gain possession of the land. Consequently, the farmer must use intensive agricultural practices to turn a profit on the land closest to market. (See Topic 5.8 for more about bid-rent and von Thünen's model.)

Intensive land-use agriculture involves greater inputs of capital and paid labor relative to the space used. (See Topic 5.1 for more on intensive agriculture.) Intensive practices are used in various regions and conditions:

- Paddy rice farming in South Asia, Southeast Asia, and East Asia is very labor intensive. Commonly used terraced fields makes using machinery difficult.

- Truck farming in California, Texas, Florida, and near large cities is sometimes **capital intensive** because it uses expensive machinery and other inputs. In addition to being capital intensive, it is nearly always **labor intensive**. These large farms produce very large quantities of vegetables and fruit, often relying on many low-paid migrant workers, to tend and harvest crops.

- **Factory farming** is a capital-intensive livestock operation in which many animals are kept in close quarters, and bred and fed in a controlled environment. The term comes from these operations running like a factory. Instead of cars or computers moving along an assembly line, it is the animals that progress from one end of the "factory" to the other end, where they are eventually processed into meat products.
- **Aquaculture (aquafarming)** is a type of intensive farming. Rather than raising typical farm animals in close quarters with a controlled environment, fish, shellfish, or water plants are raised in netted areas in the sea, tanks, or other bodies of water. (See Topic 5.11.)

Extensive land-use agriculture uses fewer inputs of capital and paid labor relative to the amount of space used. Extensive practices, such as shifting cultivation, nomadic herding, and ranching (see Topic 5.1) can be found throughout the world and across the entire spectrum of economic development.

Increasing Intensity

Regions of the world that traditionally relied on extensive agricultural techniques are under pressure because of local increases in demand for food, regional population growth, and global competition to use land more intensely. These demographic and economic forces have placed more stress on the land because they have pushed farmers to use land continuously, rather than allowing land to lie fallow and recover. This shift increases demand for expensive inputs such as irrigation, chemicals fertilizers, and improved seeds.

Those who rely on shifting cultivation have found it more difficult to continue these methods as global demand for tropical cash crops, such as coffee, tea, and cacao, compete for more land use. The timber industry has also put an economic strain on shifting cultivation. For subsistence farmers, increasing population and competition—for space to grow timber, rubber, cotton, or products that are not eaten but used in industry—have resulted in food security issues, most noticeably in Africa.

Methods of Planting

Different methods of planting increase the intensity of land use. **Double** (or triple**) cropping** is planting and harvesting a crop two (or three) times per year on the same piece of land**. Another technique, **intercropping**, also known as **multicropping**, is when farmers grow two or more crops simultaneously on the same field. For example, a farmer might plant a legume crop alongside a cereal crop to add nitrogen to the soil and guard against soil erosion.

The opposite of multicropping is **monoculture**, in which only one crop is grown or one type of animal is raised per season on a piece of land. **Monocropping,** or continuous monoculture, is only growing one type of crop or raising one type of animal year after year. As a result, these farmers purchase very specific equipment, irrigation systems, fertilizers, and pesticides designed for their one crop or animal to maximize efficiency.

Large scale monocropping farms can be thousands of acres of just wheat, corn, rice, coffee, cacao, etc. This can result in lower per-unit cost of production, higher yields, and more profits. Negative impacts include soil depletion, decreased yields over time, increased reliance on chemical fertilizers and pesticides, and increased risk since all of the farmer's resources are invested in one crop.

The Meat Industry

The economic structure of livestock raising has changed in the past few decades. Global consumption of meat increased over 50 percent between 1998 and 2018, mostly because of population growth. Growing demand accelerated the trend toward factory farms and centralized processing centers.

Today, cattle are less likely to graze on large expanses of land, but instead are raised in **feedlots**, which are confined spaces in which cattle and hogs have limited movement, also known as concentrated animal feeding operations (CAFOs). The animals grow bigger in a shorter period of time because of their reduced movement. This new practice maximizes the use of space and prepares the animal for slaughter quickly, thus maximizing profit.

The global expansion of fast-food operations and the increased demand for meat has led to larger ranching operations in the United States and South America. In the United States, the competition for space, desire for larger animals, and reduced raising time have led to an increased use of feedlots.

Some agricultural products combine extensive and intensive phases. Raising cattle in Wyoming is an example of extensive farming. The cattle roam and feed on grass in large ranches that average nearly six square miles in size. As the cattle reach maturity, the intensive phase begins. Farmers transport the cattle to feedlots in northern Colorado to fatten the animals quickly before being processed into meat for market.

REFLECT ON THE ESSENTIAL QUESTION

Essential Question: *How do economic forces influence agricultural practices?*

Economic Factor	Influence of Economic Factor

KEY TERMS

bid-rent theory	double cropping
capital intensive	intercropping (multicropping)
labor intensive	monoculture
factory farming	monocropping
aquaculture (aquafarming)	feedlots

Spatial Organization of Agriculture

Essential Question: How do economic forces influence agricultural practices?

A number of agricultural trends have changed the agricultural landscape over the past several decades. The most obvious changes involve the decline in small family farms, the development of much larger corporate farms, and the expansion of farmland into what was previously forested or wetland areas. The agricultural landscape has also been altered by the reduction in the variety of crops and the introduction of new crops to a region. Reasons for the evolving agricultural landscape are the growth of **agribusiness**, farms run as corporations, and the globalization of agriculture.

Commercial Agriculture and Agribusiness

Agribusiness involves the integration of various steps of production in the food-processing industry such as research and development, processing and production, transportation, marketing, and retail of agricultural goods. Given the enormity of this system, the largest agribusinesses are owned by **transnational corporations,** or those that operate in many countries. These large-scale operations are commercial, highly mechanized, and often use chemicals and biotechnology in raising crops and animals. The following chart compares farming at the scale of a homeowner and an agribusiness.

VEGETABLE FARMING ON TWO SCALES		
Activity	**Homeowner Scale**	**Agribusiness Scale**
Growing food	Raising vegetables in a backyard garden	Owning farms of thousands of acres that are worked by a large staff of employees
Processing food	Eating fresh, home-grown vegetables for dinner and preserving vegetables for future use	Canning and freezing products in factories that are often located near the fields
Selling food	Selling vegetables at a local market	Selling products to wholesale distributors who ship them regionally and globally
Financing the food industry	Giving some vegetables to a neighbor in exchange for using some of their land for a garden	Borrowing money from banks and selling stock to raise money for operating expenses
Researching food options	Growing different varieties of tomatoes to see which grow best	Investing in research and development of new seeds, fertilizers, and pesticides

Impact of Large-Scale Farms

Globalization has accelerated the growth of agribusiness and corporate farms during the latter half of the 20th century. Competition in agricultural products and services encouraged large-scale farms to operate more as a corporation than a family farm. Agribusinesses have often resulted from the consolidation of family farms, thus eliminating many small-scale farm operations. Many of the remaining family-owned farms have shifted to a corporate operating model.

Often, large corporate farms practice **vertical integration**, or the ownership of other businesses involved in the steps of producing a a particular good. Owning the contributing businesses gives the large farm more control of the variables and results in greater overall profits. Those businesses might include a research and development company that improves seeds, a trucking firm that transports farm products, a factory that processes the goods, and a wholesaler that distributes the food to stores.

Large-Scale Replacing Small-Scale Farms

Large-scale farms are usually specialized and practice monoculture. As farms become larger, more specialized, and vertically integrated, it becomes easier to take advantage of **economies of scale**, or an increase in efficiency to lower the per-unit production cost, resulting in greater profits. For example, consider a grain farmer who increases the size of his or her farm by purchasing an additional quarter section (160 acres). By using the existing machinery on the farm more efficiently, the farmer can successfully plant and harvest the additional acreage without the purchase of new equipment. This will increase the owner's revenues while the expenses will not increase proportionally. As a result, the cost per unit of grain will decrease and profits will increase.

Larger farms can afford the latest technology, such as better seeds or machinery, and are more likely to produce greater profits through economies of scale. Large corporate farms have made it increasingly difficult for family farms to survive since they cannot compete with the significantly cheaper costs per-unit production of large-scale farming operations.

The success and efficiency of large farms has encouraged the World Bank to fund agribusiness ventures in the developing world, often at the expense of family and subsistence farmers. Also, many family farms in the periphery have disappeared because of the rising expenses associated with Green Revolution technology and the need to adopt this technology to survive and compete in an increasingly global market.

Commodity Chains and Consumption

The transformation of agriculture has resulted in a complex system that connected producers and consumers at a global scale. This complex and enormous system enabled someone who lives in a small American town to consume bananas from Ecuador, coffee from Ethiopia, chocolate from Switzerland, and cashews from Vietnam. This transformation may be attributed to advancements in biotechnology, mechanization, transportation, and food preservation.

A **commodity chain** is a process used by corporations to gather resources, transform them into goods, and then transport them to consumers.

COMMODITY CHAIN FOR CORN

Planting: uses inputs such as seeds, fertilizer, and water

Growing: requires fertile land and adequate moisture

Harvesting: dried and stored until processed

Processing: packaged or used to create other products

Marketing: sold for animal feed, human food, or other uses

Improvements in agricultural technology, advances in transportation, and an increasingly globalized economy enables farmers to raise crops and animals far from their final market and allows consumers to still purchase the final products at low prices. Corn has numerous uses, such as livestock feed, sweetener, or fuel. Thus, the actual commodity chain of corn would be more specialized and complex than the one shown.

Additional elements of commodity chains that facilitate the process include financial institutions (banks), transportation companies, distributors, and governments. Each plays a key role in getting food from field to store. A detailed commodity chain shows the elements for milk production below.

COMMODITY CHAIN FOR MILK PRODUCTION

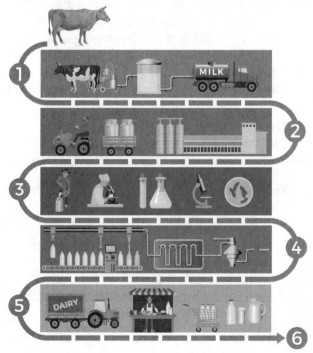

Source: Getty Images

Identify the six steps in the milk commodity chain.

Technological Improvements

The number of people that U.S. farmers can support given the available resources, or the **carrying capacity**, has risen tremendously over the past half century. In 1962, an average U.S. farmer fed an average of 26 people. Today, mostly due to technological advances, that figure has risen to 166 people. Farmers in the United States provide enough food to supply the needs of the nation, as well as many people in other parts of the world. Of course, there are other resources that are also necessary for life, such as clean air, water, and fuel.

Benefits Improvement in food production is attributed to technological advancements of the Second and Third Agricultural Revolutions. (See Topics 5.4 and 5.5.) Improvements in the quality and the use of fertilizers, pesticides, insecticides, herbicides, irrigation, soil management, and farming equipment have all resulted in higher yields. A deeper understanding of the science of plants and animals has led to efficient selective breeding programs, hybrid seeds developed through the Green Revolution, and genetically modified organisms (GMOs) created through biotechnology. These developments have had a tremendous impact on the agricultural output of farmers.

Transportation and storage advances have allowed for the more extensive use of **cool chains**, which are transportation networks that keep food cool throughout a trip. Fruits and vegetables from the tropics can be delivered fresh to the temperate climates of North America and Europe at relatively low prices for consumers.

Costs Technological advancements have created some environmental damage. The loss of wetlands and large tracts of rainforest cleared to increase farmable land have led to the loss of biodiversity and water resources. Petroleum-based fertilizers, pesticides, and herbicides have caused soil, water, and air pollution and threatened ecosystems. (See Topics 5.10 and 5.11 for more about environmental challenges due to agricultural practices.)

REFLECT ON THE ESSENTIAL QUESTION

Essential Question: *How do economic forces influence agricultural practices?*

Large-Scale Agricultural Practices	Impact of Practices

KEY TERMS

agribusiness	commodity chain
transnational corporations	carrying capacity
vertical integration	cool chains
economies of scale	

Von Thünen Model

Essential Question: How is the von Thünen model used to explain patterns of agricultural production at various scales?

It is interesting that an almost 200-year-old economic location model, the von Thünen model, is still considered essential by geographers to explain the spatial pattern of agricultural land use. Over the past two centuries there have been many changes to agriculture, as well as transportation, a key component of von Thünen's model, yet it is still used by geographers today.

Location theory, a key component of economic geography, deals with why people choose certain locations for various types of economic activity—factories, stores, restaurants, or agriculture. The **von Thünen model**, an economic model that suggested a pattern for the types of products that farmers would produce at different positions relative to the market (community) where they sold their goods, is the start of location theory. Since his original work, numerous other geographers have built on his ideas and developed their own location theories and models.

Von Thünen's Land Use Model Zones

In 1826, Johann von Thünen, a farm owner in Germany, based his rural land use model, sometimes referred to as the Isolated State model, on numerous assumptions:

- farming was an economic activity
- farmers were in business to make a profit
- there was one market where farmers sold their products
- there was one transportation system
- farmers paid transportation costs, which varied with distance
- the market was situated in the center of an **isotropic plain**, which means flat and featureless with similar fertility and climate throughout
- the area beyond the market and farmland (the Isolated State) was wilderness

The von Thünen model is based on the concept that farmers' decisions regarding what to produce were based largely upon four factors: transportation costs, land costs, intensity of land use, and perishability of the product. Distance from the market impacts the cost of transportation and land. In essence, the land closest to the market is the most valuable and the land farther away decreases in value. Farmers will use land closer to the market more intensely because it is more valuable. The farther goods are transported, the higher the cost. Perishability relates to how well a product can survive transport without spoiling or breaking.

Zones and the Von Thünen Model

In the zone closest to the market, von Thünen suggested that **horticulture**, a type of agriculture that includes market gardening/truck farming and dairy farming, would occur. Horticulture produces perishable items, and farmers need to get them to market quickly, especially important before trucks and refrigeration. Growing highly perishable crops, such as tomatoes and strawberries, and dairy farming are considered to be intensive forms of agriculture.

Von Thünen's second zone included forests. Wood was an extremely important resource in 1826, both as building material and as a source of fuel. Von Thünen thought that wood products would be close to the market because they were not only important but heavy, costly, and difficult to transport.

Farther from the market, in the third ring, were crops such as wheat and corn. Though valuable, they did not perish as quickly as vegetables and milk and were not as difficult to transport as wood. In addition, corn can be used to feed live stock located in the second and fourth rings.

The final ring was used for grazing of livestock, such as beef cattle. Livestock could be located farther from the market since they have lower transportation costs because farmers can walk them to market.

The extensive nature of grain and livestock farming meant that the farms were larger than those located in the inner ring of the model. While there is more farmland available in the larger outer rings, that was not necessarily the reason for these crops to be located there. Grain and livestock farmers could find adequate space in the innermost ring if they were willing to pay enough to acquire the land.

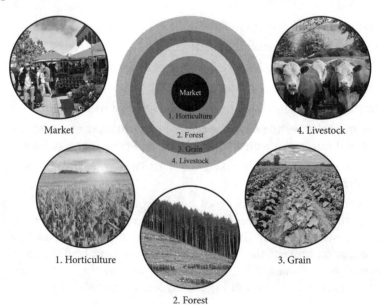

Market

4. Livestock

1. Horticulture

3. Grain

2. Forest

Land Value

The value of land was influenced by its spatial relationship to the market. Because the land in the inner ring was closest to the market, it was more valuable. Therefore, few farmers could afford large amounts of it. Consequently, only farmers who could use a small amount of land intensely and make a profit from it could be successful in the inner ring. They needed to grow high-value crops there, such as fruits and vegetables, in order to make a living.

Grain and Livestock Land farther from the market was less valuable. Because grain and livestock are less perishable than the crops in the inner ring, the farmers could locate in the area of cheaper land farther from the market and still transport the product to market successfully. Meat is perishable after it is processed, so farmers could avoid spoilage if they walked their livestock to market and had them slaughtered there. This was the common practice when von Thünen developed his model two centuries ago.

Wheat Farms in North Dakota Recent studies have shown that the distance to the market still greatly influences land prices, even for farmers who raise the same crop. One example from the 21st century is value of land for North Dakota wheat farmers. For them, the market is often the nearest grain elevator. The elevator owner purchases the grain from many farmers and then resells it to companies in the food processing business. In one study reported by the United States Department of Agriculture, land within 5 miles of a grain elevator was worth double the amount of land approximately 25 miles away. That disparity in land value grew even larger farther than 25 miles away from a grain elevator.

The Bid-Rent Curve

In the case of von Thünen's model, the bid-rent theory, which refers to the changing value and demand for land as the distance from the market increases, is used to determine what type of agriculture is located in each zone. A graph known as a **bid-price curve** or **bid-rent curve** can be used to determine the starting position for each land use relative to the market, as well as where each land use would end.

Each line on the graph reflects the farmers' willingness to pay for land at various distances from the market. Farmers are willing to pay more for land near the market than for land farther away. However, how much more varies with the types of activities. In a **free-market economy**—where supply and demand, not government policy, determine the outcome of competition for land—the farmer who will have the greatest profit will pay the most at each location to occupy the land. It is where the uppermost line on the graph intersects with the next uppermost line that represents the end of one zone and the start of another.

For example, where the strawberry line intersects the forest line indicates the end of where strawberries will be grown and the beginning of where forests will be found. Where the forest line intersects the wheat line indicates where the forest zone ends and the wheat zone begins.

BID-RENT CURVE AND VON THÜNEN'S MODEL

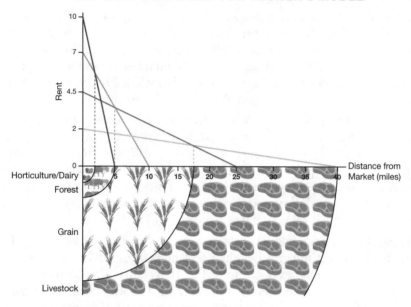

The bid-price curve is used to determine the borders of each land use. Determine the starting and ending distance for each of the four agricultural land uses shown in the graph.

Application of Von Thünen's Model

Von Thünen's model has been valuable in many ways. It has had application far beyond the topic of agriculture. His recognition of the spatial pattern in how farmers made decisions about using resources was the first economic location model. It provided the basis for the industrial location models of Alfred Weber and others who followed.

In addition, even though von Thünen created his model nearly two centuries ago, it continues to be applicable today. The basic insight of the model is still valuable, but like all models, it needs to be adapted to actual conditions and changes in technology.

Non-Isotropic Plains Von Thünen's model assumed that land was an isotropic plain—but real land includes rivers, mountains, and other physical features that make it non-isotropic. Von Thünen considered how various landscape situations would alter the shape of each land-use ring and possible impacts on transportation. For example, if a river flowed through the plain, making transportation easier and cheaper, then the zones would stretch out along the river. In addition, some areas have better climates or soil conditions for certain crops. These areas have a **comparative advantage**, or naturally occurring beneficial conditions, that would prompt farmers to plant crops differently from those predicted by von Thünen's model.

AGRICULTURAL ZONES AROUND A RIVER

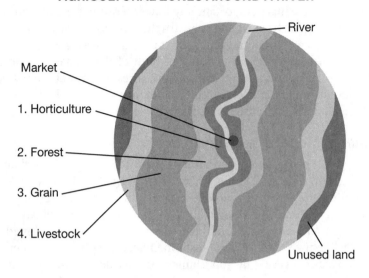

Market

1. Horticulture

2. Forest

3. Grain

4. Livestock

River

Unused land

Multiple Markets Von Thünen assumed that a farmer had one primary market, but they often have secondary markets as well. A dairy farmer might primarily sell milk to a local dairy. But the farmer might also make and sell cheese, which does not spoil as quickly as milk, in a distant market.

Changes in Transportation The development of trains, cars, planes, and storage techniques, such as refrigeration, has allowed food to be transported much longer distances without spoiling compared to 1826. As a result, the rings in the model now are wider than originally created by von Thünen. For example, rapidly perishable goods, such as strawberries and milk, can be produced much farther away from the market than in von Thünen's time. Strawberries and milk are still produced closer to the market than are grains and livestock. It is the size of the rings that has changed, not necessarily the relative position of the rings.

The cut flower market demonstrates the impact of transportation on the application of von Thünen's model. Cut flowers are very perishable and have to arrive at the market quickly, so they are similar to horticulture and dairy products that the model predicts will be produced nearby and trucked to market. However, many flowers sold in New York City are grown in the Caribbean and South America and flown to market. While air travel costs from these areas are far higher than truck transport from the outskirts of New York, other costs of flower production are much less. Land, labor, and energy costs are so much lower in the Caribbean and South America than in the outskirts of New York City that the savings outweigh the extra transportation costs. Therefore, producers can grow flowers for New York more profitably in the Caribbean than in nearby locations.

Other Changes in Technology Changes in technology have modified demand for products. Since 1826, wood has been mostly replaced by oil, natural gas, and electricity as fuel for heating homes, so forests as a source of fuel are not particulary important any longer. Forests were also important for producing lumber required for construction of homes and barns. Today, transport trucks can easily and efficiently bring the necessary lumber to the market from distant forests. As a result of both of these changes, forests are rarely located near communities today. Now, forested land at a city's edge is probably highly valued as a *greenbelt*, an area of recreational parks or other undeveloped land (see Topic 6.8), rather than a source of fuel or lumber.

Von Thünen Model at a National Scale

The improved transportation and storage methods have created changes in the use of the von Thünen model today. Since agricultural products are now transported much greater distances to markets, the model can be applied at a much larger scale than von Thünen allowed. The image below illustrates what the general pattern of agricultural land use in the continental United States would look like if the zones were positioned according to the farmer's rent-paying ability, as suggested by von Thünen. The model assumes that the New York City area is the market, and thus the rings radiate away from there. Also, the map recognizes that there are climatic variations across the country and therefore indicates some pockets of specialty crops as well as distorted rings.

AGRICULTURAL LAND USE IN THE UNITED STATES

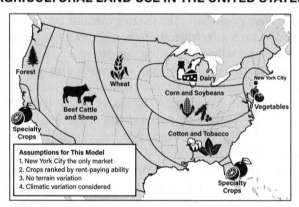

What would be similarities between von Thünen's model and this agricultural land-use map for the United States? How might they differ?

Von Thünen's model was based upon southern Germany, a much smaller region than the United States. His assumption of an isotropic plain does not apply well to the diversity of physical features and climate of the United States. Also, von Thünen's assumption of a single market is true for virtually no farmers in the United States or anywhere in the world.

Special Circumstances No model accounts for every variation that occurs in practice. For example, von Thünen's model does not fit some areas of specialty farming, such as citrus farming in Florida or the variety of crops grown in the Central Valley of California. Nor does it explain the decisions by developers who speculatively purchase land close to a city and use it for less-intensive agriculture. These developers usually want to invest as little money as possible into the farmland while they wait for the optimal time to build homes, retail space, or commercial structures on it.

Criticisms of Von Thünen's Model

Many of the criticisms of the model involve the assumptions made by von Thünen.

VON THÜNEN MODEL	
Assumptions	**Limitations**
Farming was an economic activity	Government policies can interfere with a free-market economy and effect farmers' decisions.
Farmers were in business to make a profit	Simply to provide enough food for his or her family, not profit, is the goal for many farmers, especially in less-developed areas.
There was one market where farmers sold their products	Modern agriculture systems have multiple markets; rarely is just one market available.
There was one transportation system	Planes, trains, and trucks (especially modern refrigerated transportation) have changed distance considerations for farmers.
The market was situated in the center of an isotropic plain	Differences in land formation, soil fertility, and climate exist in agricultural regions, making isotropic plains uncommon

REFLECT ON THE ESSENTIAL QUESTION

Essential Question: *How is the von Thünen model used to explain patterns of agricultural production at various scales?*

Concepts of the von Thünen Model	Application of the Concepts

KEY TERMS

location theory
von Thünen model
isotropic plain
horticulture

bid-price curve (bid-rent curve)
free-market economy
comparative advantage

The Global System of Agriculture

Essential Question: How is there interdependence among regions of agricultural production and consumption?

Globalization has become a firmly entrenched aspect of the economy of most countries, particularly in food production. Part of this has been the spatial expansion of the **supply chains,** all the steps required to get a product or service to customers. The physical distance from producers to consumers can cover thousands of miles. For example, research and development of new seeds might take place in a laboratory in the United Kingdom. The new seeds could then be sent to Ghana where the crop is grown and harvested. After some minor processing or refining in Ghana the product could be frozen and transported to China where it is manufactured into a finished product. Once packaged, it could be sent to the United States where it is sold to consumers.

The level of interdependence, or connections among regions of the world, has increased greatly. If one country experiences a problem such as crop failure, damaged infrastructure, or disruptions in trade due to political decisions, the repercussions could be significant for many countries.

Regional Interdependence

The globalization of agriculture has increased interdependence among countries of differing levels of development. Developed countries such as the United States rely on producers in Mexico, other countries with warm climates, and ones in the Southern Hemisphere, for fresh fruits and vegetables year-round.

Food on a Global Scale

Developed countries also sell food to around the world. For example, nearly half of U.S.-grown soybeans are exported. Purchasers of significant amounts of U.S. agricultural products include China, Mexico, and countries in Europe.

Low-latitude countries with tropical climates produce crops such as coffee, tea, bananas, and pineapples that are desired in core countries. **Luxury crops** are not essential to human survival but have a high profit margin. These crops including cocoa beans, which are eventually processed into chocolate, are often grown on large plantations commonly controlled by transnational companies. Plantations usually practice monoculture, specializing in only one crop. The transnational companies, which are usually controlled by shareholders in core countries, provide the capital necessary to develop and run the plantations. They take advantage of the opportunity for inexpensive land and labor, and a favorable climate. In some situations, they also take advantage of weak labor and environmental laws, which allow them to reduce costs and increase profits.

COCOA BEAN PRODUCTION, 2012

Cocoa bean production is shown as a percentage of the world's top producer, Côte d'Ivoire (1.65 million metric tons)

○ 100   ◐ 10   • 1

Source: Wikimedia Commons

As with most plantation agriculture of luxury items, cocoa is produced in the periphery but consumed primarily in the core.

For periphery and semiperiphery countries, the globalized commodity chain provides both markets for products and problems:

- Farmers who produce luxury crops might not be able to afford to purchase what they produce.

- As the supply of locally grown food decreases, prices for local consumers can increase. A farmer in Honduras who grows chili peppers for the global market is not growing corn, beans, or other foods for local consumers.

- Countries may become very dependent on one or two export commodities. When global markets shift these countries' economies become vulnerable and unstable.

- Competition to sell products might cause farmers to follow practices that cause soil erosion or chemical pollution, which endanger the long-term use of the land.

Political Systems, Infrastructure, and Trade

The efficient exchange of food around the world depends on effective political systems, strong infrastructure, and supportive trade policies. These conditions have evolved over time to make agricultural trade vital in most countries.

Colonialism and Neocolonialism Many connections that exist between Europe and the developing world were established through colonization. Although there are very few colonies in the world today, the economic relationship between core countries and periphery and semiperiphery countries resembles certain aspects of colonialism. **Neocolonialism**, the use of economic, political, and social pressures to control former colonies, can be one way to describe the current state of global food distribution.

For example, while growing and processing coffee beans is expensive, the profit margin in selling brewed coffee drinks is very high. Most of the revenue generated from coffee remains with the transnational corporation based in the wealthy country while very little revenue finds its way back to the coffee growers in developing countries.

The image shows a coffee plantation in Brazil. People who live in nearby villages provide the labor for the plantation.

Fair Trade In recent years, many consumers have become more aware of the disparity between the high incomes of those in developed countries, who manage trade, and the low incomes of the producers in the developing world. One result of this awareness is the **fair trade movement**, which started with the Fair Trade certificates for coffee in 1988. It is an effort to promote higher incomes for producers and more sustainable farming practices. Other fair trade agreements between retailers and producers have been reached for crops grown in the developing world, including bananas, cane sugar, cocoa, and cotton. While these agreements often increased the price for consumers slightly, they provided a bigger share of revenue to producers and growers.

To reduce poverty for farmers and workers in the periphery, the fair trade movement promoted numerous basic principles:

- Direct trade that will eliminate the intermediary. Transactions directly between the producer and the importer ensure more money to the producer.
- Fair price paid promptly to farmers by importers. Also, the producer must pay workers a fair price.
- Decent conditions are provided for laborers, such as a safe working environment and no use of child or forced labor.
- Environmental sustainability that required farmers to use environmentally safe practices and prohibited genetically modified organisms (GMOs).
- Respect for local culture through shared agricultural techniques with farmers.

The fair trade industry has made significant gains since 1988. More than 1.5 million farmers and workers participate in fair trade and their standard of living has improved, particularly for those in the coffee industry. However, the movement faces the challenge that many consumers feel they cannot afford to pay higher prices for fair trade products.

Government Subsidies and Infrastructure Governments across the world often provide **subsidies**, or public financial support, to farmers to safeguard food production. Examples of directly subsidized crops include rice in Japan, wheat and corn in the United States, and soybeans in China. The subsidies are designed to achieve these goals the goeevernment believes are in the best interest of the public:

- protect national security by ensuring a dependable food supply
- help farmers by increasing agricultural exports
- help consumers by reducing food costs

Transportation infrastructure is critical to move agricultural products locally, nationally, and globally. **Infrastructure** includes the roads, bridges, tunnels, ports, electrical grids, sewers, telecommunications, etc. of a country. Global systems of agriculture would not be possible without this infrastructure. Governments, communities, and companies pay to build and maintain a quality infrastructure.

For example, the U.S. government indirectly subsidizes the exports of corn, soybeans, and other agricultural products from the Midwest by spending money to make the Mississippi River navigable for barge traffic. Because water transportation is inexpensive compared to land travel, these products enter the global food supply chain with a lower price than they would have without government support. Because of subsidies, consumers in Mexico City can purchase corn more cheaply from the United States than from rural Mexico. These U.S. policies help people in Mexico City, but at the expense of Mexican farmers.

Similarly, Canada protects its dairy farmers from competition with U.S. dairy producers. This helps Canada's farmers, but raises costs for Canadian consumers.

Most infrastructure improvements in developing countries connect resources to ports so goods can be exported. Often, other infrastructure in the country is lacking. As the map of the west African country Ghana on the next page shows, the major rail lines in the country connect the interior, where resources are located, to the ports where they can be exported to the developed world.

Ghana has significant mineral and agricultural resources. However, much of revenue from selling these resources leaves the country. Agricultural products commonly exported from Ghana include cocoa, cotton, coffee, palm oil, and cassava, and gold is the main mineral export. Consequently, there was little money to spend on additional infrastructure, and the population received few benefits from the mineral wealth. See Geographic Perspectives: Ghana as a Case Study in Development (page 327), to learn more about its development strategies.

TRANSPORTATION ROUTES IN GHANA

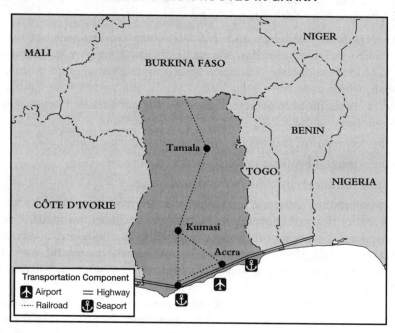

Ghana's major rail line connects ports to the mines and agricultural regions in the interior of the country.

REFLECT ON THE ESSENTIAL QUESTION

Essential Question: *How is there interdependence among regions of agricultural production and consumption?*

Causes of Increased Interdependence	Effects of Increased Interdependence

---

KEY TERMS

supply chain
luxury crops
neocolonialism

fair trade movement
subsidies
infrastructure

In the mid-1990s, the president of Ghana presented a framework known as Ghana Vision 2020, which included long-term plans for economic and social development policies, including agricultural and industrial programs. The goal was to raise Ghana into the ranks of the middle-income countries of the world by 2020. For example, the plan stated, "by the year 2020, Ghana would have achieved a balanced economy and middle-income country status and standard of living, with a level of development close to the present level of development in Singapore."

In addition to social development, Ghana Vision 2020 focused on rapid economic growth. Ghana attempted to accelerate economic growth with improvements such as modernizing agricultural inputs, increasing private investment, and developing transportation infrastructure. The purpose of these efforts was to raise income and improve living conditions for Ghanaians, thereby stabilizing the economy.

Ghana does not appear to have fully reached all of its goals for 2020, but it is poised to continue its social and economic development in the future. Offshore oil has generated significant new wealth and could provide a boost in the future to the country's development efforts—as long as the revenue from the petroleum is well managed and stays within the country. A February 2020 report from Bloomberg Opinion recognized the gains of the past two decades and suggested that Ghana is Africa's top candidate for an economic leap. The country's continued dependence on raw materials is the biggest obstacle that has to be overcome.

Source: Wikimedia Commons

A busy street in the capital city of Accra, Ghana, with bustling markets, cars, and economic activity.

1. Explain why Ghana wants to diversify its economy and not rely on just mining or agriculture.

2. Explain the importance of transportation infrastructure for Ghana's economy.

At the scale of a country, Mexico is a vitally important region for the food that people in the United States eat. Around 45 percent of the vegetables imported by the United States come from Mexico. But at the scale of states in Mexico, the distribution of food throughout the country is not even, nor are the exports consistent throughout the year. Mexico exports twice as much in the six months from December through May as it does in the other six months of the year.

Use the map to answer the questions below.

EXPORTS OF FRUITS AND VEGETABLES FROM MEXICAN STATES

1. Suggest one or more possible reasons to explain why Mexican exports have the seasonal pattern you see on the map.

2. What might explain the spatial pattern in Mexican exports?

3. The state of Veracruz has a climate similar to part of the east coast of India. Why does Veracruz export more fruits and vegetables to the United States than do similar regions in India?

CHAPTER 13 REVIEW:
Spatial Arrangement of Agriculture

Topics 5.6–5.9

MULTIPLE-CHOICE QUESTIONS

1. The von Thünen model has changed because of developments in transportation. The change that is most evident is that the

   (A) market is no longer at the center

   (B) width of the rings has increased

   (C) width of the rings has decreased

   (D) rings now stretch along rivers

   (E) model now includes a ring for transportation

Question 2 refers to the image below.

BID-PRICE CURVE

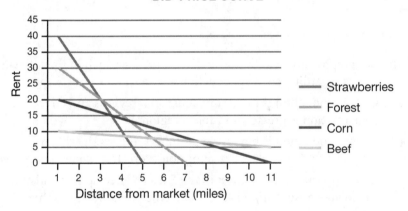

2. Based upon the bid-price curve above, in which zone should corn be grown?

   (A) 1.0 mile to 11.0 miles

   (B) 3.5 miles to 4.5 miles

   (C) 4.5 miles to 7.6 miles

   (D) 7.6 miles to 11.0 miles

   (E) 4.5 miles to 11.0 miles

3. One result of the development of cool chains is that they
   (A) eliminated the need for air transport of agricultural products
   (B) decreased the use of high-speed rail for transporting food
   (C) increased the distance that fresh fruits and vegetables could travel
   (D) reduced agricultural productivity
   (E) caused a need for large ships to transport meat products

Question 4 refers to the graphs below.

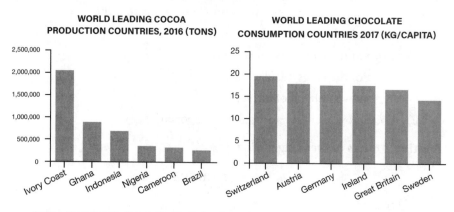

Source: International Institute for Sustainable Development

4. The two graphs shown above provide support for which of the following statements regarding cocoa production and chocolate consumption?
   (A) Cocoa production is highest in equatorial regions and chocolate consumption is greatest in tundra regions.
   (B) Cocoa production is highest in periphery and semiperiphery countries and chocolate consumption is greatest in core countries.
   (C) Cocoa production is highest in the Eastern Hemisphere and and chocolate consumption is greatest in the Western Hemisphere.
   (D) Cocoa production is highest in core countries and and chocolate consumption is greatest in semiperiphery countries.
   (E) Cocoa production is highest in the Northern Hemisphere and and chocolate consumption is greatest in the Western Hemisphere.

5. Which statement best explains why a large quantity of agricultural products are imported into the United States from Chile?

(A) Inexpensive labor in Chile reduces the cost of production.

(B) The growing season in Chile allows U.S. consumers to have fresh fruits and vegetables in the winter.

(C) Subsidies in the United States make agricultural products cheaper.

(D) Better technologies have increased Chile's agricultural output.

(E) The number of U.S. farmers has declined so significantly that the country cannot produce enough food for consumers.

6. Which lists products in the order in which they will be produced, starting closest to the market, according to von Thünen's model?

(A) Grain, forest, beef cattle, dairy cattle

(B) Tomatoes, grain, forest, beef cattle

(C) Dairy cattle, beef cattle, forest, grain

(D) Dairy cattle, forest, grain, beef cattle

(E) Forest, tomatoes, beef cattle, dairy cattle

7. A very large corporate farm in the United States is most likely to take advantage of which of the following opportunities?

(A) Fair trade certifications

(B) Traditional farming techniques

(C) Local markets to sell its products

(D) Vertical integration strategy

(E) Low-wage child labor

1. There are a variety of types of agriculture that occur around the world and range from commercial to subsistent. Coffee is one of the world's most valuable traded commodities and is considered a luxury crop.

COFFEE PRODUCTION, 2016	
Country	Production (in tons)
Brazil	3,019,051
Vietnam	1,460,800
Colombia	745,084
Indonesia	639,305
Ethiopia	469,091
World total	9,221,534

Source: FAOSTAT of the United Nations

(A) Describe the difference between subsistence agriculture and commercial agriculture.

(B) Identify TWO globally traded crops other than coffee that are currently grown on commercial plantations today.

(C) Using any of the countries listed in the sources, describe ONE advantage it has in the production of coffee.

(D) Identify a world region where most of the coffee is grown for export.

(E) Explain ONE problem facing countries when they dedicate large tracts of land to the production of a luxury export crop, such as coffee.

(F) Explain the view that coffee production is neocolonialism.

(G) Describe the primary goal of fair trade in coffee production.

CHAPTER 14

Challenges and Consequences of Agricultural Practices

Topics 5.10–5.12

Topic 5.10 Consequences of Agricultural Practices

Learning Objective: Explain how agricultural practices have environmental and societal consequences. (IMP-5.A)

Topic 5.11 Challenges of Contemporary Agriculture

Learning Objective: Explain challenges and debates related to the changing nature of contemporary agriculture and food-production practices. (IMP-5.B)

Topic 5.12 Women in Agriculture

Learning Objective: Explain geographic variations in female roles in food production and consumption. (IMP-5.C)

For hunger is a direct affront not only to the physical integrity but also to the very dignity of the human person. Hunger is an insult to the fundamental values of the international community.

—UN Secretary-General, Boutros Boutros-Ghali,
World Food Summit, 1996

Source: Alamy

In Malawi, Africa, women receive training on farm equipment, such as this hand tractor, which allows them to be more productive farmers. (See Topic 5.12 for more on the changing role of women in food production.)

Consequences of Agricultural Practices

Essential Question: What are the environmental and societal consequences of agricultural practices?

In the modern era, commercial agriculture has almost completely replaced subsistence farming. Many farming operations evolved from small enterprises owned by a single family into large-scale, capital-intensive businesses. This shift has put more stress on the environment than ever before.

In addition to dealing with the environmental consequences, agricultural challenges now include, developing new farmland, growing more food, and managing agriculture at a different scale. It is not simply changing subsistence farmers into commercial farmers, but how all farmers alter their practices to accommodate the changing needs and desires of the population.

Women have always played a crucial role in food production, and in recent years, their contributions have become even more important. Women are often the leaders in finding methods to improve the productivity of farms, in spite of the obstacles of gender inequality.

Environmental Effects of Modern Food Production

Although there are tremendous differences in the efficiency of farming practices throughout the world, most practices have evolved to effectively use the soil quality and climate in various locations. Technological innovations have allowed for massive increases in food production, but at a cost. It is usually modern and intensive forms of farming that have the greatest environmental impact. Regardless of the type of farming practiced, humans have an impact on the environment when they alter natural ecosystems.

Land Cover Change

Changes in land use occur as the world's population grows, due to increased pressure to grow more food and develop more land for homes. **Land cover change** is the study of how land is used and the impact of changing land use. Geographers are particularly interested in loss of natural land areas to agriculture and the loss of agricultural land to the expansion of urban areas. (See Topics 5.11 and 6.11.) Geographers use data and satellite images to map and analyze changes in land use.

Images taken from space show parts of western Brazil in 2000 (left) and 2012 (right). Deforestation and agriculture have impacted the rainforests of this region. The dark areas are forest and the light areas are farmland. Describe the changes of land use from 2000 to 2012.

Pollution

Pollution is often associated with industrial processes, but farming also contributes to air, water, and soil pollution. The most intensive forms of agriculture are usually responsible for the worst agricultural pollution. Farmers' use of chemical fertilizers, insecticides, pesticides, and herbicides has increased tremendously over the past several decades, and resulted in polluted air, water, and land. Their use has also resulted in health issues for those exposed to the chemicals. To ensure minimal damage to the environment and people, many governments have regulated the amount and types of chemicals that can be used, in addition to how and when they can be applied.

Desertification

Alteration of the natural vegetation in arid areas causes fertile land to become infertile, or **desertification**. For example, desertification is caused by the removal of forests or overgrazing livestock which can allow for increased wind erosion and result in the loss of the topsoil. Even common farming practices, such as plowing or irrigation, done irresponsibly can expose the soil to excessive erosion.

Soil Salinization

Improper use of irrigation or water high in salt content can cause salinization of the soil. **Salinization** occurs when salts from water used by plants remain in the soil. Salinization decreases a plant's ability to uptake water and nutrients, which results in lower yields and may render soil useless. Evaporation also leaves salts behind in the soil, so if there is excess water, either in the soil or on the surface, salinization rates increase.

Protecting Natural Ecosystems and Conservation Efforts

Economic benefits of agriculture conflict with conservation and environmental efforts in many regions. In response, an increasing number of individuals, non-government organizations, and government agencies are becoming involved with conservation efforts. Their goal is to counter the damaging effects of destroying the natural landscape, and the various flora and fauna that inhabit it, through the expansion and development of farmland.

National and local governments have instituted regulations on the use of agricultural chemicals, development and possible destruction of fragile natural environments, and preservation of valuable farmland. Governments have also educated farmers and the general public on the environmental effects of farming.

Individual farmers effect change by pursuing more environmentally friendly practices, such as reducing the use of agricultural chemicals, using more natural pest control solutions, monitoring irrigation usage, and growing crops organically. Individual consumers show support for farmers who use more sustainable practices by purchasing their products, even at higher prices.

Another practice to defend the environment is to create protected zones, forests, or preserves where development is not allowed. Some countries set aside land that has biodiversity or endangered species in order to preserve and protect the land, plants, and animals. Debates about how much protection is warranted and what types of activities should be allowed in protected areas occur on a local, national, and global scale.

An example of environmental protection at a global scale occurred in the 1980s. People from many nations joined the "Save the Rainforest" movement that supported farming and logging practices that did not damage the Brazilian rainforest.

Humans Altering the Landscape for Agriculture

Ever since the first humans began to farm, they altered the landscape to their advantage. Things that people now consider natural—building earthworks, redirecting streams, or removing natural obstacles—were at one time innovations. Far from natural, these undertakings were fresh, creative solutions to challenges faced by the earliest agriculturalists.

Terracing

One of the earliest human alterations of the landscape was **terrace farming**, in which farmers build a series of steps into the side of a hill. This creates flat surfaces, which have several benefits over steeply graded hillsides:

- The amount of arable land increases in areas with steep hillsides.
- The land collects rainfall that sustains the crops, rather than allowing it to run down a sloped hillside.
- The reduction in water running down the hillside limits soil erosion.

However, if terraces are not carefully maintained, a heavy rainfall can cause disastrous and deadly mudslides.

Terrace farming has long been used throughout the world. In East Asia, terrace farming is often used to grow rice. In South America, potatoes and maize (corn) are the main crops. In northern Africa, people often grow fruit and olive trees on terraced land.

Managing Water

The process of applying controlled amounts of water to crops using dams, canals, pipes, sprinkler systems, or other manufactured devices rather than relying on just rainfall, is called **irrigation**. Humans have used irrigation to increase food production and increase their standard of living for thousands of years. In modern times, the successful use of large-scale irrigation contributed greatly to feeding the rapidly growing population of the world. Irrigation systems can turn deserts and semi-arid regions into productive farmland. An example is California, particularly the dry central and southern regions of the state.

Types of Irrigation Systems Dams turn streams or rivers into reservoirs that are used to maintain large quantities of water throughout the year. While beneficial to preserve and distribute water, dams destroy river ecosystems and people are often displaced from their land when the reservoirs are created.

Aquifers are underground reserves of fresh groundwater which can be used to water crops. Wells must be built to access the water and then it is piped to the fields. Overuse of aquifers is a concern because the supply of water is often limited.

A system developed in the mid-20th century is **center-pivot irrigation,** in which watering equipment rotates around a pivot and delivers specific amounts of water, fertilizer, or pesticides to the field. These systems create large circular patterns in fields, which are visible from the sky. (See image on page 270.) This capital-intensive system is common with large-scale commercial farming because of its efficiency.

Problems From Irrigation When misused, irrigation can cause severe problems. It can disrupt the natural drainage of water and reduce the normal regeneration of soils caused by natural flooding. Irrigation can reduce the amount of surface water in rivers and lakes. Overwatering leads to water contaminated with chemicals seeping into rivers and underground water systems.

In the 1960s, the Soviet Union tried to divert water from rivers that flowed into the Aral Sea to increase cotton production in the region. The Aral Sea, once the fourth-largest lake in the world, was reduced to 10 percent of its former size by 1997. The project was poorly done and much of the water went to waste. The water that remained was extremely saline, which destroyed a flourishing fishing industry and caused economic hardship for the population that lived near the lake. Some of the former lakebed is now classified as a desert and cannot be farmed.

In recent years, the government of Kazakhstan has been successful in revitalizing one small part of the lake. The destruction of the lake has provided a lesson regarding the consequences of manipulating the natural environment.

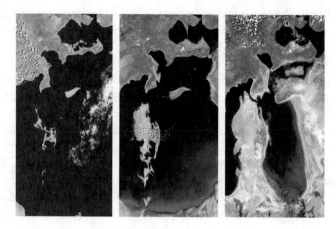

The Aral Sea evolved into four smaller lakes as it dried up over several decades. As the process continued, the lakes became progressively smaller and the easternmost lake completely disappeared.

Draining Wetlands

Low-lying areas that contain a significant amount of water at or near the surface are **wetlands**. Many people viewed wetlands as not serving any useful role. Therefore, when developers looked for land, the fertile soil of wetlands is seen as a viable option to be converted into other land use, especially for farmland.

When wetlands are converted to agricultural or other land use, numerous benefits are lost. There are many positive impacts of wetlands:

- providing a significant biodiversity in both plants and animals
- acting as natural filters that protect surface water and groundwater quality
- trapping sediment and protect against shoreline and stream bank erosion
- averting flood damage during periods of potential flooding by holding and then slowly releasing water
- buffering the local water supply by holding water during periods of drought
- reducing greenhouse gases by building and storing soil carbon

Clearing Trees and Other Vegetation

The removal of large tracts of forest, or **deforestation**, has occurred throughout human history as a common solution to the need for additional farmland. Northern and central Europe were once heavily forested. Now, the region is mostly farmland and urban areas. Deforestation today occurs mostly in Southeast Asia, parts of Africa, and, most notably, in the rainforests of South America.

Cutting down trees can result in local problems, such as soil erosion, decreased rainfall, warmer temperatures, and desertification. In addition, it can cause devastating global environmental damage. In particular, the rainforests absorb so much carbon dioxide that shrinking them leads to an increase in atmospheric carbon dioxide, which contributes to worldwide climate change.

Shifting Cultivation

Slash-and-burn agriculture, an early agricultural practice and type of shifting cultivation (see Topic 5.1), takes place when all vegetation in an area of forest is cut down and burned in place. The ash provides nutrients to the soil, and the land can be farmed for a few years before the soil becomes depleted and the plot is abandoned. The plot then returns to a natural, if somewhat altered state, while the farmers move on to burn and plant in a new space. Because slash-and-burn agriculture requires people to move regularly, it is classified as shifting cultivation. On a small scale, this system is beneficial to humans, but the environment recovers slowly. However, as population pressure increases, slash-and-burn agriculture on a large scale does not allow the ecosystem to recover, causing permanent damage.

One such environmental damage from shifting cultivation is soil erosion. Farmers usually remove vegetation by burning it, cutting it down, pulling it out, or killing it with herbicides. On the Great Plains and prairies of the United States, farmers removed the tall prairie grasses in order to plant wheat and other grains. These new crops lacked the extensive root systems of prairie grass. Without the anchor of strong roots and with dry conditions, valuable topsoil simply blew away. During this period, known as the Dust Bowl, it is estimated that nearly 35 million acres of arable land became useless. This era was one of the worst ecological disasters in U.S. history.

Pastoral Nomadism

Nomadic herding (see Topic 5.1) is an extensive agricultural activity that involves groups of people moving often and raising animals as their main means of survival. A herder's willingness to move frequently allows for a much larger number of animals to be kept, which reduces danger of the lose of a few animals. With pastoral nomadism, the farmer will keep the animals in one area only until the supply of food reaches the point that further grazing will do permanent damage to the land. If the livestock are not moved at that point, then overgrazing can lead to desertification since the animals will have eaten much of the grass, and even pulled up the roots. This makes the soil susceptible to wind erosion. This type of environmental pressure is occurring in the Sahel region of Africa.

It may appear as if pastoral nomadism is an undesirable and inefficient type of agriculture. In reality, if practiced in an environmentally sensitive way, it is an extremely efficient way to use poor quality land. The families that depend on this practice use the livestock in numerous ways. They use hides for clothing and shelters, consume meat and milk for nutrition, and trade animals when other necessities are required.

Similar to slash-and-burn agriculture, pastoral nomadism is not as common as it once was. Individuals involved in both do not usually own the land they use but rely on customary systems of communal land usage. Since governments rarely recognize these systems, maintaining these lifestyles has been difficult.

Societal Effects of Agricultural Practices

The development of agriculture has altered landscapes and resulted in environmental challenges that have had a substantial impact on society. It has influenced the size of the world's population, dietary practices, the role of women in society, economic development, and globalization.

Changing Diets

A challenge of the global food supply is the changing dietary preferences of people, especially in semiperiphery countries. As the citizens of these countries enjoy improved standards of living, they seek a more western-style diet involving meat, dairy products, and processed and convenience foods. The demand for and the use of these products can lead to significant problems.

Animals are inefficient food converters since they consume more calories than they produce. Farmers feed approximately 35 percent of the world's crops to livestock so these animals, which are used to produce meat and dairy products, will grow larger in size and number. This means fewer crops are available for human consumption.

Livestock production also puts much more demand on the environment than crop production does. Two environmental issues with raising livestock are the large amount of fresh water required by the animals and disposal of the waste they produce.

As processed food is prepared, it can be cooked, canned, frozen, packaged, or modified with preservatives. Some foods are minimally processed such as canned vegetables, while others are heavily processed such as frozen pizzas. Large agricultural food companies efficiently process food in the field or factory. These companies then advertise the convenience and cost effectiveness of ready to eat foods. Processed foods have changed peoples' diets in many communities. Agriculture continues to change to address growing concerns about the effects of diets heavy in processed foods, such as high blood pressure, elevated cholesterol, and obesity.

Role of Women in Agricultural Production

Women play an important role in agriculture throughout the world, especially in periphery and semiperiphery countries. Traditionally, women helped men in the fields and in processing and storing the harvest. Also, women performed the task of selecting the best seeds to plant the following year.

Recent economic development in periphery and semiperiphery countries has resulted in jobs in different sectors of the economy. Men are more likely to leave the farm and accept these jobs in urban centers. If the centers are close enough to commute to on a daily basis, then men might continue to be involved in the family farm. If the jobs are in centers that require men to leave their homes, then women take on much larger roles in running and managing family farms.

This feminization of agriculture has led international aid agencies to recognize that agricultural education and training, and more financial assistance, should be extended to women. The International Assessment of Agricultural Knowledge, Science, and Technology for Development (IAASTD), an initiative of the World Bank, found that women tend to be more cautious than men in making economic decisions and are less likely to accept high-risk ventures. Therefore, women are unlikely to invest in capital-intensive, large-scale commercial operations to compete in international markets.

Even if female farm owners were willing to purchase the inputs for a larger-scale operation, it is unlikely that banks or lending institutions would provide loans to them. The IAASTD has suggested that if women had equal access to production resources as men, productivity would likely rise by 20 to 30 percent.

In core countries, women usually have more opportunities to work in nonagricultural jobs than in non-core countries. There is a large number of women in rural areas of the United States who have found employment off the farm. As large agribusinesses become more common, there is an increasing number of agriculture-related jobs in management, research and development, operation of sophisticated machinery, processing, distribution, and marketing. Many of these jobs are filled by women. As agricultural changes, so do the related jobs and the mixture of people who do them.

Economic Purpose

Agriculture is an important part of most countries' economies. Agricultural products are used as food, fiber, fuel, and raw materials. Each use adds to the economic value of agricultural goods. For example, the fibers of cotton are used to manufacture clothing and other textiles, trees for building materials, corn and sugar for ethanol, and other plants are used to make medicines. Some of these products are at a local scale, near where they are grown. However, most are produced for national- and global-scale trade economies.

Agriculture contributes to the Gross Domestic Product (GDP) of countries, or the dollar amount of all final goods and services produced within a country in one year. (See Topic 7.3.) As seen in the table on the following page, agriculture is responsible for a small percentage of U.S. and Canadian GDPs. Yet, this is a small percentage of two very large GDPs (over $22 trillion in 2019), so the actual value of agriculture is over $200 billion. The Afghani and Ghanaian GDPs are so much smaller ($85 billion together), that even a large percentage of those countries' GDPs equals a smaller total value of agricultural goods compared to the United States and Canada.

AGRICULTURAL DATA, 2017 (from selected countries)		
Country	Percentage of GDP from Agriculture	Percentage of Labor Force in Agriculture
United States	0.9	1.3
Canada	1.6	2.0
Afghanistan	23.0	44.3
Ghana	18.3	44.7

Source: CIA World Factbook

Agriculture in the United States and Canada makes up a tiny percentage of the GDP, yet in Afghanistan and Ghana it is a much larger percentage. A similar situation exists for the percentage of the labor force working in agriculture among the four countries. What does this mean about the importance of agriculture in Afghanistan and Ghana?

In both the United States and Canada, food producers do a significant amount of processing to food, which adds to the total value of agriculture. In Ghana and Afghanistan, very little value is added to the agricultural products through manufacturing.

In terms of the percentage of the labor force, the low numbers in the United States and Canada reflect the significant amount of mechanization used on farms, so the labor force required is very small. In Afghanistan and Ghana, farms use much less mechanization and there are far fewer job opportunities in other sectors of the economy, so the percentage of people involved in agriculture is very high.

REFLECT ON THE ESSENTIAL QUESTION

Essential Question: *What are the environmental and societal consequences of agricultural practices?*

Agricultural Practices	Impact on Environment or Society

KEY TERMS

land cover change	center-pivot irrigation
desertification	wetlands
salinization	deforestation
terrace farming	slash-and-burn agriculture
irrigation	

Challenges of Contemporary Agriculture

Essential Question: What are the challenges and debates related to the changing nature of contemporary agriculture and food-production practices?

Many different patterns of agricultural production and consumption have developed across the globe as a result of how farmers respond to various factors. For each of the different factors, farmers decide how to take advantages of opportunities and how to overcome challenges to be successful.

Perhaps the most obvious factor influencing the patterns of production and consumption is the physical environment. How a farmer uses a flat piece of land with good soil and favorable weather will obviously be different from a rugged landscape with poor soil and unfavorable weather. Other factors that can influence the patterns of production and consumption include government policies, transportation linkages within the region and beyond, the level of economic well-being of the citizens of the region, social and cultural traditions and expectations, access to the results of agricultural research, and the proximity to large markets.

Agricultural Innovations

During the Third Agricultural Revolution, scientists researched ways to increase yields to feed growing populations, improve foods' nutritional value, and increase the profitability of farming. While agricultural innovations often accomplish at least one of these three goals, people disagree if negative consequences are outweighed by the benefits. As noted in Topic 5.5, the Green Revolution was both successful and controversial. Similarly, other innovations often raise concerns.

Biotechnology and Genetically Modified Organisms

Biotechnology is a recent controversial innovation that is used to improve the quality and health of plants and animals. Biotech includes the development of **genetically modified organisms** (GMOs), which are plants or animals that scientists have modified by extracting genes of one species and inserting them into the DNA of another species. Compared to traditional foods, GMOs can be more nutritious, resistant to weather and pest-related damage, and less susceptible to spoilage. The use of GMO seeds usually results in farmers drastically reducing chemical usage to control disease, weeds, and pests.

While the term genetic modification is commonly used, the terms genetic engineering and genetic improvement are also used. Biotechnology can also involve other sophisticated practices that advances peoples' health, such as molecular markers, molecular diagnostics, vaccines, and tissue culture.

GMO crops were first produced in the 1970s and started becoming widely used in the 1990s. The majority of scientists have found these processes safe for humans. Today, most corn, soybeans, and cotton grown in the United States, are GMO varieties. However, only a few other countries, such as Brazil and Argentina, produce large amounts of GMO crops. Many countries, particularly in Europe, have restricted the use of GMOs due to concerns:

- GMO seeds are too expensive for poor farmers to use, in part because they are often sterile, so new seeds must be purchased each year.

- GMO seeds that are resistant to pests and herbicides might lead to the development of superpests or superweeds.

- GMOs might have potential long-term risks to consumers, such as organ problems or reduced immunity to diseases, that have yet to be identified and studied.

Aquaculture

Population growth has increased the demand for food which has led to overfishing, or the depletion of fish in oceans and lakes. In response, **aquaculture,** or **aquafarming**, the practice of raising and harvesting fish and other forms of food that live in water, has become more common. People in China and Southeast Asia have practiced aquaculture for thousands of years, but it is newer in the rest of the world. Often referred to as the **Blue Revolution**, the practice is now the fastest growing form of food production on the planet and responsible for approximately 50 percent of the world's seafood.

As with other forms of food production, there are environmental concerns related to aquaculture. Critics of open-pen systems—in which a cage or net is moored to the seafloor and the fish are able to interact with the wild surroundings to some extent—point out numerous problems:

- High fish density in enclosures means diseases and parasites thrive and spread easily.

- Parasites and diseases can easily spread from fish in the enclosures to the nearby wild stock.

- Chemicals and antibiotics used to counter parasites and diseases can damage the ecosystem around the enclosures.

- Fish can escape pens and may breed or compete with native stocks of fish.

- Excess feed and the concentration of fish waste can produce dangerously high levels of organic matter in local bodies of water.

THE GROWTH OF AQUACULTURE

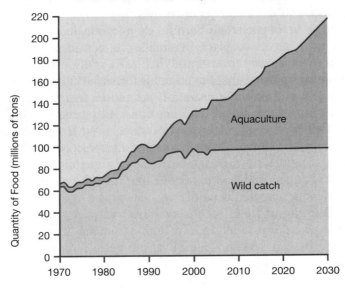

Source: futuretimeline.net

Describe the trend of both aquaculture and wild caught seafood since 1970.

There are also social concerns regarding aquaculture. The installation of fish farms can challenge traditional fishing and lead to conflicts between the two groups of fishers, disrupting the local way of life. Another concern is that owners of the aquaculture operations may unethically exploit the local labor and local environment. Some people are concerned that fish from fish farms contain high levels of pesticides that could harm humans.

Debates continue on issues of sustainability of both wild seafood and aquaculture. Without aquaculture, demand for wild caught fish increases stress on ocean and sea ecosystems. Quotas, regulated fishing seasons, and zones have helped wild seafood stock to rebound, but challenges remain. As the world's demand for seafood increases, striking a balance between the two systems will be critical to maintain a sustainable system.

Environmental Issues Related to Agriculture

Modern agriculture has dramatically modified the natural landscape. Some of these changes constitute significant environmental damage.

Agricultural Chemicals and Fossil Fuels

Much of the environmental impact of farming comes from the use of chemicals. Farmers have long used fertilizers to replace nutrients in the soil. Traditionally, the fertilizer was human or animal waste. When used properly, these products provided the soil with nutrients and disposed of wastes. While some farmers still use waste as fertilizer, most rely more on chemical fertilizers. If too much is applied, the excess contaminates nearby water supplies, causing significant environmental damage, including growth of toxic algae that uses the oxygen in the water, which kills fish and other organisms.

A second group of potentially harmful chemicals includes those designed to kill unwanted insects or plants. Pesticides, insecticides, and herbicides destroy parts of the natural ecosystem. When used or disposed of incorrectly, they can cause significant damage to other life forms, including humans.

Another group of powerful chemicals are those given to livestock, such as antibiotics to prevent disease and hormones to promote growth. Many consumers fear the consequences of consuming meat from animals given these chemicals. The primary concern is that the practice can lead to the development of antibiotic resistant bacteria, or superbugs, that could be transferred to humans and lead to serious illnesses. There is not agreement within the scientific community on the associated risks.

Modern farming machines, such as combines and tractors, run on fossil fuel. The use of these machines results in air pollution from the exhaust, depletion of fossil fuel reserves, and leaks or spills of various petroleum products that can contaminate soil and water.

Depletion of Water Supplies

The misuse of water by farmers can also damage the environment. On a worldwide scale, approximately 70 percent of all accessible fresh water is used for agriculture. Some of this water is wasted through inefficient irrigation. At times, farmers are wasteful with water by using more for crops than needed, using irrigation systems with pipes that leak, or growing crops in arid places that require excessive amounts of water. Poor irrigation can cause several problems including salinization and water depletion. (See Topic 5.10.)

Loss of Biodiversity

Changes in agriculture often reduce biodiversity. As improved varieties of crops are developed, farmers often abandon older varieties. In addition, farmers grow fewer varieties of crops than ever before. Specializing in one crop, which is known as monocropping, or monoculture, then reduces the diversity of the insects, animals, and other organisms that depend on other varieties of plants. Biodiversity also decreases as land cover uses change from wild ecosystems to agriculture or urban uses. (See Topic 5.10.)

Soil Degradation and Erosion

Many people believe grazing animals has very little impact on the natural landscape. In a large open area, the animals will simply wander from area to area seeking grass and allow the grazed areas time to recover. In restricted areas, farmers move their herds between enclosures to allow for the recovery of the grasslands.

However, if the density of animals is greater than even expansive grasslands can support, animals will **overgraze** in the search for food. This damages the grasslands to the extent that the vegetation will not refresh itself even after the animals leave. Overgrazing most often occurs when farmers or herders have too many animals, they control too little land, or climatic conditions worsen and there is less pasture available than usual. With the right combination of overgrazing and environmental circumstances, soil erosion become a danger. The Sahel region of Africa is an example of where this pressure is occurring.

Overgrazing is increasing in pastoral nomadism as the amount of land available to herders and their families has shrunken in recent decades. Since there is less land available for the migratory herders, they have to remain longer in fewer locations, significantly increasing the risk of overgrazing. Several changes have decreased the availability of pastureland, which makes overgrazing more likely:

- Governments have become more protective of their borders, which makes it difficult for some herders to follow their traditional migratory routes that often cross international borders.
- Some former pastureland is now irrigated and used for growing crops and housing permanent residents.
- Areas of former pastureland are now used for mining and petroleum operations.

Once overgrazing occurs, the grasses will not recover as quickly, if at all. Similar results occur when soil is overtilled, or poor plowing techniques are used. When farmers drain the soil of nutrients from practices such as overuse, lack of crop rotation, or failure to replace nutrients, the soil loses its ability to support plant growth. All of these practices can result in soil being susceptible to erosion by wind and water.

Sustainability and Agriculture

Farmers today face many challenges to operate in ways that are sustainable in the long term. Maintaining soil fertility without degrading the soil is possible, but it takes careful planning. Sustainable grazing and tilling practices help to minimize soil erosion. Managing chemical levels and sedimentation in bodies of water, conserving water, employing renewable energy resources, and preserving biodiversity are all part of an environmentally sustainable perspective. Farmers have to constantly analyze their decisions in order to strike a balance between immediate profitability and long-term sustainability.

Farmers face many challenges as they maintain sustainable agriculture. Today, they use GIS software to manage chemical application, reduce the impact of plowing techniques on soil, and slow runoff and soil erosion.

Changes in Food Production and Consumption

The broad trends in agriculture over the past century have been toward larger farms, corporate ownership, intensive use of machinery and chemicals, and higher output. However, smaller trends are also evident, such as the increase in fair trade, organic farming and value-added crops.

Fair Trade

Some consumers support the fair trade movement. The goal of this movement is to get more money into the hands of the small farmers in poor countries, rather than supporting large transnational corporations that manage trade in agricultural products. The most widely sold fair-trade products are bananas, chocolate, coffee, and tea. (See Topic 5.9 for more on the fair-trade movement.)

Organic Foods

In the United States, people spent more than $50 billion for organic food in 2020—an increase of almost 5 percent from the previous year. In order to be classified as an **organic food**, crops must be non-GMO, produced without pesticides or synthetic fertilizers, and use sustainable growing practices. According to the USDA, animals must be fed 100 percent organic feed and ranchers cannot administer antibiotics or hormones to the animals.

Many consumers believe that organic is healthier for them and safer for the environment. Since organic farming tends to be more labor-intensive than other forms of agriculture, it creates more jobs, but the food produced is more expensive.

Organic agriculture has possible drawbacks. One potential environmental cost is the need for more land to produce the same quantity of food. Also, some organic production of commodities, such as milk, cereal, and pork, create more greenhouse gases than conventional farming techniques. And while organic farming regulations prohibit the use of synthetic pesticides, they do allow farmers to use naturally occurring chemicals that can also be harmful to humans and other life forms.

Value-Added Specialty Crops

Increasing revenue and profits is a goal of all businesses. Farmers' and ranchers' profit margins have been in decline, so they have tried new approaches, such as raising value-added specialty crops or practicing value-added farming. **Value-added crops** are those for which consumers are willing to pay more because of special qualities or because they are difficult to acquire:

- organically grown crops and meats
- rare subtropical plants, such as passion fruit, cherimoya, longan, and star fruit
- grass-fed beef and free-range chickens and eggs

Value-added farming occurs when farmers process their crops into high-value products, rather than simply selling it as it comes from the field. The tremendous growth in grape production and the development of small wineries is a good example. Turning strawberries and other fruits into jams and jellies or using tomatoes and peppers to produce salsa, are also examples. Dairy producers create added value by making and selling their own cheese or ice cream.

Local-Food Movement

Another trend among some consumers is a **local-food movement,** or seeking out food produced nearby. Advocates, sometimes called "locavores," have pointed out that this supports local farmers and reduces the use of fossil fuel used to transport products. Starting in the 1990s, farmers markets, where consumers can purchase fruits, vegetables, and other food items directly from farmers, became more popular. Many farmers cater to local consumers by producing specialty crops, such as herbs, mushrooms, and eggs from free-range chickens, in small quantities but at relatively high prices.

Urban Farming

Urban farming refers to the production of farm goods within an urban area with the goal of providing locally grown food. It may be practiced in different forms, but all assume a level of commerce—meaning the products will be sold and not used for personal consumption. The greatly reduced distances between producer and consumer allow consumers to enjoy fresh products. Farms may be owned by a traditional farmer but could follow a nontraditional ownership model, such as a few friends, a nonprofit group, or a neighborhood group. The food produced could be sold locally at grocery stores, restaurants, or farmers' markets. Additionally, the food could be used at a local soup kitchen, church, or shelter. Cities like Detroit, Michigan, have large urban farming communities.

An increasingly popular variation of the urban farming model is **community gardens**. People use community gardens to share agricultural products with family, friends, and perhaps those in need rather than as a business. These garden plots allow people to grow and harvest their own fresh food, grown organically, if they wish. They also allow economically disadvantaged citizens to acquire high-quality food that otherwise they would have unlikely been able to access. These plots of farmland may be found in many different areas in the city such as parks, abandoned lots, or even on top of buildings.

A new type of urban farming is called vertical farming. **Vertical farms** grow crops inside in stackable trays, using greenhouses, artificial lights, and hydroponics. **Hydroponics** allows crops to grow without soil using mineral-enriched solutions. These processes use less water and less land since trays can be stacked vertically. One criticism is the substantial amount of energy needed to power the lights to grow the crops.

Source: Wikimedia Commons
Much less space is needed to grow crops using vertical farms.

Community-Supported Agriculture

One strategy used within the local-food movement is **community-supported agriculture (CSA)** that brings producers and consumers into a type of partnership. Consumers buy a share, or subscribe to a certain quantity of crops for a season. The food is made available to the consumer throughout the growing season. This ensures the consumers a local supply of fresh products and the farmer receives revenue throughout the season, rather than only at the end. It also allows for a connection between consumers and producers because consumers can often participate in the process of growing and harvesting the food. Consumers usually develop an appreciation of the challenges of production, while producers develop a better understanding of consumer wants.

Challenges of Feeding a Global Population

The development of agriculture of all types has resulted in the availability of massive amounts of food. There is enough food for everyone in the world, yet almost 1 billion people do not get sufficient food. Factors causing the food shortages include food distribution networks and the cost of the food. A distribution network is challenged by transportation difficulties, storage problems, political unrest or conflicts, or when large amounts of food are diverted to feed animals. Also, much of the food produced in developing countries is exported to wealthy countries. When food is available, people in the greatest need often cannot afford to purchase sufficient food or it can be denied because of local conflict or government corruption.

Food Insecurity

When households lack access to adequate food because of limited money or other resources, they experience **food insecurity**. People who experience food insecurity often have to make the choice between between purchasing food or other necessities. Children are particularly vulnerable to food insecurity since it hinders their ability to learn and negatively affects growth.

This problem does not exist in only periphery and semiperiphery countries. The United States is one of the richest countries in the world, yet it is estimated that over 50 million people, or more than 14 percent of the population, suffer from some level of food insecurity. In the periphery and semiperiphery regions of the world, the rate of food insecurity is approximately 30 percent. In sub-Saharan Africa, 55 percent of the people experience food insecurity. As a result of the COVID-19 pandemic, food insecurity numbers increased dramatically around the world.

The underlying causes of food insecurity in the United States—poverty, unemployment, and under-employment—are interconnected. Poverty and employment situations are also causing food insecurity in periphery and semiperiphery countries. Additional problems in non-core countries, such as high population growth, political instability, and environmental challenges, intensify food insecurity.

Food insecurity rarely exists to the same degree throughout an entire country. In the United States, it is most prevalent in poor neighborhoods and among the homeless of both major cities and rural areas. It is least noticeable in suburban areas and smaller cities.

In poorer countries, the landless poor and female-headed households in both urban and rural settings are most vulnerable. When people move from farms to find a job, they can no longer grow the foods to support their family, and often lack the financial resources to afford food. Additionally, assistance programs in the periphery often lack the resources to combat food insecurity.

FOOD INSECURITY AND SEVERE FOOD INSECURITY, 2017

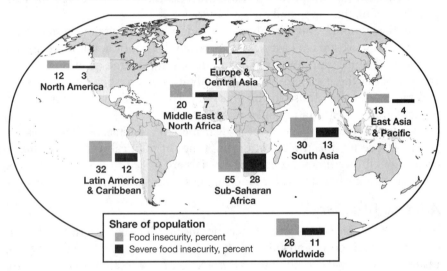

There is a tremendous variation in the levels of food insecurity between the core, the periphery, and the semiperiphery. Countries at war or dealing with high levels of poverty are particularly vulnerable.

Food Deserts

A neighborhood where residents have little to no access to healthy and affordable food is a **food desert**. The USDA defininition involves two elements. The first is the area has low income and high poverty. The second element is an urban area with 33 percent of the population located more than 1 mile from a grocery store, or more than 10 miles away in a rural area.

These neighborhoods are usually home to racial and ethnic minorities or large percentages of elderly or disabled people. Due to economic and physical constraints, the residents often do not have the means to travel to grocery stores outside of their area of the city. Car ownership may be rare and city buses may be too expensive or not readily available. As a result, the residents are forced to shop in their own neighborhoods. Often, grocery chains have eliminated stores in these neighborhoods due to lower than acceptable levels of profits. What usually remains are small independently-owned grocery stores and convenience stores. It is challenging for these small stores to maintain selections of healthful food at affordable prices. Consequently, many of the residents suffer from poor diets and the ensuing health issues.

Problems with Distribution Systems

A network of trade and transportation that get food from farms to consumers is a **food distribution system**. Food distribution challenges exist at multiple scales. At the local scale, both farmers and consumers are hindered by their inability to get to a market. If farmers cannot reach the market with their surplus products, the food will go to waste. If people require additional food beyond what they can grow, but cannot access the closest market, then the problems of malnutrition and hunger emerge.

At the regional and global scale, modern transportation systems and advances in food storage have vastly improved distribution, but there are still obstacles. A ship, transport truck, or train can move large quantities of food efficiently, but these systems work well only if there are suitable ports, roads, and rail lines. Often those in the greatest need of food live in remote areas without good transportation links.

Governments can affect food distrubution systems. Political leaders will often use food as a weapon during times of political unrest to suppress opposition. Other times, govenment officials are forced to make decisions on food allocation when accessible food supplies are insufficient.

Adverse Weather

Farmers are intense weather watchers because a slight change in the weather can impact their crops and animals. In core countries, farmers often have crop insurance to provide some financial protection from weather disasters. Crop insurance is not nearly as common in non-core regions. In regions with little surplus that can be stored for future needs, the loss of crops and livestock can have a devastating impact on the population unless another region can step in and quickly deliver necessary food to the affected population.

Farmers are among those who could be most affected by global climate change. However, scientists are unsure of how this trend will express itself over the next several decades. Climate change might increase the frequency and intensity of droughts and severe storms, threatening crop yields and livestock. In areas which already have suitable weather, warmer weather could cause problems of drought and for livestock farmers heat-wave deaths, reduced milk production in dairy cattle, and reduced weight gain for beef cattle.

Global warming could have positive effects for farmers in some regions. For farmers practicing at the fringes of agricultural zones, an extended growing season due to shorter and milder winters could allow farmers to be more successful. Warmer weather could also benefit livestock farmers in these areas through lower feed costs, increased survival rates of the young animals, and reduced energy costs.

Land Use Lost to Suburbanization

Existing farmland is threatened by the expansion of cities and suburbs. Millions of acres of farmland worldwide are converted to land use for suburban housing, shopping centers, business parks, or other types of urban development. Many view the continual loss of fertile land as a significant threat to the ability to feed a growing population.

Because most cities originally developed as agricultural centers, these cities are located near fertile land. The region of Canada with the best soil and most productive farms have recently experienced growth. This growth has consequently placed tremendous pressure on the surrounding farmland. Each time a new subdivision or some other urban land use is created, hundreds, even thousands, of acres of Canada's best farmland is lost to development.

Similar problems exist in nearly all expanding towns and cities surrounded by agricultural land around the world. Land-use planners are aware of these concerns and try to control the expansion of cities, but growing populations and the associated houses, businesses, and infrastructure have to be nearby. One solution to alleviate urban expansion issues and loss of farmland is to find ways to increase the densities within the existing cities, thus containing the growing population.

Factors Affecting Food Production

The decisions farmers make are influenced by numerous factors, including the location of food processing facilities and markets, economies of scale, distribution systems, and government policies.

Location of Food Processing Facilities and Markets

The transformation of agricultural products into food or taking food items and transforming them into a different type of food is **food processing**. One example is taking wheat and milling it into flour, which then can be either sold to consumers or sold to factories for making bread. Transportation systems and relative distance from the processing location are important factors and can vary depending on the product. The von Thünen model introduced some elements of this concept. (See Topic 5.8.) Core countries have advanced infrastructure that can move agricultural products rapidly with minimal waste. In periphery countries, product loss can be substantial because of poor transportation infrastructure and lack of access to processing plants.

Traditionally, companies located food processing facilities in rural areas or small towns. By locating facilities close to where the harvest occurs, companies could work with fresh products and benefit from the lower labor and land costs in rural areas. However, improvements in roads, truck efficiencies, and storage techniques have prompted many companies to close older, smaller facilities and open new, more-efficient ones. These larger and more-modern facilities allow companies to process more product at a lower cost per unit, thus taking advantage of economies of scale.

Economies of Scale

In farming, as in any business, taking advantage of economies of scale allows producers to increase profits. This occurs at every scale, although it is often associated with larger farming operations. The key is to alter farming practices to make the operation more efficient, and reduce the cost per unit of production. On a smaller farm, the farmer might take advantage of economies of scale by increasing the level of fertilization and irrigation of a crop. By doing so, the farmer increases expenses by 10 percent, but if the harvest increases by 25 percent, then the cost per unit will decrease, and once again, profits will increase.

Distribution Systems

In commercial farming, people have to transprot products from farm to market before consumers can purchase them and suppliers can make profits. That means the products have to arrive at a food processor, wholesaler, and eventually, market in a timely manner.

If the crops are perishable, such as tomatoes or strawberries, the distribution system from the farm to the market must allow for frequent pickup and delivery to the market. If this is not possible, then the farmers and the shipper must have access to a storage system that can preserve the quality of the crop for a few extra days. However, agricultural industries, like other industries, have adopted a system of *just-in-time delivery* to reduce the need for storage space. The COVID-19 pandemic illustrated that when just-in-time delivery systems were interrupted and product shortages occurred.

In the case of regional and global distribution, different markets might demand different products, and therefore, farmers have to adapt their production accordingly. The differences in the demand could relate to preparation and storage options available at the destination, eating traditions and taste preferences, and religious beliefs.

However, if bad weather, transportation breakdowns, or other problems delay a delivery to a grocery store, then the consumers will often have to do without the desired product. With food, this might be an inconvenience or a a serious concern, especially in a region where the population is struggling to survive.

Government Policies

Food is vital to national security, so governments often adopt policies to protect agriculture. However, many governments let market forces determine exactly what and how much farmers produce. Government policies can influence food production and farmers in several ways:

- Regulations governing migrant workers who often work in food production industries
- Financial assistance, such as low-interest loans and transportation subsidies

- Investment in transportation and storage (grain elevators) infrastructure to increase efficiency and storage capacity
- Regulations on the amount of a product grown or sold to prevent surplus or shortages
- Taxes to discourage production and use of products considered unhealthy, such as tobacco
- Changes in environmental and health regulations influence which products farmers will grow

International politics can also lead to changes in production. A trade agreement with another country could open new markets for farmers and encourage increased production. As part of a larger trade deal, a country might have to reduce exports of a certain crop which could lead to less production. On occasion, countries will impose a **tariff** (tax on imports) or a **quota** (limit the quantity of a good imported) to protect domestically produced goods. These trade restrictions raise the price of imports and make domestic goods more competitive in price within the country in which they were produced. If these restrictions continue for an extended period, farmers alter their production of crops. Between 2018 and 2020, the United States and China both raised their tariffs on traded products. (See Topic 7.6.)

REFLECT ON THE ESSENTIAL QUESTION

Essential Question: *What are the challenges and debates related to the changing nature of contemporary agriculture and food-production practices?*

Contemporary Agriculture and Food-Production Practices	Associated Challenges With Practices

KEY TERMS

genetically modified organisms (GMOs)
aquaculture (aquafarming)
Blue Revolution
overgraze
organic foods
value-added crops
value-added farming
local-food movement
urban farming
community gardens

vertical farms
hydroponics
community-supported agriculture (CSA)
food insecurity
food desert
food distribution system
food processing
tariff
quota

Women in Agriculture

Essential Question: What are the variations in female roles in food production and consumption?

Women play a crucial role in global agriculture. This role has changed and is continuing to change as women become more important in the world's efforts to eliminate hunger. The importance of women's role in agriculture is reflected in the following suggestion made in a report by the UN's Food and Agriculture Organization, "if women farmers gain access to the same resources as their male counterparts, the entire world will eat, too."

Gender Roles in the Food System

In most cultures throughout history, males and females had distinct roles in producing and preparing food. However, some of these roles have changed as technology has changed.

Food Production Women have played a major role in agriculture since humans first started farming. Today, they make up about 40 percent of the world's agricultural labor force. In regions where subsistence farming remains common, that figure is 70 percent, and the contributions of women are changing regardless of the type of farming:

- In many areas of the developing world, men migrate to urban areas in search of employment, while women stay at home and work their farms along with children. In operations where farmers sell their products at local market, women are often the sellers.

- Where farming has modernized and machines have been introduced, women have become less involved with the field work.

- In large-scale agribusinesses, women have taken on additional roles. Besides raising crops, tending animals, and processing products, they work in management, sales, distribution, and research.

Food Preparation As people have changed where they live and work, they have changed how they prepare food. As people moved from rural areas to urban areas, they grew less food and purchased more of it. Today, women are more likely to work outside the home, so they spend less time preparing food than in previous generations.

People purchase more convenience foods than previously, from cake mixes to entire meals that simply need to be heated. The demand for these foods has grown so much that food companies are committing significant research money to developing visually appealing, tasty, and healthful food products. In addition, men have become more involved in food preparation in the regions of the world with greater gender equality, particularly in households where both partners are working. Another result is that people eat in restaurants more than ever before. In 2015, for the first time in history, Americans spent more money eating out than they spent on groceries.

Gender Equality and Agriculture: Hope for the Future

The unequal opportunities, treatment, or rights of a person based on gender is considered **gender inequality.** It is a reality throughout all parts of the world and affects all aspects of society, such as educational and leadership opportunities, reproductive rights, employment options, and property ownership. Over the past few decades some progress toward gender equality has occurred, but not in all countries. (See Topic 7.4.)

In agriculture, the lack of gender equality has a very significant impact on productivity. Especially in periphery countries, where the majority of economically active women are employed in farming, women have assumed increased responsibilities. Increasingly, men are taking nonfarming jobs in urban areas, leaving women to run the farm and care for children. In spite of the added work and responsibility, women still often have little authority in the eyes of the government officials, businesses, society, or male farmers.

Women face **gender-specific obstacles,** or discriminatory practices that prevent female farmers from reaching their potential productivity:

- Women are denied access to finance and capital. It is much more difficult for women to secure the necessary financing for farm inputs, such as machinery and agricultural chemicals. Therefore, female farmers are often not able to modernize and increase productivity.
- Women are denied training and education. Women are often excluded from opportunities to become familiar with new and improved practices to improve productivity and safety on their farms.
- Women are denied property ownership. Female property ownership is rare throughout the world, especially in the peripheral countries.
- Women have limited mobility. In cultures where women face restrictions to their mobility, such as needing their husbands' or fathers' consent to leave their homes, it is difficult for women to either take farm products to the market to sell or trade, or to go to the market to acquire food .
- Women lack political power. When development projects are planned, women are rarely allowed leadership positions or consulted. Consequently, plans are implemented without the knowledge and ideas of the women who will play a role in shaping the plan's success or failure.

In terms of productivity, the lack of gender equality has resulted in a **crop gap** of 20 to 30 percent between male- and female-run farms. Female-run farms are much less productive because of gender-specific obstacles. The worst food insecurities in the world are found in the periphery, the same area where the gender-specific obstacles are the most prevalent. The Food and Agricultural Organization (FAO) of the United Nations estimated that if gender equality existed, the crop gap would disappear, and that female-run farms could even exceed the productivity of male-run farms. This would result in tremendous economic growth and increase the amount of food available in the periphery.

PROPERTY RIGHTS FOR WOMEN, 2017

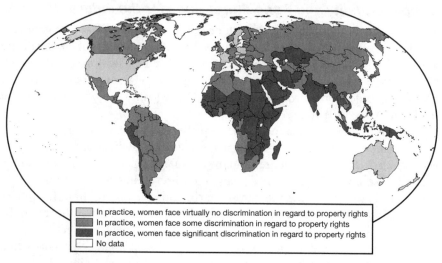

- In practice, women face virtually no discrimination in regard to property rights
- In practice, women face some discrimination in regard to property rights
- In practice, women face significant discrimination in regard to property rights
- No data

Source: womenstats.org

Describe the patterns of property rights of women. What is the relationship between the patterns and gender equality in agriculture?

REFLECT ON THE ESSENTIAL QUESTION

Essential Question: *What are the variations in female roles in food production and consumption?*

Challenges Due to the Role of Females in Food Production and Consumption	Contemporary Solutions

KEY TERMS

gender inequality

gender-specific obstacles

crop gap

Farmers, like business owners, try to utilize their resources and attract new sources of revenue and profit. Two strategies to increase revenue are agritourism and organic farming.

Agritourism

An additional potential revenue source for farmers is the growing trend of agritourism—where tourists visit farms for recreational reasons. It has become more common for farms to provide entertainment and hospitality experiences for consumers. Agritourism is especially important to smaller family farms.

Tourists may be involved in U-pick activities or purchase fresh products from a farm stand. The farm may provide experiences such as a corn maze, a petting zoo with farm animals, or a hayride. Educational opportunities for school groups or interested individuals might be another service the farm provides. Some farms host overnight stays to allow the guests to experience a true farm lifestyle, whether it is waking up to the crowing of a rooster, gathering fresh eggs to cook for breakfast, or helping with chores.

Farmers benefit from the revenue collected from agritourism activities such as a corn maze. Agritourism is also a great way for the non-farming public to become educated about farming practices and gain an appreciation for where food comes from

Organic Trends

Organic agricultural sales have boomed over the past decade with revenue in 2019 of nearly $50 billion in the United States. While non-organic modern agriculture produces food for the masses and is often sold globally, organic food has been largely seized upon by local-food movements. Organic farming—which is more expensive—has proven to be profitable because many people will pay more for organic foods.

The Distribution of the Organic Food Market

The location of organic food consumption can be best explained through the spatial analysis of economic factors, such as income. The concentration of organic food sales is predictably uneven. Farmers markets and supermarkets that offer organic foods are largely found in wealthier regions. Almost half of all organic food is sold and consumed within 100 miles of its production. Moreover, most consumption and production in the United States takes place around wealthy urban areas and organic hotspots along the West Coast and in the Northeast.

1. Describe TWO ways that farmers are trying to increase revenue.
2. Describe why some farmers are choosing to grow organic crops.
3. Explain why organic farming is unlikely to work on a global scale.

THINK AS A GEOGRAPHER: *USE SCALE TO ANALYZE FAIR TRADE*

FAIR TRADE IMPORTS TO THE UNITED STATES, 1998–2015				
Year	Coffee	Tea	Cocoa	Sugar
1998	76,059	no data	no data	no data
2000	4,249,534	no data	no data	no data
2005	44,585,323	490,645	1,036,696	271,680
2010	105,251,476	1,483,666	4,392,674	18,146,124
2015	163,630,275	2,347,699	38,492,988	38,173,065
Total, 1998 to 2015	1,359,418,892	16,002,044	129,087,925	151,248,397

Source: *Fair Trade USA 2015 Almanac. Quantities measured in pounds or other units.*

The concept of scale is useful to analyze how the principles of fair trade work in practice. The underlying principle of fair trade is to ensure that agricultural producers are fairly compensated for their work. Other principles of fair trade include fair pricing, poverty alleviation, mutual benefit (seller-producer), gender equity, safe working conditions, and environmental responsibility.

At the global scale, fair trade works when consumers in core countries desire fair trade products from the periphery countries of the world. The concept can also be applied at the neighborhood or family scale. (See Topic 5.9 for more on fair trade.)

Apply the concept of scale to the principle of fair trade in each question.

1. At the household scale, how does a family that grows food in a garden for their own consumption demonstrate some, but not all, of the principles of fair trade?

2. At the community scale, how does a farmers market demonstrate the principles of fair trade?

3. At the global scale, how does the data suggest that the idea of fair trade is becoming more widespread?

4. How does the practice of fair trade affect each of the following groups: producers in periphery countries, multinational companies, and consumers in highly developed countries?

CHAPTER 14 REVIEW:
Understanding the Challenges and Consequences of Agriculture

Topics 5.10–5.12

MULTIPLE-CHOICE QUESTIONS

Questions 1 and 2 refer to the following image.

1. Which concept is demonstrated in the picture above?
   (A) The results of the enclosure movement
   (B) The impact of the Green Revolution
   (C) The significance of carrying capacity
   (D) The use of terrace farming
   (E) The effects of deforestation

2. Which is a major concern related to the practice shown in the image?
   (A) The amount of arable land is increased
   (B) The practice decreases the efficient use of water resources
   (C) Soil erosion increases dramatically
   (D) Maintenance of the fields is difficult
   (E) The use of large-scale capital-intensive machinery to grow crops

3. Deforestation has resulted in

(A) more farmland in some places but more desertification in others

(B) more farmland in some places and less desertification in others

(C) less farmland in some places but more desertification in others

(D) less farmland in some places and less desertification in others

(E) no noticeable change in the amount of farmland or desertification

4. In which group of countries are GMOs used most widely?

(A) United States, Brazil, and Argentina

(B) France, Germany, and the Netherlands

(C) Kenya, Tanzania, and Ethiopia

(D) India and Bangladesh

(E) Australia and New Zealand

5. Slash-and-burn agriculture is often used in areas that have

(A) soil that lacks sufficient nitrogen to grow food crops quickly

(B) a climate of extremes, with very hot summers and very cold winters

(C) a shortage of rain throughout the year, such as an arid region

(D) very high elevations, such as in mountain ranges

(E) a combination of climate and physical features that result in crops growing very slowly

6. What is the main reason that female farmers in periphery countries are not as productive as male farmers?

(A) Gender inequalities prevent female farmers from access to the same resources as male farmers.

(B) Male farmers have more farming experience and their farming knowledge is passed down from fathers to sons.

(C) Men have a greater natural talent (aptitude) for farming.

(D) Farming is a physically demanding activity and males are stronger.

(E) Women in periphery countries consider farming as a hobby and just practice it in their spare time.

Question 7 refers to the following graph.

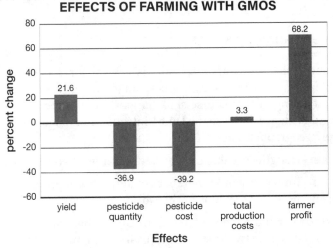

EFFECTS OF FARMING WITH GMOS

Source: Science in the News

7. What does the graph indicate about the effects of farming with genetically modified crops?

   (A) The use of both pesticides and fertilizer drop significantly.

   (B) Farm revenue goes up but production costs go up more.

   (C) Yields increase and farm profits increase even more.

   (D) Total production costs drop because pesticide costs decrease.

   (E) Farm profits go up due to increased prices internationally.

FREE-RESPONSE QUESTION

There have been many changes in the production, distribution, and marketing of food over the past few decades.

   (A) Explain why farmers using GMOs often use less insecticides and pesticides than farmers growing traditional crops.

   (B) Explain why some people consider supporting the local-food movement to be more environmentally friendly than purchasing food from a large grocery chain.

   (C) In order to increase profits some farmers are relying on value-added farming. Identify an example of value-added farming.

   (D) Describe how community-supported agriculture typically works.

   (E) Describe TWO differences between a coffee plantation and a fair-trade coffee farm.

   (F) Compare the food purchasing options available to people living in a food desert and a suburban area of a city.

UNIT 5 REVIEW:
Connecting Course Skills and Content

APPLYING GEOGRAPHIC SKILLS

Applying and utilizing geographic skills is critical for success on the AP® Exam. For each skill listed, write a one-paragraph response that illustrates your understanding of that course skill. Support your response with specific examples and evidence. Refer to the Unit 1 introduction (pages 3–8) for tips on how to apply geographic skills.

1E Explain strengths, weaknesses, and limitations of von Thünen's Model.

2D Explain similarities and differences of agricultural processes in the core and periphery regions of the world.

3B Use one map and one data table from Unit 5 that contains quantitative data and describe two spatial patterns for each map and table.

4C Choose one of the sets image in Topic 5.10 (western Brazil or the Aral Sea) and explain a pattern and change within the images. Also, explain a reason for and an impact of the pattern or change.

5C Compare how large-scale global food production is different than small-scale subsistence farming. Describe one way the two systems can interact on a local scale.

WRITE AS A GEOGRAPHER: *USE RELEVANT INFORMATION*

One problem students face when answering a free-response question is to decide what information actually supports their claim. Students should leave out all other information that is not clearly, directly related to the question. For example, a free-response question might ask: Explain how farmers in Mexico make decisions about what crops to grow.

Which of the following statements are relevant to answering this question? For ones that are not, explain why they are not.

1. Most of southern Mexico has a warm, moist climate that supports growing many fruits and vegetables.

2. Brazil has areas of heavy rainfall that are excellent for growing sugar and rice.

3. Improvements in the ports in New Orleans and on the Florida coast reduced the cost of importing goods.

4. Concerns about the long-term effects of soil erosion and fertilizer runoff have persuaded some farmers to consider changing the crops they grow.

5. Von Thünen's model can be used to study decisions by farmers.

6. The primary language spoken throughout Mexico is Spanish.

UNIT 6

Cities and Urban Land-Use Patterns and Processes

Unit Overview

Cities and the suburbs around them are constantly changing—in how they are laid out, how they work, and how large they are. One of the most basic questions geographers study is why people move into, within, or out of various parts of urban areas.

Models of Urban Areas

Geographers create models to show the distribution and size of cities. They identify patterns that help explain why cities grow to various sizes and how people in different cities are connected to each other. Other models help geographers analyze how cities are organized and develop. Cities generally have zones for commerce, housing, and other functions.

Urban Landscapes and Urban Challenges

People express their attitudes and values through the landscapes they build and how they organize social spaces. The choices people make, such as how closely they live to others and where to build an airport, reflect what they consider important.

Large concentrations of people can produce both great opportunities for progress and great challenges. Some challenges result from decline, such as the movement of industry out of cities. Others result from sustainability, such as how to keep air and water clean.

ENDURING UNDERSTANDINGS

(PSO-6)   The presence and growth of cities vary across geographical locations because of physical geography and resources.

(IMP-6)   The attitudes and values of a population, as well as the balance of power within that population, are reflected in the built landscape.

(SPS-6)   Urban areas face unique economic, political, cultural, and environmental challenges.

Source: *AP® Human Geography Course and Exam Description.* Effective Fall 2020. (College Board).

CHAPTER 15

Origin, Distribution, and Systems of Cities

Topics 6.1–6.4

Topic 6.1 The Origin and Influences of Urbanization

Learning Objective: Explain the processes that initiate and drive urbanization and suburbanization. (PSO-6.A)

Topic 6.2 Cities Across the World

Learning Objective: Explain the processes that initiate and drive urbanization and suburbanization. (PSO-6.A)

Topic 6.3 Cities and Globalization

Learning Objective: Explain how cities embody processes of globalization. (PSO-6.B)

Topic 6.4 The Size and Distribution of Cities

Learning Objective: Identify the different urban concepts such as hierarchy, interdependence, relative size, and spacing that are useful for explaining the distribution, size, and interaction of cities. (PSO-6.C)

Cities are extremely local and intimate places.... At the same time they are the product of complex interactions with other places near and far away.

—David Lanegran, *The Introductory Reader in Human Geography*

Source: David Palmer

Cities develop and change over time as illustrated by the contrast of the historic core and contemporary skyscrapers of London. (See topic 5.1 for factors that influence how cities develop.)

The Origin and Influence of Urbanization

Essential Question: What are the processes that initiate and drive urbanization?

The permanently inhabited portion of the earth's surface—what the classical Greeks called the **ecumene**—is a variety of community types with a range of population densities. As humans increasingly settled in permanent locations, classifications of settlements emerged:

- **Rural** areas (farms and villages) with low concentrations of people
- **Urban** areas (cities) with high concentrations of people
- **Suburbs** that are primarily residential areas near cities

Factors Driving Urbanization

A **settlement** is a place with a permanent human population. The first agricultural settlements appeared around 12,000 years ago. Before that, people survived by hunting and gathering, so they lived in temporary or movable shelters. The first permanent settlements were small enough that the inhabitants could all farm and subsist on the surrounding fields. Over time, in several places around the world, small agricultural settlements began to develop characteristics that made them the first true urban settlements, or cities:

- the presence of an agricultural surplus
- the rise of social stratification and a leadership class or urban elite
- the beginning of job specialization

A food surplus became available as irrigation, farming, and domestication of animals and plants developed. These changes enabled increasing numbers of people to live in the same location. A ruling class emerged to control the products that were accumulated and the people living in the community. Because not everyone was needed to produce food, some people specialized in making things, such as tools, weapons, and art. Others specialized as accountants or religious leaders—the first members of a service sector. As a result, cities developed as economic centers of services, manufacturing, and trade.

Urbanization

The process of developing towns and cities is known as **urbanization**, an ongoing process that does not end once a city is formed. Urbanization also involves the causes and effects of existing cities' growth. Describing a region as urbanized indicates that cities are present there. A common statistic associated with regions, countries, and even continents is **percent urban**—an indicator of the proportion of the population that lives in cities and towns as compared to those that live in rural areas.

Urbanization is one of the most important phenomena of the 19th and 20th centuries, and geographers continue to study its development. Today, more than 50 percent of the world's population lives in cities. Demographers estimate that by the year 2030, 60 percent will live in cities, and nearly 70 percent by 2050. Most of those people will be in the less-developed countries (LDCs) of the world's periphery and semiperiphery. While urbanization can be positive for both individuals and societies, the challenges may be overwhelming if a city is not prepared to grow or if urbanization occurs too rapidly.

Influence of Site and Situation on Cities

The location of where cities develop is a critical aspect of urban geography. The concepts of site and situation, introduced in Topic 1.4, play a key role in explaining this process. **Site** describes the characteristics at the immediate location—for example, physical features, climate, labor force, and human structures. In contrast, **situation** refers to the location of a place relative to its surroundings and its connectivity to other places. Examples would include near a gold mine, on the coast, or by the railroad. Important factors of site and situation today are different than past cities.

The site and situation of a city influences its function. Specialized functions of cities include defense, religion, trade, education, finance, transportation, government, manufacturing, retirement, entertainment, residential housing, or service centers. Larger cities often have multiple functions. Cities near natural ports, such as Boston or New York City, started as centers of trade but provide multiple functions today.

Early City-States

Historically, a **city-state** consisted of an urban center (the city) and its surrounding territory and agricultural villages. A city-state had its own political system and functioned independently from other city-states. The population in the surrounding villages and territory received services and protection from the urban center. These communities were often raided by other groups for their wealth. As a result, defense was a primary consideration, and military leaders evolved into political rulers, or kings.

Early city-states emerged in several locations around the globe in an **urban hearth**, or area generally associated with defensible sites and river valleys in which seasonal floods and fertile soils allowed for an agricultural surplus:

- the Tigris-Euphrates Valley (Mesopotamia) in modern Iraq
- the Nile River Valley and Nile Delta in modern Egypt
- the Indus River Valley in modern Pakistan
- the Huang-He floodplain in modern China

Other urban centers also emerged in Mesoamerica (in modern Mexico) and in the Andean region of South America.

Examples of city-states through history include those of Classical Greece (Athens, Sparta, Corinth), those of the Middle Ages in Europe, and Venice and Italian city-states during the Renaissance. Monaco, a city-state located entirely within the boundaries of Italy, has endured to modern times. Vatican City and Singapore are also modern city-states, though they did not evolve from previous agricultural settlements, but from religious influence. City-states eventually coalesced to form early states and empires. The ancient Babylonian Empire grew from the original city-state of Babylon.

Centers for Services

As cities grew, more people developed specialized skills other than producing food. This changed the relationship between cities and the areas around them. City residents depended on farmers for food. In return, people in cities focused on supplying services for their inhabitants and the inhabitants of surrounding regions.

Early cities often specialized in particular services. Some emerged as administrative centers from which the elite ruled. Others, often associated with important shrines, became religious centers. Defensive strongholds, university towns, and centers of specialized production—located at resource sites—also emerged.

Defining Cities

Most definitions of a city describe a place with a relatively high concentration of people. Cities are places where people come together to build a nucleated, or clustered, settlement. An **urban area** is usually defined as a central city plus land developed for commercial, industrial, or residential purposes, and includes the surrounding suburbs.

Legal Definition of a City

Definitions of what constitutes a city vary greatly, but the easiest way to define a **city** is a higher-density area with territory inside officially recognized political boundaries. This definition is useful for determining the precise population, taxing residents, providing services, and establishing and enforcing laws. Most large cities today, as defined legally, share boundaries with adjacent cities, yet those boundaries are visible only on a map. On the ground, people leaving one city might have no idea they were entering another legal city.

Metropolitan Areas

A collection of adjacent cities economically connected, across which population density is high and continuous is a **metropolitan area**, sometimes called a **metro area**. Most large cities in the world today are really metro areas of a series of legally defined cities, but they are referred to using only the name of the largest city. For example, the metro area of Denver, Colorado, consists of the cities of Denver, Aurora, Lakewood, Englewood, Greenwood Village, and other neighboring, legally defined cities.

In the United States, the term **metropolitan statistical area** (MSA) is another way to define a city. An MSA consists of a city of at least 50,000 people, the county in which it is located, and adjacent counties that have a high degree of social and economic integration, or connection, with the urban core. Similarly, **micropolitan statistical areas** are cities of more than 10,000 inhabitants (but less than 50,000), the county in which they are located, and surrounding counties with a high degree of integration. Note that this designation is really one in which a city is defined as a **nodal region**, or focal point in a matrix of connections.

Morphology, or physical characteristics, such as the buildings, streets, public places, and home, can also describe an urban area:

- The built-up area is where the landscape has a high concentration of people and structures.

- The places where built-up areas begin to give way to open spaces and underdeveloped areas are the outskirts of the city.

- This end of the continuously built-up area is often considered an urban border, whether or not it coincides with a legally defined city boundary.

THE DENVER METROPOLITAN AREA

- ● Major City in the Denver Metro Area
- ▨ Denver
- ▨ Denver-Aurora-Broomfield Metropolitan Statistical Area

The shaded-lined area shows the metro area of Denver and includes several cities. Investigate a map of your city (or a large city near you) and attempt to define its metro area and see how it differs from the MSA.

Population Characteristics

People are drawn to urban areas often from rural areas, other regions, or other countries, looking for jobs and opportunities. For these reasons, **social heterogeneity** is particularly high in cities, meaning that the population of cities, as compared to other areas, contains a greater variety of people. Diversity in cultural interests, sexual orientations, languages spoken, professional pursuits, and other characteristics are present in cities to a much larger degree than in small towns or rural areas.

Immigration One reason cities are diverse is because they are centers of immigration. For example, in several large cities around the world, 40 percent or more of the population is foreign born. Among these are Miami and San Jose in the United States, Toronto and Vancouver in Canada, and Sydney and Melbourne in Australia.

Diversity Because of the higher population density and the relative anonymity of cities, urban residents are generally more accustomed to diversity than are people in non-urban areas. Walking through the streets of cities such as New York, London, or Amsterdam, one can see signs in numerous languages, restaurants that serve food from around the world, and buildings representing many religious traditions. Such diversity is less common in more sparsely populated areas.

One result of this diversity in cities is that it leads to more diversity. Cities have always attracted individuals with less common cultures, interests, or ways of life. They are more likely to find people whom they share traits with in cities.

Transportation and Communication

Improvements in transportation and communication have aided the growth of cities in size and number. Urban areas have expanded as trains, buses, and cars have enabled people to move farther from the center of the city, but still visit or work in the city. That change illustrates how **time-space compression** (see Topic 1.4), in the form of transportation improvements, has led to urban growth. The development of the Internet—to transport ideas rather than people—has allowed more and more people to work from home, which has increased the distance people can live from the center of a city.

Borchert's Transportation Model

Geographer John Borchert developed **Borchert's transportation model** to describe urban growth based on transportation technology. Each new form of technology produced a new system that changed how people moved themselves and goods in and between urban areas. He divided urban history into four periods, which he called epochs. Each epoch had profound effects on the local scale related to a city's form (shape), size, density, and spatial arrangement. Additionally, transportation had profound impacts on the distribution and connectivity of cities on a regional, national, and global scale. The epochs are shown in the table on the following page.

BORCHERT'S MODEL OF URBAN GROWTH		
Epoch	Time Period	Conditions and Effects
Sail-Wagon	1790–1830	• Water ports became very important. • Poor road conditions made long-distance travel between cities difficult.
Iron Horse	1830–1870	• Steam engines powered boats, which promoted the growth of river cities. • Regional rail networks connected cities. • Rail lines connected resources and industrial sites.
Steel Rail	1870–1920	• Transcontinental railways emerged. • Cities emerged along rail lines in the interior of continents.
Auto-Air-Amenity	1920–1970	• Cars allowed cities to spread out. • Airport hubs emerged. • Cities became far more interconnected.

While Borchert's model ends in 1970, it could be expanded. Since 1970, some cities have encouraged mass transit (rail lines), biking (separate bike lanes on roads and new bike paths), and walking (car-free areas in cities). Additionally, the expansion and importance of jet air travel is not fully captured in the model.

Transportation's Impact on Cities

Changes in transportation infrastructure within cities has also had important effects on the urban structure. The earliest urban centers were **pedestrian cities**, or cities shaped by the distances people could walk. A horse-and-buggy era allowed for city size to increase as people could move farther from the center and its concentration of services and jobs. Streetcar systems encouraged the movement of the population even farther from the center of a city, and growth became concentrated along the lines of these small urban rail systems. **Streetcar suburbs**, communities that grew up along rail lines, emerged, often creating a pinwheel shaped city.

The advent of the automobile had profound effects on the growth of cities. Using cars and the highways built to facilitate movement, the population of cities spread out over ever-increasing distances from the urban core. The lower density suburbs that emerged around original cities developed as separate legal cities but functioned as part of the metropolitan area focused on the central, or original city. Additionally, with the U.S. interstate highway system, cities connected to highways have situational advantages of accessibility to road networks to transport goods or services more efficiently.

Today, major cities that hope to grow economically must have access to multiple modes of national and international transportation, as well as trade networks with air travel becoming increasingly important. Individual cities will often focus economic development policies to increase connectivity from the local to the global scale. Therefore, transportation methods have profound effects on the growth and shape of cities.

Communication Networks

Changes in communication technology have dramatic impacts on the growth and development of cities. Historically, cities connected to trade routes received information first. However, as telecommunication technology developed—with the telegraph, telephone, cell phones, and the Internet— early adopting cities benefitted.

Cities are nodal regions that require connectivity in order to thrive. New communication technologies diffused hierarchically to large cities first. In the early 2000s, cities that lagged in building new communication infrastructure fell behind cities that were on the cutting edge of technology, like Tokyo, Chicago, London, and New York City. Today, advanced communication networks are essential to attract large corporations, factories, or high-tech companies to an urban area in order to encourage further economic growth. In 2020, according to *U.S. News & World Report*, the city with the best communication network (or *smart city*) was Singapore.

Population Growth and Migration

Rural-to-urban migration is an important concept to understand the growth of cities. Population growth pressure, cultural tension, environmental strain, and lack of economic opportunities create push factors in agricultural communities. Cities promise the hope of economic opportunities and cultural freedoms. Consequently, billions of people have migrated from agricultural regions to urban areas over the past 100 years. People are attracted to more densely populated cities to obtain higher paying jobs and more government services.

Today, the most rapid rural-to-urban migration occurs in periphery and semiperiphery countries of the world, including China, India, and Brazil. The vast majority of this migration pattern occurs domestically, or within the country. For example, millions of people continue to migrate from rural northern and western Brazil to the rapidly expanding cities of Sao Paulo and Rio de Janeiro in southeast Brazil. This rapid growth has stretched resources and created challenges for cities, such as substandard housing, overcrowding, and stressed infrastructure (transportation, sanitation and water systems).

In core countries, such as the United States, rural-to-urban migration has slowed but domestic and international migration to cities in the west and south has increased. The increase is due to the perception of economic opportunity, cost of living, and quality of life in those regions. Urban areas, such as Atlanta, Tampa, and Charlotte in the South; and Denver, Dallas, and Phoenix, in the West, have experienced rapid urban population growth that has created challenges for local communities, governments, and residents. (See Topics 6.10 and 6.11.)

Economic Development and Government Policies

Increasingly, cities are viewed as engines of growth for a country's economy. Consequently, economic and political leaders, at the national and local scale, develop policies to guide and encourage the growth of cities. Cities can have a variety of different functions and economic emphases. Cities in the Midwest of the United States, such as Cleveland, Pittsburgh, and Chicago, were often focused on attracting manufacturing jobs; while cities in Florida, such as Orlando and Tampa, promoted development based on retirement and tourism. Local policies that created economic incentives, such as low-cost loans, lower taxes, or cheap available land, were used to encourage economic development. However, the economic function of a city can change over time. Today, Pittsburgh has changed its economic development policies to attract high-tech industries, such as Google and Uber, to take advantage of the highly educated students graduating from Carnegie Mellon University and the University of Pittsburgh. Within the high-income countries of the world, cities often compete with each other to attract companies and jobs.

Policies at the national scale can also impact the growth and development of cities. In 2014, China implemented the New Urbanization Plan that developed specialized cities and designated the eastern coast of the country for urbanization. The plan used a variety of methods such as tax incentives, land grants, and the creation of a series of connected cities, each with an economic focus. An example would be Shenzhen, a city near Hong Kong where the Chinese government has invested heavily in higher education and the high-tech industry to create a global financial center and its own Silicon Valley.

REFLECT ON THE ESSENTIAL QUESTION

Essential Question: *What are the processes that initiate and drive urbanization?*

Identify the Processes That Initiate and Drive Urbanization	Explain the Processes That Initiate and Drive Urbanization

---

KEY TERMS

ecumene	city-state	nodal region
rural	urban hearth	social heterogeneity
urban	urban area	time-space compression
suburbs	city	Borchert's transportation
settlement	metropolitan area (metro	model
urbanization	area)	pedestrian cities
percent urban	metropolitan statistical area	streetcar suburbs
site	(MSA)	
situation	micropolitan statistical area	

Cities Across the World

Essential Question: What are the processes that initiate and drive urbanization and suburbanization?

The process of urbanization and suburbanization appears differently on the cultural landscape in different regions of the world. In North America after World War II, changes in transportation, demographics, and the economy dramatically changed how cities developed. In the periphery and semi-periphery, rapid population growth of cities has affected how geographers classify and study the urban areas of the world.

Suburbanization

A suburb is a largely residential area adjacent to an urban area. **Suburbanization** involves the process of people moving, usually from cities, to residential areas on the outskirts of cities. There, they form communities that are connected to the city for jobs and services. However, suburbs are often less-densely populated and less-ethnically diverse than inner cities.

Causes of Suburbanization

Several causes contributed to the growing suburbanization in North America after World War II. Among these were economic expansion, greater purchasing power for many families, the growth of a car-centered lifestyle, and the government's construction of a vast system of new highways that allowed workers to commute from their city jobs to suburban homes. In the United States, the Federal Housing Administration provided mortgage loans for families to move to the suburbs, which were newly zoned for single-family housing.

Racial tensions provided another impetus for suburban growth. As African Americans came to the North in search of jobs and better education during and after World War II, many White Americans moved to the suburbs in what became known as "White flight." Continued government investment in suburban growth, along with a lack of investment in inner cities, hastened both urban decline and suburban growth. Industries and jobs left the cities, and residents followed. In addition, highways were sometimes built in locations that uprooted or divided existing urban communities.

Shifting Trends

The process of suburbanization is one effect of urban growth. In the developed world, especially North America, it has been the most prominent change in urban areas since the middle of the 20th century. In 1960, the U.S. population was roughly equally divided with about 60 million people living in each of the three types of areas—urban, suburban, and rural. According to the Pew Institute, in 2016, 55 percent (175 million) of Americans lived in suburban counties, 31 percent (98 million) in urban, and 14 percent (46 million) in rural counties. Suburbs are now the dominant form of residential living in the United States.

As economic and residential activities continue to decentralize into the suburbs, cities spread out horizontally, creating a sprawling landscape. **Sprawl** is the rapid expansion of the spatial extent of a city and occurs for numerous reasons:

- growth of suburbs
- lower land costs in suburbs compared to inner cities
- lower density single family housing
- weak planning laws
- the continuing growth of car culture

In the United States, sprawl is most common in fast-growing areas in the Southeast and West. A specific process that encourages sprawl is **leap-frog development**, where developers purchase land and build communities beyond the periphery of the city's built area. As a result of sprawl, the urban footprint of American cities, such as Atlanta, grew larger than those of more populated cities in other regions of the world. Atlanta now covers over 8,300 square miles and contains 6 million people. In contrast, cities in other parts of the world are much smaller in physical size. For example, Mexico City is 580 square miles but contains over 21 million people, resulting in a much more compact and densely populated city.

New Forms of Land Use

As a result of the suburbanization process, new land-use forms have been created. **Boomburbs,** or boomburgs, are rapidly growing communities (over 10 percent per 10 years), have a total population of over 100,000 people, and are not the largest city in the metro area. This type of community develops differently than a traditional city and usually do not have a dense urban center. Examples include Mesa, Arizona; Plano, Texas; and Riverside, California.

Another new land use is found near key locations along transportation routes that has mini downtowns of hotels, malls, restaurants, and office complexes. Modern geographers have dubbed these **edge cities,** which are nodes of economic activity that have developed in the periphery of large cities. They usually have tall office buildings, a concentration of retail shops, relatively few residences, and are located at the junction of major transportation routes.

While cities are the destination for many of the world's migrants, the counter-flow of urban residents leaving cities is known as **counter-urbanization** or **deurbanization**. Many of these migrants are relocating to **exurbs**, the prosperous residential districts beyond the suburbs. Contributing to exurbanism is the ability of people to work remotely via technology, which removes the need to commute. Other factors include relative affordability of land in these areas and cultural preferences. These *exurbs* tend to have expansive lots and large single-family homes. People who live in these areas want tranquility and privacy while still having connections to an urban center.

Suburbanization has affected rural areas by increasing population density, building homes and businesses on former farmlands, and adding new residents from urban backgrounds to communities. However, suburbanization itself is currently changing in North America, as some suburbanites return to live in the city, in a process called **reurbanization**.

POPULATION CHANGE IN NEW YORK CITY AND ITS SUBURBS

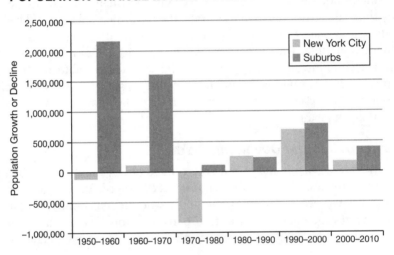

Source: Adapted from Wendell Cox, "The Accelerating Suburbanization of New York." New Geography, 2011.

The graph of city and suburb growth in New York illustrates the massive growth of suburbs after World War II as well as the later process of reurbanization.

Megacities and Metacities

Megacities and metacities are the world's largest cities. **Megacities** have a population of more than 10 million people. Because of the rapid growth of cities in the 21st century a new type of city has emerged—the metacity. **Metacities**, sometimes called hypercities, are defined in two ways:

- continuous urban area with a population greater than 20 million people
- attributes of a network of urban areas that have grown together to form a larger interconnected urban system

These urban giants can spread across political borders and exert an influence that is felt regionally, and even worldwide. This influence is due to the size of their populations, but in other cases, their influence is derived from the city's political, economic, and cultural power. The world's first and largest metacity is Tokyo, Japan, with a current population of over 37 million. New York City is the tenth largest with just over 20 million people. An emerging metacity near Shenzhen, China, is predicted to exceed 120 million people by 2050.

Megalopolis

The term **megalopolis** goes back to the early 1900s and describes a chain of connected cities. It became more common after 1961, when French geographer Jean Gottman used it to describe the continuously developed string of cities from Boston—through New York City, Philadelphia, and Baltimore—to Washington, DC. The "Bos-Wash Corridor" now includes nearly 50 million residents.

These cities had grown until they essentially merged into a single **conurbation**, an uninterrupted urban area made of towns, suburbs, and cities. The cities crossed state boundaries and exceeded the definition of a metropolitan area, which is focused on a single, urban center. Gottman noted that, although legally the major cities remained separate, they and their suburbs had become a single region that had taken on some characteristics of a single, massive city.

Since that time, with urban growth increasing across the planet, other cities have combined into megalopolises. The corridor in California from San Diego through Los Angeles to San Francisco is a single, growing metropolitan corridor on the West Coast of the United States. Tokyo through Yokohama is a megalopolis in Japan.

Urbanization in the Developing World

Megacities were once found at only the centers of large empires or the most powerful countries. However, that pattern has changed. In the past century, megacities have become more common in less-developed countries because of high birth rates and increased rural-to-urban migration. Of the 20 largest urban areas in the world in 2020, 15 were in semiperiphery or periphery countries.

WORLD'S LARGEST URBAN AREAS, 2020

Megacities in relatively poor countries face the same challenges as megacities in wealthy countries, but without as many resources to respond. Social problems between ethnic groups, joblessness, lack of infrastructure, inadequate housing, and environmental problems—such as Mexico City's severe air pollution—are common in all megacities.

REFLECT ON THE ESSENTIAL QUESTION

Essential Question: *What are the processes that initiate and drive urbanization and suburbanization?*

Processes That Influence Urbanization and Suburbanization	Effects of Those Processes

KEY TERMS

suburbanization

sprawl

leap-frog development

boomburbs

edge cities

counter-urbanization (deurbanization)

exurbs

reurbanization

megacities

metacities

megalopolis

conurbation

6.3

Cities and Globalization

Essential Question: How do cities influence the processes of globalization?

Cities are becoming increasingly larger in population and physical size, as well as the economic engine of the global economy. The influence of cities is an important area of study for geographers. An analysis of the influence of urban systems is critical to understand the concepts of world cities and urban hierarchy.

World Cities

The world's largest cities are not always the most influential. Cities such as New York, London, Tokyo, and Paris are **world cities**, or **global cities**, that exert influence far beyond their national boundaries. All are currently media hubs and financial centers with influential stock exchanges, banks, and corporate headquarters. Many are the headquarters of international organizations. For example, New York is home to the United Nations. World cities are the control centers for the global economy where key decisions about products, manufacturing, banking, cultural trends, marketing and information originate.

Researchers rank a city's influence based on its financial power, innovation, academic resources, cultural influence, livability, connectivity, accessibility, and political influence. The top 10 world cities in 2020 according to the Global Power City Index are shown in the map below.

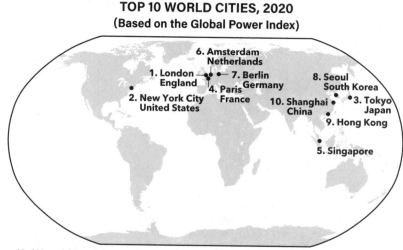

TOP 10 WORLD CITIES, 2020
(Based on the Global Power Index)

6. Amsterdam Netherlands
1. London England
7. Berlin Germany
4. Paris France
8. Seoul South Korea
2. New York City United States
10. Shanghai China
3. Tokyo Japan
9. Hong Kong
5. Singapore

Source: Mori Memorial Foundation

The decisions made by leaders in world cities impact all people, even those in a rural areas or small towns. World cities are the most powerful of all urban centers and drive globalization. These influential cities are very interconnected via transportation and communication networks. Leaders of world cities typically wield political power on a national and international scale that rivals the power of leaders of entire countries.

Connectivity and Urban Hierarchy

Cities at all scales of geography do not function in isolation, rather they are a part of a larger urban system. Systems of cities have an **urban hierarchy,** or ranking, based on influence or population size. (See Topic 6.4.) For a city to be influential, it must have *connectivity*, or be connected to regional, national, and global networks. World cities operate on a global scale but also have connectivity to smaller cities within a country's urban system.

Nodal cities are command centers on a regional and occassionally national level. Cities like Denver, Phoenix, or Minneapolis are not as influential as world cities but possess significant power within a region of the country. These cities will have some corporate headquarters and numerous regional offices for transnational companies, while they also serve as major entertainment, cultural, and economic centers within their regions. In order to maintain global connectivity, these cities have developed road systems, large airports, and advanced communication networks that connect to smaller cities in their regions and to world cities, such as New York, Chicago, or Los Angeles.

Cities specializing in certain functions are another level of the urban hierarchy. Examples include Austin, Texas (government); Las Vegas, Nevada (entertainment); Elkhart, Indiana (manufacturing); and Norfolk, Virginia (military).

REFLECT ON THE ESSENTIAL QUESTION

Essential Question: *How do cities influence the processes of globalization?*

Characteristics of Cities	Global Influence of Characteristic

KEY TERMS

world cities (global cities)	urban hierarchy	nodal cities

The Size and Distribution of Cities

Essential Question: What are the different urban concepts such as hierarchy, interdependence, relative size, and spacing that are useful for explaining the distribution, size, and interaction of cities?

Today, cities range in size from just a few thousand inhabitants to those that have populations of over 20 million, such as Karachi, Pakistan. Often a city exists in an **urban system**—an interdependent set of cities that interact on the regional, national, and global scale. Models have been developed to help explain the distribution, or location, and interaction of these urban systems.

Urban Hierarchy

Systems of cities have an *urban hierarchy* or ranking based on influence or population size. (See Topic 6.3.) On the global scale, world cities are at the top of the hierarchy regarding influence or power. Megacities and metacities are on the top of the urban hierarchy when considering population. On a national or regional scale, the concepts of rank-size rule and primate city are utilized to determine the hierarchy within a country's urban system.

Rank-Size Rule

The **rank-size rule** describes one way in which the sizes of cities within a region may develop. It states that the nth largest city in any region will be $1/n$ the size of the largest city. That is, that the rank of a city within an urban system will predict the size of the city. For example, the third-largest city in a system that exhibits the rank-size distribution would be approximately one-third the size of the largest city.

Geographers consider rank-size distributions to be characteristic of well-developed regions or countries. Such distributions are also more common where federal governments typically share power with other levels of government. A rank-size distribution includes cities of all sizes in the system. This implies that there are cities with a wide variety of services available within the system, from very high-order services in the largest cities to lower-order services in the smaller cities. **Higher-order services** are usually expensive, need a large number of people to support, and are only occasionally utilized. Examples include major sports teams, large malls, luxury car dealerships, and large specialized research hospitals. **Lower-order services** are usually less expensive than higher-order services, require a small population to support, and are used on a daily or weekly basis. Examples include gas stations, local grocery stores, or small restaurants.

As a general rule, geographers consider rank-size distribution to be an indicator of an urban system that can efficiently provide needed services to its population. Countries that demonstrate the rank-size rule include the United States, Canada, Australia, and India. The model is not exact and applies better to some countries than others. Limitations of the model are that it does not explain the distribution of cities nor does it take into account the distance or interactions between cities. Problems can arise when comparing city systems in multiple countries because places define cities differently. In general, the model works better when using metropolitan area population.

Primate Cities

If the largest city in an urban system is more than twice as large as the next largest city, the largest city is said to have primacy, or be a **primate city**. A primate city is more developed than other cities in the system, and consequently, disproportionately more powerful. Primate cities are the social, political, and economic hub for the system and offer a wider range of services than do the many smaller cities. In primate city urban systems, medium sized cities are often not present. In addition, countries that follow a unitary form of government, or extremely strong central government, often follow a primate city model.

The United Kingdom exhibits urban primacy. London is by far the largest city in the country. However, the relatively small size of the country, its unitary government, and its well-developed transportation infrastructure, all reduce the need for a number of medium-sized cities. In the United Kingdom, people can get to London for higher-order services relatively easily. Northern Scotland is less than a two-hour flight from London.

Mexico illustrates a different model for a country with a primate city. Mexico City provides many services that are not as easily available to portions of the population. Across large portions of northern Mexico, people would have to travel great distances to receive even mid-level services due to the lack of medium-sized cities. Because of Mexico City's primacy, people often migrate to the city in search of economic opportunity and greater services.

Trait	United Kingdom	Mexico
TWO PRIMATE CITIES: LONDON AND MEXICO CITY		
Largest urban area: Population	London: 14.0 million	Mexico City: 21.2 million
Second largest urban area: Population	Manchester: 2.6 million	Guadalajara: 4.3 million
Distance from primate city to farthest edge of country	675 miles	1,750 miles
Transportation network (buses, trains, planes)	Excellent	Poor
Population density	660 people/sq. mi.	148 people/sq. mi.

Both the UK and Mexico have primate cities. What evidence in the chart indicates the existence of a primate city? What influence does Mexico's transportation network have on people's ability to acquire services?

Gravity Model Interactions

The **gravity model** states that larger and closer places will have more interactions than places that are smaller and farther from each other. This model can be used to predict the flow of workers, shoppers, vacationers, migrants, information, mail, products, economic activity, and nearly any other flow between cities. The model holds that there are more numerous flows to bigger cities and between nearer cities. Assumptions of this model include locations with no barriers, which is also considered a limitation. Other limitations with the model include not accounting for how political (borders), physical (walls or rivers), or cultural (language) barriers influence the interactions between cities.

Interactions between cities are complicated by factors beyond size and distance. Cities such as Orlando, Florida, and Las Vegas, Nevada, are tourist destinations that attract far more visitors than their size and their distance from other cities alone could predict. Similarly, religious sites such as Jerusalem and Mecca, government centers such as Washington, DC, and various cultural destinations distort effects predicted by the gravity model. However, the basic theory applies to most places.

Central Place Theory

In 1933, Walter Christaller, a German geographer, proposed the **central place theory** to explain the distribution of cities of different sizes across a region. The model used consumer behavior related to purchasing goods and services to explain the distribution of settlements. Christaller defined a **central place** as a location where people go to receive goods and services. It might be a tiny community, such as a hamlet, with only lower-order services, such as a convenience store, post office, and religious center. Or it might be a slightly larger village, town, or small city with more stores and services. Or the central place might be a major city, where one can get lower- and higher-order services, such as direct air flights to other major cities or watch a touring Broadway musical. In Christaller's model, each size of settlement would be evenly distributed across space.

The model accurately concludes that larger cities will be farther spaced from each other than smaller town or villages. This conclusion is evident across multiple locations but particularly when viewing the distribution of cities in the eastern United States. (See North America at night map, page 5.) Large cities like Chicago and Atlanta have a series of medium cities between them that are roughly the same distance from each other.

The Shape of Market Areas

A **market area**, or zone that contains people who will purchase goods or services, surrounds each central place. Higher-order services have larger market areas than lower-order services. Christaller chose to depict these market areas as **hexagonal hinterlands** because this shape was a compromise between a square—in which people living in the corners would be farther from the central place—and a circle—in which there would be overlapping areas of service. Nesting hexagons allowed for central places of different sizes to distribute themselves in a clean pattern across the region.

CHRISTALLER'S CENTRAL PLACE THEORY

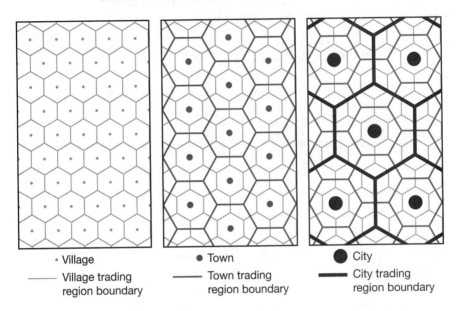

· Village
——— Village trading region boundary

● Town
——— Town trading region boundary

● City
——— City trading region boundary

Threshold and Range

What determines which services will be available in any central place? How far apart should central areas of the same population size be located? Central place theory uses the concepts of threshold and range to answer these questions.

The size of population necessary for any particular service to exist and remain profitable is the **threshold**. Services with a very low threshold, such as a convenience store or a gas station, are present even in very small central places. Restaurants, hospitals, high schools, and department stores have higher thresholds, so they require a larger population within the market area to survive economically. Only in the largest market areas can services appear that depend on the support of huge populations—stock market exchanges, major sports teams, symphony orchestras, and elite research centers. As cities grow in size, the number and variety of available services increase with the population.

The distance people will travel to obtain specific goods or services is **range**. People will travel very far for higher-order services such as wedding rings and heart transplants, but they are less likely to travel very far for basic services such as fast food or toothpaste. This helps explain why fast-food restaurants can be found in nearly any town but a shop dealing in diamond jewelry would be found only in larger cities.

Limitation of Central Place Theory

A limitation of the model is that it assumes a flat, featureless plain. It does not take into account the effects of natural landscapes of rivers, mountains, or other barriers on the distribution of cities. Nor does it consider the influence of transportation systems (rail, road, water, and air) and how the availability of those types of transportation can expand the market area.

REFLECT ON THE ESSENTIAL QUESTION

Essential Question: *What are the different urban concepts such as hierarchy, inter-dependence, relative size, and spacing that are useful for explaining the distribution, size, and interaction of cities?*

Urban Concepts	Application of Concepts for Cities

KEY TERMS

urban system	central place theory
rank-size rule	central place
higher-order services	market area
lower-order services	hexagonal hinterlands
primate city	threshold
gravity model	range

A century ago, approximately 10 percent of the world's population lived in cities. By 2008, the world passed a milestone: more than half the populace was urban. While urbanization and suburbanization continue to expand in more-developed countries (North America and Europe), the pace remains slow and steady.

American Cities

In the United States, as millennials have started families, they have relocated out of central cities into enclaves inspired by new urbanist designs. These "urban burbs" offer walkable streets, local markets, public transit, and less-expensive accommodations than central business districts (CBDs). In the future, self-driving cars and other new technology could reduce the friction of distance. If so, edge cities and exurbs will likely expand.

Experts predict that immigration will likely continue, making the population more diverse. Voluntary segregation will likely continue, and the number of ethnic neighborhoods will flourish.

Megacities in Asia and Africa

The megacities of the less-developed countries of Asia and Africa will likely get even larger. The economic, social, and educational opportunities these cities offer will continue to pull in migration from rural areas. However, if growth exceeds carrying capacity, the standard of living will deteriorate. In addition, the increasingly dense concentration of people will increase the impacts of deadly epidemics, natural disasters, environmental changes, immense pollution, criminal networks, terrorist activity, and civil unrest.

These megacities are already home to more than one-billion squatters, and many people breathe unhealthy air and lack access to safe drinking water. Without dramatic economic and political changes, these problems seem likely to worsen. However, efforts to address these problems have had some success, which suggests that megacities may become more livable in the future.

1. Describe TWO ways that you think U.S. cities will change over the next 20 years.
2. Describe TWO challenges that megacities in Asia and Africa could face in the future.

THINK AS A GEOGRAPHER: *COMPARING METROPOLITAN REGIONS*

Comparing similar places, regions, or trends is one way to highlight significant elements in phenomena. For example, comparing the size of the largest cities on Earth suggests patterns in urban developments. Over the past 12,000 years, the size of the largest cities in the world has generally increased. The first cities to reach a population of 100,000 were probably in Iraq around 2000 B.C.E. By the beginning of the Common Era, several cities were approaching or had passed 1 million residents. Sometime in the late 1800s, London probably exceeded 5 million residents. Today, more than 30 urban areas, which include several neighboring cities, have more than 10 million residents.

POPULATION OF WORLD'S LARGEST URBAN AREAS, 2020		
City	**Entire Urban Area**	**Main City Only**
Tokyo, Japan	37 million	9 million
New Delhi, India	29 million	11 million
Shanghai, China	26 million	18 million
Mexico City, Mexico	22 million	9 million
Sao Paulo, Brazil	22 million	12 million
Mumbai, India	21 million	12 million
Osaka, Japan	20 million	9 million
Beijing, China	20 million	12 million
New York, United States	20 million	8 million
Cairo, Egypt	18 million	7 million

1. Based on the data for these ten urban areas, which region of the world has the most megacities?

2. Seven of the ten largest urban areas are in periphery and semiperiphery countries. Explain two factors that contributed to the growth of megacities in these countries.

3. Estimate the typical ratio between the relationship in size between the entire urban areas and the main cities alone. What factors of political or physical geography might explain the variations in ratios?

CHAPTER 15 REVIEW:
Origin, Distribution, and Systems of Cities

Topics 6.1–6.4

MULTIPLE-CHOICE QUESTIONS

Question 1 refers to the following chart.

BORCHERT'S MODEL OF URBAN GROWTH		
Epoch	**Time Period**	**Conditions and effects**
Sail-Wagon	1790–1830	• Water ports became very important. • Poor road conditions made long-distance travel between cities difficult.
Iron Horse	1830–1870	• Steam engines powered boats, which promoted the growth of river cities. • Regional rail networks connected cities. • Rail lines connected resources and industrial sites.
Steel Rail	1870–1920	• Transcontinental rail emerged. • Cities emerged along rail lines in the interior of continents.
Auto-Air-Amenity	1920–1970	• Automobiles allowed great expansion of city size. • Airport hubs expanded. • Cities became far more interconnected.

1. Which generalization does the chart above support?

   (A) Each new form of transportation technology slowed urban growth by leading to suburbanization, reurbanization, and exurbanization.

   (B) Some new forms of transportation technology slowed urban growth in peripheral countries and other factors slowed it down.

   (C) Each new form of transportation technology spurred urban growth by allowing more people to live and work in the central city.

   (D) Each new form of transportation technology spurred urban growth by producing a new system for moving people and goods.

   (E) Some new forms of transportation technology spurred urban growth and other factors slowed it down.

2. The term "percent urban" means the

(A) population of people living in a city

(B) ratio of people living in cities compared to rural areas

(C) percent of people who work in cities

(D) amount of land devoted to buildings versus green areas

(E) number of cities in a given area

3. Singapore is an example of a modern city-state because it

(A) is a city and surrounding territory with its own independent government

(B) has survived for centuries in an important trading center

(C) has historical connections to the Italian city-states of the Renaissance

(D) is located entirely within the boundaries of the independent nation of Malaysia

(E) is a self-governing city that has never fully gained independence from the British

4. Which statement most accurately describes the urban hearths where the first city-states developed?

(A) Any urban center and its surrounding territory and fertile agricultural lands.

(B) A location that was a service center, producing tools, dwellings, and weapons.

(C) A river valley where floods and fertile soil aided production of an agricultural surplus.

(D) A location where a city-state has endured to the present, such as Monaco and Vatican City.

(E) A city-state in the Tigris-Euphrates Valley, Mesoamerica, or the Andes of South America.

5. Which term most accurately describes a city with a population of approximately 60,500 in 2016 that was strongly integrated with its adjacent counties, socially and economically?

(A) Metropolitan area

(B) Metropolitan statistical area

(C) Micropolitan statistical area

(D) Primate city

(E) Suburban area

Question 6 refers to the following chart.

LARGEST CITIES IN OHIO		
City	Population	Population (rounded)
Columbus	787,033	800,000
Cleveland	396,815	400,000
Cincinnati	296,943	300,000
Toledo	287,208	300,000
Akron	199,110	200,000
Dayton	141,527	150,000
Parma	81,601	100,000
Canton	73,007	100,000

6. Which concept is most clearly demonstrated by the population information shown in the chart?

   (A) Primate city

   (B) Rank-size rule

   (C) Central place theory

   (D) Forward thrust capital

   (E) Unitary state

7. Which feature would most distort the predictions of the gravity model of flow and interaction among urban areas?

   (A) St. Peter's Cathedral in New York City

   (B) The Mississippi River shore in St. Louis, Missouri

   (C) Lake Michigan in Chicago, Illinois

   (D) Raleigh, the capital city of North Carolina

   (E) Disney World in Orlando, Florida

1. The geography of urban areas around the world is rapidly changing. Megacities and world cities are a way of clarifying different types of cities today.

LARGEST METACITIES IN THE WORLD, 2018	
City	Population
Tokyo, Japan	37 million
New Delhi, India	29 million
Shanghai, China	26 million
Mexico City, Mexico	22 million
Sao Paulo, Brazil	22 million

TOP 5 WORLD CITIES, 2018
London, United Kingdom
New York City, United States
Tokyo, Japan
Paris, France
Singapore

(A) Define a metacity.

(B) Explain the concept of world city using either economic or political characteristics.

(C) Using the tables, compare the distribution of metacities to world cities.

(D) Choose ONE of the world cities from the table and explain an economic reason why the city has become such a powerful city.

(E) Choose ONE of the metacities from the table and explain either an environmental or social problem it faces.

(F) Explain ONE political or social reason why suburbanization has occurred so prevalently in United States cities since the 1950s.

(G) Describe the role that transportation has played in the suburbanization of United States cities since the 1950s.

CHAPTER 16

Urban Structure

Topics 6.5–6.7

Topic 6.5 The Internal Structure of Cities
Learning Objective: Explain the internal structure of cities using various models and theories. (PSO-6.D)

Topic 6.6 Density and Land Use
Learning Objective: Explain how low-, medium-, and high-density housing characteristics represent different patterns of residential land use. (IMP-6.A)

Topic 6.7 Infrastructure
Learning Objective: Explain how a city's infrastructure relates to local politics, society, and the environment. (IMP-6.B)

Like a piece of architecture, the city is a construction in space, but one of vast scale.

—Kevin Lynch, *The Image of the City*, 1960

Peripheral areas of cities in southeastern Brazil exhibit many of the visible landscape elements typical of favelas—steep slope, dense population, and poor construction. (See Topic 6.5 for more on the structure of cities around the world.)

The Internal Structure of Cities

Essential Question: How do various models and theories explain the internal structure of cities?

Cities are enormously complex and important centers for much of the world's population. Since cities first emerged in human civilization, they have been centers of economic, political, and cultural power. They have been places of innovation. Cities are growing faster today than ever before in history and that trend is projected to continue.

Urban Models

Like most other models used by geographers, urban models are based on observations of real places. Though models vary, all models share certain functions:

- classifying and categorizing land use in urban areas
- describing how various urban land uses are segregated spatially
- offering explanations for the location of different urban land uses

Urban Zones

One principle underlying all urban models is **functional zonation**, the idea that portions of an urban area—regions, or zones, within the city—have specific and distinct purposes. The various zones fit together like a puzzle to create the entirety of the city. However, unlike a puzzle, the pieces of a city are not clearly delineated, and geographers have tried to identify and classify them with models. The resulting urban models provide geographers with a framework to describe, understand, and analyze cities. Urban areas around the world share three basic zones: the central business district, industrial/commercial, and residential.

Central Business District A vital part of any urban model is the **central business district (CBD)**, which is the commercial heart of a city. Often located near the physical center of a city, or the crossroads where the city was founded, the CBD is the focus of transportation and services. The **bid-rent theory** explains agricultural land use, just as it helps explain land use in central business districts. This theory explains that land in the center of a city will have higher value than land farther away from the city's center. Therefore, land use will be more intense and costs will be higher closer to the CBD. This means high-order services often dominate the CBD.

BID-RENT THEORY FOR CENTRAL BUSINESS DISTRICTS

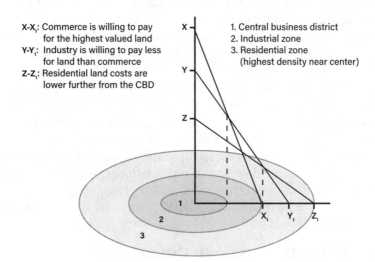

X-X$_1$: Commerce is willing to pay for the highest valued land
Y-Y$_1$: Industry is willing to pay less for land than commerce
Z-Z$_1$: Residential land costs are lower further from the CBD

1. Central business district
2. Industrial zone
3. Residential zone (highest density near center)

Competition for valuable space in the CBD gives it certain characteristics:

- In some countries, including the United States and Canada, the CBD has skyscrapers and "underground cities" that might include facilities for parking, shopping, and rapid transit.

- In Europe, many CBDs are located in the historic heart of the city where buildings are shorter but services are still concentrated.

- Because the cost of land is high in CBDs, manufacturing activities are rarely located there.

- High costs and limited space often result in residential portions of CBDs having high-density housing, such as high-rise apartment buildings.

The cultural landscape Chicago's CBD is characterized by high rise office buildings, with few examples of residential life— single-family homes, parks, grocery stores, or schools.

Industrial/Commercial Zone The zone outside the central business district is dedicated to industry. These industrial zones may include manufacturing, warehousing, and transportation. Industrial zones are generally separated from residential areas because they are associated with air and noise pollution.

Commercial areas with lower-order services and less-intensive land use are also found outside the CBD. Law firms might locate in the CBD, but department stores usually prefer commercial shopping zone with land values.

Several factors influence the choice of locations for businesses within the commercial zone. First, the land is zoned for commercial use so they are legally allowed there. Second, some industries have a **commensal relationship**, which is when commercial interests benefit each other. For example, restaurants and theaters benefit by being in the same zone, as do clothing stores and shoe stores.

Residential Zone All cities have **residential zones,** areas where people live. These are generally separate from the CBD and industrial zones either legally—through government zoning—or simply by the choices of inhabitants.

The different residential zones are distinct from one another. They may be segregated by density, income level, ethnic group, religion and culture, social status, or other characteristics. Which characteristic distinguishes the residential zones depends on the world region where the city is located.

Models of North American Cities

Three models describe typical urban areas in North America—the concentric zone model, sector model, and multiple-nuclei model. These "classic models" were based on the city of Chicago. It was a good place to examine urban structure without the complications caused by irregular topography.

Concentric Zones

The **concentric zone model** describes a city as a series of rings that surrounds a central business district. It is known as the Burgess model because sociologist E. W. Burgess proposed it in the 1920s. The first ring surrounding the CBD is a transition zone that mixes industrial uses with low-cost housing. Manufacturing benefits from proximity to the city-center workers and affordable land. Housing in this zone is often high-density, consisting of older, subdivided homes.

The next three rings are residential. Moving outward, one is for working-class housing, then one of more expensive housing, and finally, one of larger homes on the edge of the city and in the suburbs. With greater distance from the CBD, land is more plentiful and affordable, so residences are larger and of higher quality, and population densities decrease.

Sectors

In the 1930s, economist Homer Hoyt developed the **sector model,** also called **Hoyt's model**. While Burgess used land-use rings that grew outward from the CBD, Hoyt described how different types of land use and housing were all located near the CBD early in a city's history. Each grew outward as the city expanded, creating wedges, or sectors of land use, rather than rings.

Hoyt's model describes sectors of land use for low-, medium-, and high-income housing. The model locates the sectors for the low-income, lower-quality housing next to these industrial and transportation zones, and it places high-income residences extending in a wedge away from these zones along wide tree-lined boulevards or on higher ground. The model also notes a sector for transportation extending from the city's center to the edge. This sector would contain rail, canal, and other transport networks within it. The transportation sector would also favor an adjacent zone of manufacturing.

Multiple Nuclei

Geographers Chauncy Harris and Edward Ullman developed the **Harris and Ullman multiple-nuclei model** by studying changes in cities in the 1940s. This model suggested that functional zonation occurred around multiple centers, or nodes. The characteristics of each node either attracted or repelled certain types of activities. The result was a city that consisted of a patchwork of land uses, each with its own center, or nucleus.

In the multiple-nuclei model, the CBD and related functions continued to exist but were joined by smaller business districts that emerged in the suburbs. A zone of industry could be in a variety of locations, including the traditional CBD or port, or it could move to new outlying locations near an airport or other transportation junction. This industrial zone would attract related industries and an area of higher density housing. A university or a business park might attract nearby restaurants, theaters, and other amenities. As a result, people might create a district of student housing or high-quality homes nearby.

The **peripheral model**, a variant of the multiple-nuclei model, describes suburban neighborhoods surrounding an inner city and served by nodes of commercial activity along a ring road or beltway. This model's name derives from the role of the service nodes with the related suburbs that develop on the periphery of the original city.

URBAN LAND-USE MODELS

Concentric Zone Model

Central business district
Transition zone
Low-cost residential
Moderate-cost residential
Commuters' zone

Sector Model

Central business district
Low-cost residential
Moderate-cost residential
High-cost residential
Industrial
Transportation
Education and recreation

Multiple-Nuclei Model

Central business district
Light manufacturing
Low-cost residential
Moderate-cost residential
High-cost residential
Heavy manufacturing
Outlying business district
Suburban residential
Suburban industrial

Galactic Cities

Beginning in the 1950s, suburban growth in the United States skyrocketed as governments built highways that improved transportation in and out of cities and subsidized home purchase. Based on this process in Detroit, Chauncy Harris developed the **galactic city model.** In it, an original CBD became surrounded by a system of smaller nodes that mimicked its function. As suburbs grew, they took on some CBD functions. At key locations along transportation routes, people created mini-downtowns of hotels, malls, restaurants, and office complexes. Some of these nodes grew large enough to become **edge cities** (see Topic 6.2.), but they left behind a declining inner city.

GALACTIC CITY MODEL

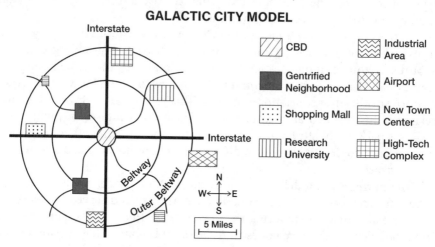

The image above illustrates the geographic distribution of zones in a galactic city.

World-Regional Models

Geographers have also developed models to describe cities outside of North America. Rings, sectors, and multiple-nuclei are found in these models, along with some additional elements. But the models share the same basic characteristic of North American models, that of functional zonation.

European Cities

Many of today's cities in Europe grew out of medieval and pre-industrial cities. City walls, which were built for protection before the wide use of gunpowder weapons, restrained growth. These cities grew slowly and with little planning for centuries. The result is now a dense mix of commercial and residential land use with narrow, winding streets. Distinct land-use zones are difficult to find in the core areas of these cities. Later urban renovations cut through areas to produce elegant, wide boulevards with high-quality housing and shops.

CBDs in Europe differ in important ways from those in North America. Attempting to preserve their historic urban cores, city leaders have limited new construction and restricted the height of buildings. Often, former palace grounds have become large urban parks. European CBDs also have many more

Source: Getty Images

Aerial view of Paris with Eiffel Tower and skyscrapers of La Defense. Paris is a planned city with the historical districts in the center of the city. The newer skyscraper business district is outside the city center.

residents living in relatively low-rise apartment buildings. As a result of the larger population living downtown, commercial uses go beyond those in North America and include many more small businesses such as vegetable markets, bakeries, and butcher shops. The result supports a very walkable lifestyle.

Also in contrast to North America, European suburbs are likely to have a higher percentage of tall buildings. Most are apartment buildings, so population densities are higher in the suburbs of Europe compared to North America. International immigration creates ethnic diversity in the suburbs, and this diversity often reflects the colonial heritage of the country. For example, suburban London includes a large number of South Asians and their descendants, and suburban Paris includes people of North African heritage.

Middle Eastern and Islamic Cities

The spread of Islam shaped many cities in the Middle East, North Africa, and parts of Spain, East Africa, and Southeast Asia. Dominating these cities is a central mosque that includes one or more tall and highly visible minarets, or tall slender towers. The principal **mosque** in the center of an Islamic city is usually surrounded by a complex of structures to serve the public, such as schools and soup kitchens. As cities grew, additional mosques were added in outlying neighborhoods.

Many Islamic cities were built with a defensive **citadel**, a fort designed to protect the city, with its related palace and barracks for soldiers. Walls with gates and towers were typical in earlier times and they, or their remnants, still survive in many modern Islamic cities. Major roads connect the gates of the citadel to the city center. Along these roads are traditional outdoor markets or covered bazaars, called **suqs**. These markets often exhibit spatial differentiation with shops selling luxury items near the center of the city, with bulkier, less-valuable materials for sale near the wall and gates.

Explain the similarities and differences between the market in the photo and a local grocery store or convenience store.

Residential neighborhoods often reflect differences in ethnicity or branch of Islam in their organization and architecture:

- Streets and alleys are usually twisting and often dead-end.
- Homes have central courtyards rather than yards in front or back.
- Windows are small and located above eye level.

The above features create shady areas, which suggests they might be cultural adaptations to the sun and heat of the Middle East. These features also imply that privacy is an important value within Islam.

Latin American Cities

The **Griffin-Ford model** is often used to describe Latin American cities. It places a two-part CBD at the center of the city—a traditional market center adjacent to a modern high-rise center. The most desirable housing in the city is located there, next to the developed center of the city. This high-quality housing extends outward from the urban core, accompanied by a **commercial spine** of development. Theaters, restaurants, parks, and other amenities are also located along this spine, or corridor. The spine ends in a growing secondary center, also called a **mall**.

In contrast to the concentric zone model in North America, as distance increases from the center of Latin American cities, the quality of housing decreases. Public transportation, the urban water supply, and access to electricity all decrease farther away from the center, sometimes disappearing altogether. Often, Latin American cities have a zone of *in situ accretion* that acts as a transitional area between the older areas of the central city and the peripheral outer ring. The outer ring of the city, the **periférico,** shows poverty, lack of infrastructure, and areas of poorly built housing known as **shantytowns**. Often, the residents of shantytowns are recent migrants to the city. The model notes the possible presence of an industrial node closer to the commercial spine.

Many Latin American cities include **favelas**, or **barrios**, which are neighborhoods marked by extreme poverty, homelessness, and lawlessness. Most favelas are in **disamenity zones**, areas not connected to city services and under the control of criminals. They are often in physically unsafe locations, such as on steep, unstable mountain slopes. Structures are poorly constructed, often by the residents themselves, and densely packed together.

African Cities

Large cities were rare in most of Africa until the 19th century, when Europeans colonized the continent. But in recent decades, urban areas in Africa have grown rapidly. New cities have been built next to or on top of existing ones. These new cities can include several identifiable regions:

- The **traditional CBD**, which existed before European colonization, has small shops clustered along narrow, twisting streets. It includes the formal economy—permanent stores with full-time jobs that comply with local regulations and have set wages.

- The **colonial CBD** has broad, straight avenues and large homes, parks, and administrative centers.
- The **informal economy zone** thrives with curbside, car-side, and stall-based businesses that often hire people temporarily and do not follow all regulations. This zone also includes **periodic markets**, where small-scale merchants congregate weekly or yearly to sell their goods.
- A zone of mining and manufacturing is often found in cities.
- Residential zones are often based on ethnicity. These mirror the multi-ethnic makeup of African countries.

The periphery of cities often consists of densely populated **informal settlements**, called **squatter settlements.** They often lack sufficient public services for electricity, water, and sewage. Similar to Latin American favelas, they face problems with drugs, crime, and disease. One of the largest squatter settlements in the world is Kibera, on the western edge of Nairobi, Kenya.

Southeast Asian Cities

The **McGee model** describes the land use of many large cities in Southeast Asia, where the focus of the modern city is often a former colonial port zone. This export-oriented zone shares commercial uses similar to the CBD in North American cities. Additionally, these cities might include a government zone. If the city is a national or regional capital, it might have a commercial zone dominated by foreign merchants and ambassadors. A belt of market gardening often surrounds and supplies these cities.

Cities in Southeast Asia have a history of Chinese immigration and commercial interest that dates back a few centuries. As a result of this immigration, many cities include a secondary commercial zone dominated by Chinese businesses. As the importance of industry in Southeast Asia has risen in the last few decades, industrial parks and regions of manufacturing have emerged on the peripheries of some cities.

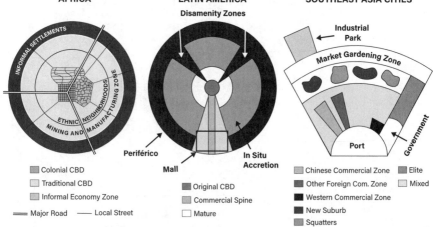

WORLD REGIONAL CITY MODELS

REFLECT ON THE ESSENTIAL QUESTION

Essential Question: *How do various models and theories explain the internal structure of cities?*

Model or Theory	City Structure Within Model

KEY TERMS

functional zones
central business district (CBD)
bid-rent theory
commensal relationshhip
residential zones
concentric zone model
sector model (Hoyt's model)
Harris and Ullman multiple-nuclei model
peripheral model
galactic city model
edge cities
mosque
citadel
suqs

Griffin-Ford model
commercial spine
mall
periférico
shantytowns
favelas (barrios)
disamenity zones
traditional CBD
colonial CBD
informal economy zone
periodic markets
informal settlements
squatter settlements
McGee model

Density and Land Use

Essential Question: How do low-, medium-, and high-density housing characteristics represent different patterns of residential land use?

Residential zones have different population and building densities. These differences can reflect the city's culture, landscape and lifestyle preferences, and social divisions.

Local Regulations on Land Use

Sometimes individuals or groups have conflicts over how to use land in a city. For example, most homeowners want a place that is quiet at night so they can sleep. However, a factory owner might want to continue production, which can be noisy, around the clock. To balance competing desires, cities and counties use **zoning ordinances**, regulations that define how property in specific geographic regions may be used. Local governments use three general zoning categories:

- residential, where people live
- commercial, where people and businesses sell goods and services
- industrial, where businesses make things

Governments use zoning ordinances as a tool of **urban planning**, a process of promoting growth and controlling change in land use. Zoning laws can result in very clear land-use segregation. However, not all cities have zoning ordinances, and most include undeveloped areas yet to be zoned.

Residential Zones

Those areas of a city devoted to where people live rather than to commercial or industrial functions are **residential zones**. Ordinances set limits on the density and size of houses within specific zones. For this reason, some residential neighborhoods contain only large homes and lots, while others are composed of small homes and lots, and still others contain apartment buildings.

Zoning can create various types of neighborhoods that appeal to people with various housing needs and lifestyles. However, it can also be used to prevent socioeconomic diversity or ethnic diversity in a neighborhood.

In North America, residential areas surrounding the CBD are known as the **inner city**. Apartment buildings and townhomes dominate the residential zone, which has the highest population density of the zones. As one moves farther from the inner city, population and housing-unit density declines, and types of housing change. This variation is known as the **residential density gradient**.

Suburbs are often characterized by single-family detached houses. More than half of all Americans now live in suburbs. Many suburbs are noticeably homogenous in terms of housing size and style. However, in recent years, homeowners have been tearing down existing homes and building new ones that are much larger. These new homes, known as McMansions, do not always conform to the style of other homes in the neighborhood.

Source: David Palmer

When homes age or people of higher income move into a neighborhood, older homes may be torn down and replaced. What are the advantages and disadvantages of this process?

Cycles of Residential Zones

Neighborhoods undergo transformations over time as existing residents move out and new ones move in. Through a process known as **filtering**, houses pass from one social group to another. This usually occurs when people with less wealth move into the houses after wealthier residents move. This creates a ripple effect down the social scale. The filtering process might include changing the use of a house. For example, a home built for a single family might be subdivided for use by two or more families or replaced with apartments.

Filtering is most noticeable when an ethnic enclave neighborhood changes to another group. The term **invasion and succession** refers to the process by which one social or ethnic group gradually replaces another through filtering. An important result of filtering is a changing landscape through the process of sequent occupancy. (See Topic 3.2.)

The rise of *gated communities* (see Topic 6.10) is another example of change in suburbs and occasionally in cities. These neighborhoods are planned to control access and promote aesthetics within the community. They are fenced, or walled, with a limited number of streets going in and out. Security guards and cameras are sometimes found at the entrances. The landscaping, housing styles, and other visual elements of the community are strictly regulated.

Many communities today use **urban infill** in suburbs as one way to reduce urban sprawl on the outer edges of the city. Urban infill is the process of increasing the residential density of an area by replacing open space and vacant housing with residences. As land becomes more valuable in a suburb, bid-rent may make it profitable to replace lower-density houses with the large yards of higher density housing, multi-family housing, or even apartments.

Another change involves the availability of businesses. Suburban residents have always been able to find shops for food and necessities in their neighborhoods. In recent decades, there has been an increase in the number and size of businesses in suburbs:

- Strip malls and shopping malls have become common.
- Big-box retail stores have been successful.
- Offices and business services have moved to the suburbs.

All of these changes are part of the **suburbanization of business**, the movement of commerce out of cities to suburbs where rents are cheaper and commutes for employees are shorter. As a result, many cities have faced declines in job opportunities, consumer choices, and services.

Residential Land Use Outside North America

Outside of the United States and Canada, the residential density gradient does not usually run from higher to lower the farther one goes from the CBD. Instead, population density tends to increase in the suburbs even though land is more plentiful. In Europe, as explained earlier, the centers of cities contain many historic structures, and population densities are fairly low. The suburbs on the edges of the central cities contain multistory apartment complexes and have very high population densities.

In Latin America, the peripheral areas of cities may contain suburbs typical of the United States, with single-family houses and lower densities, and also suburbs similar to Europe with high-rise apartments. In addition, very densely settled squatter settlements, or favelas, are where the poorest residents live. Gated communities are increasingly common in Latin America as the region develops. Because of their popularity with wealthy urban elites, these security-minded neighborhoods are emerging in residential areas in all regions of the world today.

REFLECT ON THE ESSENTIAL QUESTION

Essential Question: *How do low-, medium-, and high-density housing characteristics represent different patterns of residential land use?*

Type of Residential Land Use	Characteristics

KEY TERMS

zoning ordinances	inner city	invasion and succession
urban planning	residential density gradient	urban infill
residential zones	filtering	suburbanization of business

Infrastructure

Essential Question: How does a city's infrastructure relate to local politics, society, and the environment?

Critical to the functioning of any city is its **infrastructure**, the facilities and systems that serve the population. The infrastructure of any city has many elements:

- transportation features, such as roads, bridges, parking lots, and signs
- communications features such as cell phone towers, television cables, and Internet service
- distribution systems for water, gas, and electricity
- buildings, such as police stations, courthouses, and fire stations
- collection systems for sewage and garbage
- entertainment venues, such as museums, theaters, and sports facilities
- open spaces, such as public parks and town squares

Building, repairing, and replacing infrastructure is costly and, in a busy urban setting, disruptive to people who live and work there. The infrastructure of older cities around the world is often in poor condition.

Deciding who pays for elements of infrastructure, where they should be built, and what economic and social benefits they offer are usually hotly debated issues. For example, using public resources to build sports stadiums is particularly controversial, and the results are difficult to predict. In Denver, building a baseball stadium for the Colorado Rockies served as an anchor for economic development that helped revitalize a dilapidated area. In Atlanta, building a stadium displaced African American neighborhoods and provided limited economic benefits to the community.

Political Organization and Infrastructure

A city is a political entity. The term **municipal** refers to the local government of a city or town and the services it provides. For example, a mayor and city council make up the core of the municipal government, and the local water supply is the municipal water supply. **Municipality** refers to a local entity that is all under the same jurisdiction. The municipal government is responsible for managing infrastructure at the local scale, although the federal government often subsidizes large expenses.

As cities have grown in the past two centuries, they have expanded in physical size, pushing their boundaries farther from the original core. When these settled areas move beyond the legal boundaries of the city, the inhabitants may be left without political representation or services from the city. The process of adding land to a city's legally defined territory is known as **annexation**. Annexation generally requires a vote by residents in the affected areas.

Sometimes, residents who live beyond the legal boundaries of the city do not desire to become part of the central city. In such cases, residents may choose the option of **incorporation**, the act of legally joining together to form a new city. One reason is that the newly-created municipality is smaller and political representation is more "local" than if the residents had opted for annexation. Often many of these peripheral municipalities are cities only in terms of legal and political considerations. They usually lack a true CBD and continue to function as **bedroom communities**, or commuter suburbs, within the larger metro area.

Some populated regions do not fall within the legal boundary of any city or municipality. These are known as **unincorporated areas**. On a political map, these are the areas between the legal boundaries of cities. Usually a nearby municipality provides their services and administration, through some higher division of civil government such as a county, borough, parish, or province. Over time, people of these areas may consider annexation by an existing city or incorporation as their own city.

Infrastructure and Economic Development

Economic wealth is not evenly distributed across the globe. Some cities are located in wealthier countries and, therefore, can spend more money on developing, maintaining, and improving infrastructure.

Frankfort For example, Frankfurt, Germany, is centrally located in Europe and is within a two-hour flight to most European capitals. The Frankfurt airport provides service to more than 100 countries. Its rail transportation is highly developed with nearly 1,800 trains that move people about the city each day. In addition, telecommunications are an integral part of the city's infrastructure. At the national scale, Frankfurt is considered the most important Internet exchange center in Germany. At the global scale, the city is one of the world's largest and most reliable data transfer sites.

Lagos By comparison, Lagos, Nigeria, with almost 20 million people, is one of the world's most populous megacities. Lagos is a vibrant city with a significant amount of commerce, accompanied by dynamic music, fashion, and film industries.

However, due to extensive unplanned population growth, Lagos faces significant obstacles in the areas of public transportation, utilities, and sanitation. Roads are in severe disrepair, and often become nothing more than pathways of mud when heavy rains occur. The lack of sufficient roads limits the movement of residents and commerce in many parts of the city. While the city of Lagos has planned to improve communication infrastructure, it still lacks much of the technology of more-developed regions.

Infrastructure and Social Development

Urban planning and smart-growth policies are often implemented as urban and suburban populations continue to grow. *Smart-growth policies* (see Topic 6.8) encourage sustainable development economically and socially to increase efficiencies and protect the environment. Many aspects of smart-growth are illustrated in the infrastructure and social development of a city. Creating more walkable areas (both paved and nature trails), bike lanes, and common public spaces encourages a sense of place and community belonging.

Improvements in infrastructure dramatically improve the living conditions in the poorest areas of the world. More indoor plumbing can help improve the sanitation conditions of people in some of the more densely populated cities like Kolkata, India; Port-au-Prince, Haiti; and Nairobi, Kenya. Expanding access to educational opportunities and healthcare, especially for females, helps to strengthen society. People with more educational opportunities tend to have higher earning potential over the course of their lifetimes, which means they are more likely to have the financial resources to meet basic needs such as housing and healthcare.

Transportation and Urban Infrastructure

Running a city is complex and a challenge to all levels of government, especially smaller less-funded municipal governments. Local governments have to provide services that meet the needs of sometimes rapidly growing populations. Governments must build and care for infrastructure, maintain order, and mediate competing interests for the benefit of the entire population.

Public Transportation

The dense population of cities, combined with the high number of suburban residents who commute to central cities for jobs each day, places great demands on the transportation system. The use of large numbers of individual automobiles creates a multifaceted problem:

- environmental—air pollution and excessive use of nonrenewable energy sources
- social—congested roads and long commute times
- economic—valuable real estate used for parking areas and costs associated with car ownership

One solution to moving people around an urban area is **public transportation**—buses, subways, light rail, and trains that are operated by a government agency. Some cities in the United States—such as New York City, Washington, DC, and San Francisco—are known for the success of their mass transit systems. However, few cities have extensive systems and ridership is often low in these cities so fares rarely cover operating costs.When fares increase, passenger numbers decline and the poor, who need public transportation the most, are often not able to use the system.

In contrast, governments in other countries have placed a higher priority on building, maintaining, and promoting the use of public transportation. A much higher percentage of the population of cities in Europe, Latin America, and parts of Asia rely on public transportation. Of the ten most-used urban train systems in the world, only New York City is in the United States. Of the top 50, only New York City and Washington, DC, are in the United States.

Automobiles in Urban Areas

Along with the importance of public transportation, automobile ownership has continued to grow in the 21st century. Collecting data about automobile use and applying it to improve traffic flow is critical to transportation in large cities. The use of this data by cities is an example of applied geography.

Traffic patterns change throughout the day as commuters come into the city in the morning and leave again in the afternoon. Lunch rush hours, weekends, and holiday data is also collected.

Once a city knows when and where the traffic issues are, the primary tool used to encourage efficient flow is the traffic signal. Cameras mounted at intersections and along major transportation arteries allow cities to adjust traffic flows in response to vehicle accidents and weather in real time. Emergency vehicles benefit from the data collected in both setting up signal patterns ahead of time and adjusting them from real-time data collection. A great deal of planning goes into decisions about signal lengths and coordination to keep cars moving efficiently.

REFLECT ON THE ESSENTIAL QUESTION

Essential Question: *How does a city's infrastructure relate to local politics, society, and the environment?*

Element of Infrastructure	Importance to Society

KEY TERMS

infrastructure	incorporation
municipal	bedroom communities
municipality	unincorporated areas
annexation	public transportation

One basic geographic decision that nearly every person makes is where to live. Since they have more money than others, wealthy people have more options. The choices they make reflect what people value in a particular culture. In turn, these choices shape the spatial distribution of public services.

Different Places, Different Choices

In Europe and Canada, wealthy people have traditionally chosen to concentrate in densely-populated central cities. They have always valued having a short commute to their place of work, as well as easy access to concerts, plays, museums, and other forms of entertainment.

In contrast, in the United States, wealthy citizens have been more likely to choose to live in suburbs where population densities are lower. The attractions of spacious homes, large yards, and clean air have outweighed the longer commute to work. Smart-growth approaches have transformed large swaths of sprawled suburbia into lively, walkable, and wealthy neighborhoods.

The Impact of Choices

The distribution of wealth, by area, affects the distribution of political power. The strong core of wealthy residents in central cities in Europe and Canada has created political pressure on governments to provide excellent public transit and other public services to these areas. In U.S. cities, without as many wealthy people, the pressure for those services has been less—but pressure to provide suburban rail lines and freeways has been greater.

Geographers study how changes in work and public policy affect choices about where people live. As more people work at home, they worry less about a long commute to an office. And as more people fly for work, living near an airport becomes a bigger benefit. For these reasons, more wealthy people in Europe and Canada are moving to the suburbs.

At the same time, increasingly strict pollution regulations have cleaned up the air and water in central cities, making them more desirable places to live. Since families are smaller today, the desire for a large house and yard is less important than it once was. For these reasons, in recent decades more wealthy people in the United States are moving downtown, and these areas are increasing their political power.

1. If you just graduated from college and have accepted your first professional job offer in a major metropolitan area, describe where you think the most desirable place to live would be.

2. How do level of education, cultural perceptions, and income level affect a person's choice about where they live?

3. Explain the types of public services each of the following groups of people living in the United States often want in urban areas in which they live:

   - married couple, both recent college graduates, no kids

   - single parent with a teenager, an elementary-age child, and a baby

   - retired couple in good health

	COOK COUNTY, ILLINOIS	MARION COUNTY, INDIANA
Area, in Square Miles	1,635	403
Number of Municipalities	135	1
Major City	Chicago	Indianapolis
Population	5,238,000	939,000
North-South Distance	c. 48 miles	c. 20 miles
East-West Distance	c. 32 miles	c. 20 miles

1. Explain how the different physical shapes of the counties might affect how each county is governed.

2. Describe the borders within each county and what that suggests about the role of county government.

3. How might the difference in population explain the differences in the number of municipalities?

4. How does the number of communities in each county affect how the government operates?

CHAPTER 16 REVIEW:
Urban Structure

Topics 6.5–6.7

MULTIPLE-CHOICE QUESTIONS

Question 1 refers to the photograph below.

1. Which phrase best describes the urban central business district (CBD) shown in the photograph?

   (A) European CBD that mixes low-rise historic buildings with new skyscrapers

   (B) Latin American CBD that mixes traditional markets with modern high-rises

   (C) European suburban CBD with high-rise residential buildings and high population

   (D) African colonial CBD with broad avenues, large homes, and administrative centers

   (E) North American CBD near the city's center, offering commercial space, parking, and transportation

2. Which best provides a general explanation of functional zonation?

   (A) Urban areas pass laws to define how property in specific areas can be used in order to separate commercial and residential spaces.

   (B) A city is made up of a series of rings that surrounds the central business district, each having a different function.

   (C) Different portions of an urban area have specific and separate purposes, which fit together to create the entirety of the city.

   (D) In cities around the world, residential areas are based on ethnicity, and cities are thus divided into ethnic enclaves.

   (E) An urban area's inner city has its highest population density, and population density declines in areas farther from the city.

3. Which urban model would best describe a city that includes edge cities along its beltways?

   (A) Galactic city

   (B) Concentric zone

   (C) Multiple-nuclei

   (D) Sector

   (E) Griffin-Ford

4. Why do many African cities contain multiple commercial districts?

   (A) Colonial central business districts emerged separately from the traditional commercial centers.

   (B) Africans were traditionally not allowed to use the central business districts used by Europeans.

   (C) African governments promoted multiple central business districts through urban planning.

   (D) One central business district is not enough to serve Africa's fast-growing urban population.

   (E) Locations of Africa's business districts were poorly chosen, requiring multiple downtowns.

5. Which of the following represents a key difference between European cities and North American cities?

   (A) European cities do not contain suburbs.

   (B) North American suburbs have a higher population density.

   (C) European CBDs are less walkable than North American CBDs.

   (D) Public transportation is better developed to serve North American cities.

   (E) European suburbs are more ethnically diverse.

6. The wide, tree-lined avenues, tall office buildings, and mansions of Mexico City's Paseo de la Reforma, illustrate what feature of many large Latin American cities?

(A) Disamenity zone

(B) Periférico

(C) Favelas

(D) Commercial spine

(E) Zone in transition

7. Which best explains why European central business districts have largely resisted the construction of skyscrapers and the resulting impressive skylines that typify American cities?

(A) Competition for valuable commercial space is not as keen in European cities as it is in the United States.

(B) European culture prefers lower buildings and has negative attitudes toward commercialism and skyscrapers.

(C) The centers of European cities contain many historically significant buildings that leaders choose to preserve.

(D) The European Union regulates the height of buildings and has forbidden tall buildings because of safety concerns.

(E) European cities tend to have stronger mass transit systems, so people do not need to be as concentrated in CBDs.

1. The diagrams show three early models of urban development and land use in North America.

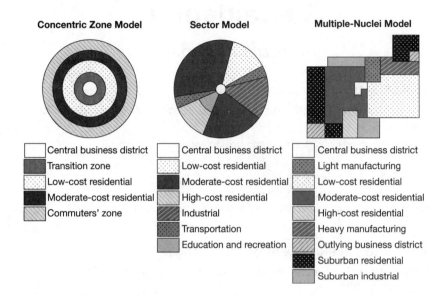

Concentric Zone Model   Sector Model   Multiple-Nuclei Model

Concentric Zone Model	Sector Model	Multiple-Nuclei Model
Central business district	Central business district	Central business district
Transition zone	Low-cost residential	Light manufacturing
Low-cost residential	Moderate-cost residential	Low-cost residential
Moderate-cost residential	High-cost residential	Moderate-cost residential
Commuters' zone	Industrial	High-cost residential
	Transportation	Heavy manufacturing
	Education and recreation	Outlying business district
		Suburban residential
		Suburban industrial

(A) Using the sector model, explain the rationale for the location of the industrial sector.

(B) Choose one of the models and explain in detail the rationale for a different specific land use location.

(C) Describe TWO similarities that North American models share in how they describe land use.

(D) Using the multiple-nuclei model, explain why some businesses relocate near the suburbs.

(E) Compare these models with one pattern of urban development and land use on a continent other than North America and account for the differences.

(F) Describe ONE positive of zoning regulations related to urban planning.

(G) Describe ONE negative of zoning regulations related to urban planning.

CHAPTER 17

Urban Challenges and Sustainability

Topics 6.8–6.11

Topic 6.8 Urban Sustainability

Learning Objectives: Identify the different urban design initiatives and practices. (IMP-6.C)

Explain the effects of different urban design initiatives and practices. (IMP-6.D)

Topic 6.9 Urban Data

Learning Objective: Explain how qualitative and quantitative data are used to show the causes and effects of geographic change within urban areas. (IMP-6.E)

Topic 6.10 Challenges of Urban Changes

Learning Objective: Explain causes and effects of geographic change within urban areas. (SPS-6.A)

Topic 6.11 Challenges of Urban Sustainability

Learning Objective: Describe the effectiveness of different attempts to address urban sustainability challenges. (SPS-6.B)

> *Whenever. . . societies. . . prospered rather than stagnated and decayed, creative and workable cities have been at the core of the phenomenon. Decaying cities, declining economies, and mounting social troubles travel together. The combination is not coincidental.*
>
> —Jane Jacobs, *The Death and Life of Great American Cities*, 1961

Source: Getty Images

The image shows the Kibera slum in Nairobi, Kenya. In the background are numerous gated residential communities. (See Topic 6.10 for more on housing in periphery countries.)

Urban Sustainability

Essential Question: What are urban design initiatives and practices and what are the effects of those initiatives and practices?

Using the earth's resources while not causing permanent damage to the environment is referred to as **sustainability.** Maintaining the sustainability and long-term viability of cities has become an increasingly important discussion for city planners, developers, and citizens.

Sustainability and the Future

Modern cities face numerous challenges from urban sprawl to access to services to environmental injustice. (See Topics 6.10 and 6.11.) New development concepts are shaping the debate about sustainability and city landscapes in both the United States and around the world.

Smart-Growth Policies and Greenbelts

Urban planners and policymakers have developed **smart-growth policies** to combat urban sprawl and create a new vision for cities that are more sustainable and equitable. Smart growth focuses on city planning and transportation systems of an urban region.

One major goal of smart-growth policies is to slow sprawl by creating concentrated growth in compact centers. These policies suggest spatial arrangements that focus on encouraging a mix of building types and uses with a variety of housing and transportation options available within communities. Smart growth also includes several other goals:

- to create attractive residential neighborhoods that are walkable, meaning they provide amenities that people can walk to easily
- to develop a strong sense of place among residents
- to increase livability by making the community easy and safe to navigate
- to involve residents and stakeholders in decisions that impact the community

In London and other European cities, smart growth policies that preserve farmland and other open, undeveloped spaces near the city have existed for over one hundred years. These **greenbelts,** areas of undeveloped land around an urban area, have been created to limit a city's growth and preserve farmland. At the same time, they provide an area for people to enjoy recreation and the environment.

This photo of Feltham, England, located in West London, shows the edge of the greenbelt that surrounds much of the city of London. What purposes does the greenbelt serve?

Many communities in the United States have adopted greenbelt policies to limit growth similar to those in Europe. Under the principles of smart growth, cities are allowed to annex (legally add) land only in areas specifically designated by laws. New Jersey, Rhode Island, Washington, Tennessee, and Oregon have all enacted smart-growth policies.

Some cities desire to slow the population growth and development that could consume and alter their communities. **Slow-growth cities** adopt policies to slow the outward spread of urban areas and place limits on building permits in order to encourage a denser, more compact city. Protecting local sense of place and natural landscapes has also motivated governments to embrace slow-growth policies. The cities of Boulder, Colorado, and Portland, Oregon, are considered slow-growth cities that have aggressively applied these policies.

New Urbanism

A group of developers in the 1990s created a set of strategies called **new urban design** to put smart growth into action within communities. Some strategies of new urbanism include creating human-scale neighborhoods (designed for optimum human use), reclaiming neglected spaces, giving access to multiple modes of transportation, increasing affordable housing, and creating **mixed-use neighborhoods.** Unlike the clear separation between residential and commercial uses created by zoning in most cities, these neighborhoods would have a mix of homes and businesses. A mixed-use neighborhood is vibrant, livable, and walkable. Homes would include a variety of sizes and price ranges to create a socially diverse community. Shared open spaces and community gathering spaces are also common.

New urbanism has succeeded in many communities that have tried the strategies in spite of two large obstacles:

- The existing system of zoning (see Topic 6.6) created segregated areas by land use, and thus contributed to sprawl.

- People accustomed to traditional land-use patterns in cities were not easily convinced that the new urbanism was an improvement.

Stakeholder involvement is an important aspect of new urbanism. For example, in Denver, a new urban neighborhood that was built on the site of a closed major airport was recently renamed. The airport was originally named after a former politician who had supported racist and discriminatory policies, but the neighborhood decided to change its name Central Park in 2021. New urban design can occur in the suburbs as a new development or within the city practicing the concept of urban infill.

Urban Infill

The opposite of leapfrog development (see Topic 6.2) and sprawl is **urban infill**, the process of building up underused lands within a city. Most cities have areas of vacant or undeveloped land of varying sizes. These may be remnants of shut down industrial areas, airports, military bases, hospitals, or malls. The space could be unused because of difficult terrain or poor planning. Because infill uses vacant or discarded land rather than expanding the edge of a city, it is considered smart growth.

The communities of Central Park, Colorado, and Civita, California, are examples of both urban infill and new urbanism. The Civita master-planned community was built on the site of a former quarry located in the Mission Valley section of San Diego. Today, Civita includes a mix of housing types, parks, community centers, and commercial zones, and is well connected by public transit. The community also promotes sustainability by using renewable building materials, solar panels, electric vehicle charging stations, and energy management tools for residents and businesses.

Source: David Palmer

Denver's Central Park Neighborhood is an example of both new urban design and infill. The former airport control tower is in the background and the neighbors share a common open space. Notice the single-family homes and higher density townhomes in the background. Shops are two blocks away.

Transit-Oriented Development

New urban and other smart growth developers have embraced the concept of **transit-oriented development (TOD),** which locates mixed-use residential and business communities near mass transit stops, resulting in a series of more compact communities which decreases the need for automobiles. Increasingly TOD includes multiple forms of transportation including train, bus, and light rail.

Getting public transit riders the last mile from a transit stop to home or work is challenging for city planners. Micro-transport options such as taxis, electric street scooters, bicycles, and shared rider apps (such as Uber or Lyft) help solve the last mile problem. These types of transportation exist in most major world cities and have varying levels of success. The cities of Singapore, London, Paris, and New York City are rated as some of the most successful cities in transit-oriented development.

Source: David Palmer

Transit-oriented development (TOD) often includes multiple forms of transportation. Union Station in Denver includes train, bus, light rail, and many micro-transport options.

Livability

A concept that has recently gained traction with sustainable urban development is livability. **Livability** refers to a set of principles that supports sustainable urban designs. Livable communities have affordable and equitable housing, access to employment and community services, multiple and accessible transportation modes, and social and civic engagement.

Other Changes

Cities adapt to their growing and evolving populations. For example, the creation of pedestrian zones where street fairs, festivals, and public events are held help make inner cities both safer and more desirable destinations. The addition of bike lanes and an increase in bike usage reduces traffic congestion and parking needs while encouraging a healthful lifestyle. In addition, increasing the number of running paths, community gardens, and dog parks further promotes the health and well-being of residents. Many cities are actively developing relationships with local farmers, which benefits both urban and rural citizens through the spread of farmers' markets and the promotion of a more sustainable local economy.

Criticisms of Smart Growth

While smart growth has proven successful in many cities, it is not without critics. Opponents make economic and social arguments against smart growth:

- It is not affordable to families because of increases in the cost of land and housing. It also contributes to congestion and noise within cities
- Smarth growth limits peoples' choices for single-family housing, a suburban lifestyle, quality schools, and the autonomy of car ownership.
- It creates high-population density areas that often have higher crime rates and provides less privacy for residents.
- Smart growth can result in unintended segregation both ethnically and economically.
- It promotes the displacement of low-income and ethnic communities, and the destruction of historical buildings and unique places.

Specific criticisms of mass transit are that it has large upfront costs and is slow to adjust. Rapid growth and change often make it difficult for city planners to predict where mass tranist will be most useful. Also, mass transit often does not connect all parts of a city so people still need cars to get to work, services, or school.

REFLECT ON THE ESSENTIAL QUESTION

Essential Question: *What are urban design initiatives and practices and what are the effects of those initiatives and practices?*

Urban Design Initiatives and Practices	Effects of Initiatives and Practices

---

KEY TERMS

sustainability
smart growth policies
greenbelts
slow-growth cities
new urban design

mixed-use neighborhoods
urban infill
transit-oriented development (TOD)
livability

6.9

Urban Data

Essential Question: How are qualitative and quantitative data used to show the causes and effects of geographic change within urban areas?

Cities are large, diverse, and dynamic. People live in cities for two primary reasons: access to jobs and public services. In the late 20th century, total urban population worldwide grew larger than rural population. The most significant reasons for urban growth were ample job opportunities and a changing economy. This rapid growth led to dynamic and increasingly diverse cities. The ability to analyze the changes and needs within cities requires accurate and local scale quantitative and qualitative data.

Quantitative Data

Quantitative data is information that can be counted, measured, or sequenced by numeric value. For example, geographers count the total population of a country and sequence it with the total populations of other countries. This allows for comparison based on that particular data.

In the United States, a census is required by law every ten years. Census data, as well as other data, provides **population composition**. In addition to showing where people live, population composition gives a description of people's income, age, gender, ethnicity, race, family size, and other details. That information is valuable to governments to determine what services are needed, such as public libraries, schools, and neighborhood parks, and where they should be located.

Quantitative data helps identify the need for and location of other public services such as local emergency medical help providers (EMS), police, fire, and public utilities (trash and sewer services). Each have specific site and situation factors (see Topic 6.1) that influence its ideal location.

GEOGRAPHIC CATEGORIES IN THE CENSUS			
Category	**2010 Census**	**Increase over the 2000 Census**	**Average Number of People in the 2010 Census**
Population	308,745,538	9.7%	-----
Census Tracts	73,057	11.8%	4,226 people/tract
Block Groups	217,740	4.3%	1,418 people/group
Blocks	11,078,297	35.0%	28 people/block

Source: Bureau of the Census

Notice that each subdivision gets smaller in total number of people. What are the advantages and disadvantages of data at each scale of analysis? Assuming you had income data for each category, describe how the data could be used at each scale.

Population Data in Urban Areas

U.S. census data is available at many scales. Urban areas in many countries are divided into **census tracts**, contiguous geographic regions that function as the foundation of a census. In the United States, a census tract typically consists of between 4,000 and 12,000 people. Each tract is subdivided into block groups, which are further subdivided into blocks. A **census block** in a densely populated urban area is often very small, consisting of a single block bounded by four streets. In suburban and rural areas, because of their lower population densities, a census block typically covers a larger area.

Using the proper scale of data is critical. Deciding where to build a new playground in a neighborhood requires data such as number of children per household at the block level. Country-level data would be useless in this case. Block-level information might be of some value in deciding where to build an airport but data of the metro area or a national-scale map would be critical.

Researchers and businesses use data to identify potential goods and services that people desire. Merchants and business owners, such as those who own grocery stores and car dealerships, could also use this information to determine the best locations to serve the needs of the population. Census data is usually gathered per household but can be aggregated at multiple scales.

The chart below shows a sample of some of the types of data that are gathered in the U.S. census. National and local scale data are both shown. Many statistics such as household size and income also have corresponding data (not shown) down to the block or census tract scale. Geographers compare local data with that at the national scale to analyze patterns, trends, and processes within communities.

SELECTED QUANTITATIVE DATA OF THE UNITED STATES AND THE DETROIT MSA, 2019		
	United States	**Detroit MSA**
Average household size	2.61	2.51
Household income ranges	Over $200,000 8.5%	Over $200,000 6.6%
	$150,000-199,999 7.2%	$150,000-199,999 6.8%
	$100,000-149,999 15.7%	$100,000-149,999 15.2%
	$75,000-99,999 12.8%	$75,000-99,999 12.5%
	$50,000-74,999 17.4%	$50,000-74,999 17.0%
	$25,000-49,999 20.3%	$25,000-49,999 21.6%
	Under $25,000 18.1%	Under $25,000 20.3%

Source: US Census Bureau, 2019.

Identify the scale of the data presented. Would this data be useful for determining the local population composition or income of a neighborhood? Explain your response.

Qualitative Data

Qualitative data is based primarily on surveys, field studies, photos, video, and interviews from people who provide personal perceptions and meaningful descriptions. Questions and study topics help those who gather information learn how individuals and communities feel about urban growth, zoning changes, local government, crime rates, and other topics that affect people living in the city. Questions have to be carefully worded to be objective so responses are accurately reflected. They can also be worded in such a way to elicit value judgements:

- Would you support the city spending money to make more sidewalks?
- Would you like to have new playground equipment in your neighborhood park? Why or why not?
- Would you rather see the city pay for more street lights or a community recreation center? Why or why not?
- Would you support a 2-cent tax increase to pay for a police substation in your neighborhood? Why or why not?

Qualitative data is important to geographers and is often used to verify quantitative data. Cities are diverse and there are often many perspectives related to urban issues. For example, when a new housing development is being built in a neighborhood, researchers seek out multiple viewpoints about the project. Business and property owners may view this as positive as it will increase economic activity, while longtime apartment residents may view it as a negative because it will cause higher rent.

Geographers use qualitative and quantitative data to analyze changes in the spatial relationships of an urban setting. Recognizing patterns and locations of urban growth can help city planners meet the social, economic, and infrastructural needs of its citizens. However, researchers must always be aware that data can be flawed or inaccurate. Factors such as who gathered the information, the type of questions asked, the scale of the data, how often or when the data was gathered, and if the people who responded answered accurately, influence the quality of the data.

REFLECT ON THE ESSENTIAL QUESTION

Essential Question: *How are qualitative and quantitative data used to show the causes and effects of geographic change within urban areas?*

Uses of Urban Quantitative Data	Uses of Urban Qualitative Data

KEY TERMS

quantitative data	census block
population composition	qualitative data
census tracts	

Challenges of Urban Changes

Essential Question: What are the causes and effects of geographic change within urban areas?

Cities are nodes, complex places characterized by interconnections, and are often centers for innovation, cultural diversity, and art. They are often engines of economic growth and centers of political power. But the dense concentration of people combined with many complicated systems of cities can make solving problems difficult. Cities can be places of poverty, violence, and environmental decay.

The world is more urbanized than ever, and experts expect the percentage of people living in cities to continue growing. Consequently, understanding and solving urban challenges will continue to be important work for geographers.

Urban Challenges

While people with great wealth concentrate in cities, so do people with little wealth. Urban poverty exists throughout the world. It is found from inner cities of core countries to squatter settlements and favelas of less-developed countries. According to a United Nations report, about one-sixth of the world's population lives in urban poverty, and mostly in developing countries.

The role of cities in more-developed countries has changed rapidly, shifting from centers of industry to centers of services. Conversely, in less-developed countries, cities have experienced problems brought on by rapid industrialization and growing numbers of new migrants.

Urban Housing Issues in Core Countries

In the developed world, housing for inner-city poor residents is characterized by at least three problems—poor quality, insufficient availability, and significant unaffordability. Often the physical conditions of the buildings need updated to be safe. Proper maintenance and repairs of plumbing, electrical systems, roofing, stairwells, and heating systems are often unaffordable to inner city residents. Landlords often delay making expensive repairs, so over time, the overall quality of the housing suffers.

This process is often visible in the transitional areas of cities, as well as in ethnic enclaves, since both have a high percentage of renters. In European cities, these issues often occur near the edge of cities where mass transit lines end and rent is less expensive. Some geographers contend that in many European and North American cities, poorer residential areas are concentrated near industrial regions built on the eastern side of cities. Rents are lower in these areas in part because the wind usually blows east, sending air pollution and industrial smells through these neighborhoods.

Women are more numerous than men in large, central cities in North America. One reason for this disparity is the high number of female-headed households. These women and their children are more likely to be poor than men. According to the U.S. Census Bureau in 2018, 56 percent of the U.S. population living in poverty were women. Hence, women concentrate in areas where housing is the least expensive, even if these areas often have higher crime rates. The lack of good schools, parks and playgrounds, and available of day care options, compound the problems faced by women and their children.

Housing Discrimination and Segregation in the United States

For the poor in the United States, housing opportunities have suffered because of decay in central cities. Neighborhoods go through cycles of change (see Topic 6.6), culturally and in land use. During much of the 20th century in the United States, housing discrimination was legal.

At the neighborhood scale, **redlining**, the process by which banks refuse loans to those who want to purchase and improve properties in certain urban areas, was common. Historically, minorities and the poor were the predominant inhabitants of neighborhoods where loans were commonly denied. Banks and federal government loan agencies considered investments in these areas too risky. The term originated as these lending institutions identified these no-loan areas by red lines on maps. Redlining reinforced the downward spiral of struggling and predominately minority neighborhoods. Minorities' inability to get loans significantly limited homeownership and often resulted in higher poverty rates. Laws now restrict redlining so that denial of a loan cannot happen for racial or cultural reasons.

Other discriminatory laws and practices existed. It was legal for landowners or real estate agents to deny selling or renting property to people based on race, ethnicity, gender, marital status, or religion. Most of the suburban neighborhoods in the United States denied minorities the right to buy homes. This practice prevented minorities from buying less-expensive homes in the suburbs, thereby forcing them to rent because they could not afford the more expensive land and houses closer to the city center.

These practices are now illegal in the United States because of the Fair Housing Act of 1968, but discriminatory policies have impacted the spatial arrangements of U.S. cities dramatically. Most economists argue that home ownership is a key factor for individual wealth. While minority homeownership has improved, the legacy of discriminatory policies still exists according to U.S. census data:

- In 1900, fewer than 20 percent of African Americans owned a home compared to over 46 percent of White people.
- In 2019, over 73 percent of White Americans owned the home they lived in compared to 42 percent of African Americans and 47 percent of Hispanics and Latino Americans.

Racial segregation in housing occurs when people live in separate neighborhoods based on their ethnicity or race. Segregation can occur voluntarily (see Topic 3.2) but often occurs involuntarily. In particular, throughout U.S. history, many communities had neighborhoods where African Americans could live and neighborhoods where they could not. Such segregation was enforced through real estate practices, traditions, and violence.

One of these practices was **blockbusting**. This is when people of an ethnic group sold their homes upon learning that members of another ethnic group were moving into the neighborhood. In U.S. history, often middle-class White families left when African American or Hispanic families moved into neighborhood. Investors would buy houses at low prices and either resell or rent them to minorities for a large profit.

Segregated neighborhoods can sometimes become **ghettos**, areas of poverty occupied by a minority group as a result of discrimination. Residents who live in ghettos often feel trapped because of social or political factors or a lack of economic opportunities. These neighborhoods have a high percentage of residents who rent, poorly maintained buildings, fewer businesses, and underfunded education and other government services.

Government Support for Affordable Housing

Governments have responded to the shortage of low-income housing in various ways. The federal government provides financial subsidies to help low-income residents with the cost of housing. London, New York City, Denver, and other cities have rent control policies that keep some affordable units available when a neighborhood improves. **Inclusionary zoning** practices offer incentives for developers to set aside a percentage of housing for low-income renters or buyers. However, critics point out that these policies reduce incentives for investments in new housing.

One reason for the shortage of affordable housing in urban neighborhoods is the cost of constructing and managing a new building can be greater than the profits a business can make. Governments and charitable groups, in both the United States and other countries, often step in to provide assistance, either by building and operating housing or by providing subsidies for others to do so.

These public housing developments—sometimes called "projects"—were first built in areas of the inner city where other structures had been torn down. Many provided decent housing and a solid sense of community. However, these buildings were often high-rise apartments, which concentrated poverty in a small area within the city. These areas experienced problems common in other urban neighborhoods where the poor were clustered, such as drug use, high crime rates, and poor maintenance.

In some cities, community leaders used a **scattered site** approach to alleviate the problems of public housing. In this approach, of the city or government provided rental assistance for individuals to dispurse public housing throughout the area. This allowed children access to better local schools and older residents access to amenities in wealthier neighborhoods.

The scattered-site approach has faced opposition from the "not-in-my-backyard" response. People fear that adding public housing near them will reduce property values and create problems for local communities and schools.

Urban Renewal

As residents in the United States moved to the suburbs after World War II, inner cities suffered from urban decay, high crime rates, and increased poverty. During the 1960s and 1970s, many city governments in the United States adopted the policy of **urban renewal**. The policy allowed governments to clear out the blighted inner-city slums, which usually displaced the residents to low-income government housing complexes, and built new development projects.

Governments often use the legal concept of **eminent domain** which allows the government to claim private property from individuals, pay them for the property, and then use the land for the public good. The practices of urban renewal and eminent domain happen in all countries but they most disproportionately affect minorities and the poor in periphery and semiperiphery countries.

Gentrification

During the 21st century, large numbers of people desired to leave the suburbs and move closer to the urban core. **Gentrification** is the process of converting an urban inner-city neighborhood from a mostly low-income, renter-occupied area to a predominately wealthier, owner-occupied area of a city. Often gentrifying areas are of mixed-use development and include art districts, coffee shops, commissioned street art, dog parks, and trendy bars and restaurants. Also, these neighborhoods are near the central business district and its many amenities are available by public transportation.

Gentrification occurs mostly in the cities of core countries but is increasingly happening in cities in the periphery. Often the households in gentrified areas are dual-income, no-kids regardless of the level of development of the city in which they are located. The newcomers to gentrified areas are often a combination of three groups:

- young urban professionals with high-paying jobs
- LGBTQ+ looking for neighborhoods that are more inclusive, accepting, and safe
- older couples whose children have moved out

While gentrification includes positive aspects, there are also negative ones. These neighborhoods experience changes in racial and cultural diversity. Gentrification can displace residents, create space that excludes minorities or the poor, and eliminate the historical cultural landscape of previous residents.

As land values rise in inner cities along the growing edge of the central business district, low-income and often minority urban residents are pushed out by rising rents or rising taxes. Older residents who own their home, but live on fixed incomes, can no longer afford to pay taxes and often have to sell their homes and move.

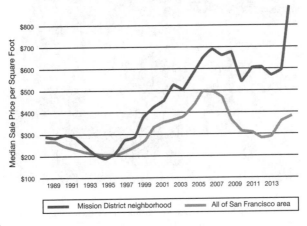

GENTRIFICATION IN SAN FRANCISCO

Median Sale Price per Square Foot

$800
$700
$600
$500
$400
$300
$200
$100

1989 1991 1993 1995 1997 1999 2001 2003 2005 2007 2009 2011 2013

—— Mission District neighborhood   —— All of San Francisco area

Source: Dataquick

The graph shows how property values increased in the Mission District neighborhood in San Francisco. Describe a positive and a negative of rising property values.

Housing in Periphery Countries

Urbanization has rapidly expanded the population of cities in periphery countries, which has highlighted a lack of quality housing, especially for poorer residents. The periphery of cities often consists of **informal settlements**, densely populated areas built without coordinated planning and without sufficient public services for electricity, water, and sewage. Residents often lack **land tenure,** or the legal protection of contracts to show ownership of the land or structures. These areas are also known as urban slums, favelas or squatter settlements in different parts of the world. (See Topic 6.5.) Residents construct housing from whatever materials are available. Bricks and concrete blocks are more durable, but sheets of tin and plastic are also used. Living in these buildings can be dangerous because of questionable building materials and rarely enforced housing codes. In 2013 in Mumbra, India, 74 people died when an apartment building collapsed.

Most *informal settlements* are in *disamenity zones* (see Topic 6.5), abandoned land, or undeveloped open spaces such as parks. **Zones of abandonment** are areas of a city that have been deserted by their owners for either economic or environmental reasons. In some extreme cases, entire cities have been abandoned usually because of disasters such as the nuclear reactor meltdowns in Chernobyl, Ukraine (1986), and Fukushima, Japan (2011).

In most cases, abandonment is the result of economics and impacts different aspects of an urban region. The area will often have empty decaying buildings, poor sanitation, high crime rates, and vandalism. Examples occur in all regions of the world including Detroit, Michigan, or Kowloon, near Hong Kong. Another specific type of abandonment is a *brownfield*, created when factories leave an area. (See Topic 6.11.)

Source: Wikimedia Commons

Kowloon Walled City near Hong Kong was a zone of abandonment, then a slum, and was torn down in 1993 to make room for urban renewal and a park.

A problem facing many poor communities worldwide is **environmental injustice**, sometimes referred to as **environmental racism,** the disproportionate exposure of minorities and the poor to pollution and its impacts, plus the unequal protection of their rights under the law. This process is more common in urban settings where poor communities are often located near high-polluting activities. Some governments will limit new high-polluting industries and activities to poor existing neighborhoods. Residents of these neighborhoods often lack the economic and political resources to block new high-polluting development in their neighborhoods, or to even minimize the impacts.

Geographers use GIS technology to map and study the vulnerable impacted populations and some work together with communities to create solutions. Environmental injustice often results in increased health problems, such as birth defects and cancer, as well as shorter average life expectancy.

Gated or Walled Communities

The compact nature of many cities around the world has pushed informal settlements and poorer communities to live in close proximity to the wealthy. One response to this new geographic pattern is the building of walled or fenced neighborhoods with limited access and entry points, called **gated communities**. They represent a redesign of urban living with an attempt to recapture features more commonly found outside urban areas—safety, quiet, and homogeneity.

Gated communities are growing in cities all around the world. Some have referred to them as *citadels,* after historic castles and forts built to ensure safety inside the walls amid lawlessness and crime outside. The growth of gated communities can reinforce separation in economics, social status, ethnicity, and even political views. Slums and wealthy gated communities are often close to each other because residents in both groups desire access to the economic center of the city.

Homelessness

All countries of the world face the challenge of homelessness, the condition of not having a permanent place to live. While some unhoused people find temporary shelter with friends or relatives, others live on the streets. In the United States, the unhoused population was once primarily single men, but the problem expanded in the late 20th century to include more women and children. Government, religious groups, and nonprofit organizations responded by building shelters, advocating for public funding to support housing, and helping the unhoused learn new skills and gain access to health care and social services. In cities without strong public transit systems, people who are unhoused have difficulty traveling to available jobs and services.

Services

Shops and services often struggle to survive in urban neighborhoods. If the patrons are poor, prices for services must be low to maintain a customer base in the area. The result is very tight margins with little money available for shop owners to spend on maintenance or improvement of their facilities. The housing decay spreads to the service sector. Public services such as parks and swimming pools might be rare in urban neighborhoods with low tax bases. Private businesses and service providers, such as doctors and dentists, are often scarce in poor neighborhoods. They are particularly scarce in poor, heavily urbanized countries. For example, in Bangladesh, the number of doctors per capita is about one-fifth the number in the United States.

Food Deserts

Access to food stores in urban neighborhoods is often a problem. Grocery stores and supermarkets tend to favor suburban locations, where residents are wealthier and land costs less. Fresh, healthful food may be far less available than lower priced fast food. This results in few choices for poor families beyond fast food. These urban zones that lack food stores are known as *food deserts* (see Topic 5.11), and they contribute to health problems, such as obesity and diabetes, for poorer urban residents.

Many cities are developing programs and systems to bring food into urban food deserts, such as mobile grocery stores and community gardens, and incentives for grocery stores that locate in low-income areas. Some local food groups provide fresh fruits and vegetables at local pop-up markets.

Political Challenges of Urban Regions

Governing urban regions can be challenging because *metropolitan areas* (see Topic 6.1) are often a collection of adjacent cities and counties each, with its own government but environmentally, economically, and socially connected. Many urban challenges require a regional approach to governance—examples include urban growth, mass transit, road construction, pollution, and homelessness. Regional governance typically requires voluntary coalitions of city governments to address the needs and create plans for the larger region.

Occasionally, special districts (see Topic 4.7) are established to handle long-term regional needs such as transportation, fire, and police districts.

The system of federalism has many strengths but its fragmented nature of governance between states, counties, cities, and neighborhoods often makes collaboration difficult. It is challenging to get multiple levels of government to agree on and implement plans for any major project. The benefits of such cooperation are comprehensive plans and shared costs by the various levels of governance. Additionally, with collaboration, economies of scale (reduced per unit cost) are more likely to be achieved in large-scale projects.

Cities with successful regional planning include Portland, Oregon; Minneapolis, Minnesota; and Amsterdam, Netherlands. Amsterdam has developed a regional multi-model transportation system and a large-scale smart-city initiative that limits outward growth while improving the infrastructure and livability of the existing urban regions. Urban planners argue that as networked *meta-cities* (see Topic 6.2) of over 20 million people continue to increase around the world, regional planning will be required to improve the connectivity, infrastructure, and livability of these urban giants.

REFLECT ON THE ESSENTIAL QUESTION

Essential Question: *What are the causes and effects of geographic change within urban areas?*

Causes of Geographic Change in Urban Areas	Effects of Geographic Changes in Urban Areas

---

KEY TERMS

redlining	gentrification
racial segregation	informal settlements
blockbusting	land tenure
ghettos	zones of abandonment
inclusionary zoning	environmental injustice (environmental
scattered site	racism)
urban renewal	gated communities
eminent domain	

Challenges of Urban Sustainability

Essential Question: How effective are attempts to address urban sustainability challenges?

Cities are becoming the dominant landscape in the world with more than half of the world's population living in cities. The United Nations predicts that will rise to over two-thirds by 2050. Consequently, the actions of cities are key to living in a more sustainable world. Multiple levels of government will have to work together to deal with the challenges faced by urban areas.

Environmental Problems in Cities

A city and its population affect the environment in many ways. Stresses are placed on nature when people modify the environment and in the way they respond to those changes.

Environmental Effects of Cities

The physical landscape of an urban area affects the natural environment in many ways and often poses challenges to urban sustainability:

- **Urban canyons**, streets lined with tall buildings, can channel and intensify wind and prevent natural sunlight from reaching the ground.
- Soils are compacted and replaced with structures that are impermeable to water, such as buildings, streets, and parking lots. As a result, rainwater runs off instead of soaking into the ground, causing urban flooding.
- Water demand increases as people move to cities, which can strain existing water resources. Water is often diverted from agricultural use to urban use.
- The concentration of buildings and concrete in the center of a city creates an **urban heat island**, an area of a city warmer than surrounding areas.

PARIS AS A HEAT ISLAND

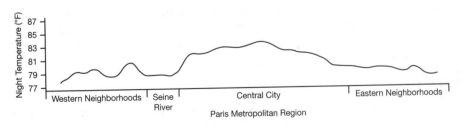

Source: Data is from the Summer of 2003, nasa.gov.

The diagram of Paris shows that the central city is relatively warm. In contrast, the Seine River, which has no buildings, is cooler. In the summer what are the negatives of the urban center being hotter than the surrounding areas?

Cities and Wildlife

Wildlife is also affected by urban areas. Cities destroy animal and plant habitats, redirect or replace natural hydrologic (water) systems such as rivers and lakes, and break up ecosystems. The interruption of continuous ecosystems makes it difficult, if not impossible, for animal species to survive. The animals that survive are often in conflict with humans:

- Native animals such as deer, coyotes, skunks, alligators, bears, cougars, monkeys, and leopards cause problems where cities have invaded or abutted their natural territories.
- **Urban wildlife** such as rats, raccoons, and pigeons can thrive in cities, but they can spread diseases and be a nuisance to people.
- Feral (wild) populations of cats, dogs, snakes, and other former pets that have escaped their human owners or have been abandoned can be dangerous or upset the ecological balance.

Pollution

Rising urbanism also degrades the environment, particularly in less-developed countries that have fewer resources to combat pollution. Industrial and human waste, concentrated in cities will, if untreated, pollute rivers, aquifers, and coastal areas. As countries develop, air pollution increases because of more industrial activity and more emissions from a growing number of cars. Poorer inhabitants in these cities burn charcoal, wood, and kerosene as fuel sources, all of which pollute the air.

In large, urban regions, automobile pollution causes serious concerns. The huge number of commuters to central business districts and surrounding edge cities creates problems beyond congestion. During **rush hour**, the commuting periods in early morning and in late afternoon or early evening when many people travel to and from work, idling cars on roads increase and concentrate air pollutants in the city. The result is smog, a severe issue in large cities such as Los Angeles, Beijing, Delhi, and Mexico City.

Climatic conditions and the physical geography of cities and surrounding areas, such as mountains, can intensify pollution. For example, mountains surround Mexico City, and during temperature inversions (when a layer of hot air sits above cool air), smog is trapped and concentrated close to the ground for days with negative effects on the health of the inhabitants. According to the World Health Organization, air pollution results in three million deaths a year. One-third of those are in China, where coal is widely used in industry and to heat homes.

Urban Sprawl

Before automobiles became popular, cities tended to grow vertically through taller buildings as population expanded. Since the mid-20th century, cities and their related environment—such as roads and commercial developments—have expanded horizontally across the landscape. This rapid spread of development outward from the inner city is called **suburban sprawl**.

In the United States, sprawl is most common in fast-growing areas in the Southeast and West. Urban areas experience sprawl for several reasons:

- the availability of automobiles
- the creation of interstate and other high-speed highways
- the presence of inexpensive land outside the urban area

As a city spreads out it has a greater impact on the environment. More land and energy per capita are needed to maintain a sprawling city as compared to a more compact city design. The physical size of of a city has a direct correlation with an **ecological footprint**, or the impact of human activity on the environment. (See Topic 7.8.)

Responses to Urban Sustainability

Urban systems continue to expand and maintain their position as the dominant location where humans live, work, and play. Therefore, geographers continue to study and propose ideas to respond to the challenges that growing cities create.

Regional Planning and Brownfields

Responses to urban challenges often require a regional planning approach (see Topic 6.10) because urban areas spread across large spaces, include multiple cities, and have wide ranging impacts. Protecting farmland from expanding cities, developing large-scale water and sewage systems, or creating responses to air pollution require collaborative efforts from multiple stakeholders.

On a local scale remediating and redeveloping land is a critical issue for cities. Industry once thrived in central cities of developed countries. Yet new technologies have decreased the need for workers, which weakened the economic strength of many cities. Also, manufacturing moved to the suburbs, where land was cheaper, and to other countries, where labor was less expensive.

Source: Wikimedia Commons

This abandoned automobile factory in Detroit, Michigan, is both a zone of abandonment (see Topic 6.10) and a brownfield. Describe two challenges of using brownfields as sites for redevelopment.

As manufacturing moved away, cities were left with unemployed residents and abandoned factories. Brownfields are visual reminders on the landscape of how the centers of cities have changed over time. A typical **brownfield** consists of dilapidated buildings and polluted or contaminated soils. These are expensive to remove or repair and often remain in cities, devaluing neighboring properties. Brownfields exist in most core countries and in some semiperiphery countries such as China.

If remediated, their locations are increasingly used as redevelopment sites. If the building remains structurally solid, an entrepreneur might renovate it for a new use and keep enough of its exterior so that people know the building's history. People have converted old factories into apartments, restaurants, recreational facilities, and artisan boutiques.

Redevelopment

The process of **urban redevelopment** involves renovating a site within a city by removing the existing landscape and rebuilding from the ground up. The process of urban redevelopment usually begins when a local government declares that an area it wishes to develop is blighted, in a deteriorated condition. Eminent domain laws (see Topic 6.10) allow the government to seize land for public use after paying owners the market value for their property. Cities often use these laws to enable the building of new roads or schools, but they can also sell the land to private groups to build hotels, hospitals, or other developments.

While redevelopment initiatives sometimes replace brownfields or low-quality housing with successful enterprises, critics point out that these efforts can cause problems. They can force poor people to leave their homes and communities. Redevelopment can break up and eliminate historic neighborhoods. Private developers are also sometimes given tax-break incentives to purchase and build. By reducing tax revenues on these projects, the city shifts the tax burden to other taxpayers.

REFLECT ON THE ESSENTIAL QUESTION

Essential Question: *How effective are attempts to address urban sustainability challenges?*

Urban Challenges	Impacts

KEY TERMS

urban canyons	rush hour	brownfields
urban heat island	suburban sprawl	urban redevelopment
urban wildlife	ecological footprint	

Humans who live in cities have an impact on the environment. Geographers have studied whether it is more sustainable to live in a city, suburb, or rural area. Many factors can influence this comparison ranging from level of development, income, consumption, or geographic location.

All three living scenarios modify the natural environment, but agricultural activities use over 50 percent of the habitable land in the world compared to less than 2 percent of the suburban and urban built-up land. In terms of resource consumption, urban areas consume the most resources in absolute value. However, if measured in per capita values, compact cities consume the least per person.

In periphery countries, air pollution is a major problem in both urban and rural areas. In urban areas, air pollution is generated by car emissions, coal, and other fossil fuels. In rural areas, the greatest threat of air pollution comes from using biomass (organic materials) as a fuel source for cooking and heating. In core countries, urban areas do have higher air-pollution rates than rural areas. However, core countries are making efforts to regulate limits on air pollution and use less-polluting sources of energy.

Water quality is usually better in urban and suburban areas of core countries because of better water treatment and purification systems than well water typically used in rural areas. However, rapidly growing urban areas have a difficult time keeping up with water demands and safe drinking water.

The question is complex and difficult to answer, but in general, compact cities in core countries are the most sustainable per capita and sprawling cities are the least sustainable. Rural areas do have a higher per capita ecological footprint, but the food production and energy resource demands placed on rural locations by cities is largely the cause. Most geographers agree that the choices made by rapidly growing cities in the periphery countries will shift the focus of sustainability and the environment in the future.

1. Explain TWO reasons why compact urban areas are more sustainable than suburbs.

2. Explain why farming is essential to maintaining cities.

3. Explain why it is difficult to answer the question: Which is more sustainable, urban or rural living?

Geographers compare data describing different regions or communities as a way to highlight what makes each place distinctive. Large cities feature diverse populations, including a variety of ethnicities, religions, income levels, forms of entertainment, and health services.

Use the information in this chart to compare life in Philadelphia, Minneapolis, and Orlando and to help you answer the questions below.

COMPARING LIFE IN THREE CITIES			
Statistic	**Philadelphia**	**Minneapolis**	**Orlando**
Population: City	1,517,550	382,618	185,951
Population: Metropolitan Statistical Area (MSA)	6,188,463	3,615,902	1,644,561
Median Household Income (Entire MSA)	$47,528	$54,304	$41,871
Murder Rate per 100,000 Population (City Only)	15.9	7.7	5.8
Median Age (City Only)	34.2	31.2	32.9

1. What are the advantages and disadvantages of living in a large metropolitan area?

2. Explain why the MSA population is larger than the population of each city.

3. Describe the scale of the data for Median Age.

4. In which of the major urban areas listed above would you prefer to live? Use the data from the chart to support your answer.

CHAPTER 17 REVIEW:
Urban Challenges and Sustainability
Topics 6.8–6.11

MULTIPLE-CHOICE QUESTIONS

Question 1 refers to the table below.

USE OF PUBLIC TRANSPORTATION			
City	Metropolitan Area Population	Daily Bus Commuters	Daily Subway Commuters
Seoul	25,000,000	4,500,000	5,600,000
New York	20,000,000	2,500,000	3,800,000
Chicago	9,500,000	1,000,000	750,000
Berlin	5,000,000	1,000,000	1,000,000

1. Which generalization comparing the use of urban transportation systems in four cities does the table support?
   (A) People in no country have placed much importance on urban public transportation.
   (B) Europeans and Asians have placed about the same importance on urban public transportation as have people in the United States.
   (C) People in the United States have placed more importance on urban public transportation than have Europeans and Asians.
   (D) European and Asian urban transportation systems serve a higher proportion of residents than do systems in the United States.
   (E) European and Asian urban transportation systems meet the needs of residents, but systems in the United States fail to do so.

2. Based on current and historical conditions, which would be most likely to help alleviate the problem of food deserts?
   (A) Encouraging food trucks that are part of the informal economy to serve food deserts
   (B) Encouraging gentrification and building upscale housing in poor neighborhoods
   (C) Establishing new farmers markets in the suburban and exurban communities
   (D) Opening upscale food stores in neighborhoods that have already gentrified
   (E) Opening supermarkets in inner city neighborhoods that have poor public transportation

3. Which has been a partially effective response to the problems of public housing?

(A) Gentrification, because it creates a safer and more diverse community

(B) Scattered-site housing, because it places families in safer areas with better schools

(C) Redlining, because it limits bad housing investments in the inner city

(D) Eminent domain, because it allows government to gain vast urban lands to develop

(E) Blockbusting, because it makes affordable housing more available

4. Which of the following scenarios is best solved using a regional planning model?

(A) Redeveloping the buildings of a brownfield

(B) Deciding to build a new entrance into a mall

(C) Choosing a location to build a new playground

(D) Building a new mass transit line

(E) Choosing where in a CBD to erect a new ten-story office building

5. The revival of downtown nightlife and an increase in street lighting are methods used by city governments primarily to

(A) deter criminal activity

(B) generate tax revenue during evening hours

(C) decrease traffic congestion during the day

(D) promote new urbanism

(E) reduce the effects of exurbanization

6. Which activity most directly uses racial prejudice to perpetuate segregation in housing?

(A) Gentrification by young professionals and suburbanites moving into the inner city

(B) Leapfrogging over suburbs by developers to expand communities far from the inner city

(C) Blockbusting by realtors who want to promote movement to the suburbs

(D) Scattered-site housing by city governments to keep the poor in the city

(E) Ideas of new urbanism applied by developers who are creating mixed-use neighborhoods

Question 7 refers to the graph below.

PRICE PER SQ FT IN SAN FRANCISCO

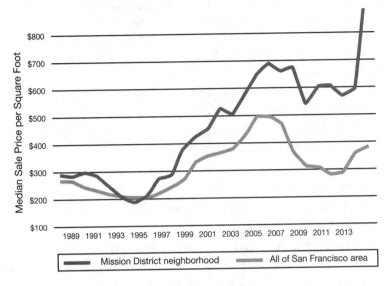

Mission District neighborhood   All of San Francisco area

7. Which of the following is the most likely impact of the changes in price of the Mission District neighborhood?

(A) Increased poor populations seeking jobs

(B) Increased minority-owned businesses

(C) Decreased young urban professional residents

(D) Increased likelihood of a food desert

(E) Increased number of dog parks and specialty coffee shops

1. The Brookings Institution, a research organization based in Washington, D.C., issued a report that stated, "Urban areas face daunting economic challenges that have increased in scope in recent years. At the same time, cities provide exciting opportunities for growth and revitalization. The interplay of these challenges and opportunities creates important tasks for policymakers and researchers."

(A) Describe ONE economic problem of urban areas today to which this quotation could refer.

(B) Explain the potential economic benefits when an older, run-down part of a city is redeveloped.

(C) Explain ONE social problem that can occur when an older, run-down part of a city is redeveloped.

(D) Describe the challenges for people who live in an urban food desert.

(E) Explain ONE potential solution to address the challenges of living in an urban food desert that does not involve relocating residents.

(F) Metropolitan areas such as Los Angeles and Chicago are often made up of multiple smaller cities, each with its own local government. Explain the problems this can create related to solving transportation issues within a metro area.

(G) Describe how cities can negatively impact the environment.

UNIT 6 REVIEW:
Connecting Course Skills and Content

APPLYING GEOGRAPHIC SKILLS

Applying geographic skills is critical for success on the AP Exam. For each skill listed write a one-paragraph response that illustrates your understanding of the question. Support your response with specific examples and evidence. Refer to the Unit 1 introduction (pages 3–7) for tips on how to apply geographic skills.

1C Compare the concepts of metacity and world city.

2D Explain a geographic land use similarity and difference between cities in core and periphery countries.

3F Explain the possible limitations of the quantitative demographic data shown in the table in Topic 6.9 (page 423) for solving an issue about locating a playground in a neighborhood.

4E Compare the images of Chicago and favelas in Brazil in Topic 6.5. Describe a pattern that is similar and one that is different between the images.

5B Using Borchert's transportation model in Topic 6.1 and urban models in Topic 6.5, explain how rail transportation influences land use of a city on the local scale and the distribution of cities across a wider regional scale.

WRITE AS A GEOGRAPHER: *GIVE FULL EXPLANATIONS*

Well-written paragraphs usually begin with a topic sentence stating the paragraph's primary claim. The other sentences then provide support for this idea, such as examples, explanations, or applications of a concept.

Below are sets of points that could be used in a paragraph in response to a question about *urban sustainability*. For each set, write a topic sentence for a paragraph that includes a claim and ties the ideas together and relates to *urban sustainability*.

1. Set A
   - a city begins a public service to help residents compost
   - a state provides incentives for consumers to use less electricity
   - a national organization runs public service ads about reducing pollution
   - countries of the world sign an agreement to combat climate change

2. Set B
   - Transit-oriented development (TOD) encourages businesses and residents to locate near mass transit stations.
   - New urbanism encourages compact and walkable mixed-use neighborhoods.
   - Walkable neighborhoods improve the health of residents.
   - Car-dependent cities create a larger ecological footprint.

3. Set C
   - United States: commuting by bike increased by 62 percent between 2000 and 2013
   - Brazil: rainforest loss in 2014 was one-sixth the rate in 2004
   - Germany: production of solar energy increased from 1 percent of all energy production in 2009 to nearly 7 percent in 2015
   - China: efforts to reduce air pollution have begun to show success

UNIT 7

Industrialization and Economic Development Patterns and Processes

Unit Overview

Great Britain was the hearth of the 18th century Industrial Revolution. As people learned to use water power and coal energy to manufacture goods, they increased their agricultural productivity, population, and wealth. In the last two centuries, industrialization has diffused throughout the world.

Measures of Development

Since the start of the Industrial Revolution, people have developed statistical measures to describe changes in society. Some measure the total output of each country, the distribution of income, rates of childbirth, the percentage of people who can read, and the different opportunities available to males and females. Scholars use this information to create models or theories of spatial patterns of economic and social development in countries around the world.

Variations in Development and World Economy

The diffusion of industrialization generally increased trade and interdependence, which improved the standard of living for most people. However, many people lost their jobs, either because of the greater use of machines or the movement of work from one place to another. As people in some countries specialized in particular types of work, an international division of labor emerged. Industrialization also damaged the environment motivating many people to push for more sustainable practices.

ENDURING UNDERSTANDINGS

SPS-7: Industrialization, past and present, has facilitated improvements in standards of living, but it has also contributed to geographically uneven development.

PSO-7: Economic and social development happen at different times and rates in different places.

IMP-7: Environmental problems stemming from industrialization may be remedied through sustainable development strategies.

Source: *AP® Human Geography Course and Exam Description.* Effective Fall 2020. (College Board).

CHAPTER 18

Industrialization and Economic Development

Topics 7.1–7.4

Topic 7.1 The Industrial Revolution

Learning Objective: Explain how the Industrial Revolution facilitated the growth and diffusion of industrialization. (SPS-7.A)

Topic 7.2 Economic Sectors and Patterns

Learning Objective: Explain the spatial patterns of industrial production and development. (SPS-7.B)

Topic 7.3 Measures of Development

Learning Objective: Describe social and economic measures of development. (SPS-7.C)

Topic 7.4 Women and Economic Development

Learning Objective: Explain how and to what extent changes in economic development have contributed to gender parity. (SPS-7.D)

A nation's growth depends, among other factors, on whether and how it educates and integrates its talent. Women make up half of the potential workforce available in any economy, and the efficient use of this talent pool is an important factor for growth, prosperity and competitiveness.

—World Economic Forum, "Gender Parity," 2016

Source: Wikimedia Commons

Containers can be loaded from trucks or trains and stacked onto large ships via the cranes shown in the images. Containers have reduced break-of-bulk costs dramatically. (See Topic 7.2 for more on containerization.)

The Industrial Revolution

Essential Question: How did the Industrial Revolution facilitate the growth and diffusion of industrialization?

Economic activity and development have brought dramatic changes to the world. **Industry,** the process of using machines and large-scale processes to convert raw materials into manufactured goods, has stimulated social, political, demographic, and economic changes in societies at all scales. Industry requires **raw materials,** the basic substances such as minerals and crops needed to manufacture finished goods.

Growth and Diffusion of Industrialization

Before the 18th century, people made for themselves most clothes, tools, and other items they used. They bought only a few items, often textiles or metal goods, in a **market,** a place where products are sold. What they did buy was usually made by other families working in their own homes who had a contract to make products for a merchant. These small home-based businesses that made goods are called **cottage industries.** These industries depended on intensive human labor since people used simple spinning wheels, looms, and other tools.

Starting in the 18th century, a series of technological advances known as the **Industrial Revolution** resulted in more complex machinery driven by water or steam power that could make products faster and at lower costs than could cottage industries. Because the new machinery was so large and required so much investment money, or capital, manufacturing shifted from homes to factories. The replacement of labor-intensive cottage industry with capital-intensive factory production reshaped not only how people worked, but where they lived and how they related to each other spatially.

CHANGES IN MANUFACTURING DUE TO THE INDUSTRIAL REVOLUTION		
Characteristic	**Cottage Industry**	**Factory Manufacturing**
Scale of Production	Small	Large
Size of Labor Force	One family	Dozens to thousands
Method of Production	Human labor	Machines
Typical Building	House or small workshop	Factory
Capital Investment	Low	Large
Speed of Production	Slow	Fast
Efficiency	Low	High
Market	Local	Local and global

The Industrial Revolution spread throughout the world. However, cottage industries remain important, especially in less-developed countries. Many families survive by producing and selling items such as hand-woven fabric and rugs in both local and global markets. Wealthy consumers are willing to pay more for high-quality handcrafted products than they would pay for mass-produced items.

Diffusion of the Industrial Revolution

Starting in the mid-1700s, the Industrial Revolution diffused rapidly on a regional scale and then a global scale. From Great Britain it moved first to nearby France and the Netherlands. By the mid-1800s, industrialization had spread east to Germany and west to the United States. By the early 1900s, it had reached all of Europe, Japan, parts of China, and South America. Today, most of the world is industrialized.

DIFFUSION OF THE INDUSTRIAL REVOLUTION

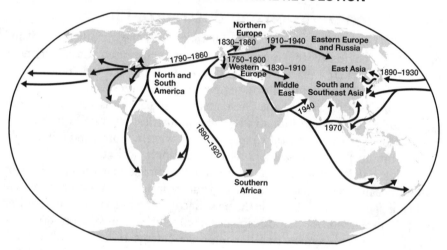

The earliest adopters of the industrialization process were the countries closest to Great Britain. Explain the relatively short time it took for the diffusion to much more distant places such as North or South America? Was distance the only factor that determined if industrialization would be adopted by a country?

On the local scale, investors originally considered three main factors in choosing where to build a factory:

- energy resources to provide power, such as rivers or coal deposits
- minerals or agricultural products needed for producing goods
- transportation routes, such as roads, rivers, canals, and ports

As new forms of transportation and electricity were developed during the 19th century, industries became less dependent on the location of local coal supplies and companies could build factories in more diverse locations.

As factories grew larger, its location near a large workforce became more important. Hence, factories began to cluster in cities. These population centers also provided a market for the products made in a factory.

As the Industrial Revolution progressed, improvements in farm machinery and farming techniques—the Second Agricultural Revolution—increased agricultural productivity. Machine power replaced human and animal power. As a result, society needed fewer people to work on farms. These displaced farm workers moved to cities in search of work. Industrialization, then, promoted greater urbanization.

Growth of Cities and Social Class Changes

The growth of cities and factories reinforced each other. Factory work drew people to cities, who provided a market for factory goods. The greater availability of goods attracted more people. For example, London grew from one million people in 1800 to six million in 1900.

Such rapid urban growth brought problems. Old systems for handling human waste, burying the dead, and cleaning up horse manure were overwhelmed. Disease was rampant. Since people burned wood and coal to heat their homes and run factories, air pollution increased to harmful, even deadly, levels. At times, smog caused the normal death rate to double. Over time, people supported stronger government action—such as building sewers and regulating cemeteries—to protect public health.

Industrialization changed the class structure of society significantly. Before industrialization, most people worked with their hands, usually on farms or sometimes in a craft. A tiny elite class of people were wealthy landowners or church leaders. In between these two classes was a small class of merchants, clergy, and others who relied more on their knowledge than on their physical skills. With industrialization, this middle class expanded rapidly. Industry needed factory managers, accountants, lawyers, clerks, and secretaries. In addition, as the demand for workers who could read and write increased, so did the demand for teachers and professors. Class differences were stark:

- In rural areas, the mechanization of agriculture drove people away, but those who were able to stay benefited from the increased productivity.

- The urban working class who were employed in factories had hard and dangerous jobs, lived in crowded conditions in polluted areas, and often could not afford to purchase the products they made.

- People in the expanding urban middle class had more comfortable lives and enough income to purchase the low-cost manufactured goods.

- Some factory owners, bankers, and others in business in urban areas became extremely wealthy.

- Landowners often maintained their control of land, but they lost much of the influence in society to the rising business-oriented class.

Physical Changes in Cities

Cities grew both outward (horizontally) and upward (vertically). Horizontally, improvements in intra-urban transportation, such as trains, cars, and trucks, allowed cities to spread out farther from the downtown core. People could live farther from their workplace and still commute to work easily. At the same time, producers could transport food from the countryside into cities to feed a growing population.

Vertically, the development of elevators, stronger and more affordable steel, and techniques to construct stronger foundations combined to allow for people to construct taller buildings. As taller buildings made city populations more dense, public health measures became increasingly important.

Colonialism, Imperialism, and the Industrial Revolution

The Industrial Revolution built on the earlier rise of imperialism, a policy of extending a country's political and economic power. (See Topic 4.2.) As countries such as Great Britain and France industrialized, they desired to control trading posts and colonies around the world. They also looked to colonies to provide various resources:

- raw materials such as sugar, cotton, foodstuffs, lumber, and minerals for use in mills and factories
- labor to extract raw materials
- markets where manufacturers could sell finished products
- ports where trading ships could stop to get resupplied
- capital from profits for investing in new factories, canals, and railroads

By the early 1900s, several European countries and the United States had colonies around the globe. The development of imperialism made wealthy countries even wealthier, leading to a greater divide between the advanced, industrialized states and the underdeveloped, nonindustrialized states.

Major Industrialized Regions of the World Today

For most of the 20th century, industrialized regions were often found in large urban areas that provided a significant workforce and along coasts or rivers which provided easy transportation to global markets. Most were part of an **industrial belt** that stretched across the midlatitudes of the Northern Hemisphere. It included the northeastern and midwestern United States, much of Europe, part of Russia, and Japan.

However, near the end of the 1900s, these areas began to **deindustrialize,** a process of decreasing reliance on manufacturing jobs. As a result of improved technology, companies needed fewer employees to produce the same quantity of goods. Further, manufacturing companies transfer production to semiperiphery countries. In places such as China, India, and Mexico, companies could pay workers lower wages and avoid regulations designed to protect workers and the environment. Workers in the deindustrializing core countries fought against this process, but with limited success. Regions that have large numbers of closed factories are called **rust belts.**

THE INDUSTRIAL BELT AND INDUSTRIAL REGIONS

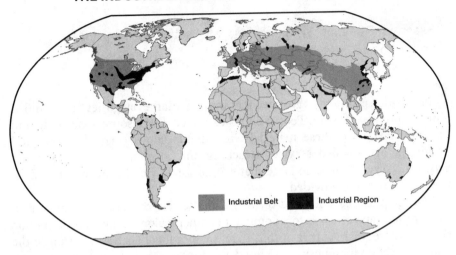

Industrial Belt   Industrial Region

The industrial belt is found in a strip of the midlatitudes in the Northern Hemisphere. What do most of the industrial regions have in common regarding their relative location? Why are they found in these relative locations?

REFLECT ON THE ESSENTIAL QUESTION

Essential Question: *How did the Industrial Revolution facilitate the growth and diffusion of industrialization?*

Reasons for Growth	Reasons for Diffusion

KEY TERMS

industry	Industrial Revolution
raw materials	industrial belt
market	deindustrialize
cottage industry	rust belt

Economic Sectors and Patterns

Essential Question: What are the spatial patterns of industrial production and development?

For decades, economists grouped jobs into three large categories that included almost all types of work. People either extracted raw resources (farming and mining), processed these materials into usable goods (manufacturing and building), or provided services (teaching and medicine). The category of providing services grew so large that economists divided it further, based on the type of services provided.

Geographers have focused on why some sectors of work are dominant in some regions and other sectors dominant in other regions. Why is any economic activity where it is? As part of this, they use locational analysis to evaluate the optimal location for a business to build a factory or other place of employment. For example, at a global scale, they study why most people in Ethiopia work in the extraction sector while most people in the United States work in the service sector. At the local scale, they study why one city has more jobs in software development than another.

Economic Sectors

Today, economists commonly divide a country's workforce into five sectors. The three main sectors are primary, secondary, and tertiary, with quaternary and quinary being additional sectors that were once part of the tertiary sector.

TRADITIONAL SECTORS OF THE U.S. ECONOMY		
Sector and Focus	**Examples**	**Economic Characteristics**
Primary extracting natural resources from the earth	• Farming • Mining • Fishing • Forestry	• Dominated the economy until the late 1800s • Includes many high-risk jobs • A small part of today's economy • Few high-paying jobs • Most jobs require physical skill
Secondary making products from natural resources	• Manufacturing • Building	• Significant growth from the 1840s to the 1960s • Wages vary greatly
Tertiary providing information and services to people	• Retail sales • Medicine • Housekeeping	• A small part of the economy until the mid 1900s • Most people in the U.S. labor force today • Wages vary widely

ADDITIONAL SECTORS OF THE U.S. ECONOMY

Sector and Focus	Examples	Economic Characteristics
Quaternary managing and processing information	• Financial analysis • Software development • Data science	• Small percentage of employees • Most jobs require advanced education or technical skills • High wages • Considered part of the tertiary sector until recently
Quinary creating information and making high-level decisions	• Research • Top managers in corporations or government	• Very small percentage of employees • Very high income • Decisions can affect millions of people • Considered part of the tertiary sector until recently

Identify which sector of the economy each of the following jobs best fits?
A) Architect, B) Tailor, C) Fisher, D) Assembly line worker at a food processing plant, and E) Chief Executive Officer of the Microsoft Corporation

Employment Sectors and Economic Development

In 1800, nearly everyone in the United States worked in the primary sector, mostly in agriculture. As the country industrialized, the agricultural sector became mechanized and efficient enough to free up workers for other jobs, and the demand for people in the secondary sector increased. The primary sector began to decrease. Today, it is less than 5 percent. Employment in the secondary sector grew until it reached a peak in the 1950s, when it began to decline.

Since then, the economy has become *postindustrial*. (See Topic 7.6.) That is, most job growth has been in the tertiary sector. The shifts in the U.S. economy reflect what has happened in most highly industrialized economies today.

STRUCTURAL CHANGES IN ECONOMIES

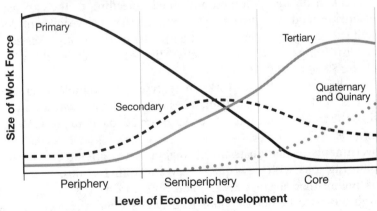

Division of labor varies by level of economic development. What happens to the percentage of workers in each sector of the economy as a country industrializes?

Because the distribution of labor by sector reflects industrialization, countries today have very different mixes in their economies. The following graph shows the percentages of people employed in each of the three sectors for Ethiopia, China, and the United States.

LABOR FORCE BY SECTOR (of selected countries)

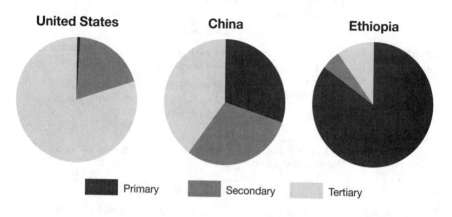

The composition of the labor force changes as the level of economic development changes. Over the next 25 years will China's graph change to look more like Ethiopia's or the United States? Why do you think so?

The Multiplier Effect

As part of this shift, countries become wealthier because wages in the secondary sector are higher than those in the primary sector. In addition to higher wages, the secondary sector jobs also have a large **multiplier effect,** the potential of a job to produce additional jobs. The secondary sector has the greatest multiplier effect of all the sectors. For example, when an auto manufacturer expands a plant and adds 100 new jobs in a community, the new workers will have more money to spend on food, clothes, and movies, leading to the expansion of other businesses and jobs. Economists estimate that every dollar of demand for manufacturers' goods generates $1.92 of demand for other services and products. In comparison, the respective figures for retail and wholesale activities are $0.54 and $0.58.

The multiplier effect also works in reverse. For example, over the past four decades in Flint, Michigan, General Motors has shut down several plants. Because of the reverse multiplier effect, far more people than just GM workers lost their jobs.

Governments in deindustrializing regions often attempt to replace lost manufacturing jobs with new quaternary and quinary jobs. Both types of jobs pay higher-than-average wages, and both can have a multiplier effect. Pittsburgh has used quaternary jobs to drive its rapidly growing economy. As research and high-tech jobs flowed in, entertainment, tourism, and education grew. One challenge of shifting from manufacturing to quaternary jobs is that many of the displaced workers do not possess the skills required for the new jobs. As a result, the displaced workers may end up in the expanding tertiary sector, but usually at less pay than both secondary and quaternary sector jobs.

Theories on Industrial Location

Geographers have developed many models explaining the geographic distribution of economic activities. Because a model focuses on the key factors, it is useful for making predictions about how changing one factor affects the entire process.

Weber's Least Cost Model

In 1909, the secondary sector was growing rapidly in Europe and the United States. German economist Alfred Weber developed an influential theory, known as the **least cost theory**, to explain the key decisions made by businesses about where to locate factories. Weber proposed that factory owners would locate their factories where they could minimize their total costs by balancing three factors:

- minimizing transportation costs, such as getting raw materials to the factory and moving finished products to where they will be sold
- minimizing labor costs, such as the wages and salaries of employees
- maximizing **agglomeration economies,** the spatial grouping of several businesses to share costs, such as an access road to a public highway or development of a workforce with special skills

The Locational Triangle

Weber's model can be shown with a **locational triangle**. The three points of the triangle are the market for a good and two resources needed to make the good.

Bulk and Industrial Location Transportation costs were often closely related to the bulk (weight and size) of the objects being transported. Weber observed that some raw materials lose bulk during processing and some do not. For example, copper is embedded in heavy rock when first mined, but it loses bulk as it is processed. So copper production is an example of a **bulk-reducing industry.** These types of industry are also known as weight-losing, raw material-oriented, or raw-material-dependent industry.

Since transporting the extracted material is more expensive than transporting the finished product, a company can save money by moving production close to the sources of that raw material. It does not need to pay the cost of shipping the full weight of the material when only part of it is needed. Most mining, lumber, and agricultural industries are bulk-reducing. This helps explain why states known for their agriculture, such as Iowa, often have a significant number of jobs in food processing facilities.

In contrast, soft drinks become bulkier as processing occurs. The heaviest component of a soft drink is water. Since water is ubiquitous (widely available), companies try to add it as close to the market as possible, rather than pay to ship the weight of the water. These factories usually locate close to the market and are considered **bulk-gaining industries** (or weight-gaining, market-oriented, or market-dependent industries).

Products are commonly made of multiple bulk-reducing raw materials. Based on a locational triangle, these relationships can be identified:

- The manufacturing site (D) will be somewhere between the locations of the two raw materials (B and C).
- The intermediate location will be closer to the one that loses the greater percentage of its weight (C in this case).
- The finished product would then be shipped directly from the processing facility (D) to the market (A).

WEBER'S LOCATIONAL TRIANGLE

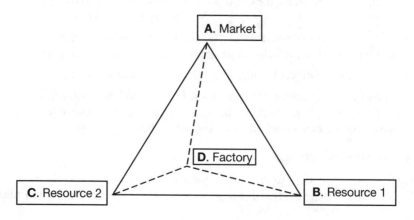

Weber's locational triangle. Considering the location of the factory at D relative to the two resources (B and C), which of the two resources loses the greater percentage of its weight when processed?

Sometimes the cost savings from either cheaper labor or from agglomeration economies could be greater than the savings derived from locating at the cheapest spot relative to transportation costs. In these cases, Weber recognized that business owners would benefit by locating where these other costs were less.

Applying Weber's Theory Like other models that simplify reality, Weber's model had the benefit of focusing attention on key parts of a complex process. However, this benefit came with limitations. In response to these limitations, later scholars refined Weber's model by adding other considerations to it. However, the basic model remains useful. It recognizes patterns that can help people make decisions about the spatial distribution of factories, offices, and all types of business that employ workers.

COMPARING WEBER'S THEORY AND REALITY		
Issue	**Weber's Assumption**	**Real Conditions**
Uniformity of Area	The area considered is an isotropic plain, which means that human and physical geographic features are uniform throughout an area.	Isotropic plains rarely exist. Mountains, densely populated urban areas, and other features can alter the transportation costs.
Labor	Sufficient labor is available in fixed locations and it is immobile.	Automation reduces the need for labor. Labor is relatively mobile.
Raw Materials	Raw materials are found only in certain fixed locations.	Raw materials are often available in many locations. The *substitution principle* allows for alternative inputs.
Number of Products and Markets	There is one good produced, and it is for a single market in a fixed location.	Goods are sold in more than one location. Globalization may result in numerous markets.
Transportation Costs	Transportation costs are directly related to the distance of travel and to the weight of the items.	Cost per mile may decrease as the distance increases. *Space-time compression* can reduce the overall cost of transportation.
Influences on Location	Economic factors dominate the decision about where to locate a factory.	Emotional factors, such as tradition, a desire to have the factory close to where the owner lives, or the presence of existing facilities can influence where a factory is opened.
Significance of Costs	Owners want to minimize costs.	Owners maximize revenue and establish predictable future costs to generate profit.

Labor Costs

Weber's original least cost model did not differentiate among different types of labor. A company in a **labor-oriented industry,** or **labor-dependent industry,** is highly dependent on a workforce and will want to be near a source of those workers. Companies more dependent on a large quantity of labor will try to locate near a community with an available potential workforce. High-tech companies that depend on highly skilled workers in the computer or engineering fields often locate close to major universities.

Importance of Energy

The history of manufacturing demonstrates the importance of a source of power for machinery. The type of power influenced where factories were built:

- Waterpower was not mobile, so early mills and factories were located on streams and rivers.

- Coal could be transported, so companies had wider options about where to locate factories. However, coal is bulky and expensive to transport. So, companies that needed vast quantities of coal also tried to locate near coalfields. Coal could also power a mobile engine, which made railroads practical. Companies became less dependent on water transportation.
- With the development of electricity in the late 19th century, power became even more mobile. It could move through wires at low costs for hundreds of miles so, the location of energy sources became less important.

Aluminum production relies on the raw material of bauxite, but it is an energy-oriented industry. Companies locate processing plants near low-cost sources of energy and ship the bauxite to the plant rather than process it near a mine where energy costs are high. Low-cost hydroelectricity in Canada and geothermal-electricity in Iceland results in large-scale aluminum processing in both countries.

Bulk, Containerization, and Transportation

The cost of shipping materials decreased dramatically in the last two centuries because of improved technology and methods. As the following table shows, various modes of transportation have various benefits.

COMPARISON OF TRANSPORTATION TYPES			
Mode	Speed	Capacity	Per Unit Cost
Airplane	High	Low	High
Train	Medium	Large	Low
Truck	Medium	Low	Medium
Pipe	Medium	Large	Low to Medium
Ocean Ship	Slow	Large	Low
River Barge	Slow	Medium	Medium

In addition to new technology, people have developed systems for speeding up the **break of bulk,** the procedure of transferring cargo from one mode of transportation to another. This is achieved through **containerization,** the system in which goods are loaded into a standardized shipping unit. The containers are **intermodal,** meaning they can be carried on a truck, train, ship, or plane. For example, a container might be loaded in a computer factory in China and not unloaded until after it has been carried by train to a port on the coast, transported across the ocean to the United States on a ship, taken by a truck to Dallas, and then finally delivered to a warehouse. By making transportation more efficient, additional regions of the world have been involved in the global trade network.

Significance of Government

Government policies and political stability influence location decisions in many ways. Tax dollars pay for much of the transportation network. Companies prefer to locate in countries and communities that are safe and peaceful, and have predictable enforcement of laws and regulations. Additionally, governments from the local to the national scale offer tax breaks, subsidies, and other incentives to encourage companies to locate their factories in specific areas.

Other Locational Considerations

One refinement to Weber's theory has been to allow for differences in industries. For example, the cost of raw materials is more influential for a steel plant than it is for a factory making high-end clothing.

Businesses use a hierarchy of locational factors in choosing where to build. The table below uses the example of a new factory being constructed in the United States that will market its product both nationally and globally. The primary location factors are used to pick a general region of the country (e.g. Southeast or state). Secondary factors are used to narrow down the location to a more specific location, such as a particular metropolitan area. Finally, another group of factors may be used to determine the exact site of the factory within a particular metropolitan area.

FACTORS IN LOCATING A MANUFACTURING FACILITY		
Scale of Analysis	Example	Examples of Site or Situational Factors
National	Southeastern United States	• Proximity to the market of the densely populated northeastern United States • Proximity to raw materials • Availability of sufficient labor with the right mix of skills • Lower than average wages for the United States • Access to global transportation network through the Atlantic Ocean and the Panama Canal • Adequate and affordable supply of power
Regional	Charleston, South Carolina	• Favorable government regulations such as tax incentives • Agglomeration economies from nearby factories • Access to global and national transportation networks: Large airport, container ship port, 2 major rail lines and 3 interstate highways • Local universities and tech schools provide skilled workers • Lower than average energy costs for the United States • High quality of education, recreational, affordable housing and medical facilities
Local	Industrial park site beside harbor	• Large, flat piece of land that is easy to build on • Adequate water and sewer lines • Waterfront access and a dock available for ships • Rail spur line connecting to the main rail system • Good road system connecting to major highways and airport • Adequate space for easy truck loading and unloading • Adequate parking space for employees

Other Models While Weber assumed business wanted to minimize costs, other geographers have started with other assumptions. August Lösch assumed that businesses would maximize profits, even if it required higher costs. Harold Hotelling focused on locational interdependence, meaning that businesses choose a location based partially on where their competitors were located.

Additional Locational Considerations

In addition to the factors described above, other factors can shape locational decisions of other sectors of the economy. These refinements show how companies have become more flexible about their locations.

Online Businesses The development of high-speed internet service greatly increased online retail selling. Since some businesses don't rely on face-to-face interactions, they can be based anywhere. However, the location of distribution centers that fulfill orders need access to transportation systems and markets.

Companies that provide informational services, such as call centers, can locate their offices anywhere with good communications systems and a group of trained people who speak the language of their customers. Over the past two decades, hundreds of call centers that serve U.S. customers have been built in rural areas of the United States and Canada, as well as in low-wage countries such as India and the Philippines. However, because locational demands are minimal, these businesses are **footloose,** meaning they can pack up and leave for a new location quickly and easily.

Prestige To signal its prominence and wealth, a corporation might want to locate its main office for its top executives on the expensive upper floors of a skyscraper in a large city. These types of spaces, known as **front offices,** are designed to impress clients. However, the company might decide to locate the rest of its employees in less expensive office spaces, known as **back offices.**

Locational Decisions and World Systems Theory

On a global scale, decisions about where to locate factories, offices, and other businesses shape the wealth and power of countries. Economic historian Immanuel Wallerstein developed what is known as World Systems Theory. (See Topic 7.5.) He grouped countries into three categories:

- Core countries are highly industrialized and wealthy. Examples include the United States, Japan, Australia, and most of Europe. They have strong government support for economic growth, so businesses often locate their quaternary and quinary sector workers in these countries.

- Semiperiphery countries are those in the process of developing industry but are less wealthy than core countries. Examples include China, India, Brazil, and Mexico. Companies often locate factories in semiperiphery countries. As these countries develop, skills and wages increase, so they add more tertiary sector jobs and lose secondary sector jobs to lower-wage countries.

- Periphery countries are more reliant on producing raw materials than on industry. Examples include Bangladesh, Bolivia, Cambodia, and most countries in Africa. Poor infrastructure makes it difficult for these countries to attract jobs in any sector other than the primary sector.

REFLECT ON THE ESSENTIAL QUESTION

Essential Question: *What are the spatial patterns of industrial production and development?*

Identify the Three Elements of Weber's Model	Description of Each Element of Weber's Model

KEY TERMS

primary sector
secondary sector
tertiary sector
quaternary sector
quinary sector
multiplier effect
least cost theory
agglomeration economies
locational triangle
bulk-reducing industries

bulk-gaining industries
labor-oriented industry
   (labor-dependent industry)
break of bulk
containerization
intermodal
footloose
front offices
back offices

Measures of Development

Essential Question: What are social and economic measures of development?

The decisions by companies about where to locate factories, call centers, and other businesses shape each country's economic development. In addition, countries make decisions that affect their own prosperity. The opening quotation of the chapter highlights a key issue in making progress: using the talents of all members of society. Even into the 21st century, many countries restrict opportunities for ethnic minorities and women which slows economic progress. Having measurable data regarding the opportunities for all groups allows people to compare success of development attempts in various regions.

Measures of Development

Geographers use several statistics to indicate the overall wealth of a country and its people. Three of the most common are Gross Domestic Product (GDP), Gross National Product (GNP), or Gross National Income (GNI). These vary slightly, based on issues such as whether money earned by a U.S. citizen working in Korea should be credited to the United States or to Korea. However, they are all attempts to measure the total output of a country.

GNP and GNI The dollar amount of all goods and services produced by a country's citizens in one year is measured in the **Gross National Product (GNP)** and the **Gross National Income (GNI)**. These terms are very similar and often used interchangeably. They involve the money generated by citizens and businesses of a country, regardless of where the citizens are, or live, when money is earned. For example, the income of American citizens working in South Korea and the profits from an American-owned factory in Mexico would both count as part of the United States' GNP and GNI. The money made by Mexican migrant workers in a foreign-owned factory on U.S. soil would not count as part of the United States' GNP or GNI.

GDP The dollar amount of all final goods and services produced within a country in one year is the **Gross Domestic Product (GDP)**. GDP is based more upon geography in the sense that it involves money generated by any business or person within a country. Only money earned in the United States, regardless of who earns it, will be used to calculate the United States' GDP. It does not matter if the money stays in the country where it was earned—the key is that the money was generated within the country. For example, the income earned by Mexican migrant workers, or the profits from a foreign-owned factory on

U.S. soil, would count as part of the United States' GDP. This is true even if the migrant workers sent much of their earnings back to family members in their home countries as **remittances**, or the profits from a foreign-owned company were leaving the country and going back to the home country.

Making Statistics More Useful To make comparisons among countries more useful, these statistics are adjusted in several ways:

- Countries use different currencies, so amounts are usually converted into U.S. dollars to make comparisons easier.

- The total size of a country's economy influences the total size of its output. To adjust for the number of people in a country, each country's total output can be divided by the country's total population. This produces an amount per person, referred to as **per capita.** For example, in 2019, the United Kingdom and India has similar total GDPs of approximately $2.9 trillion but very different GDPs per capita. In the United Kingdom, it was about $39,000. In far more populous India, it was about $1,900.

- The prices people pay for identical goods varies from country to country because of transportation costs, the value of its currency, and other factors. To adjust for the variations in the prices of goods in various countries, economists use **purchasing power parity (PPP)**, a measure of what similar goods cost in different countries. For example, in 2016, the same collection of goods that cost $1,000 in the United States, cost $590 in the Czech Republic and $1,620 in Switzerland. So, people with the same income in these three countries could afford more goods in the Czech Republic than in the other two countries.

All three measures of development are based upon money and it is generally accepted that the countries with the high GDP/capita, GNP/capita, or GNI/capita are wealthy countries and therefore highly economically developed, and those with low values are poor countries and not as well developed.

GDP (PPP) PER CAPITA, 2018

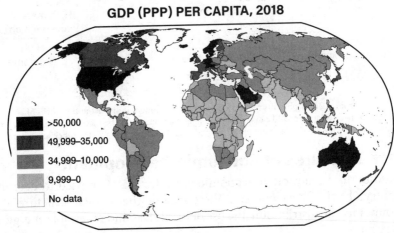

Source: Wikimedia Commons

There is a tremendous range of wealth in the world. In terms of the relative location, what do many of the countries in the lowest categories have in common? Explain how the relative location of these countries results in their low GDP per capita.

Terms of Development

The various economic measures reflect a continuum of the relative wealth and development among countries. People use various systems to categorize countries on this continuum. Each system focuses on slightly different traits of countries, so it uses slightly different terms. However, systems divide countries broadly into low-end, middle-range, and high-end categories. The table below summarizes some of these systems. World Systems Theory and Stages of Economic Growth will be discussed in more detail in Topic 7.5.

COMPARING TERMS FOR LEVELS OF DEVELOPMENT				
System	**Low End**	**Middle Range**		**High End**
Economic Level (based on GDP/capita)	Low income	Middle income		High income
Economic Development (based on overall economic characteristics)	Developing economies	Emerging economies		Advanced economies
Level of Industrialization (based on amount of industry)	Nonindustrialized	Newly industrialized country (NIC)		Postindustrial economy
Human Development Index (based on economic and social factors)	Low HDI	Medium HDI		High and very high HDI
World Systems Theory (based on the role in the world economy)	Periphery country	Semiperiphery country		Core country
Stages of Economic Growth (based on types of economic activity)	Stage 1: Traditional society Stage 2: Precondition for take-off	Stage 3: Take-off		Stage 4: Drive to maturity Stage 5: High mass consumption
Income Classification (World Bank designation)	Low income	Lower-middle income	Higher-middle income	High income

The vast number and variety of terms related to levels of development indicate the challenges of both trying to measure development and categorizing it. Suggest a reason why the Income Classification terms recently adopted by the World Bank can be considered as an improvement over the other sets of terms.

Other Measures of Economic Development

In addition to money, other economic variables are often used to determine a country's level of development. These include the sectoral structure of the economy, income distribution, the use of fossil fuels and renewable energy, and literacy rates.

Sectoral Structure of the Economy

The least-developed countries in the world have higher percentages of their labor force in the primary sector. (See Topic 7.2.) In contrast, more developed countries have higher percentages in the tertiary sector.

Another way to analyze an economy is to distinguish between the formal and the informal sectors. The **formal sector** is the portion of the economy that is monitored by government, so people in it follow regulations and pay taxes. This is the portion of economic activity measured by GDP, GNP, and GNI. The **informal sector** is the portion of the economy that is not monitored by government. It includes several types of economic activities:

- Some activities are done without any pay, such as cleaning your own house or cooking meals for a friend who is sick. Similar services done for money are part of the formal economy.
- Some activities are legal if reported to the government, but are often not reported. For example, restaurant workers can legally accept tips, but not reporting the income from tips on a tax return is illegal.
- Some activities are always illegal, such as drug dealing and identity theft.

The informal sector is sometimes called the underground economy or the shadow economy. For many people in poor countries, participating in the informal sector allows them to survive. In general, the lower the level of development, the higher the percentage of workers involved in the informal sector. In some countries, it probably includes over half of economic activity. Economists who study the shadow economy estimate that it accounts for about 10 percent of the U.S. economy.

Energy Consumption

As people become more prosperous, they consume more because they can afford to purchase more goods and they live longer. For example, the United States includes about 5 percent of the world's population but consumes about 20 percent of all resources. The spatial pattern of consumption of energy is shown in the map on the following page. At current rates of consumption, a baby born in the United States will consume in his or her lifetime more than 200 times the energy resources as will a baby born in Bangladesh.

While the spatial pattern of consumption is strongly skewed toward the developed world, the environmental impact of the consumption is spread more broadly. Many natural resources used to manufacture goods are extracted and processed in semiperiphery countries and then consumed in the core countries. Consequently, the problems with mining and manufacturing plague poor countries. For example, mining is among the most dangerous jobs in the world, and manufacturing is responsible for signficant air pollution. However, problems with using products, such as waste disposal, are more common in wealthy countries.

ENERGY CONSUMPTION AROUND THE WORLD

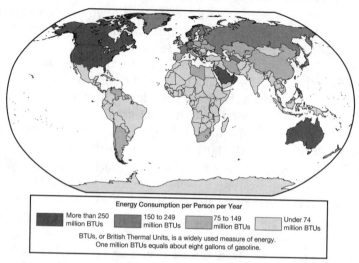

Energy Consumption per Person per Year

| More than 250 million BTUs | 150 to 249 million BTUs | 75 to 149 million BTUs | Under 74 million BTUs |

BTUs, or British Thermal Units, is a widely used measure of energy.
One million BTUs equals about eight gallons of gasoline.

What regions of the world use the most and least amounts of energy?

Income Distribution

While per capita measures of wealth are useful for comparing countries, they do not reflect the distribution of wealth. South Africa and Paraguay have similar levels of GDP per capita but very different distributions of wealth. Paraguay has a much higher percentage of middle-income people, while South Africa has more people who are either very wealthy or very poor.

One measure of the distribution of income within a population is the **Gini coefficient,** sometimes called the Gini index. The values range between 0 and 1. The higher the number, the higher the degree of income inequality. A Gini coefficient of 0 would mean the population had no inequality—everyone's income was exactly the same. A Gini coefficient of 1 would indicate total inequality—one person had all the income in a population and everyone else had none.

GINI COEFFICIENT BY COUNTRY, 2017

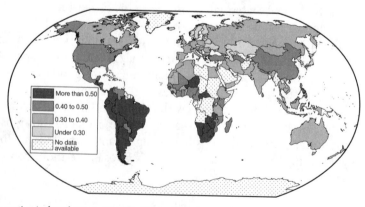

| More than 0.50 |
| 0.40 to 0.50 |
| 0.30 to 0.40 |
| Under 0.30 |
| No data available |

What connection is there between the size of the middle class, industrialization, and the Gini coefficient?

In general, periphery and semiperiphery countries have higher Gini coefficients than do core countries. Often, this reflects the small number of middle-income people in a periphery and semiperiphery country.

Patterns of Economic Development

The spatial pattern of inequality reflects more general patterns of economic development. At a global scale, some regions are wealthier than others.

Africa and South America Many African states have growing economies, but average incomes remain low compared with more-developed countries. South America has both middle- and low-income countries. These continents account for about 20 percent of the world population but only about 8 percent of global GDP.

Asia The largest income gains in the past five decades have been in Asia. First Japan, and then South Korea, Hong Kong, and Singapore, adopted policies of strong government support for education and business, which promoted prosperity. More recently, China and India have shown impressive economic developments. Asia accounts for about 60 percent of the world population and about 37 percent of global GDP.

North America and Europe These regions have been relatively prosperous over the past century. With about 16 percent of the world population, they produce about 55 percent of global GDP. Western Europe and the United States have been the wealthiest parts of this region. Central America is mostly middle income with Mexico and Costa Rica becoming more prosperous.

Uneven Development at the Regional Scale Development can be very uneven within countries. In general, rural or peripheral regions of a country are often less developed than core urban areas. In China, the three wealthiest provinces are along the heavily urbanized Pacific Coast, while the poorest provinces are all in the heavily rural western region.

Social Measures of Development

Relying on just one statistic, or "single numberitis," is not a reliable way to understand a country's level of development. Several noneconomic factors also reflect development.

- The total fertility rate (see Topics 2.4 and 2.8) is the number of babies a woman is expected to have in her lifetime. It shows a negative or inverse correlation with wealth and development. That is, as income and development goes up, total fertility typically declines.
- The infant mortality rate (see Topic 2.4) is the rate at which babies die before the age of one. It also has an inverse correlation with development.
- **Life expectancy,** the number of years a person is expected to live, has a positive correlation with development. Life expectancy is also related to the availability of adequate health care. Poor countries that have invested in health care have increased their life expectancy.

- The **literacy rate** is the percentage of population that can read and write, usually at an 8th grade level or higher. In 2015, it topped 90 percent of the world population and 99 percent in highly developed countries. Most who were not literate were females living in less-developed countries.

The Gender Gap

Differences in the privileges afforded to males and females in a society are the **gender gap.** The size of the gender gap varies tremendously among countries. These differences might appear in educational opportunities, employment options, wages, voting rights, health care, political empowerment, property rights, the ability to drive a car, inheritance rights, or the right to make contraceptive decisions.

Gender Inequality Index (GII)

Since 2010, UN's Human Development Report has reported on the **Gender Inequality Index (GII),** a composite measure of several factors indicating gender disparity:

- Reproductive health, which includes maternal mortality rates (death of a mother during birth) and adolescent (under 19 years old) fertility rates

- Empowerment, which includes the share of government seats held by each gender and the proportion of adult females and males with at least some secondary education

- Labor market participation, which includes the labor force participation rate of female and male populations aged 15 years and older

The composite score is a measure of the percentage of potential human development lost due to gender inequality. The table belows the GII for Switzerland, the United States, and Yemen. The GII for Switzerland indicates that the country lost only 2.5 percent of its potential human development as a result of gender inequality in 2019, while Yemen lost 79.5 percent.

GII WORLD RANKINGS, 2019 (for selected countries)		
Country	Rank in World	GII
Switzerland	1	0.025
United States	46	0.204
Yemen	162	0.795

Source: UN Human Development Report, 2019

The GII varies greatly among countries of different development levels. In which of these three countries would you expect the maternal mortality rate and the adolescent fertility rates to be the lowest?

A closer examination of data used to determine the GII for Switzerland, the United States, and Yemen reveals the discrepancies among the variables—shown in the table on the next page. Of particular significance are the share of seats in parliament and labor participation value. Women in Yemen are severely underrepresented in their governments, as well as in the labor force.

DIFFERENCES AMONG GII DATA, 2018 (for selected countries)			
2018 Values	**Switzerland**	**United States**	**Yemen**
Maternal Mortality Rate (Deaths/100,000 live births)	5	19	385
Adolescent Birth Rate (Births/1,000 for women ages 15–19)	2.8	19.9	60.4
Share of Seats in Parliament (Percent held by women)	29.3	23.7	0.5
Population with Some Secondary Education or More (Percent for ages 25 and older)	Female: 96.4 Male: 97.2	Female: 96.1 Male: 96.0	Female: 19.9 Male: 35.5
Labor Force Participation Rate (Percent for ages 15 and older)	Female: 62.6 Male: 74.1	Female: 56.1 Male: 68.2	Female: 6.0 Male: 70.8

Source: UN Human Development Report, 2019

Notice the very large differences among the data for these countries. Where would a female have the greatest opportunity to study and to potentially earn a seat in the country's parliament?

The Human Development Index (HDI)

Since money alone does not reflect human well-being, in 1990, a group of researchers led by Pakistani economist Mahbub ul Haq released an alternative measure of development. The **Human Development Index (HDI)** combines one economic measure (GNI per capita) with three social measures (life expectancy, expected years of schooling, and average years of schooling). The composite score for each country will range between 0 and 1, with the higher values representing greater levels of development.

HUMAN DEVELOPMENT INDEX, 2018

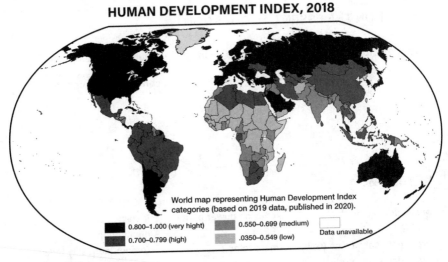

World map representing Human Development Index categories (based on 2019 data, published in 2020).

■ 0.800–1.000 (very hight)	■ 0.550–0.699 (medium)
■ 0.700–0.799 (high)	■ .0350–0.549 (low)
	□ Data unavailable

Source: Wikimedia Commons

The majority of countries with the highest HDI scores are core countries. Which continent has the most countries with very low HDI?

While most countries rank similarly on GNI per capita and HDI, some rank quite differently, as the chart on the following page shows.

HUMAN DEVELOPMENT INDEX SCORE, 2019 (for select countries)

Country	HDI Score	Rank Based Upon HDI	Rank Based Upon GNI/Capita PPP
Norway	0.954	1	6
United States	0.920	15	11
Israel	0.906	22	45
Qatar	0.848	41	1
Cuba	0.778	72	125
Niger	0.394	189	181

Source: hdr.org

*World Rankings based upon GNI/capita PPP and Human Development Index, 2019

What do the two different rankings suggest about Cuba? What do the two different rankings suggest about Qatar? Note: Niger had the lowest HDI of all countries with data in 2019.

In the table above, notice the differences between the rankings for GNI/capita PPP and HDI for the six countries:

- The rankings of countries by HDI and income are often similar (Norway and the United States). Norway ranks 1st in HDI and 6th in income.
- Some that invest heavily in education and medical care rank higher in HDI than in income (Israel and Cuba). Israel ranks 22nd in HDI but only 45th in income.
- Some countries that are rich in oil or other natural resources rank higher in income than in HDI. Qatar ranks first in the world in income, but only 41st in HDI.

REFLECT ON THE ESSENTIAL QUESTION

Essential Question: *What are social and economic measures of development?*

Social Measures	Economic Measures

KEY TERMS

gross national product (GNP)	purchasing power parity (PPP)	literacy rate
gross national income (GNI)	formal sector	gender gap
gross domestic product (GDP)	informal sector	Gender Inequality Index (GII)
remittances	Gini coefficient	Human Development Index (HDI)
per capita	life expectancy	

Women and Economic Development

Essential Question: To what extent have changes in economic development contributed to gender parity?

Females account for slightly less than half of the world's population, yet they account for far less than half of the world's earnings. Much of their work is not measured because it is unpaid work done for their family, such as raising children and cooking. When women do work in the formal sector, they are often paid less than their male counterparts. This loss of economic potential slows progress toward improving the standard of living. Many countries are trying to expand education for females so they can become fully engaged in economic development

As countries become more developed economically, the roles open to women often change. In general, higher development and higher status for females are correlated. The Gender Inequality Index (GII) is often used to measure inequality and helps monitor changes in equity over time.

Barriers to Gender Equality

The GII chart in Topic 7.3 shows gender equity at the country scale. Within countries, urban areas often have higher gender equity than rural areas. Overall, conditions are improving but obstacles to gender equity for women still exist:

- Cultural barriers often inhibit participation in the economy. (See Topics 3.2 and 3.7.)
- Lack of educational opportunities can reduce employment options. (See Topic 2.8.)
- Limited access to loans and other resources makes starting or expanding a business difficult. (See Topics 5.10 and 5.12.)

Wages for women have increased in recent decades, but there still is a global disparity in the wages between men and women, even with comparable work. In the United States, if a man and a woman do the same type of job, a man would typically make a salary that is 17.5 percent higher than a woman.

The Glass Ceiling Another trend reflecting employment discrimination toward women is that women rarely obtain upper-level jobs in companies, the civil service, or in governments, particularly in developing countries. The situation has been improving in recent years in developed countries, but the "glass ceiling," as it is often called, remains. If a country reaches a stage where the glass ceiling ceases to exist, the standard of living will rise tremendously for all of its citizens.

In top levels of corporations and in politics, women often must overcome cultural attitudes that cause people to not see them as leaders. Women such as former British Prime Minister Margaret Thatcher, U.S. Vice President Kamala Harris, and General Motors Company CEO Mary Barra are examples of women who became part of the quinary sector.

Increased Opportunities for Women

Women have made progress toward gender equality despite the significant obstacles they face. Governments of many countries, transnational corporations, non-governmental organizations, and international organizations, such as the United Nations, have aided the efforts to reduce gender inequality.

Transnational Corporations One reason for the expanded employment opportunities for women has been the efforts of transnational corporations. As these businesses have opened more factories in developing countries, they often employed women because they were available and would work for lower wages than men. Another key reason for increased female participation in the labor force is because of very low birth rates. Countries such as Japan and Singapore would face severe labor shortages if women were not accepted as an integral part of the labor force.

Increased educational opportunities for females during the past two decades also prepared more women to work outside their homes. Globally, more than 250 million additional women joined the paid workforce between 2006 and 2015. Many women who previously had low-paying domestic jobs as servants, childcare providers, and store clerks began earning significantly more in manufacturing jobs.

NGOs and Microloans Several programs enacted by governments and international non-profit agencies, known as **non-governmental organizations** (NGOs), empower women to find jobs outside the home. One example of how NGOs have helped women is through **microcredit**, or **microfinance** programs, to provide loans often to women to start or expand a business. The most well-known of these is the Grameen Bank, founded in Bangladesh in 1983. These programs have been particularly active in South Asia and South America. The repayment rate for these loans has been unusually high—more than 98 percent.

The success of microcredit programs resulted in several changes to societies where the loans are available. The increased financial clout of women gave them more influence in their homes and communities. And as working women have more voice in childbearing decisions, more money to pay for contraceptives, and less need for additional children, birth rates have decreased. Women's increased wealth also allows for the children to be better nourished, which has helped to reduce child mortality.

Sustainable Development Goals for Women The United Nations established a series of goals in 2015 to encourage sustainable development. Many targeted areas to improve the lives of females. The creators of these goals recognized that gender equality will lead to economic development. (See Topic 7.8 for more on Sustainable Development Goals and their effects on women.)

Essential Question: *What factors have contributed to gender parity?*

Social	Economic

KEY TERMS

non-governmental organizations (NGOs)   microcredit (microfinance)

GEOGRAPHIC PERSPECTIVES: *NEIGHBORHOODS FOR NEW CLASSES*

Prior to the Industrial Revolution that began in the mid-18th century, most people in Europe were farmers who lived in rural communities. A few were wealthy nobles who lived on estates or in the centers of cities. With industrialization, though, the number of people in the middle class grew tremendously and a new class of factory workers emerged. Where would they live?

Middle Class

As industrialization began, most members of the growing middle class lived and worked in urban areas, but in widely scattered locations. Some could afford to live in the center of the city. Others lived in new areas built on the outskirts of an urban area. And some lived above their shops, wherever they were located. The spatial distribution of the middle class made building a sense of unity in the new class difficult.

Working Class

The other type of job that greatly expanded in numbers was working in factories. People doing these jobs became known as the working class. They found housing in less-desirable urban neighborhoods located outside the central business districts. The spatial dimensions of their lives—toiling side-by-side in large groups in factories and living near each other in distinctive neighborhoods—created strong social bonds among them. These bonds led them to form labor unions, which gave them power to push for higher wages and better working conditions.

1. Which of the TWO rapidly expanding social classes was larger?
2. Explain why the working class resided in a more spatially concentrated pattern than the middle class.

THINK AS A GEOGRAPHER: *DEFINING DEVELOPMENT*

The Human Development Index illustrates the level of development of countries using both economic and social measures. Immanuel Wallerstein asserted that the inter-regional interaction between economically developed (core) countries and economically developing (periphery) countries was the primary influence on the global economy. Wallerstein believed the core countries had more disposable income to invest in new technologies and to train higher-skilled labor, while peripheral countries provided more low-skill, low-wage labor.

The following chart shows some of the data used to calculate the HDI score for several countries. Use it to answer the questions that follow.

HDI DATA FOR SELECTED COUNTRIES, 2015			
Country	Life Expectancy at Birth (in years)	Expected Years of Schooling	Income per Capita
Japan	83.5	15.3	$36,927
United States	79.1	16.5	$52,946
Brazil	74.5	15.2	$15,175
Bangladesh	71.6	10.0	$3,191
India	68.0	11.7	$5,497
Haiti	62.8	8.7	$1,668
Nigeria	52.8	9.0	$5,341

Source: United Nations Development Programme, Human Development Reports

1. Using the data above, which countries demonstrate characteristics more closely aligned to be a part of the global economic core?

2. Identify ONE of the countries in the chart above that would be considered in the global economic periphery.

3. Explain why life expectancy is an important indicator of development.

4. Describe the pattern that exists between years of schooling and income per capita.

CHAPTER 18 REVIEW
Industrialization and Economic Development
Topics 7.1–7.4

MULTIPLE-CHOICE QUESTIONS

Question 1 refers to the following graph.

GLOBAL GENDER GAP PERFORMANCE

Source: Based on data from the World Economic Forum, "The Global Gender Gap Report 2015."

1. The two areas that have the largest degree of gender inequality are
   (A) health and politics
   (B) health and education
   (C) economy and politics
   (D) economy and education
   (E) economy and health

2. The question most likely studied using the Gini Index is whether
   (A) a country is moving closer to gender equality
   (B) religious traditions influence educational achievements
   (C) climate influences the infant mortality rate
   (D) push or pull factors are more influential on migration
   (E) the income distribution influences economic growth

3. The Industrial Revolution's greatest impact on the social structure was
   (A) a significant increase in the percentage of upper-class citizens
   (B) the growth of a large middle class
   (C) a large increase in the percentage of people in the primary sector
   (D) a significant decline in the percentage of middle-class citizens
   (E) the development of the wealthy nobility

4. Which is the best example of a footloose activity?

(A) A steel mill

(B) An auto assembly plant

(C) A call center

(D) A large research university

(E) An aluminum smelter

5. Fishing, farming, forestry, and mining are part of the

(A) primary sector

(B) secondary sector

(C) tertiary sector

(D) quaternary sector

(E) quinary sector

6. Which statement best demonstrates why purchasing power parity is useful in comparing income and wealth in various countries?

(A) The euro is worth about $1.05.

(B) A pair of blue jeans that cost $27 in Pakistan cost $40 in Laos.

(C) Inflation is 2 percent higher in Indonesia than it is in Peru.

(D) Unemployment is 2 percent higher in Israel than it is in Japan.

(E) Germany's national debt is twice as high as Panama's.

Question 7 refers to the diagram below.

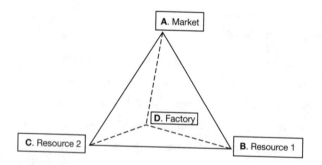

7. The diagram illustrates the optimal location of a factory for which of the following scenarios?

(A) A bulk-reducing raw material-oriented industry

(B) An energy-oriented industry

(C) A market-oriented industry

(D) A bulk-gaining raw material-oriented industry

(E) A labor-dependent industry

1. One way to analyze a region's economic system is by the type of jobs people perform there. Use the diagram below to answer the questions that follow it.

STRUCTURAL CHANGES IN ECONOMIES

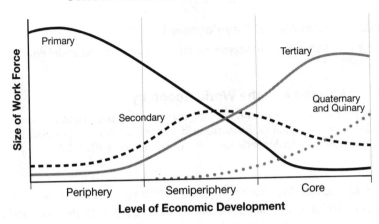

(A) Identify the category of jobs and give a specific example of a job that is most common in preindustrial countries or regions.

(B) Describe the types of jobs in the secondary sector of the economy.

(C) Explain why the percentage of the workforce in the secondary sector often declines as a country becomes more developed.

(D) Describe an additional economic impact on a local community when jobs are lost in the secondary sector.

(E) The number of people employed in the secondary sector in the United States has declined since 1975, but the overall production of goods has increased. Explain how this statement could be true.

(F) Describe tertiary sector jobs.

(G) Explain the benefit of quaternary sector jobs.

CHAPTER 19

Development and Trade

Topics 7.5–7.6

Topic 7.5 Theories of Development

Learning Objective: Explain different theories of economic and social development. (SPS-7.E)

Topic 7.6 Trade and the World Economy

Learning Objective: Explain causes and geographic consequences of recent economic changes such as the increase in international trade, deindustrialization, and growing interdependence in the world economy. (PSO-7.A)

Globalization, the increasing integration and interdependence of domestic and overseas markets, has three sides: the good side, the bad side, and the ugly side.

—Panos Mourdoukoutas, "The Good, the Bad, and the Ugly Side of Globalization," *Forbes*, 2011

Source: Wikimedia Commons

The Three Gorges dam is an infrastructure project designed to generate hydroelectric energy for China. (See Topic 7.6 for factors that influence interdependence and the world economy.)

Theories of Development

Essential Question: What are the theories of economic and social development?

Why have some countries of the world become so much wealthier than others? Geographers and others have proposed several theories of development to answer this question. Underlying it is a more general issue about equality. Can all countries grow equally prosperous, or will the world always include a mix of more- and less-wealthy countries?

Theories of Development

Topic 7.3 described various social and economic measures of development and systems for grouping countries based on these measures. While the measures and systems vary, most show that Australia, New Zealand, Japan, South Korea, and most countries of North America and Europe are more developed than most of Africa, parts of Asia, and South America. Two of the best-known theories explaining these differences were developed by Walt Rostow and Immanuel Wallerstein.

Rostow's Stages of Economic Growth

In 1960, American economist Walt W. Rostow developed a *modernization theory* that focuses on the shift from traditional to modern forms of society. He called it the **Stages of Economic Growth model**. Rostow assumed that all countries wanted to modernize, and that all would, though at different speeds. He saw economic development as a linear progression in which countries moved from one stage to the next until they reached the fifth and final stage—high mass consumption.

Like the Demographic Transition Model (DTM), the Stages of Economic Growth theory is a generalization based upon how the United States and western Europe evolved, and both identify distinct stages. However, they differ fundamentally. The DTM is a population model that focuses on changes in the number of people in a country. Rostow's theory is an economic model that focuses on how people live.

Rostow suggested that different inputs and levels of investment were required to allow countries to move from one stage to the next. The theory suggests a system for development—do this, then this, and eventually the economy of a country will become developed. The key characteristics associated with each stage are listed in the chart on the following page.

ROSTOW'S STAGES OF ECONOMIC GROWTH

Stage	Characteristics	Examples
1. Traditional Society	• Depends upon primary sector activities (farming, fishing, hunting) for subsistence • Uses limited technology • Carries out local or regional trading • Enjoys limited socioeconomic mobility	• English colonies in North America in the 17th century • Medieval Europe • No entire country is at this stage today
2. Preconditions for Take-Off	• Improves infrastructure (roads, electrical grid, water systems, etc.) • Improves farming techniques and shifts toward commercial agriculture • Exports agricultural and raw materials (international trade) • Diffuses technology more widely • Starts individual socioeconomic mobility	• United States in the early 19th century • Nigeria today • Afghanistan today
3. Take-Off	• Develops major technological innovations • Starts industrialization and primary sector begins to shrink • Spreads entrepreneurial mentality • Begins to urbanize • Initiates self-sustaining growth	• United States, mid-19th century • Japan, late 19th century • Bangladesh today
4. Drive to Maturity	• Creates new industries while strengthening existing ones • Improves energy, transportation, and communication systems • Sees economic growth greater than population growth • Invests in social infrastructure (schools, hospitals, etc.)	• United States, late 19th century • Germany, early 20th century • Brazil today
5. High Mass Consumption	• Spends money on nonessential goods (consumerism) • Purchases of high order goods become common • Desires to create a more egalitarian society • Supports a strong tertiary sector	• United States, early 1920s to present • Japan, mid-1950s to present

Notice the types of changes that have to occur to allow for a country to transition from one stage to the next. What would be a major concern if all countries reached the stage of high mass consumption?

Criticisms of Rostow's Model

In spite of being one of the most influential economic models of the 20th century, some experts have expressed concerns about Rostow's model. Critics of Stages of Economic Growth model argue it has several weaknesses.

Limited Examples The model was based on American and European examples, so it did not fit countries of non-Western cultures or noncapitalist economies.

Role of Exploitation Rostow's model led to poorer countries getting trapped in a state of dependency upon wealthier countries.

Bias Toward Progress The model suggested linear change, always in the direction of progress. However, developing countries often need the assistance, money, and technology of developed countries to develop. And in some cases, countries might regress in economic development.

Lack of Variation In his model, Rostow suggested all countries have the potential to develop, but there are significant differences among countries, such as physical size, population, natural resources, relative location, political systems, and climate, that affect their ability to develop.

Lack of Sustainability The model assumed that everyone could eventually lead a life of high mass consumption but failed to consider sustainable development or the carrying capacity of the earth.

Need for Poorer Countries Rostow's model failed to recognize that most of the countries which reached the stage of high mass consumption did so by exploiting the resources of lesser-developed countries. Countries that were still developing would have difficulty finding other countries to exploit.

Narrow Focus The model focused on domestic economies and did not directly address interactions between countries, specifically globalization.

Despite these criticisms, geographers, economists, and others continue to use the model to understand how countries have changed over the past two centuries. It has prompted people to think about economic and social change in a global context and challenged them to provide their own framework.

Wallerstein's World Systems Theory

In the 1970s, historian Immanuel Wallerstein proposed an alternative model to Rostow's, which he called the **World Systems Theory**. It is a **dependency model**, meaning that countries do not exist in isolation but are part of an intertwined world system in which all countries are dependent on each other. Dependency theory argues that colonialism and neocolonialism (see Topic 4.2) are the cause of global inequities. Both Wallerstein and Rostow attempt to explain the inequalities that exist between different countries and regions. World Systems Theory includes both political and economic elements that have significant geographic impacts.

As mentioned in Topic 7.2, Wallerstein divided countries into three types—core, semiperiphery, and periphery. As a result, his theory is sometimes referred to as the **Core-Periphery model**.

WALLERSTEIN'S WORLD SYSTEMS THEORY		
Category	**Characteristics**	**Examples**
Core	• Includes the economically advantaged countries of the world • Includes the headquarters of most large multinational companies and banks • Focuses on higher-skill, capital-intensive production • Promotes capital accumulation • Dominates semiperiphery and periphery economically and politically • Locates factories and service centers in semiperiphery and periphery countries • Benefits greatly from international trade	• United States • United Kingdom • Japan • Australia • Germany
Semiperiphery	• Includes most middle-income countries, sometimes called emerging economies • Provides the core with manufactured goods and services that the core formerly provided for itself • Shares characteristics of both core and periphery	• China • Mexico • Brazil • South Africa • India
Periphery	• Includes the least-developed countries • Maintains many jobs in low-skill, labor-intensive production and extraction • Provides the core and semiperiphery with inexpensive raw materials and labor • Receives jobs but few profits from manufacturing • Attracts jobs by having weak laws protecting workers and the environment	• Afghanistan • Zimbabwe • Bolivia • Kenya • Laos

Core Dominance Multinational companies, financial institutions, and centers of technology are mostly based in core countries, but they have signficantly influenced the economies of semiperiphery and periphery countries. Businesses and governments in non-core countries borrow money to finance large-scale projects and purchase technology from core countries. Both processes increase the *dependency* of the periphery on the core.

Changing Categories Unlike Rostow's model, Wallerstein's model does not suggest that all countries can reach the highest level of development, nor does it explain how countries can improve their position. In contrast, it indicates that the world system will always include a combination of types of countries. But countries can change categories, moving in or out of the core. For example, in 1950, South Korea and Singapore were part of the periphery. By 2020, they were core countries. In 1900, Argentina was a core country. By 2000, it had become part of the semiperiphery.

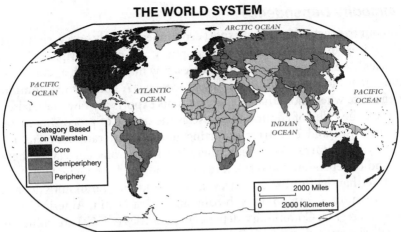

THE WORLD SYSTEM

PACIFIC OCEAN
ARCTIC OCEAN
ATLANTIC OCEAN
PACIFIC OCEAN
INDIAN OCEAN

Category Based on Wallerstein
- Core
- Semiperiphery
- Periphery

0   2000 Miles

0   2000 Kilometers

The majority of the core countries are in close proximity to each other. How can you account for the core status of Australia and New Zealand that are so distant from the other core countries?

Labor Trends Wallerstein's model provides a framework for analyzing the international division of labor by sector and location:

- Periphery countries are often where primary sector workers engaged in the extraction of raw materials and agriculture are located.
- Semiperiphery countries are often home to many workers in the secondary sector (such as factory workers) and in the tertiary sector (such as call center staff).
- Core countries include many tertiary sector workers and most quinary and quaternary sector workers.

Systems Theory at the Country Scale Wallerstein built his model for a global scale. However, geographers also apply it to smaller scales by identifying centers of power and dependency relationships. In the United States the core would be the major cities, such as New York and Chicago. The semiperiphery would be the manufacturing belt in the Midwest and parts of the South. The periphery would be the rural areas of the Great Plains and the West.

Criticisms of World Systems Theory

Much Rostow's model, the Wallerstein's model has its detractors.

Little Emphasis on Culture It focused heavily on economic influence—investments and purchases of raw materials—but it paid little attention to the pervasive influence of culture—movies, music, and television.

Emphasis on Industry It was based on industrial production, but many countries have postindustrial economies based on providing services.

Lack of Explanation It is of limited practical use, suggesting that countries can change their status, but it does not explain how.

Limited Roles It focused too much on the role of countries, governments, and corporations. As a result, it failed to recognize the role of organizations such as UN agencies and private, nonprofit charitable NGOs.

Commodity Dependence

Core countries have diversified export economies that rely on a variety of goods and services. In contrast, some semiperiphery and many periphery countries rely heavily on the export of **commodities,** raw material such as coffee, cocoa, and oil, that have not undergone any processing. A country has **commodity dependence** when more than 60 percent of its exports are raw materials.

Since the value of commodities rise as the degree of processing increases, the businesses and countries exporting unprocessed raw materials receive relatively low returns. As a result, there is a very strong correlation between commodity dependence and low levels of economic development.

More than half of the countries in the world are commodity dependent. They are most common in sub-Saharan Africa, Latin America, and the Caribbean region. Commodity-dependent countries (CDCs) are vulnerable to fluctuating commodity prices. Prices can suddenly drop for many reasons:

- a large, new supply of the commodity becomes available
- manufacturing companies finds a less-expensive substitute product
- consumer demand for the product made from the commodity falls

Some commodities, such as oil, are much more valuable than others. Even valuable commodities are vulnerable to wide, rapid price fluctuations. Between 2012 and 2020, the price of a barrel of oil dropped from $109 down to $41, then rose up to $70 before falling to $42.

The countries that have best weathered a downturn in oil prices have been those that have diversified their exports. For example, the United Arab Emirates was very dependent on oil revenues in the 20th century. The country's leaders recognized the risk in this and began to diversify its economy by expanding its transportation, financial, and tourist sectors, particularly in its major city, Dubai. When oil prices crashed around 2014, the country's economy was varied enough to withstand the potentially disastrous decline.

REFLECT ON THE ESSENTIAL QUESTION

Essential Question: *What are the theories of economic and social development?*

Development Theory	Explanation of Theory

KEY TERMS

Stages of Economic Growth model	non-governmental organization (NGO)
World Systems Theory	commodities
(Core-Periphery model)	commodity dependence
dependency model	

Trade and the World Economy

Essential Question: What are causes and geographic consequences of recent economic changes such as the increase in international trade, deindustrialization, and growing interdependence in the world economy?

In the 21st century, countries are becoming increasingly interconnected. Vast improvements in transportation and communications over the past few decades have linked people throughout the world. The political, cultural, and economic processes of each region are linked with those of other regions, resulting in a degree of global interdependence not seen before. But as Panos Mourdoukoutas indicated in the chapter opening quote, globalization includes the good, the bad, and the ugly. Consider the impact of moving manufacturing jobs from core countries to semiperiphery and periphery countries:

- The good might be that in core countries, corporations can increase their profits and consumers can purchase goods at lower prices, resulting in more jobs in non-core countries.
- The bad might be that in core countries, factory workers often lose their jobs and, as a result of the multiplier effect, other people do as well.
- The ugly might be that in semiperiphery and periphery countries, laborers suffer from poorly regulated working conditions and entire populations are endangered by weak environmental regulations.

Trade and Interdependence

Trade occurs when one party desires a good or service that it does not have or cannot produce and another party has the desired good or service with which it is willing to part. Trade sometimes occurs through **barter**, a system of exchange in which no money changes hands. This is most common between individuals. In the book-turned-movie *To Kill a Mockingbird*, the main character, a lawyer, provides legal services to a poor farmer in exchange for bags of food.

Comparative Advantage and Complementarity

Trade usually occurs with an exchange of money. Parties tend to trade goods or services in which they have a **comparative advantage,** or the ability to produce a good or service at a lower cost than others. For example, China's workers recieve lower wages than do U.S. workers, so Chinese companies can manufacture goods at a lower cost. This gives them a comparative advantage.

When a country has the income, goods, or services that the another country desires, they have **complementarity**. For example, Canada, with its cold winters and forests of maple trees, is a leading producer of maple syrup but it produces no coffee. Costa Rica, with its tropical climate and rugged terrain, is famous for its coffee, but it produces no maple syrup. Canadian merchants import coffee from Costa Rica while Costa Rican merchants import maple syrup from Canada.

When complementarity does not exist, trade is heavily weighted in one direction. For example, U.S. consumers desire and can afford to purchase many products made in China, yet Chinese consumers desire and can afford far fewer U.S. products. This trade imbalance has created political tensions.

Technology and Trade

One of the most significant changes in the world in the past several decades has been the increase in international trade. In the United States, trade increased from 5 percent of the total economy in 1960 to 28 percent in 2018. Globally, in 1970, trade accounted for about 27 percent of global GDP. In 2019, it accounted for 60 percent. A combination of changes in technology and changes in policies have promoted trade.

Larger and faster ships, containerization, improvements to major canals and new port facilities, and increases in air cargo have made moving goods less expensive. These transportation advancements have helped overcome the spatial barriers and distances that, for many years, minimized trade among distant countries. (See Topic 7.2.) They have had the effect of making the world seem smaller and people more interconnected.

The Internet increased the efficiency of trade and transportation information systems. Online sales have expanded markets for both consumers and producers resulting in increased demand and trade.

Government and Trade

Like improved technology, government influences trade. Over the past century, governments have increasingly taken steps to influence trade.

Policies Increasing Trade In the late 19th century and early 20th century, most industrializing countries, including the United States, imposed trade barriers to protect their young industries from foreign competition. As these countries grew wealthier, they adopted **free trade** policies, or laws, that reduced barriers to trade. Since the end of World War II in 1945, most core countries have promoted freer trade because of its benefits to corporations and consumers. Support for free trade was a cornerstone of **neoliberal policies,** a set of reforms that reduced government regulations and taxation. In the 1980s, U.S. President Ronald Reagan and U.K. Prime Minister Margaret Thatcher were leading advocates of neoliberalism.

Countries that industrialized in the late 20th century, such as China and other countries in East Asia, followed the pattern of the United States and

Europe. While developing, they restricted imports and promoted exports. As these countries developed, they reduced trade barriers.

Factors Decreasing Trade In recent years, trade barriers have often reflected political and economic decisions. Since 2016, the United Nations has used economic sanctions more than 30 times, mostly to pressure countries to reduce human rights abuses.

In 2018, the U.S. government increased tariffs on many Chinese-made goods sold in the United States. By making these goods more expensive for U.S. consumers, the government hoped Americans would buy more U.S.-made goods and China would relax its barriers on U.S. imports. China responded by reducing its purchases of U.S. farm products and increasing tariffs on U.S. goods. In 2019, the gap between U.S. imports from China and exports to China was almost identical to what it had been in 2016.

Another factor that can decrease trade is health problems. Just as globalization made trade of goods easier, it also provides pathways for diffusion of disease. In 2020, global trade decreased sharply because of COVID-19. The dangers of the virus caused factories to shut down, disrupted transportation networks, and reduced consumer demand for many products.

Government Development Initiatives

Because of the desire for economic development, governments at all levels provide various incentives to encourage the expansion of existing economic activities or the creation of new ones. The type of incentive varies depending upon the nature of the economic development and what level of government is supporting the development. In most cases, the government that provides the incentives insists the company which receives the incentive must achieve certain targets such as providing a certain number of full-time jobs. There are several common incentives used to stimulate economic development that are shown in the table below.

GOVERNMENT EFFORTS TO PROMOTE ECONOMIC GROWTH	
Type of Incentive	**What Businesses Receive**
Tax Breaks	• A tax holiday (a temporary exemption from some taxes) • A tax break for money invested in research and development
Loans	• Forgivable loans (part or all of the loan doesn't have to be repaid) • Money to borrow at below-normal interest rates
Direct Assistance	• Land or building use free of charge • Infrastructure such as roads and sewers paid for by government • A subsidy for each full-time job created
Changes in Regulations	• Legislation that weakens unions • Legislation that reduces environmental rules
Tariffs	• Taxes imposed on imported products make these products less attractive and domestically produced goods more attractive

These government incentives may be applied at different scales. For example, national, state, and county governments all may offer their own version of incentives.

Supranational Trading Blocs

Because of the increasing importance of trade, many countries have strengthened their relationships with their most important trading partners. This resulted in the formation of **trading blocs,** groups of countries that agree to a common set of trade rules. (See Topic 4.9.) Some examples include the U.S.-Mexico-Canada Agreement (USMCA), the Organization of the Petroleum Exporting Countries (OPEC), and **Mercosur** or *Southern Common Market*, which includes several South American countries.

The European Union (EU) is also a trading bloc, but it is unlike most othe ones. It also has *open borders,* which means it allows free movement of people as well as goods from one country to another.

Most trading blocs occur within regions. However, the **World Trade Organization (WTO)** is a global organization. It was created in 1995 to monitor the rules of international trade by providing a forum for negotiating trade deals, settling disputes between its members, supporting the needs of developing countries, and helping companies follow similar international trade policies. As of 2020, the WTO included 164 member countries that accounted for 98 percent of global trade. Another 20 countries have applied for membership.

Manufacturing in Semiperiphery Countries

One aspect of globalization and trade has been that companies have moved industrial production from core countries to semiperiphery countries. The speed of phone and Internet communications means that decision makers of transnational corporations can easily maintain contact with the management of new processing plants in the semiperiphery world. The ease of transportation results in frequent travel between the head offices and the factories in the semiperiphery. The manufactured goods can also be easily shipped to markets in core countries and the rest of the world.

Impacts of Economic Interdependence

Increased interdependency has strengthened the links among the countries' economies. Growth in one country can result in new economic opportunities in other countries. For example, as China grew wealthier, it purchased more grains and meat from U.S. farmers, bought more cars from companies headquartered in the United States, and sent more students to U.S. colleges and universities. However, China's growing industries also competed with U.S. manufacturers, and many companies layed off U.S. workers and moved jobs to China.

Similarly, an economic downturn in one country can lead to economic challenges elsewhere. When the price of oil dropped in mid-2014, consumers everywhere enjoyed lower gas prices and manufacturers lowered their production costs on every product that used oil. However, economies in all oil-producing regions suffered:

- Oil companies lost revenue. For example, Royal Dutch Shell, based in the Netherlands, saw its earnings fall 80 percent from 2014 to 2015.
- Workers in oil related industries lost jobs. About 250,000 people across several occupations became unemployed.
- Governments in oil-dependent countries, such as Venezuela, lost tax revenue, forcing them to lay off employees and reduce services.
- Investors in energy industry companies saw the value of the holdings plummet. In the second half of 2014, the 24 energy producers in the Fortune 500 lost $263 billion in market value.
- Workers for coal companies lost jobs. As coal could not compete with lower-cost oil, mines reduced production and laid off workers

Responses to Global Financial Crises

Numerous international financial institutions (IFIs) assist struggling countries with financing and provide professional advice on development. Most IFIs are partnerships among several countries. While all encourage development opportunities, some focus on particular regions or types of projects.

International Monetary Fund (IMF) The best known IFI is the **International Monetary Fund (IMF)**, which was created in 1945 to aid countries caught in need of financial assistance. Recognizing how quickly a financial crisis can lead to social and political instability, the IMF promotes economic stability for countries dealing with financial struggles. The assistance can take several forms from new, more manageable loans to assistance in overhauling the country's economic system. With 190 member countries, the IMF also works to promote monetary cooperation, facilitate international trade, increase employment, encourage sustainable growth, and reduce poverty.

Two recent examples of IMF interventions involve the destabilization of the Argentinian economy in 2018 and the COVID-19 crisis of 2020. In the case of Argentina, the IMF provided $57 billion worth of loans to the country. In response to the COVID-19 pandemic, much needed emergency funding was provided to 76 countries.

Large-Scale Projects Many projects funded by IFIs involve multimillion- or even multibillion-dollar deals to build big projects, such as hydroelectric dams or new transportation systems When successful, these projects can be extremely beneficial to a country's economy and to thousands of people.

However, large-scale projects are risky, and some do not work as planned. Failures can create additional problems for an already struggling country as it now must repay an even larger debt. Dependency theorists criticize periphery countries for borrowing money from the core. High debt-to-GDP ratios make periphery countries more dependent on core countries and defaults on loans increase potentially resulting in a debt crisis and larger economic problems.

Small-Scale Projects In contrast to these big loans, some NGOs focus on *microlending*. (See Topic 7.4.) Microloans are designed to help entrepreneurs with small-scale businesses by providing small loans, usually less than $2,000.

KEY TERMS

trade

barter

comparative advantage

complementarity

free trade

neoliberalism

trading blocs

Mercosur

World Trade Organization (WTO)

International Monetary Fund (IMF)

GEOGRAPHIC PERSPECTIVES: *THE NEW GLOBAL WORLD*

In an age of globalization, every problem affects multiple countries. In particular, the economic policies of the financially powerful core states have large spillover effects on semiperiphery and periphery economies. Geographers study how these effects diffuse from one place to another, and how globalization can make them more or less damaging.

Thailand's Fragile Prosperity

In 1997, a crisis in the periphery country of Thailand threatened first that country, then its neighbors, and eventually the rest of the world. Thailand's economy had been growing an impressive 10 percent per year for over a decade. However, it relied heavily on foreign investments, particularly from the United States and Japan, and high exports.

When the Thai economy started to slow, concern quickly spread. The Thai stock market crashed, and the currency lost its value. Many companies had trouble paying their employees and laid off numerous workers.

Diffusion and Distance Decay

What followed was the runaway hierarchical and contagious diffusion of market disturbances from one country to another. In line with the concept of distance decay, the ripple effect of Thailand's financial crisis hit its neighbors the hardest—Indonesia, Malaysia, Singapore, the Philippines, and South Korea. The interdependent economies of these countries then faced similar financial woes. This crisis threatened to spread beyond Asian markets and create a global economic panic.

The Role of Globalization

This crisis—made worse by globalization—ended when the International Monetary Fund (IMF) stepped in and offered loans to the weakened countries. With these loans, confidence was restored and the economies began to grow again.

1. Applying the concepts of distance decay and diffusion, describe the patterns of impacts on other countries.

2. What are some of the impacts that could be expected if a Toyota Corolla manufacturing assembly plant in Mississippi shut down?

THINK AS A GEOGRAPHER: *ANALYZE TARIFF INFORMATION*

Geographers study patterns of interaction among people who live in different places. One of these interactions is trade in goods and services. Many non-core countries hope that trade will provide them an opportunity to create jobs and improve the lives of their citizens. The experience of the United States in economic development might provide a model for some countries to follow.

Use the graph showing average U.S. tariffs (taxes on imports) to answer the questions about the role of trade in economic development.

AVERAGE TARIFF RATE IN THE UNITED STATES, 1792 TO 2010

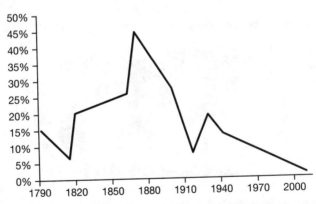

1. Describe the general level of tariff rates between 1792 and 1860.

2. How did tariff rates between 1860 and 1910 compare to earlier and later tariff rates?

3. Describe the trend in tariff rates since 1942.

4. Explain why the post-1990 data supports the adoption of neoliberal policies in the United States.

CHAPTER 19 REVIEW
Development and Trade

Topics 7.5–7.6

MULTIPLE-CHOICE QUESTIONS

1. A developing country that exports nearly 75 percent of all its raw materials has

(A) a comparative advantage

(B) complementarity

(C) commodity dependence

(D) neoliberal policies

(E) locational interdependence

2. Based upon Wallerstein's World Systems Theory, which of the following countries best fits the description of a periphery country?

(A) Brazil

(B) Germany

(C) Mali

(D) China

(E) Japan

Question 3 refers to the map below.

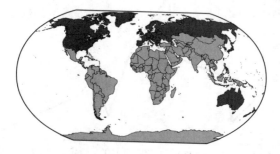

3. Which phrase best describes the countries shown in the darkest shade?

(A) Periphery countries

(B) Semiperiphery countries

(C) Core countries

(D) Least-developed countries

(E) Developing countries

4. Which stage of Rostow's Stages of Economic Growth model does the United States best fit today?

(A) Preconditions for take-off

(B) Drive to maturity

(C) High mass consumption

(D) Take-off

(E) Traditional society

5. Modernization models such as Rostow's suggest that

(A) there will always be a combination of more developed countries and less developed countries

(B) owners of industries will always try to locate plants to take advantage of agglomeration economies

(C) geographic factors, such as the availability of natural resources, determine a country's level of development

(D) it is possible for all countries to reach a high level of economic development

(E) governments should not provide stimulus for economic development

6. Which of the following changes most directly increased globalization?

(A) Greater use of tariffs and other trade restrictions

(B) More frequent political disputes among world leaders

(C) Greater time-space compression

(D) Decreased use of containerization

(E) Decreased complementarity among countries

Question 7 refers to the map below.

7. Which organization illustrating globalization is shown on the map?

(A) Mercosur

(B) USMCA

(C) OPEC

(D) IMF

(E) NATO

1. Two theories of economic development are Rostow's Stages of Economic Growth and Wallerstein's World Systems. Rostow's theory argues that all countries can attain higher levels of development by progressing through a five-step process. Wallerstein argues that the world will remain divided among periphery, semiperiphery and core regions.

(A) Identify TWO countries or regions of the world on which Rostow's model was based.

(B) Using the Rostow model, explain why improving a country's infrastructure is a precondition for economic development.

(C) Describe the types of economic products that the periphery supplies to the core and semiperiphery.

(D) Explain the economic role that semiperiphery countries often provide for core countries.

(E) Explain why world systems theorists often argue that multinational corporations act as a neocolonial economic force.

(F) Describe ONE change that has increased gender equality in the past 20 years.

(G) Describe ONE challenge that societies still face in achieving gender equality.

CHAPTER 20

Changing Global Economy and Sustainability

Topics 7.7–7.8

Topic 7.7 Changes as a Result of the World Economy

Learning Objective: Explain the causes and geographic consequences of recent economic changes such as the increase in international trade, deindustrialization and growing interdependence in the world economy. (PSO-7.A)

Topic 7.8 Sustainable Development

Learning Objective: Explain how sustainable principles relate to and impact industrialization and spatial development. (IMP-7.A)

Anyone who believes in indefinite growth of anything physical on a physically finite planet is either a madman or an economist.

—Kenneth Boulding, economist, 1953

Source: Wikimedia Commons

Women complete the labor-intensive manufacturing of clothing in a maquiladora in Mexico. (See Topic 7.7 for maquiladoras and other changes in the global economy.)

Changes as a Result of the World Economy

Essential Question: What are the causes and geographic consequences of recent economic changes such as the increase in international trade, deindustrialization, and growing interdependence in the world economy?

Globalization is firmly entrenched as part of daily life, largely due to vast improvements in transportation and communication technologies. People no longer depend solely upon products made close to home or decisions made by local, or even national, politicians. The world is so interconnected that a any decision can have significant implications for people across the globe. In addition to the growing interdependency of countries and their economies, the types of jobs, in core, periphery, and semiperiphery countries has changed. The economic landscape has transformed from local to global scales.

The Changing Global Economy

To take advantage of improved transportation and communication, and in search of lower labor costs, companies have changed spatial distribution of manufacturing and business services. At the global scale, many companies have moved manufacturing plants from highly developed core countries, such as the United States, to less-developed periphery and semiperiphery countries, such as the Malaysia and Brazil. At the regional scale, factories in the United States have moved from the Northeast and Midwest to the Southeast and Southwest.

Outsourcing and Offshoring

To reduce costs, many companies use **outsourcing,** contracting work to noncompany employees or other companies. The contracted company might be less expensive because it specializes in the work and does it more efficiently. Or, it might pay workers lower wages or provide fewer benefits. Companies often outsource manufacturing work and administrative functions such as handling payroll and paying taxes.

As with multinational manufacturing companies, some tertiary and quaternary sector companies move their back offices to other countries, a process known as **offshoring**. Companies will locate services or manufacturing in other countries if the costs of doing business are lower and worth the risk of moving some operations overseas. Many software and manufacturing companies in the United States and Europe locate facilities in India and China to take advantage of the highly skilled but lower-cost labor.

Labor unions and government officials have pressured some companies into reshoring, returning jobs to the business's home country. Because of the multiplier effect (see Topic 7.2), this benefits others in the country as well.

Sometimes companies will both offshore and outsource, as Boeing did with the 787 Dreamliner airplane. Boeing designed the planes in Seattle, the nose section was outsourced to a company in Kansas, wing tips were made in South Korea by Korean Air, wings were assembled by Boeing in Canada, and final assembly was done by Boeing outside of Seattle. The final product demonstrated outsourcing, offshoring, globalization, and the international division of labor.

Economic Restructuring

Globalization has increased competition among companies based around the world. In response, many have adopted new technology that needs fewer employees to operate. They also have shifted jobs from core countries to the periphery and semiperiphery ones with lower wages. As a result of these changes, many workers in core countries have lost jobs or had their wages cut.

While workers have suffered, consumers have benefitted. Lower production costs have resulted in lower prices for retail goods.

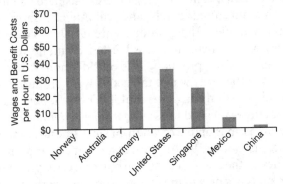

MANUFACTURING COSTS, 2012 (for selected countries)

Based on the graph, how much more expensive are wages and benefits in Norway than in China? Wages and benefits are much cheaper in Mexico and China than in the United States. With the costs much less in China, why have so many U.S. companies chosen to locate in Mexico?

Globalization has created a **new international division of labor**, a changed system of employment in the various economic sectors throughout the world:

- In core countries, people design and develop products for the global market. Tertiary, quaternary, and quinary jobs have increased in the core.

- In semiperiphery countries, people often manufacture goods that are marketed in core countries. Consequently, employment in the secondary sector has increased. Employment in the primary sector has declined.

- Periphery countries, such as Bangladesh, Angola, and Papua New Guinea, have large primary sectors and export minerals and resources to core and semiperiphery countries for further processing and consumption.

STRUCTURE OF THE U.S. LABOR FORCE, 1940 AND 2020

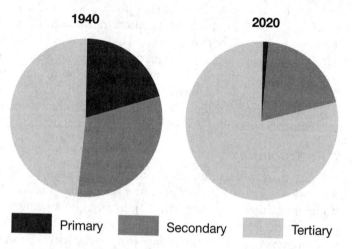

1940

2020

■ Primary ■ Secondary ■ Tertiary

The percentage of employees in all three sectors of the labor force has changed tremendously since 1940. Why has the percentage of workers involved in the primary sector dropped so drastically?

Basic and Non-basic Activities

Actions that creates new wealth for a region are considered a **basic economic activity**. Most manufactured goods and commercial farm products are examples of basic activities. These products are usually sold beyond the area where the factory or commercial farm is located, so money from outside the area is used to purchase the products. This outside money is considered new money which makes the areas where the goods were produced wealthier and leads to additional growth through the multiplier effect. For this reason, basic activities are sometimes referred to as *city-forming activities*.

A grocery store is an example of a **non-basic economic activity** because it does not generate new money for the area. Instead, it allows for recirculation of the existing money in the area. Most people buy groceries near where they live, so the money spent is not new to the region. Non-basic activities are important since they provide services or goods such as food and clothing. However, they do not play a significant role in bringing money into the local economy, so non-basic activities are also referred to as *city-serving activities*. There is a limited multiplier effect for non-basic activities.

Community leaders in core countries are concerned about the loss of manufacturing jobs since they are often basic activities and generate new wealth. If a company relocates offshore, often the displaced workers find replacement jobs in the tertiary sector, which contains primarily non-basic jobs, and the community will lose out on much-needed new money.

Quaternary sector jobs are more desirable since they have higher salaries and are more likely to be basic activities with a greater multiplier effect. Consider a software developer or a research scientist. The products or information these workers produce will generate income from far beyond their own community, and thus, generate new money which leads to economic growth.

Transnationals, Multinationals, and EPZs

Businesses that operate in multiple countries are known as **transnational corporations (TNCs)** and **multinational corporations (MNCs)**. Because of the jobs and wealth these corporations can bring to a country, government compete with each other to entice them to their shore. Over 100 countries in the world have attracted TNCs and MNCs by using special manufacturing zones, commonly referred to as **export-processing zones (EPZs)**.

These EPZs offer foreign corporations major tax savings, inexpensive labor, fewer environmental regulations, well-serviced industrial sites, and proximity to good transportation networks that allow for easy delivery of raw material and shipping of finished products. EPZs are often near international airports, seaports, or land borders from where the products can be exported easily.

Tax Incentives One incentive that countries use in EPZs is tax breaks. Transnationals typically do not pay taxes on any item they import into an EPZ as long as these items are re-exported or used to make products for export. This regulation protects existing businesses that cater to the local market. For example, if a resident entrepreneur employs 20 people producing T-shirts to sell locally, a new T-shirt factory in the EPZ will not drive the resident owner out of business with cheaper products. The existing jobs in the locally owned factory will remain in addition to the jobs added by the foreign-owned factory.

Functions Initially, most of these special zones were occupied by factories that manufactured goods. However, some also acted as *transshipment* points (transfer containers) and recently, as sites for tertiary and quaternary sector activities. For example, the largest share of businesses established by TNCs and MNCs in India offer professional, scientific, and technical services.

EPZs first appeared in the 1960s, and by 2015, 130 countries were home to 4500 of these special zones and employed an estimated 68 million people worldwide. Special manufacturing zones are known by different names— **special economic zones (SEZs)** in China, **maquiladoras** in Mexico, and **free-trade zones (FTZs)** in Singapore—but have similar functions.

In China, the original SEZs were situated in coastal cities near major ports, allowing easy access to international markets. First created in 1979, the Chinese government has increasingly used the incentives of SEZs to attract foreign trade and businesses.

Changes in Maquiladoras There was a surge of American-owned maquiladoras factories after the North American Free Trade Agreement (NAFTA) was signed in 1994. Maquiladoras are now the second-largest source of income in Mexico after petroleum. The maquiladoras were originally all positioned in a single district in northern Mexico, near the United States-Mexico border to minimize transportation costs into the United States.

In recent years, the number of maquiladoras has decreased due to the increased competition for these international corporations as more countries adopt the creation of EPZs as a development strategy. Despite the decrease, there are still approximately 3,000 foreign-owned factories and over 1 million employees working in Mexican maquiladoras.

Free-Trade Zones (FTZs) These are locations where a foreign company can store, warehouse, transfer, or process without additional taxation or duties if goods are exported. Major seaport cities like Singapore, London, Amsterdam, and Hong Kong have FTZs. Similar to FTZs, but on a larger scale, are free-trade regions such as the European Union.

Ethics and Societal Changes Related to EPZs

People disagree about whether EPZs are ethical. Critics charge that the transnational corporations are taking advantage of the workers and paying them a fraction of what they would pay workers in their home countries. Proponents of EPZs believe that the wages are reasonable for the region and thousands of people, mainly women, have access to paid employment at better wages than would otherwise be available to them. In addition, low wages keep the cost of manufactured items low, which allows lower-income people to purchase them.

One of the most significant changes related to the development of EPZs is the role of females in society. Typically, the majority of workers hired in EPZs are female. As women earn wages, they become less dependent upon men and are more likely to be heard by government. In addition, birth rates decline as more women gain employment.

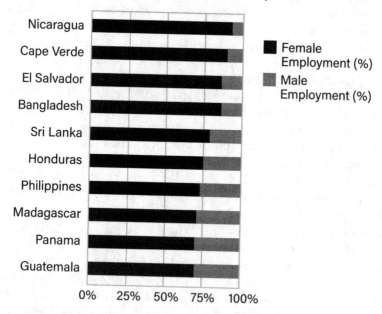

FEMALE WORKERS IN EPZS, 2007

- ■ Female Employment (%)
- ▨ Male Employment (%)

Nicaragua, Cape Verde, El Salvador, Bangladesh, Sri Lanka, Honduras, Philippines, Madagascar, Panama, Guatemala

0% 25% 50% 75% 100%

Source: United Nations

Women dominate the labor force in most EPZs. Why are women much more likely to be employed in EPZs than men?

The Postindustrial Landscape

As the types of economic activities that exist in a region evolve, so does the economic landscape. Many wealthier core countries now have a **postindustrial economy**, one that no longer employs large numbers of people in factories but has people who provide services and process information. The shift from an industrial to a postindustrial economy changes the landscape of a country.

Post-Fordist Methods of Production

In the 19th century, production increased with the shift from a system of cottage industry to factory production with machines powered by water or coal. However, most products were still made individually.

Early in the 20th century, Henry Ford advanced productivity by developing the **assembly line**—in which an item is moved from worker to worker, with each repeatedly performing the same task. The use of assembly lines allowed companies to rapidly produce more standardized products and with less-skilled workers than ever before. This system of mass production, known as **Fordism**, changed manufacturing and became standard practice across industries.

As globalization increased, so did the need for flexibility from industries in the production process. In modern factories, the **substitution principle**, in which businesses maximize profit by substituting one factor of production for another, has been applied to the labor force. In the late 20th century, increased automation, or replacing workers with machines, allowed assembly line production to greatly increase. However, automation, also known as mechanization, has also forced many workers to become unemployed. The remaining workers are often trained to do more than one job, so they can rotate among a few different workstations during a day, reducing the risk of injuries. This industrial adaptability was the basis of the **post-Fordist** system.

Economies of Scale

Although expensive to install, mechanization saves a company money over the long term and creates *economies of scale* (see Topics 4.9 and 5.11) by allowing business owners to increase output with improved efficiency. Machines can work 24 hours a day without breaks or vacations, and they produce consistent, high-quality work. For example, U.S. industrial output doubled between 1984 and 2015, but industrial employment declined by one-third.

Just-in-Time Delivery

Auto assembly plants make use of **just-in-time delivery**, a system in which the inputs in the assembly process arrive at the assembly location when they are needed. This system reduces the expensive storage costs of extra inventory—but at the risk of running short on inputs. It works only if a factory owner has confidence in his or her suppliers, communications and transportation systems, and ability to accurately predict production needs.

Agglomeration Economies

In some cases, the location decision for one factory is dependent upon the location of other related factories, referred to as **locational interdependence**. Being near similar factories allows businesses to use the same services, such as transportation companies or accounting firms that might specialize in providing service to the industry. It also allows businesses to observe their competition and to occasionally hire away talented young employees from another company.

In addition, the finished product from one factory could be an input at another factory. In this case, it is a market-dependent situation. For example, an auto assembly plant is the market for the output from an auto parts factory. Consequently, the location of the parts factory is very dependent upon the location of the assembly plants.

Most businesses, whether they are secondary, tertiary, or quaternary businesses, locate in proximity to similar businesses to take advantage of **agglomeration economies**. (See Topic 7.2.) Large shopping districts are an example of agglomeration and the *gravity model*. (See Topics 3.3 and 6.4.)

Certain stores locating close together can be more attractive to customers because they have easy and efficient access to many products. The larger the mall, the more pull, or gravity, it will have to draw customers from farther away. Fast-food restaurants will often agglomerate, or cluster, on the corners of busy road intersections because each wants to be visible and accessible to potential customers. For factories, agglomeration is usually close to transportation systems, parts suppliers, or near available skilled workers.

Technopoles

Just as agglomeration economies can encourage the spatial grouping of manufacturing plants, stores, and offices, the same principles can apply to technology companies. A **technopole** is a hub for information-based industry and high-tech manufacturing. The proximity of companies allows for benefits such as the sharing of certain services and attracting highly skilled workers to the area. Often these technopoles are located near universities well known for their computer, mathematics, engineering, science, and entrepreneurial business programs:

- Silicon Valley, near the Universities of California-Berkeley and Stanford
- Route 128, near Harvard University and the Massachusetts Institute of Technology
- The Research Triangle, near Duke University, North Carolina State University, and the University of North Carolina, Chapel Hill
- The Technology Triangle near the University of Waterloo and the University of Guelph in Ontario, Canada

Because of the economic stimulus associated with the technopoles, they often act as **growth poles**, or **growth centers**. The concentration of high-value economic development in the growth pole attracts even more economic development. Once the process starts, the cumulative causation effect means it tends to feed upon itself. Each time new businesses are attracted to the growth pole, the "magnet" becomes even stronger and attracts more businesses.

Growth poles often have **spin-off benefits,** or **spread effects,** which are positive economic outcomes beyond the growth pole. For example, farmers that are 100 miles away from a growth pole should have expanded markets in which to sell their produce, resulting in increased sales and profits. The *multiplier effect* (see Topic 7.2) of job creation is also another potential benefit.

The possible downsides of growth poles are the **backwash effects,** or negative effects on one region that result from economic growth in another region. A typical backwash effect is the loss of the highly educated young people from distant communities who migrate to growth poles for employment. As a result, the distant communities can face depopulation, loss of tax revenue, and the closure of various services.

In China, the impressive growth in prosperity for people in large urban areas in the eastern part of the country has pulled in people from rural areas in the west. One backwash effect of this has been that the rural western areas sometimes face a shortage of working-age people and those who care for elderly family members.

The Fate of Brownfields

The stereotyped image of a postindustrial landscape is one of deteriorating buildings surrounded by weeds, marked by broken or boarded-up windows, and rusting metal. These sites of abandoned factories are known as **brownfields.** Because of the rusting metal, the region of the United States hit hardest by deindustrialization—the Northeast and lands around the Great Lakes—is often called the **Rust Belt.** In reality, old buildings are usually torn down, so brownfields are often empty. (See Topic 6.11 for more on brownfields.)

Corporate Parks and Campuses

It is not just the existence, removal, or repurposing of old factories that typifies a postindustrial landscape. New service sector jobs also help to shape the postindustrial landscape. As a result of this growth, office buildings and other commercial spaces are more likely to be evident on the landscape. Increasingly, these office buildings congregate in **corporate parks,** or **business parks,** where they can take advantage of agglomeration economies.

Some very large corporations create their own corporate parks where they are the only tenant. Samsung has its headquarters, known as Samsung Digital City, in a park 13 miles south of Seoul, South Korea. The campus covers an area about equal to 40 city blocks. About 35,000 people work there, and it includes 135 buildings, of which four are large office towers. Other facilities include research laboratories, gymnasiums, swimming pools, medical offices, a heliport, daycare facilities, and housing for guests and visiting employees.

Working Remotely and COVID-19

The work people do and how they do it determines where they do it. While people in primary and secondary sector jobs often need to be present at their jobsite to tend crops or build homes, many workers in the tertiary sector do not. They can do their jobs anywhere they have a computer and an internet connection. As the U.S. economy has changed, more and more people have begun working from home.

This trend of working from home picked up momentum when the COVID-19 pandemic struck. By the spring of 2020, more people were working from home than ever before. If the trend to remote working continues, the built environment will change to reflect it:

- Central business districts will include fewer large office buildings, fewer parking lots for commuters, and fewer diners for workers eating lunch.
- Retail companies will close stores and replace sales clerks with online representatives and delivery people.
- Residential houses will identify areas dedicated to office space.

REFLECT ON THE ESSENTIAL QUESTION

Essential Question: *What are the causes and geographic consequences of recent economic changes such as the increase in international trade, deindustrialization, and growing interdependence in the world economy?*

Causes of Global Economic Changes	Consequences of Global Economic Changes

---

KEY TERMS

outsourcing	export processing zones (EPZs)	locational interdependence
offshoring		agglomeration economies
reshoring	special economic zones (SEZs)	technopoles
new international division of labor	maquiladoras	growth poles (growth centers)
basic economic activity	free-trade zones (FTZs)	spin-off benefits (spread effects)
non-basic economic activity	postindustrial economy	
transnational corporations (TNCs)	assembly line	backwash effects
	Fordism	brownfields
multinational corporations (MNCs)	substitution principle	Rust Belt
	post-Fordist	corporate parks (business parks)
	just-in-time delivery	

Sustainable Development

Essential Question: How are sustainability principles related to and impact industrialization and spatial development?

In the 21st century, many people, businesses, organizations, and governments around the world have begun to recognize and act on the dangers development poses to the environment. In 2015, the United Nations adopted a new vision that acknowledges resources are necessary for human life but also for economic prosperity. Some of the goals of this vision were to eliminate poverty, create prosperity, promote equality, and preserve the earth and its resources.

Sustainable Development

Using the earth's resources without doing permanent damage to the environment is **sustainability**. The goal of **sustainable development** is to address problems caused by depletion of natural resources, mass consumption of goods, pollution of air and water, and the impact of climate change. People can apply the concept at any scale:

- At the household scale, individuals might set thermostats to use less energy heating and cooling their homes.
- At the local level, city and town governments might operate composting programs and shopping malls might reduce unneeded lighting.
- At the country scale, the government might fund research into products that use less energy and industries might recycle their waste.
- At the global scale, countries might cooperate to protect ocean habitats for marine life.

Ecological Footprint and Consumption

A small percentage of the earth's population uses most of the resources and generates most of the waste products. For example, 7 percent of the world's population produces 50 percent of the carbon dioxide. In general, people with more wealth have a larger **ecological footprint**, or impact on the environment. One measure of an ecological footprint is how much land is needed to provide one person with resources and to handle the person's garbage.

For example, the ecological footprint per person in the United States is 20.0 acres. An American football field is 1.3 acres in size, so 5 billion football fields of productive land are needed to support consumption of the U.S. population. The world average is 6.4 acres.

ECOLOGICAL FOOTPRINT PER PERSON, 2017	
Qatar	36.1
United States	20.0
Germany	11.6
Brazil	6.9
Madagascar	2.2

Source: footprintnetwork.org

There is a wide range between countries. What factors account for the differences? Describe a reason why Qatar has such a high ecological footprint compared to other countries.

Resource Depletion

When people overuse resources, development becomes unsustainable. For example, farmers traditionally maintained the fertility of land by regularly allowing a field to lie fallow (unused). In recent decades, farmers have often used all available land every year. As a result, land has become less productive, a trend that cannot be sustained. To counter the loss of natural fertility, farmers have become more dependent on chemical fertilizers.

Similarly, people have depleted resources such as fossil fuels (coal, oil, and natural gas), forests, and fish in either particular regions or the world in general. This has prompted people to develop alternatives, such as solar and wind energy, tree farms, and fish farms.

Pollution

Pollution contaminates air and water with smoke, chemicals, and waste products. It has numerous causes:

- Some, such as volcanic eruptions, are natural events that humans do not influence.

- Some are a mixture of natural events and human actions. For example, dust storms occur naturally in some dry regions. However, they are more likely to occur after farmers have removed the deep-rooted natural vegetation that holds soil in place.

- Some are completely the result of human actions. For example, people pollute the air when the burn wood, coal, or oil. They pollute water when they dump waste from industries or allow farm chemicals to flow into rivers or lakes.

The Impact of Pollution Pollution has large impacts on plants, animals, and humans. According to the Global Alliance on Health and Pollution, in 2015, pollution caused 16 percent of deaths worldwide. Over 90 percent of these deaths occurred in low- or middle-income countries, and most who died were children. Pollution strains the economies of countries by increasing health care costs and causing people to miss school and work because they are ill or taking care of someone who is. The worldwide costs of pollution are estimated to be $4.6 trillion annually, or around 6 percent of global economic output in a year.

Efforts to Control Pollution One reason pollution is difficult to control is because it spreads so easily. Often, the person or business causing the pollution is not the one who suffers its effects. The people who feel the affects of pollution might live hundreds of miles away from where it originates. In addition, pollution travels across political boundaries. Hence, one government has an interest in letting the pollution continue and a different government wants to stop it.

In the mid-1900s, pollution released by factories in the Midwest drifted eastward and mixed with water in the atmosphere. When it fell as "acid rain" it began destroying forests in New York and New England. The companies causing the pollution had no incentive to stop. The problems caused by the pollution were far from their factories. If one company voluntarily took the costly steps needed to pollute less, its production costs would increase, as would the prices it charged for its products. In a competitive market, it would risk losing sales and possibly going out of business.

The solution was to force every company to reduce emissions. Under pressure from organized citizens, the federal government passed stricter laws on air pollution. With the passage of the Clean Air Act in 1970 and its subsequent amendments, the country reduced the emission of six major types of air pollution by over 70 percent. Besides helping protect the forests, the act resulted in fewer premature deaths, fewer hospitalizations, and fewer days of school missed because of breathing ailments. Similarly, government regulations have made lakes, rivers, and drinking water cleaner than they once were.

Climate Change

Between 2011 and 2020, worldwide temperatures were the warmest on record. Organizations such as NASA, and the National Academy of Science, and the Intergovernmental Panel on Climate Change agreed that human actions were a major cause of climate change. Scientists also concluded that the rise in temperature contributed to more frequent and more destructive wildfires, hurricanes, floods, and droughts. They predicted that climate change would have widespread consequences in the future:

- Diseases once confined to areas around the equator could spread to new areas.
- Ocean levels could rise as glaciers melt, which will threaten the homes and safety of the 40 percent of the global population that lives near coasts.
- Refugee crises could become more common as more frequent floods and droughts cause millions of people to move in search of food, water, and safety.

At the current rate of greenhouse gas emissions, temperatures could be 3.2°C (5.8°F) warmer by the end of this century. Scientist believe that increase could be a low as 1.5°C if countries reduce emissions to levels based on international agreements. In general, core countries has been more able to reduce emissions than have non-core countries. Core countries have greater wealth to pay for cleaner technology and higher standards of living so they can better absorb changes. In addition, many of the world's manufacturers have moved from core countries to non-core countries, which resulted in these countries increasing their greenhouse gas emissions.

Ecotourism

One example of sustainable development is **ecotourism**, travel to a region by people who are interested in its distinctive and unusual ecosystem. The money spent by ecotourists and the jobs created can provide incentives to people to protect these rare areas rather than convert them to agriculture or industry. It can also fund conservation efforts to protect these regions from damage by developments elsewhere. Some popular ecotourism sites include:

- rainforest wildlife in Costa Rica
- mountain gorillas of Rwanda
- coral reefs in Australia
- whale watching in Kaikoura, New Zealand
- new species of marine and terrestrial life on the Galapagos Islands
- fire and ice landscape (volcanoes and glaciers) in Iceland

Ecotourism is designed to be sustainable. However, carries risks. If too many people visit a fragile ecosystem, they can damage it even as they learn to appreciate it.

UN Sustainable Development Goals

In 2000, the United Nations identified the most challenging barriers to development and eight key steps to overcoming them. Known as the Millennium Development Goals (MDGs), they helped countries with low levels of human development improve the lives of their citizens.

The UN released an analysis of progress toward meeting these goals, the Millennium Development Goals Report, in 2015. The report found that by focusing on very specific and globally accepted goals, countries had cooperated to lift nearly one billion people out of extreme poverty, reduce hunger, and increase the number of girls attending school. This global effort was the most successful anti-poverty program in history.

Despite the success of the MDGs, world leaders still had concerns over the environmental unsustainability of many practices. In 2015, after extensive consultation with representatives of the 193 member states, academics, scientists, private sector leaders, and humanitarian organizations the UN created a new set of goals to replace the MDGs. The 17 new goals were called the **Sustainable Development Goals** (SDGs). The SDGs were intended to finish the job that the MDGs has begun, but with more awareness of environmental challenges and ways to overcome them. As with the MDGs, the UN gave countries 15 years to achieve the goals.

The SDGs targeted all countries, whereas the MDGs had focused on periphery and semiperiphery countries. As summarized in the table below, countries did not make as much progress in the first five years as people in 2015 hoped for. When the COVID-19 pandemic hit in 2020, progress toward many goals virtually stopped. In several cases, gains made during the first four years were nullified as countries redirected funds to battle the pandemic. With hopes that progress would resume, officials began referring to the period starting in 2021 as the Decade of Action.

| UN SUSTAINABLE DEVELOPMENT GOALS, 2016–2030 ||
Goal	Changes 2016–2020
1. End poverty in all its forms everywhere	Decline in poverty from 10 percent to 8.2 percent worldwide
2. Achieve food security, improve nutrition and promote sustainable agriculture	Increase of 60 million people who suffer from food insecurity since 2016
3. Ensure healthy lives and promote well-being for all at all ages	Increasing life expectancy and reducing common diseases but limited by COVID-19
4. Ensure inclusive and equitable quality education for all	Increasing access to education but 260 million school-age children not in school in 2018
5. Achieve gender equality and empower all women and girls	Fewer child marriages and more women in politics
6. Access to clean water and sanitation for all	Slight increase in percentage of people who have clean water and safe sanitation
7. Access to affordable, reliable, sustainable and modern energy for all	More access to electricity in poorer countries and more renewable energy use worldwide
8. Economic growth, productive employment and decent work for all	Stagnating or declining per capita income for 1 in 5 countries worldwide in 2019
9. Increase investment in infrastructure to achieve sustainable development	More investments in research, infrastructure, and mobile connectivity in non-core countries
10. Reduce inequalities within and among countries	Fewer inequalities at the national scale but within countries vulnerable populations at risk
11. Make cities and human settlements inclusive, safe, resilient, and sustainable	More people live in slums than ever before—up to 828 billion people in 2020
12. Ensure sustainable consumption and production patterns	Some progress globally but as population increases, current trends will not be enough
13. Combat climate change and its impacts	Minor reductions in emissions in core countries and increased emissions in non-core countries
14. Conserve and sustainably use oceans and marine resources	Progress in reducing illegal fishing but fewer sustainable fishing practices put species at risk
15. Protect and restore terrestrial (land) ecosystems and halt biodiversity loss	32 percent of countries on track, 50 percent making limited progress, 8 percent no progress
16. Promote just, peaceful, and inclusive societies	More than 70 million refugees in 2018—highest number in nearly 70 years
17. Improve global partnership for sustainable development	Increasing global partnerships in trade but limited by COVID-19

Sustainable Development Goals in Action

Each SDG addressed a major problem facing Earth's population, and the problems were seen as interconnected. Success or failure in meeting one goal would shape success or failure in meeting others. For example, achieving Goal 3 (ensure healthy lives and promote well-being for all) would require success in Goal 1 (poverty), Goal 2 (hunger), Goal 4 (education), Goal 5 (gender equality), and Goal 6 (clean water and sanitation).

Each SDG was broken down into more focused targets. For example, Goal 11 was to make cities and human settlements inclusive, safe, resilient, and sustainable. The writers of this goal recognized that development of public transportation projects was essential to meeting the goal. Only half of the world's population had convenient access to public transportation.

In many Latin American cities, many of the poorest people who most needed public transportation resided at the edge of the city where public transit often did not travel. Yet most of the potential jobs for these people were in the downtown area. If impoverished people had no public transportation, overcoming poverty became much harder.

An additional target of Goal 11 was to reduce the environmental impact of cities, specifically to improve air quality. Mexico City, one of the world's most polluted cities, opened a bus-based rapid transit system (BRT) in 2005 that used low-emission or electric buses. The stations were designed like train stations and the buses could be boarded like a subway, increasing capacity and efficiency. In addition, the buses had the flexibility of using dedicated bus lanes and roads so they cost less to develop and could reach many more people. Cities around the world began modeling their mass transit systems after Mexico City's.

REFLECT ON THE ESSENTIAL QUESTION

Essential Question: *How are sustainability principles related to and impact industrialization and spatial development?*

Sustainability Principles	Impact of Sustainability Principles

---

KEY TERMS

sustainability
sustainable development
ecological footprint

ecotourism
Sustainable Development Goals

The economic fortunes of Argentina and South Korea have been influenced by their physical locations as well as their roles within global trading networks. Argentina is situated along the Atlantic Coast of South America, so trade with the East Coast of the United States is convenient. Korea is between China and Japan, two large markets.

Conditions in the Early 20th Century

A century ago, Argentina was a much wealthier nation than Korea (the country was not divided between North and South Korea then). Argentina's income per worker made it one of the top 10 economies in the world. Its industrial growth created significant pull factors, and migrants poured in from Europe, particularly Italy. Korea was a heavily agricultural country, and its income per worker ranked it toward the bottom quarter of all countries.

Conditions Today

Currently, about 60 percent of the workers in each country are employed in the service sector. Beyond that, the economies differ greatly.

Argentina, like many countries in Latin America over the past half century, suffered periods of massive inflation, military dictatorships, and heavy foreign debt. These factors combined with massive loan defaults and a poor development plans resulted in a collapsed economy in the 1990s from which the country is still trying to recover. Today, Argentina is a semiperipheral state that relies heavily on agricultural exports such as beef, fruit, and grains.

In contrast, Korea has been a success story of modern economic development, as have many countries in East Asia. Through a combination of intense education, heavy government subsidies, tough trade restrictions, and strong corporations, Korea focused on making products it exported. The plan worked. Today, Korea is a high-tech industrialized economy and exports— mostly manufactured goods—account for nearly half of its GDP. Its levels of health, wealth, and education rank it as a core state, with about 2 percent of its population involved in primary activities and about 40 percent in secondary activities.

1. Describe THREE reasons why Argentina dropped from being a core country to a semiperiphery country.

2. Explain South Korea's plan to improve their economic development.

3. Using one of the SDGs describe a process that South Korea could use to make their development sustainable into the future.

THINK AS A GEOGRAPHER: *INDUSTRIAL GROWTH AT DIFFERENT SCALES*

One way to understand the process of industrialization at different scales is to analyze the opening or closing of a factory. At the local, national, and global scales, starting up a new factory or shutting down an existing one will have economic, social, political, and environmental effects (ESPN). Consider potential impacts you have learned in this chapter and unit.

1. Review the chart and note the effect at each scale. Identify each effect as either economic, social, political, or environmental.

2. Describe an additional effect for each scale of analysis and identify it using ESPN (economic, social, political, natural/environmental).

IMPACT OF AN AIRCRAFT FACTORY		
Event	**Effect**	**Additional Effects**
Aircraft Factory Closes	Local: The amount of empty space in the community's industrial area increases.	1. Local
	National: The federal government funds a program to retrain unemployed workers.	2. National
	Global: The supply of aircraft decreases, which causes airplane prices to increase.	3. Global
Aircraft Factory Opens	Local: The unemployment rate decreases, and total income in the community increases.	4. Local
	National: Total federal tax revenue increases.	5. National
	Global: The supply of aircraft increases, which causes airplane prices to decrease.	6. Global

CHAPTER 20 REVIEW
Changing Global Economy and Sustainability

Topics 7.7–7.8

MULTIPLE-CHOICE QUESTIONS

Question 1 refers to the following chart.

EMPLOYMENT IN SELECTED EXPORT PROCESSING ZONES

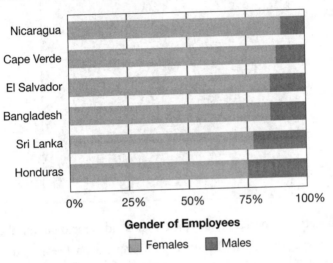

Gender of Employees

Females ■ Males ■

Source: International Labor Organization, 2007.

1. Which statement about the employment of men and women in EPZs is most clearly supported by the graph above?

   (A) Unemployment is probably an acute issue for men in these countries.

   (B) Women make up the vast majority of each country's secondary sector employees.

   (C) Men generally prefer to work in quaternary sector positions than in the positions found in these EPZs.

   (D) The governments of these countries will be more likely to listen to the concerns of the women.

   (E) Resource consumption by women working in EPZs will surpass that of men in these countries, causing great social change.

2. Silicon Valley is an example of a technopole because it

(A) takes its name from the material used to make microchips

(B) demonstrates the concept of agglomeration economies

(C) is a center for developing new ideas that generate growth

(D) has attracted new universities to locate in the region

(E) reuses brownfield sites that were once industrial factories

Question 3 refers to the map below.

3. Which statement best describes the darker shaded region in the above map?

(A) Growing prosperity in this region over the past several decades has had a spin-off effect on nearby regions.

(B) Industries in the region have a comparative advantage over ones in the South and Southwest regions in recent years.

(C) Brownfields are one sign of the economic recovery occurring in the region.

(D) The region is known as the Rust Belt because of the many closed factories in it.

(E) The region has always had a shortage of jobs in the secondary sector.

4. Which is most responsible for deindustrialization in highly developed countries?

(A) Easy capital financing available in developing countries

(B) Low wages in developing countries

(C) Labor shortages in developed countries

(D) The lack of strong unions in developed countries

(E) The shortage of raw materials in developed countries

5. The main benefit for countries that host export processing zones (EPZs) is that these zones

(A) create thousands of relatively high-paying jobs for their citizens

(B) increase availability of manufactured products for their citizens

(C) attract thousands of foreign workers, which results in millions of extra dollars in tax revenue

(D) increase opportunities for the citizens to work for American companies and to learn English

(E) provide an efficient way to increase imports from the United States

Question number 6 refers to the graph below.

CO$_2$ EMISSIONS PER CAPITA, 2017 (of selected countries)

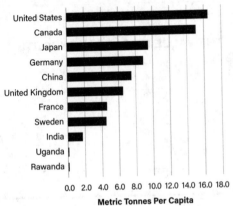

Metric Tonnes Per Capita

Source: World Bank

6. Based upon the graph above, which of the following factors corresponds the most closely with the amount of CO$_2$ emissions per capita?

(A) Gross Domestic Product of the country

(B) Size of the country (mi.^{2} or km^2)

(C) Amount of fossil fuels extracted in the country

(D) Population of the country

(E) Longitudinal position of the country

7. Which of the following business activities will have the greatest multiplier effect?

(A) Growing grain crops

(B) Manufacturing cars

(C) Serving fast-food

(D) Raising fish in a fish farm

(E) Repairing computers

FREE-RESPONSE QUESTION

1. Neoliberal policies and greater complementarity have caused dramatic changes in global trade since the 1950s. National governments set the rules, but companies are the most common trading partners, not countries. The values in the table below are percentages of travel and communication costs using the 1930 costs as 100 percent.

COSTS OF INTERNATIONAL TRAVEL AND COMMUNICATION					
Cost	1930	1950	1970	1990	2005
Sea Freight	100	57	45	26	22
Air Passenger Transport	100	45	23	18	15
International Phone Calling	100	20	18	2	1

Source: Organization for Economic Cooperation and Development Economic Outlook, 2007

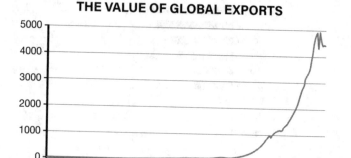

THE VALUE OF GLOBAL EXPORTS

Values reflects changes in the amount of trade compared to 1913. Trade in 1913 represented 100.

Source: Federico, G., Tena Junguito, A. (2016). "World trade, 1800-1938: A New Data-Set," EHES Working Papers in Economic History, n. 93.

(A) Using the concept of complementarity, explain why companies in different countries trade with each other.

(B) Use the table to explain the pattern of global exports in the graph.

(C) Using a specific method of transportation, describe the benefit of using this mode of transportation for trade.

(D) Describe how export processing zones (EPZ) or special economic zones (SEZ) work to lower the cost of trade.

(E) Describe ONE positive economic impact of increased international trade on a local community.

(F) Describe ONE negative economic impact of increased international trade on a local community.

(G) Explain how women in developing countries often benefit from international trade.

UNIT 7 REVIEW:
Connecting Course Skills and Content

APPLYING GEOGRAPHIC SKILLS

Applying geographic skills is critical for success on the AP Exam. For each skill listed write a one-paragraph response that illustrates your understanding of the question. Support your response with specific examples and evidence. Refer to the Unit 1 introduction (pages 3–7) for tips on how to apply geographic skills.

1C Explain TWO advantages of locating a car manufacturing plant in Ohio or Mexico that will sell the cars in the United States.

2C Using the U.S. Rust Belt as an example, explain how the multiplier effect can work in a negative way.

3D Using the Gini Coefficient and Human Development Index maps in Topic 7.3, describe one similar and one different spatial pattern.

4E Explain how the image of containers on page 446 relates to the concept of globalization and the new international division of labor.

5D Use examples to help explain the degree to which the concept of income inequality explains the different standards of living experienced by people at the international, national, and local scale.

WRITE AS A GEOGRAPHER: *GIVE FULL EXPLANATIONS*

Answers to free-response questions can be very basic—or they can be fully explained for additional credit on an exam. Consider the question, "Why did Chicago develop where it did?" The basic answer is that Chicago grew into a major city because it is located where two water transportation networks come together—the Great Lakes and the Mississippi River system. This is correct but basic. A fuller explanation would include claims that explain the context and the details to give significance to these basic facts. It would explain:

- the importance of water travel in the 1800s
- the wealth of food—wheat, corn, beef, and pork—produced in the Midwest
- the increasing demand in the East and Europe for food as industrial cities grew
- the increasing demand in the Midwest for manufactured goods produced in the East

For each question, write a basic answer in one or two sentences. Then list three additional points that would provide a fuller explanation.

1. Explain why purchasing power parity is a more useful refinement of gross national income.

2. Which criticisms of Rostow's Stages of Economic Growth model could also be made against Wallerstein's World Systems Theory?

3. What are the costs and benefits of sustainable growth?

AP® Human Geography
Practice Exam

MULTIPLE-CHOICE QUESTIONS

Questions 1 and 2 refer to the map below.

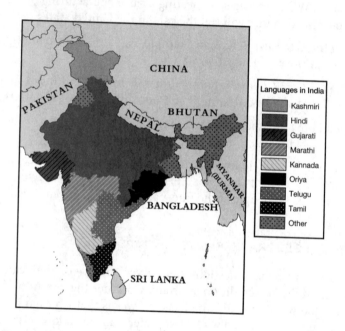

1. Which subfield of human geography is illustrated by the map shown?
   (A) Population
   (B) Culture
   (C) Economics
   (D) Urban areas
   (E) Politics

2. Which argument does the map shown most clearly support?
   (A) All languages in India are part of the Indo-European family.
   (B) All Indians grow up multilingual.
   (C) A lingua franca could help communication.
   (D) Each caste in India has its own language.
   (E) India's languages have shaped its diverse climate

Question 3 refers to the image below.

3. This aerial photograph is useful to geographers because it shows
   (A) a defined boundary
   (B) geographic information systems (GIS)
   (C) relative location
   (D) random distribution
   (E) qualitative spatial data

Questions 4 and 5 refer to the image below.

4. Based on its architecture, the worship site shown is probably used by people of which religious tradition?

   (A) Christianity

   (B) Judaism

   (C) Islam

   (D) Hinduism

   (E) Buddhism

5. Which geographic concept is best illustrated by the image shown?

   (A) Mental map

   (B) Gravity model

   (C) Urban hearths

   (D) Cultural landscape

   (E) Agricultural density

Question 6 refers to the map below.

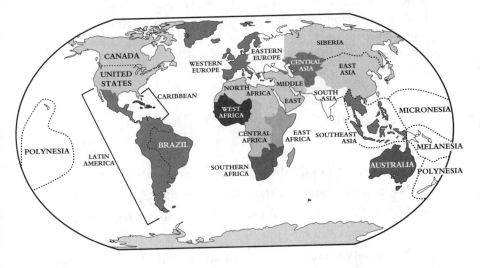

6. Why is regionalization as shown in the map, sometimes a challenge for geographers?

   (A) The boundaries of many world regions can be defined in several different ways, producing overlapping areas.

   (B) Geographers do not all agree that the concept of region is an appropriate way to look at the world.

   (C) Large areas of the world are unpopulated or only sparsely populated and therefore do not fit well in any type of region.

   (D) Distortion on map projections makes the accurate portrayal of world regions difficult.

   (E) The process of how people create regions has not been studied in depth.

7. Modern dairy farms are often located in places other than where the von Thünen model suggests. What invention or development has most directly led to this?

   (A) GMOs

   (B) Aquaculture

   (C) The Green Revolution

   (D) Agribusiness

   (E) Refrigeration

8. In 2014, Russia invaded and annexed a region of Ukraine that had earlier been part of Russia and where many people spoke Russian as their primary language. This suggests that the annexation was an example of

(A) ethnic separatism

(B) terrorism

(C) horizontal integration

(D) subnationalism

(E) irredentism

9. Which best describes the difference between nationality and ethnicity?

(A) Nationality relates to a state while ethnicity relates to culture.

(B) Nationality relates to culture while ethnicity relates to a state.

(C) Nationality relates to language while ethnicity relates to religion.

(D) Nationality relates to cities while ethnicity relates to rural areas.

(E) Nationality relates to religion while ethnicity relates to urban enclaves

10. What effect does emigration usually have on the demographics of the country of origin?

(A) Average age increases because most people who migrate are older.

(B) Demographics skew toward males, as women leave to work abroad.

(C) Population becomes less urban as people remaining can own larger areas of land.

(D) Population skews toward older residents as working-age people leave to work abroad.

(E) Demographics change little, as immigrants replace the emigrants.

Questions 11 and 12 refer to the graphic below.

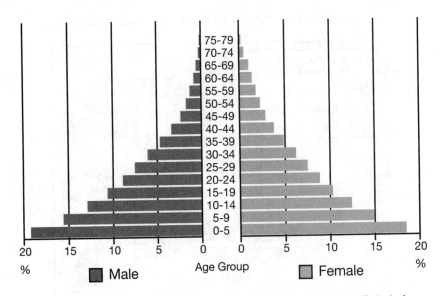

Source: Population Analysis for Policies and Programmes. Paris: International Union for the Scientific Study of Population.

11. The population pyramid shown is typical of countries
   (A) with a large migrant work force
   (B) in Europe and North America
   (C) in the economically less-developed regions
   (D) with a stable population size
   (E) with a shrinking population

12. Which of the following best describes the likely demographic and economic characteristics of the country shown in the graphic?
   (A) High birth rate, high death rate, and a large manufacturing sector
   (B) High birth rate, low death rate, and a highly skilled quaternary sector
   (C) Low birth rate, low but rising death rate, and very high income
   (D) High birth rate, high but declining death rate, and large agricultural sector
   (E) Declining birth rate, rising death rate, and large tertiary sector

Questions 13 and 14 refer to the map below.

RELOCATION OF PEOPLE AFTER HURRICANE KATRINA

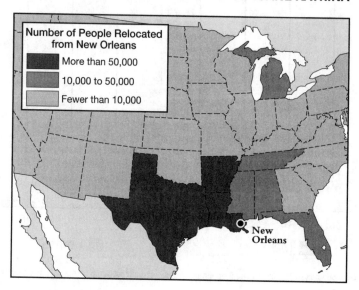

Number of People Relocated from New Orleans
- More than 50,000
- 10,000 to 50,000
- Fewer than 10,000

New Orleans

13. Based on the information on the map, which is the most appropriate term to describe the people who were forced to move away from New Orleans after Hurricane Katrina in 2005?

(A) Refugees

(B) Asylum seekers

(C) Voluntary migrants

(D) Chain migrants

(E) Internally displaced persons

14. The pattern shown on the map of the movement of people out of New Orleans after Hurricane Katrina demonstrates the concept of

(A) distance decay

(B) outsourcing

(C) random distribution

(D) reverse hierarchical diffusion

(E) time-space compression

15. Filtering is the process of a housing unit or neighborhood being occupied by progressively lower-income people over time. How are filtering and gentrification related?

(A) They both lead to similar changes in the average income in a neighborhood.

(B) They both occur more in rural areas than in urban areas.

(C) After years of filtering, a neighborhood might experience gentrification.

(D) Gentrification is one step in the filtering process.

(E) Filtering and gentrification are the same thing.

Question 16 refers to the image below.

16. The above sign, which is in both English and Welsh, represents the effort by the people of Wales

(A) to guard against the development of a creole language

(B) to develop a lingua franca in the country

(C) to help preserve their traditional language

(D) to replace their traditional language with English

(E) to use two languages that are not closely related

17. Why is French often considered a lingua franca, while some other languages that are spoken by far more people are not?

(A) French is an easier language to learn than are most other languages.

(B) French is widely used in many of France's former colonies around the world.

(C) People in Europe and the Americas never learned non-European languages such as Arabic and Mandarin.

(D) French is used around the world by artists and musicians, so it is widely known in the international community.

(E) French never merged with other languages to create vast numbers of creole speakers.

18. Exurbanization is the process of people moving to large homes in rural areas just outside of the suburbs. Which factor is strongest in promoting this process?

(A) Subsidies for mass transit have made commuting to central city offices more expensive.

(B) Increases in land prices have made living on the edges of metropolitan areas more costly.

(C) Improvements in communications technology have made working from home easier.

(D) Decreases in family size have made living in central cities more affordable.

(E) Reductions in air pollution have made living in central cities more pleasant.

19. Which best explains why the Spanish language diffused widely in Latin America?

(A) Indigenous people had long tried to develop a lingua franca.

(B) Indigenous people found it easier to learn than other languages.

(C) Spanish was the first Indo-European language in the Americas.

(D) Spain was one of two major imperial powers in the region.

(E) Spanish developed out of a creole language.

Question 20 refers to the table below.

THE CULTURE OF GREECE		
Category	Greek	Other
Ethnicity	93%	7%
Language	99%	1%
Religion	98% (Greek Orthodox)	2%

Source: World Factbook

20. Based on the data in the chart, Greece is best described as

(A) a nation but not a state

(B) a member state of the European Union

(C) a nation-state

(D) a multinational state

(E) a federal democratic state

21. In the 1990s, the southeast European country of Yugoslavia became

(A) a united country through the centripetal force of opposition to Soviet control

(B) an independent country and member of NATO

(C) two independent countries through the Velvet Divorce

(D) several autonomous, self-governing regions within one country

(E) shattered into several independent countries as a result of centrifugal forces

22. Which would cause an increase in carrying capacity?

(A) Emigration increases the number of people living in the area.

(B) Farmers use new techniques to increase the wheat production per acre.

(C) People begin delaying marriage, so the total fertility rate decreases.

(D) The number of people moving to cities to take secondary sector jobs increases.

(E) Improved health care increases the percentage of elderly people in a population.

23. As shown on the map, Argentina and Uruguay share a boundary formed by the river and estuary of the Rio de la Plata. Which of the following is most likely NOT a challenge of a using a river as a border?

(A) Competing claims of freshwater resources

(B) Rivers can change course over time

(C) Rivers act as obvious, easily identifiable borders

(D) Sharing control of transportation on the river

(E) Sharing responsibility for maintaining a deep channel for navigation

24. Which of the following types of farming is most likely to use a large number of migrant workers?

(A) Beef farming on the plains of Wyoming

(B) Truck farming in California

(C) Nomadic herding in a semi-arid region of Africa

(D) Shifting cultivation in the Amazon region of Brazil

(E) Grain farming in the Canadian Prairies

25. The clearest example of relocation diffusion is the spread of a

(A) new clothing style as seen on television

(B) Tik Tok video throughout the world

(C) religion acquired through books and letters

(D) religion to a new area by immigrants

(E) religion by missionaries who move somewhere temporarily

26. The Arctic Council, an association of eight states and indigenous people that attempts to coordinate policies related to the Arctic region, is an example of

(A) globalization

(B) a nation-state

(C) irredentism

(D) supranationalism

(E) subnationalism

27. What often happens to an industrial site after many of the factories close?

(A) In older industrial areas, it often becomes a brownfield site.

(B) In EPZs, it is almost always reclaimed as a recreational site.

(C) In the Great Lakes region, it usually attracts new industry.

(D) In the South and West of the United States, it usually remains vacant.

(E) In most periphery countries, it often becomes an office park.

28. The percent of the population of the United States that lives in cities rather than rural areas is growing. What effect will this change have?

(A) The agricultural density of urban areas will increase.

(B) Environmental stress may reduce the carrying capacity of the country.

(C) Additional infrastructure will be required in growing cities.

(D) The physiological density of rural areas will increase.

(E) The arithmetic density at the national scale will decrease.

29. Governments design natalist policies in order to discourage or encourage families from having more or fewer children. Which of the following natal policies is justified by the data?

(A) Expanded education for woman, CBR 38 and CDR 26

(B) Families paid a bonus for each child born, CBR 32 and CDR 9

(C) Increased spending on health care in urban areas, CBR 42 and CDR 35

(D) Campaigns that encouraged families to have fewer children, CBR 10 and CDR 14

(E) Laws that limited families to one child, CBR 13 and CDR 12

30. What type of landscape modification is shown?

   (A) Cutting and burning of forests

   (B) Terracing

   (C) Draining of wetlands

   (D) Destruction of grasslands

   (E) River diversion

31. Which of the following sets of characteristics best describes a food desert?

   (A) A poor area of a city with only a convenience store nearby for groceries

   (B) An area of the city built on very poor soil, so gardens are not possible

   (C) A part of an urban park where city inhabitants are not permitted to plant gardens

   (D) Area at the edge of the city that farmers have abandoned due to future urban growth

   (E) The central business district of a city where multiple tall office buildings are located

32. All of the following were positive consequences of the Green Revolution EXCEPT
    (A) increased crop yields
    (B) increased use of traditional farming methods
    (C) reduced hunger and famine
    (D) reduced crop losses from diseases
    (E) reduced dependency on food imports

33. Traditionally, North American cities have been more likely than European cities to have a higher percentage of
    (A) historic buildings in the central business district
    (B) wealthy people living near the central business district
    (C) tall buildings in the central business district
    (D) poor residents living in high-density suburbs
    (E) workers who use public transportation to go to work

34. Which is most likely to decrease as a neighborhood becomes gentrified?
    (A) Property tax rates
    (B) Enrollment in private high schools
    (C) Number of older buildings
    (D) Average household income
    (E) Specialty coffee shops and dog parks

35. Which change would LEAST affect capital intensive commercial farmers?
    (A) Decreased demand for beef in urban areas
    (B) Decreased available farmland
    (C) Increased global demand for cash crops
    (D) Increased cost of water
    (E) Increased rural-to-urban migration

36. These fields of rapeseed in China, as shown in the image, illustrate which agricultural concept?

(A) A greenbelt

(B) Monoculture

(C) A supply chain

(D) Vertical integration

(E) Desertification

37. What type of agriculture practice is shown in the image?

(A) Commercial

(B) Subsistence

(C) Slash-and-burn

(D) Double cropping

(E) Shifting cultivation

Questions 38 and 39 refer to the image below.

38. The assembly of the car shown in the image reflects which sector of the economy?

   (A) Primary

   (B) Secondary

   (C) Tertiary

   (D) Quartenary

   (E) Quinary

39. Which of the following statements best reflects an impact of automation shown in the image?

   (A) Many additional quinary sector jobs are created and many of the primary sector workers in the plant lose their jobs.

   (B) The capital expenditure on technology decreases, and labor costs increase.

   (C) Jobs are lost in the factory and the cost of production increases.

   (D) The number of quaternary jobs increases, and economies of scale is improved.

   (E) The number of both primary and secondary sector jobs at the factory increase.

40. A U.S. government agency, the Army Corps of Engineers, regularly dredges the Mississippi River so that large vessels can transport grain and livestock at low cost. This is an example of

(A) providing public assistance to farmers

(B) helping the freshwater fishing industry

(C) promoting the fair-trade movement

(D) encouraging the market for luxury products

(E) maintaining access for importing agricultural products

Question 41 refers to the table below.

ORGANIC FOOD SALES IN THE UNITED STATES	
Year	Total Sales (in billions of dollars)
2004	11
2005	13
2006	15
2007	17
2008	19
2009	21
2010	22
2011	24
2012	26
2013	29

Source: farmxchange.org

41. If the trend shown in the table continues, the most likely consequence will be an increase in

(A) the development of superpests

(B) the number of jobs in the agricultural sector

(C) the amount of topsoil lost to erosion

(D) the use of chemical fertilizers

(E) the use of chemical pesticides

Question 42 refers to the image below.

42. The system of aquaculture as shown in the image often leads to all of the following EXCEPT

(A) the reduction in parasites that live on fish

(B) the spread of diseases to wild fish stock

(C) the use of antibiotics that can damage ecosystems

(D) the escape of fish that can breed with native stocks of fish

(E) the increased availability of fish protein

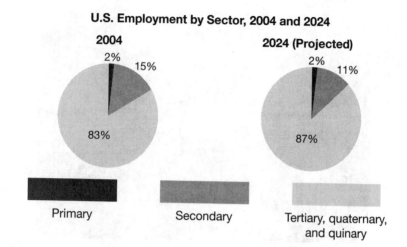

U.S. Employment by Sector, 2004 and 2024

2004

2%   15%

83%

2024 (Projected)

2%   11%

87%

Primary   Secondary   Tertiary, quaternary,
and quinary

Source: U.S. Bureau of Labor Statistics.

43. Which projected change in the percentage of workers in each employment sector as shown in the graphs, concerns economic development analysts the most?

(A) The stability in the primary sector even though natural resources are becoming increasingly scarce

(B) The decline in the secondary sector because these jobs pay high wages and have a strong multiplier effect

(C) The decline in the secondary sector because this points to the increased use of human labor

(D) The growth in the tertiary and quaternary sectors because they indicate a decrease in productivity

(E) The growth in the quaternary and quinary sectors because these jobs pay low wages

44. A limitation of the data shown in the graphs is that it

(A) includes three sectors of the economy

(B) is from an unreliable source

(C) shows a comparison for two different years

(D) shows structure of jobs within an economy

(E) excludes informal jobs

45. Which of the following best describes the geographic scale of analysis of the data shown in the graphs?

(A) Local

(B) Regional

(C) Sectoral

(D) National

(E) Global

46. The best example of a job in the quinary sector of the economy is

(A) chef at a top-rated restaurant

(B) short-order cook at a diner

(C) maintenance engineer at a tire plant

(D) athletic trainer for a professional sports team

(E) minister of finance in a national government

47. Which is the most common result of the global, interconnected nature of today's economy?

(A) Disparities in consumption patterns between the core and periphery countries are becoming very small.

(B) Financial crises that arise in one region of the world can now be

(C) isolated to that region.

(D) Major economic fluctuations in one part of the world can affect workers and investors worldwide.

(E) Transnational corporations have moved many primary and secondary sector jobs from periphery countries to core countries.

(F) Brownfields and other signs of a postindustrial landscape have become less common in core countries.

48. Which accurately explains a difference between the HDI composite index and GDP as measures of development?

(A) HDI is always reported as a per capita measure but GDP rarely is.

(B) HDI includes life expectancy and educational variables, while GDP focuses on only economic development.

(C) HDI does not include indicators of health, but GDP does.

(D) HDI is used more for analyzing less developed countries, while GDP is used mostly for more developed countries.

(E) HDI shows Latin America is more developed than Europe, while GDP shows the opposite.

GINI COEFFICIENT BY COUNTRY

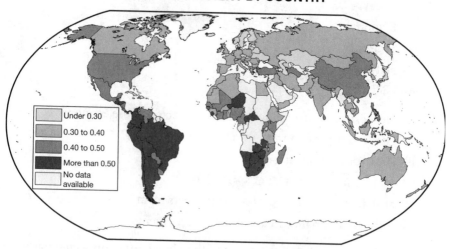

Legend:
- Under 0.30
- 0.30 to 0.40
- 0.40 to 0.50
- More than 0.50
- No data available

49. Based on the data in the map shown, which region generally has the greatest degree of income inequality?

    (A) Western Europe

    (B) North Africa

    (C) East Asia

    (D) Australia

    (E) South America

50. Which of the following best describes the characteristics of countries with high income equality?

    (A) Low-income states with their economies based heavily on oil and gas reserves

    (B) Low-income states with large numbers of subsistence farmers who are primarily women

    (C) High-income states with a large percentage of highly educated males and females

    (D) States with large land areas and with rapidly emerging economies

    (E) Middle income, smaller land-area states with excellent access to seaports

51. According to Ravenstein's laws of migration, which statement explains why men are more likely than women to migrate internationally?

(A) Men usually care more about democracy than women and therefore will more likely migrate in search of it.

(B) Men are better educated than women and they can more easily learn the new language of the country they move to.

(C) Women are less likely to find work in the destination country, so they are more reluctant to migrate.

(D) Women usually have greater job opportunities in their local communities than men do, so they are less likely to migrate.

(E) Women usually stay in school longer than men do, so they can find better jobs without the need to migrate.

52. Which best represents the concept of a metacity as defined by the United Nations?

(A) Melbourne, Australia, is one of the largest cities by land area outside the United States.

(B) Taipei, Taiwan, is one of the most densely populated cities in the world.

(C) Jakarta, Indonesia, has a population of 32 million.

(D) Luanda is the largest city in Angola and the country's most important industrial area.

(E) Islamabad is the capital of Pakistan and part of the Islamabad Capital Territory.

| SENEGAL'S MOST POPULOUS CITIES ||
City	Population (estimated)
Dakar	2,476,000
Pikine	874,000
Touba	529,000
Thiès Nones	252,000
Saint-Louis	176,000

53. The information in the table shows that Dakar can be classified as a
    (A) city-state
    (B) megacity
    (C) world city
    (D) primate city
    (E) nodal region

54. According to the rank-size rule, the population of Touba should be
    (A) one-half the size of Dakar
    (B) one-half the population of Pikine
    (C) one-third the size of Dakar
    (D) twice the size of Thiès Nones
    (E) the size of Thiès Nones and Saint-Louis combined

55. The Kurds are considered a stateless nation because they
    (A) lack a common cultural heritage that unites them
    (B) migrate often so they do not consider any country their homeland
    (C) are not a majority of any country in which they reside so they lack control of a country
    (D) have failed to be recognized as a distinct cultural group by other countries
    (E) have political control over one country but live in many countries

Question 56 refers to the diagram below.

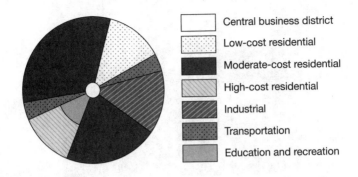

56. Which mode of transportation most influenced the land-use patterns shown in the sector model?

(A) Airplanes and subways

(B) Automobiles and elevated rail

(C) Buses and taxis

(D) Cargo ships and airplanes

(E) Rail and streetcars

57. A typical megacity of the periphery is best described as

(A) an urban area facing numerous challenges, as rapid growth brings many social problems

(B) a megalopolis that exerts international influence and power far beyond its boundaries

(C) a world city with economic and cultural dominance over a wide area

(D) a city with a concentration of global corporations and media hubs

(E) a vast suburb where housing, food, and services are easy to obtain

58. Which option below gives the term that best describes the human landscape shown in the image, and the region that is associated with the highest concentrations of these human landscapes?

(A) A transnational corporation and region A

(B) A maquiladora and region B

(C) An urban brownfield and region C

(D) An export processing zone and region D

(E) An industrial site and region E

Question 59 refers to the map below.

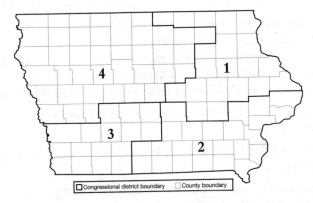

59. The map shown of federal congressional districts in Iowa is best described as one that

   (A) shows why the Constitution requires redistricting after each census

   (B) demonstrates how reapportionment can favor one party

   (C) suggests strong support for irredentism

   (D) provides little evidence of gerrymandering

   (E) reflects the idea of open boundaries

Question 60 refers to the diagram below.

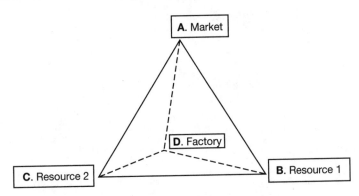

60. Which reason explains why, according to the Weberian analysis, an automobile assembly plant is most likely to be located at an intermediate location such as D in the diagram above?

   (A) Automobiles are a weight-gaining industry made of multiple parts.

   (B) Cars are expensive to import because of high tariffs.

   (C) The weight-loss element of cars requires a location near a resource.

   (D) Environmental regulations require cars to be assembled near cities.

   (E) Labor costs are usually lower in high population areas.

1. In 1983, Sudan erupted into civil war that lasted more than 20 years and resulted in the creation of the country of South Sudan in 2011. Then in 2013, political struggles plunged South Sudan into civil war. The wars have had significant domestic, regional, and international impacts. The UN estimated that both wars created millions of refugees and internally displaced persons.

   (A) Compare the concepts of refugees and internally displaced persons (IDP).

   (B) Describe ONE economic impact of either refugees or IDPs at the country scale.

   (C) Compare the concepts of centrifugal and centripetal forces in relation to political stability of a country.

   (D) Explain ONE centrifugal force in relation to the Sudan or South Sudan civil wars.

   (E) Explain the degree to which the concept of balkanization or shatterbelt explains the region of the Sudan

   (F) Explain how a unitary government could increase tension within a country.

   (G) Describe how wars or violent boundary disputes can impact the food security of an international region.

2. The model shown is a representation of the galactic city model within the United States. Use the model to help respond to the questions.

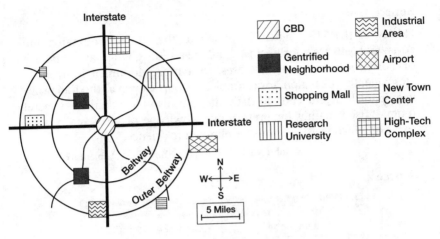

(A) Identify the mode of transportation that most influences the shape of galactic cities.

(B) Explain ONE reason why the airport is located where it is as opposed to near the central business district (CBD).

(C) Explain ONE economic reason why new town centers form near the periphery of the city.

(D) The map shown is incomplete in the southeastern part of the city, near the beltway. Explain ONE reason a specific land use, other than a new town center, is likely to occur on the southern end of the city between the two beltways.

(E) Explain to what degree the galactic city model accurately describes the location of commercial land use in cities within the United States.

(F) Describe ONE negative environmental impact of the land-use patterns shown in the galactic city model.

(G) Describe ONE challenge of using public mass transit with the land-use patterns shown in the galactic city model.

3. Lingua franca languages often threaten endangered languages. Use the excerpt and the chart to answer the questions that follow.

Source 1:

"Many of the 113 languages spoken in the Andes Mountains and Amazon basin are poorly known and are rapidly giving way to Spanish or Portuguese, or in a few cases, to a more dominant indigenous language. In this region, for example, a group known as the Kallawaya use Spanish or Quechua in daily life, but also have their own secret tongue, used mainly for preserving knowledge of medicinal plants, some of which were previously unknown to science."

—John Noble Wilford, *New York Times*, September 18, 2007

Source 2:

PRIMARY LANGUAGES OF PEOPLE IN PERU	
Language	**Percentage of Population**
Spanish	84.1%
Quechua	13.0%
Aymara	1.7%
Ashaninka	0.3%
Other Languages	0.9%

Source: The World Factbook

(A) Explain ONE reason why languages such as that used by the Kallawaya are becoming extinct.

(B) Explain ONE historical factor that explains how Spanish diffused to Peru or the greater South American region.

(C) Describe ONE economic reason why Spanish or English have become the dominant lingua franca of many countries.

(D) Describe ONE political policy that local governments can use to preserve endangered languages.

(E) Describe ONE way that technology is being used to preserve threatened languages.

(F) Using a language different from ones previously discussed, identify a region or country in the Eastern Hemisphere and its lingua franca.

(G) Using a language different from ones previously discussed, identify a region or country in the Western Hemisphere and its lingua franca.

Index

P

Paris Agreement on climate change, 256
Paris as heat island, 433*f*
Pastoral nomadism agricultural practice, 275–276, 339–340
Pattern distribution
circular, 15
clustered or agglomerated, 15
dispersed, 15
geometric, 15
linear, 15
random, 15
Pedestrian cities, 372
Per capita, 462, 463
Percent urban, 368
Perceptual regions, 44
Periférico, 400
Periodic markets, 401
Peripheral model, 397
Periphery countries, 461, 467, 483
Peters projection, 16, 16*f*
Philippines, 207
Physical consequent boundary, 221
Physical environment, 271
Physical geographic boundaries, 218
Physical geography, 244–245, 271
Physical landscape, 138
Physiological population density, 58–59
Pilgrimage, 179
Placelessness, 138
Plantation agriculture, 275–277
Plant domestication, 282
Political boundaries/border, 218–219, 221
exist to separate bodies of water, 223
functions of, 223
Political enclaves, 226
Political entities, types of, 194–197
Political map (contemporary), evolution of
colonialism (*see* Colonialism)
geopolitical forces influence, in present day maps, 201–205
imperialism (*see* Imperialism)
modern nation-state, 198, 199*f*
world map, 198
Political map (contemporary), structure of
independent states as building blocks, 193–194
political entities (*see* Political entities)
Political organization of urban regions, challenges of, 431–432
Political power, 206–207
Political units, 193
Pollution, 434, 506–507

Popular culture, 134–136
Popular demand, 24
Population change
demographic balancing equation, 77
life expectancy, 78–81
number of births, measurement of, 77–78
number of immigrants and emigrants, 77
Population composition, 422
age composition, 64
sex composition, 64
Population density, 55, 279
calculation, reason for, 58
dependent groups, composition of, 70
spatial distribution, 70
time influence on, 60
types of, 58–60
Population density, consequences of
economic, 61–62
environment, 62–63
infrastructure, 62
natural resources, 62–63
political, 61–62
social, 61–62
urban services, 62
Population distribution, 55
changes in populations, 53
governments' influence on, 57
human factors, 57–58
human factors influencing, 56–57
physical factors influencing
low-lying areas, 56
midlatitudes, 56
other factors, 56
reasons for people movement, 53
scale of analysis, 57–58
social stratification, 57
world, 56*f*
Population distribution, consequences of
economic, 61–62
environment, 62–63
infrastructure, 62
natural resources, 62–63
political, 61–62
social, 61–62
urban services, 62
Population dynamics. *See also* Demographic transition model (DTM)
explosion of world population, 76, 76*f*
growth in human population before 19th century, 76
Population, growth and decline of, 103
Population policies
anti-natalist policies of China, 93–95
to encourage population growth, 95
government programs to control, 93